W9-COM-567

ROOM {1219}

THE LIFE OF
FATTY ARBUCKLE,
THE MYSTERIOUS DEATH OF
VIRGINIA RAPPE,
AND THE SCANDAL THAT CHANGED
HOLLYWOOD

GREG MERRITT

An A Cappella Book

SOMERSET CO. LIBRARY
BRIDGEWATER, N.J. 08807

Copyright © 2013 by Greg Merritt
All rights reserved
Published by Chicago Review Press Incorporated
814 North Franklin Street
Chicago, Illinois 60610
ISBN 978-1-61374-792-6

Library of Congress Cataloging-in-Publication Data

Merritt, Greg, 1965–

Room 1219 : the life of Fatty Arbuckle, the mysterious death of Virginia Rappe, and the scandal that changed Hollywood / Greg Merritt.

pages cm

Summary: "Part biography, part true crime narrative, this painstakingly researched book chronicles the improbable rise and stunning fall of Roscoe "Fatty" Arbuckle from his early big screen success to his involvement in actress Virginia Rappe's death, and the resulting irreparable damage to his career. It describes how during the course of a rowdy three-day party hosted by the comedian in a San Francisco hotel, Rappe became fatally ill, and Arbuckle was subsequently charged with manslaughter. Ultimately acquitted after three trials, neither his career nor his reputation ever recovered from this devastating incident. Relying on a careful examination of documents, the book finally reveals what most likely occurred that Labor Day weekend in 1921 in that fateful hotel room. In addition, it covers the evolution of the film industry—from the first silent experiments to the connection between Arbuckle's scandal and the implementation of industry-wide censorship that altered the course of Hollywood filmmaking for five decades"— Provided by publisher.

Includes bibliographical references and index.

ISBN 978-1-61374-792-6 (hardback)

1. Arbuckle, Roscoe, 1887–1933. 2. Motion picture actors and actresses—United States—Biography. 3. Rappe, Virginia, 1895–1921. 4. Murder victims—California—Biography. 5. Murder—California—Los Angeles. I. Title.

PN2287.A68M48 2013
791.4302'8092—dc23
[B]

2013015168

Interior design: Jonathan Hahn

Printed in the United States of America
5 4 3 2 1

In loving memory of
Laurie Carrico

CONTENTS

INTRODUCTION

This is a mystery story. It began on Labor Day of 1921 in room 1219 on the top floor of a San Francisco hotel. Only two people were present. One was Roscoe "Fatty" Arbuckle—a movie superstar. The other was actress Virginia Rappe. Afterward, Rappe suffered wrenching pains for four days and then died. More than nine decades later, the mystery remains: What happened in that room? Did Arbuckle assault Rappe or otherwise contribute to the injury that led to her death, or did he only happen to be near when her injury became evident? Was she his victim, or were they both victims of circumstance?

When Arbuckle was arrested for the murder of Rappe, a mania raged as newspapers competed to print the most startling front page. One simply shouted (in the largest possible letters): ARBUCKLE, THE BEAST. Others predicted the previously beloved performer's death on the gallows. He was not just tried and convicted in the press but also sentenced and punished, again and again.

So was Hollywood. Once the public's appetite for scandal was whetted, it could not be sated. For weeks in the autumn of 1921, newspapers dredged up or concocted stories of movie industry depravity. A typical headline read, ARBUCKLE AFFAIR NO SURPRISE AFTER ORGIES OF FILM COLONY. A new narrative took hold. Previously, the "film colony" lifestyle was presented in fan magazines and newspaper gossip columns as a carefree extended adolescence. Suddenly, this characterization had a dark counterpoint: Hollywood was filled with spoiled idlers, living beyond society's norms, going from party to party, fueled by jazz music, alcohol, narcotics, and deviant sex. The editorialists had a field day.

The public, which had begun over the previous few years to learn about their favorite actors' houses and families and vacations, now started to learn about their adultery and wild parties and drug use. It's a straight line from the tabloid-style coverage of the Arbuckle case to *Confidential* magazine in the 1950s to today's *National Enquirer* and TMZ. In the years following Arbuckle's arrest, studio publicity machines continued to paint performers in the most favorable light. However, now that a superstar actor had appeared in story after story as a "beast"—the host of an orgy to which he lured starstruck young women, one of whom he raped and killed—there was no turning back; the following year, tales of a director's mysterious murder and an actor's doomed fight with drug addiction would fill front pages.

The relentless coverage of the Arbuckle case sparked loud condemnations of Hollywood's allegedly decadent ways from editorialists, religious leaders, and a new and powerful voting bloc—women. That trifecta was part of the coalition that had successfully lobbied for Prohibition, and they intensified their fight against motion pictures, another "intoxicant." In fact, many restated an argument they made against alcohol: movies cast those who imbibed them under a dreamlike spell that could loosen morals and foster criminality. The defenders of tradition were pitted against the purveyors of modernity. On one side, the Victorian era. On the other, the Jazz Age. It was the first great battle in a culture war that has persisted in various forms to the present day.

Arbuckle was a casualty of this war. On the day of the fateful party, he had seven feature films playing in theaters and two more in the can; he was the top star at the top studio. Less than a week after his arrest, his films had been pulled from every screen in America. Later, his image was effectively banned from American cinemas by Will Hays—the head of the motion picture industry's new self-policing organization. No artist in American history has been censored more than Roscoe "Fatty" Arbuckle.

Before Rappe's death, Arbuckle had been among the most beloved of all celebrities. His "Fatty" movie character was typically a scamp bumbling in and out of trouble, mischievous and sometimes corrupt but easy to laugh at and root for. The actor made news for charitable giving and for appearances and purchases that highlighted the wealth and leisure of the elite few in the new motion picture industry. With the passage of time and the proliferation of myths, the true story of Roscoe Arbuckle was lost. He was remembered as a killer or a victim and nothing more. To the present day, his name reappears when a celebrity is publicly entangled in a matter of sex or violence, yet invariably nothing is said about his film career other than that it was "ruined." We learn nothing about his forty-six years of life other than his association with a tragic death.

The best introduction to him is via his movies, and it's easier than ever to watch them today. Much of his finest work—silent shorts made between 1914 and 1919—can be viewed free via the Internet. Techniques feel fresh, because they were forgotten long ago. Ludicrous situations and slapstick antics build in the manner of cartoons. Arbuckle was a veteran of the vaudeville stage, and you see that medium's aesthetic brought to cinema: deliver as much varied entertainment as possible. There are visual puns, pratfalls and chases, exaggerated violence, broad emotional eruptions, tender love scenes, risqué and macabre humor, wild stunts, subtle parodies, and camera and editing tricks. Shots of printed text, now known as intertitles, replicate spoken lines and sometimes provide a wry commentary.

Not every Arbuckle movie has aged well. Comedic bits can fall flat in even his best movies. Some of the humor is shockingly adult, but most of it is childishly silly, and an adult has to accept that silliness to fully enjoy it. Unfortunately, few potential viewers ever realize what they've been missing. The contributions of Roscoe Arbuckle—the ingenious comedic actor and adroit filmmaker—have been virtually forgotten, as if erased by whatever occurred in that hotel room in 1921.

This book's first mystery is just that: what *did* occur in room 1219? Its second mystery helps us solve its first: who was Roscoe Arbuckle, and was he capable of the crime for which he was tried three times? His career took him from Wild West vaudeville stages to some of the first motion pictures shot in Los Angeles, to the heights of young Hollywood, to the depths of his ostracism, and to a long-delayed comeback in the sound era. He worked closely with fellow legends Charlie Chaplin, Mabel Normand, Mack Sennett, and Buster Keaton. He was one of the first people to fully experience the Hollywood lifestyle, including a fleet of trophy cars, a mansion and servants, and worldwide fame—as well as frequent parties, marital separations and divorces, and drug addiction.

But Roscoe Arbuckle's life story is not the only one to have been eclipsed by the events of Labor Day 1921. The real story of Virginia Rappe, the only other person in that hotel room, was buried so deep beneath the accumulated lies and exaggerations that it seemed it would never be found again. The prosecution and the newspaper accounts portrayed her as an innocent, while Arbuckle's defense team questioned her character. However, it was only decades after her death that the strongest attacks on her reputation were launched. She was presented in histories as a "slut" if not a "whore," sleeping her way through Hollywood, riddled with venereal diseases, and suffering from the lingering effects of a botched abortion. Rappe came to represent the movie industry's underbelly and the licentious Jazz Age in the same manner Arbuckle had in 1921. However, virtually everything I first learned from books and websites about Rappe was wrong, starting with her year of birth and ending with her cause of death. Beyond the inaccurate sexual and medical histories, there was precious little written about her. That's why it was surprising to find so much about her published during her lifetime.

Overcoming an impoverished childhood, she became a celebrated model, an inventive clothing designer, and a moderately successful film actress. She was entrepreneurial, idealistic, and outspoken. Using her fame in the fashion world, she championed feminism and pacifism. She traveled to Europe and throughout America. She was frequently engaged but never married. But all of that and more was seemingly erased the moment she died—except it wasn't. This book's third and final mystery is: who was the real Virginia Rappe?

A missing chapter remains, however, in the biographies of both Virginia Rappe and Roscoe Arbuckle. And that returns us to the first mystery. What happened in room 1219 has been obscured not just by conflicting testimony and the passage of time but also by the proliferation of myths. The most prevalent of these is that Arbuckle punctured Rappe's bladder by raping her with a bottle. Today if a person knows only one thing about Fatty, it is probably the bottle legend. When previous histories did not merely print this fiction or some variation, they blamed the victim, highlighting lies about her to further their thesis that Arbuckle was innocent.

In this book, I revisit Labor Day 1921 and present the details we know for certain, what each side said, and, ultimately, what likely caused Virginia Rappe's death. I avoided forming an opinion about this ultimate mystery until I had read the available testimony and reportage, consulted with experts, and thoroughly researched the lives of Arbuckle and Rappe. When I realized that pertinent information had been missed or marginalized, it became clear that fragments of the most reliable accounts fit together like pieces of a jigsaw puzzle. Ultimately, a new picture took shape. The most comprehensive, objective narrative of what likely occurred on September 5, 1921, in room 1219 of the Hotel St. Francis is presented in these pages.

My aim has been to peel away the accumulated fictions and present the true story of one of the neglected giants of cinema, an unfairly pilloried woman, and the greatest of all Hollywood scandals. This is a mystery story, but it's much more than that. It surveys the birth of the movie industry and its development from the earliest experiments to the sound revolution. It examines the practice and business of making comedy. It covers a monumental censorship debate and early battles in the culture war. It looks at how the press reported on celebrity and scandals. It is a story about fate and how two lives were decimated, only because they briefly connected.

{1}

LABOR DAY

> As would become a lifelong habit for most of us, we longed to witness both spectacular achievement and mortifying failure. Neither of these things, we were discreetly certain, would ever come to us; we would instead be granted the frictionless lives of the meek.
>
> —Thomas McGuane, "Ice"

The road followed, approximately, El Camino Real ("the Royal Road"), a trail blazed beside the Pacific by Spanish missionaries. It had been pounded for generations by boots, hooves, wagon wheels, and eventually automobile tires as explorers and enterprisers traveled between the preeminent West Coast metropolis of San Francisco and the lazy town of Los Angeles. California had started surfacing the future Route 101 in 1912. Nine years later, many stretches remained unpaved, and the narrow road took treacherous turns on hills—the risks to travelers compounded by the primitive machinery of the average driver's Ford Model T.

Roscoe Arbuckle did not own a Model T. His personal fleet included a silver Rolls-Royce, a Renault roadster, a Cadillac town car, a Hudson limousine, a Locomobile Sportif (priced at a then-staggering $9,500), and, everyone's favorite, a custom-built right-hand-drive Pierce-Arrow Model 66 A-4 touring car. At a time when Ford's ubiquitous creation sold for $370, Arbuckle's P.A. had set him back ninety-two times as much: $34,000. Although the oft-published assertion that the car included a backseat toilet is false, it was appointed with many luxuries, including a cabinet ideal for hiding illegal liquor. Painted iridescent purple-blue with a gray cloth convertible top and creamy all-white tires tricked out with silver rims and varnished wooden spokes, the colossal and flamboyantly ostentatious Pierce-Arrow was the Batmobile of the Jazz Age, and it drew crowds wherever it went. It was famous throughout Southern California as "Fatty's car."*

This was the car Arbuckle drove on the future Route 101 from Los Angeles to San Francisco on September 3, 1921, the Saturday before Labor Day. At thirty-four, he was by most criteria the world's number-two actor, bested by only Charlie Chaplin. Having appeared in over 150 films over the previous thirteen years and having starred in all but the first few—often with his adopted name, Fatty, in the title—he was immensely famous around the globe. As the director of at least seventy-eight films, he was celebrated for his cinematic artistry. And as the first screen actor signed to a contract worth $1 million annually ($13 million in today's dollars), the former vaudeville vagabond was by then wealthy beyond his wildest dreams.

Before the third day of September, Arbuckle had honored that contract by starring in nine feature-length films for Paramount Pictures, all of which were produced over the previous twenty-one months. The seventh, *Crazy to Marry*, had only just premiered. *Variety* enthused:

> To attempt to describe in cold, unfeeling print the story of a "Fatty" Arbuckle comedy is a well-nigh futile task. And if, perchance, some descriptive writing genius succeeded, he would only be spoiling a bunch of fun for those unfortunate to read it. . . . This is so funny that Tuesday at the Rialto the laughter was so loud as to give the impression the auditorium was being cannonaded. . . . "Crazy to Marry" will make the whole world laugh.

---

* From 1910 to 1918, approximately 1,250 Pierce-Arrow Model 66s were produced. Fourteen are known to survive today. One is Arbuckle's, which was fully restored in recent years.

The man who made the whole world laugh had wrapped production on *Freight Prepaid* three weeks prior and was planning his next feature. Meanwhile, the fourth annual "Paramount Week" was beginning that Labor Day weekend. During the seven-day celebration, Paramount Pictures pulled out all stops to publicize its wares, and many more theaters than usual booked its movies exclusively. Admission was typically free. On Labor Day, the studio's stars were to parade through Los Angeles, with the highlight being Arbuckle in his "twenty-five-thousand-dollar gasoline palace" (his $34,000 Pierce-Arrow). Later that same day, Arbuckle was to appear at a screening of his film *Gasoline Gus* at the lavish Million Dollar Theatre in downtown Los Angeles. But despite protestations from Paramount studio head Adolph Zukor, Arbuckle would make no such appearances. He wanted a vacation, and the long Labor Day weekend was the perfect opportunity for a jaunt to San Francisco.

Not joining him was his wife, Minta Durfee, herself a prolific actress. Married for thirteen years, they had been separated for the past four and a half. Also not joining him was his best friend, the famous comedic actor Buster Keaton, a companion on previous trips to San Francisco. Keaton had married actress Natalie Talmadge three months before, and they were planning to sail a yacht to Catalina Island for a relaxing weekend. They invited Arbuckle.

Arbuckle declined. He was seeking neither communion with the ocean nor the company of newlyweds. He wanted to party, and for that San Francisco was the ideal destination. It had been *the* West Coast metropolis since the Gold Rush seventy-two years prior, and it had fashioned itself the "Paris of the West," with world-class hotels, restaurants, and theaters. It learned early how to house, feed, and amuse not only princes but also paupers—the frontier fortune-seekers who overtook the big city on Saturdays in search of hard liquor and soft flesh.

By 1921, San Francisco's businesses still readily accommodated society's high and low visitors, but sentiments there had chilled toward Los Angeles since its recent population explosion; the 1920 census was the first in which the population of Los Angeles exceeded that of San Francisco (577,000 to 507,000). Northern California's elite looked down on the rubes to their south, mostly transplants from small towns in the heartland, and they also resented the nouveau riche celebrities of the moving pictures treating their city as the Las Vegas of the day.

When nightlife was on the agenda, Arbuckle was almost always accompanied by an entourage. He was the headliner; they were his supporting cast. He called the shots, he attracted the greatest attention, and he picked up the tabs. Keaton and other usual members of that group were not accompanying Arbuckle as he journeyed north, but he wasn't about to go to San Francisco alone. The two men riding with him, Lowell Sherman and Fred Fishback, were not close friends of his, but they were the type who expanded his clique on late nights in Los Angeles. They knew that the best parties always seemed to follow Fatty.

The handsome Sherman, thirty-two years old, was a dramatic film actor. He played mostly dashing playboys, dastardly knaves, or a combination of the two, and he had only recently begun to distinguish himself, most prominently as a cad in *Way Down East*, the smash of 1920. A note in a newspaper column on that fateful Labor Day read, "Lowell Sherman is the name of a gentleman who is being styled as 'the screen's most polished villain.'"

Twenty-seven-year-old Fishback was born in Bucharest, Romania. Formerly a minor film actor and then Arbuckle's assistant director, by September 1921 he was under contract at Universal Pictures and a prolific director and writer of comedies.

The three men, each of whom was married, set out early on September 3, 1921. Filling stations, general stores, and roadside cafés were rare but welcome sights, and when the Pierce-Arrow parked it likely stirred up some commotion.

Those general stores were probably selling the latest issue of the celebrity magazine *Photoplay*. Inside was an article attributed to Roscoe "Fatty" Arbuckle, salaciously entitled "Love Confessions of a Fat Man," in which he stated, "I am convinced that the fat man as a lover is going to be the best seller on the market for the next few years. He is coming into his kingdom at last. He may never ring as high prices or display as fancy goods as these he-vamps and cavemen and Don Juans, but as a good, reliable, all the year around line of goods, he's going to have it on them all." Maybe the three Hollywood men laughed about the jibes at the likes of "Don Juan" Douglas Fairbanks and the new superstar, "he-vamp" Rudolph Valentino. Maybe this part struck them as ironic: "Nothing is so humiliating to an efficient woman these days as an unfaithful husband. Fat men tend to be faithful." Or this: "A man's ideal is most of the things most men want to come home to—slippers, drawn curtains, a bright fire, peace, praise, comfort, and a good, hot dinner." So said the fat man, long estranged from his wife, who was journeying to party in San Francisco. The article also included a peculiar musing from Arbuckle: "It is very hard to murder or be murdered by a fat man."

As the ride progressed, Arbuckle, an avid baseball fan, may have chatted about Babe Ruth, for if baseball came up, Ruth surely did. He was in the midst of the best year of his vaunted career. Alcohol may have been consumed during the lengthy trip. The basement of Arbuckle's Los Angeles mansion was stocked with the finest liquors, and twenty bottles were along for the ride. More could be purchased in San Francisco—despite the fact that Prohibition was the law of the land.

The Eighteenth Amendment had been in effect for nearly twenty months, so buying, transporting, or selling any drink with more than a tinge of alcohol could earn you a stiff fine or six months in a brick room. But for the wealthy, like Roscoe Arbuckle and the planets that revolved around him, the main effect was to impart drinking with a sheen of outlaw glamour. There were passwords and secret knocks, private shindigs and underworld connections. Drinking was a pursuit worthy of a 350-mile excursion, and though the charms of illegal imbibing were bringing more and more women into nightclubs, such an excursion was cause to leave the wives at home. After all, there were women in San Francisco.

Along with Tijuana, where alcohol was still legal, San Francisco was a common weekend destination for Roscoe Arbuckle. He had lived there in his teenage years, employed as a singing waiter at an exclusive café. In April 1915 he directed and, with frequent comedic foil Mabel Normand, costarred in a nine-minute film, *Mabel and Fatty Viewing the World's Fair at San Francisco, Cal.* It featured the rotund star clowning with San Francisco mayor (and California's future governor) James Rolph, and it presented "the Grand Dame of Union Square." Intertitle: "Hotel St. Francis, One of the Largest Hotels on the West Coast." An establishing shot presented Union Square with its ninety-seven-foot-tall Dewey Monument, and then the camera panned up and rightward to take in the great height and breadth of the hotel, as wide as a city block.

The St. Francis was not merely one of but *the* largest hotel on the West Coast—and, with the nearby Palace Hotel, one of the two most prestigious lodging destinations west of the Mississippi River. The 450-room St. Francis was modeled after the great hotels of Europe, and after two years of construction at a cost of $2.5 million, it was an immediate sensation when it opened in 1904. Construction of a third wing began soon thereafter to meet the demand for rooms. The fire following the 1906 earthquake decimated the hotel's interior, but the building suffered no structural damage, and the Grand Dame of Union Square reopened twenty months later. (In contrast, the older Palace Hotel had to be torn down and rebuilt.) In 1913 a fourth wing upped the room total to 629.

The St. Francis featured pneumatic tubes by which rooms could exchange messages with the front desk. Rooms also had their own telephones, a rare high-tech luxury for travelers then. Engines in the basement fed vacuum outlets in each room, replacing the hotel's air with fresh air every eight minutes. The hotel had its own orchestra, which played on the mezzanine; its own school for young guests; its own Turkish baths with heated saltwater pumped in from the bay. Its most distinctive feature was the ten-foot-tall Magneta grandfather clock from Vienna, which controlled all other clocks in the hotel. When the St. Francis became the place in San Francisco to be seen, the clock's location in the resplendent rococo lobby was a popular meeting place, celebrated in lore.

The Hotel St. Francis was also the place to eat. From 1904 to 1926, Victor Hirtzler was the head chef.* His menu was noted for its encyclopedic variety: traditional French dishes, American favorites, and local foods like bay oysters, artichokes, and avocados. Breakfast options included 203 egg dishes, among them "eggs Moscow" (poached eggs stuffed with caviar). By publishing cookbooks, naming dishes like "celery Victor" after himself, and scoring publicity for greeting celebrity guests, Hirtzler became the most famous chef in America during his twenty-two years at the St. Francis. He was the Wolfgang Puck of the Progressive Era.

As the St. Francis was celebrated for its grandeur, unique luxuries, and cuisine, it attracted the rich, famous, and powerful. The list of those who stayed there before September 1921 includes Presidents Theodore Roosevelt, William Taft, and Woodrow Wilson and such Hollywood celebrities as Charlie Chaplin, Douglas Fairbanks, Mary Pickford, John Barrymore (who tumbled out of a bed during the 1906 earthquake), and Cecil B. DeMille. The hotel's brochure in the early 1920s listed three famous guests, likely chosen to represent the variety of mega-celebrities who slept and ate there: World War I commander General John Pershing; Billy Sunday, the most celebrated evangelical preacher of the era; and Roscoe Arbuckle.

In the late afternoon of Saturday, September 3, Arbuckle's "gasoline palace" pulled up beside the four granite pillars that marked the entryway to the Hotel St. Francis. Arbuckle's live-in secretary had reserved three adjoining rooms in the south wing of the hotel's uppermost floor, its twelfth:

- 1219, a rectangular room with one window facing south, a bathroom, and a closet

* The French-born Hirtzler had been the personal chef to Nicholas II, emperor of Russia, and Carlos I, king of Portugal, and oversaw the legendary kitchens of Sherry's and the Waldorf-Astoria in New York City before those of the St. Francis.

- 1220, a larger, squarish room with one window facing south and one facing east (toward Union Square and, a mile away, the bay), and a fireplace but no bathroom or closet
- 1221, another rectangular room, with two windows facing east and one facing north (toward the center wing), and a bathroom but no closet

Each room had a door connecting it to the hallway, and doors connected 1219 to 1220 and 1220 to 1221. Room 1220 was typically used as a second bedroom for either 1219 or 1221, thus the absence of a bathroom, but on this weekend it also lacked a bed. Instead, a single bed for Fishback was added to 1219, while Arbuckle slept in the room's double bed. Sherman slept in a double bed in 1221. Room 1220 was their lounge, with furnishings including a couch and a love seat.

That Saturday evening, a deliveryman carried four bottles of gin and Scotch from nearby Gobey's Grill into the St. Francis and up to the three rooms on the southeast corner of the top floor. If the hotel staff noticed, nothing was said, for alcohol was a common commodity there. One unpublicized feature of the hotel was a fully stocked speakeasy in the basement.

On Sunday, after an afternoon of sightseeing in Arbuckle's Pierce-Arrow and visiting with Bay Area friends, Arbuckle and his two movie industry companions dined and danced at the Tait-Zinkand Cafe, located just one block from their hotel. Along with the restaurant in the Hotel St. Francis, Tait's was one of the two most prestigious dining destinations in the city. The café also had a cabaret show, and alcohol was served to discreet customers. The three patrons from Los Angeles stayed late.

Lowell Sherman invited one of Tait's chorus girls, Alice Blake,* to come to the top floor of the St. Francis for drinks the next day. Twenty-six-year-old Blake was the daughter of a prominent Oakland flour-mill magnate. At age seventeen in 1912, she made the news for her elopement and, at her father's behest, the marriage's prompt annulment. She

---

* Actual name: Alice Westphal. She likely went by "Blake" to disguise her café career.

had high aspirations for a dancing and acting career and, in accepting Sherman's invitation, probably envisioned the hotel social affair as a Hollywood networking opportunity. She had a dancing rehearsal the next afternoon but agreed to stop by the hotel suite beforehand.

That same Sunday evening, three other visitors from Los Angeles checked in to the nearby Palace Hotel: small-time film publicist Alfred Semnacher, his friend Maude Delmont, and film actress Virginia Rappe. The German-born Semnacher was forty-three years old and had been estranged from his wife for nearly a year; he had filed for divorce because of her "undue attentions" to another man, and the hearing was scheduled for a Los Angeles courtroom on September 15. Semnacher had known Delmont for years and ran into her a few days earlier leaving the Pig'n Whistle restaurant in Hollywood. She was either thirty-eight or thirty-nine. She admired his car, and he suggested a trip. Semnacher also invited his friend Rappe to ride along and stay a week in San Francisco. Rappe, who turned thirty that summer, had been spending too much time alone. A vacation in her former home of San Francisco sounded invigorating. Maybe she could catch up with old friends; maybe she could foster new friendships. Semnacher introduced her and Delmont just before the trio headed north.

Also staying at the Palace Hotel was Ira Fortlouis—an unlikely catalyst for Hollywood's greatest scandal. He was a thirty-four-year-old salesman from the Northwest. He formerly sold hardware and sewing machines but was now focused on women's clothing. And he knew Fred Fishback.

On Monday morning, Labor Day, Fortlouis was just about to leave the Palace for an 11 AM meeting with Fishback when he saw Semnacher, Delmont, and Rappe in the lobby. Forever on the lookout for women to model the gowns he sold, he asked a bellboy about the dark-haired and stylish beauty in the striking green outfit and was told she was "Virginia Rappe, the movie actress."

At the Hotel St. Francis, Fred Fishback invited Fortlouis into the twelfth-floor suite. Fishback was fully dressed, but Sherman and Arbuckle were still in pajamas and robes. The four men chatted, and Fortlouis asked if they knew an actress he had just seen in the Palace lobby: Virginia Rappe. All did, having encountered her on a studio set or at a Hollywood party. Fishback phoned the Palace and had an attendant hand Rappe a note, inviting her over to 1220. Rappe told Semnacher and Delmont, "I'll go up there, and if the party is a bloomer I'll be back in twenty minutes."

Around noon, Rappe entered the suite. A former model and fashion designer, she wore the same self-made clothes she had at the Palace: a jade skirt and jade sleeveless blouse over a white silk shirt adorned with a string of ivory beads. Her hair was up and under a white Panama hat trimmed with a thin ribbon of jade.

Twenty minutes later, Rappe spoke to Delmont by telephone. It wasn't yet much of a party, but there was plenty of alcohol. At her invitation, Delmont came up. Shortly thereafter, another guest arrived: Alice Blake, the chorus girl Lowell Sherman had invited the night before. Blake was followed twenty minutes later by her friend Zey Prevost, also a chorus girl, a brunette in her midtwenties, and an aspiring actress.* Unlike Blake, however, Prevost came from modest means; she was a child of Portugese immigrants. At the time of the 1920 census, she lived in a hotel and worked in a cafeteria pantry.

"Let's have some music, a piano or something," Rappe suggested.

"Who can play a piano?" Arbuckle asked.

No one. And so Arbuckle ordered a Victrola, which the hotel staff delivered with some 78 RPM records. From the phonograph's brass horn wailed the tinny clamor of popular songs like "St. Louis Blues" by the Original Dixieland Jazz Band, Paul Whiteman and His Orchestra's "Everybody Step," and "Ain't We Got Fun?" as sung by Van and Schenck. This last song, released in April, was quickly becoming the devil-may-care anthem of the Jazz Age. "*Times are bad and getting badder, still we have fun.*" They drank. They danced.

Around 1:30 PM, Fishback left. He took Arbuckle's Pierce-Arrow to a nearby beach to observe seals he was considering shooting for an upcoming movie. There were then four women and three men in 1220.

---

* Actual name: Sadie Reiss. She chose the exotic "Zey Prevost" to bestow upon herself some Hollywood-style glamour.

Arbuckle asked Sherman to tell one of those men, Fishback's acquaintance Ira Fortlouis, to leave. The traveling salesman had overstayed his welcome. He departed.

Shortly after Fishback took the car, a friend of Arbuckle's named Mae Taube arrived at the party. Taube was the wife of a cattle buyer and the daughter-in-law of popular evangelist Billy Sunday, who was a vocal proponent of Prohibition. The day before, Taube had stopped by the suite and Arbuckle had invited her to take a ride in his Pierce-Arrow that Labor Day. Arbuckle later described her as "peeved" to find a party in full swing.

"Who are all these people?" she asked.

"Search me. I don't know them," Arbuckle replied.

But he did introduce Taube to Rappe. Not wanting to join the drinking, Taube agreed to return later for the promised ride. Meanwhile, Al Semnacher appeared with the intention of picking up Rappe and Delmont, but both women were having too much fun to leave; Rappe was drinking orange blossoms (Arbuckle's favorite cocktail), and Delmont was wearing a pair of Sherman's pajamas and downing a great many double scotches. Instead, Semnacher drove Alice Blake the one block to her dance rehearsal at Tait's. Upon discovering the rehearsal was canceled, Blake returned to the party a short time afterward.

Blake's need to attend a rehearsal was probably the initial reason for the Labor Day gathering's early launch, and the gathering was likely intended as a pre-party get-together. Arbuckle had planned to spend the early afternoon taking Mae Taube for a ride, and most invited guests were scheduled to arrive at the suite later in the day. But as the afternoon wore on and the drinking continued, the prelude became the main event. Present then were Arbuckle, his suitemate Lowell Sherman, chorus girls Alice Blake and Zey Prevost, and Virginia Rappe and her traveling companion Maude Delmont. Ice, orange juice, and food were brought in. The deliveryman from Gobey's Grill returned to drop off twelve additional bottles of booze—most from Canada, some moonshine.

Arbuckle remained clothed in pajamas and a plush purple bathrobe. His attire would later be used to paint him as sort of a Jazz Age Hugh Hefner, a circumventor of society's norms. Perhaps the pajamas did signify that he hoped to be out of them and into bed with one of the women. With Delmont putting on a pair of Sherman's pajamas, supposedly because she was hot, and Sherman presumably still in pajamas himself, it had become a sort of pajama party. Still, Arbuckle wore a thick brocade robe over silk sleepware: a long-sleeve shirt and long pants. The robe reached his ankles. It would have revealed no more flesh than a suit and tie.

In one-on-one conversations, Arbuckle was prone to shyness, but he came alive when performing before a group—whether in a vaudeville theater, on a movie set, or at a party. He knew how to command an audience, regaling all with humorous showbiz tales, clowning about with a drink in one hand and cigarette in the other, and fox-trotting to jazz records on the Victrola. "Roscoe liked nothing better than playing host to all comers," Buster Keaton recalled.

Arbuckle jokingly announced he would leap out of one of 1220's two windows if anyone there would join him. "If I would jump out of the twelfth-story window, they would talk about me today, and tomorrow they would go to see the ball game. So what is in life after all?"

Ain't we got fun?

At some point, Arbuckle and Rappe sat together on a sofa. They likely talked about the movie industry. His acting career was now soaring, while after some initial promise, hers was sputtering. They had moved in the same Hollywood circles. They knew some of the same people—especially movie director Henry Lehrman. He had been Rappe's boyfriend for two and a half years. The relationship had halted with an argument that spring, but emotions were still simmering. Early in his film career, Arbuckle had been directed by Lehrman many times. Rappe may have thought getting to know Arbuckle better could boost her career, as had her relationship with Lehrman. Movie industry success was often launched via personal connections.

They may have spoken about San Francisco. They had both lived there previously, though not at the same time. Both had attended the World's Fair. And Rappe, like Arbuckle, had likely been to Tait's and other local nightlife destinations. They may have spoken about Los

Angeles. They had likely danced in the same Southern California nightclubs and previously attended the same parties.

They had other things in common. Both had traveled to some of the same cities and made ocean journeys to Europe. They had both lived in New York City. They had lost their mothers at nearly the same age: she at eleven, he at twelve. She never knew her father; his had been absent for most of his childhood and was now deceased. And they had each launched public careers in their youth: she was a model, he a stage actor and then a singer.

As the music played and they sat together in room 1220, drinking, they probably flirted. He likely prefixed some of his sentences with "Gee"—his favorite expression, and one that made him seem endearingly childish, like his film characters. But he may also have made risqué jokes and quips, as he sometimes did, and this too was reminiscent of his usual movie role—for on-screen the childlike Fatty had adult preoccupations.

Then or some time after then, Rappe tried to enter the bathroom in room 1221. The door was locked. She heard Maude Delmont inside and asked if she could enter. The answer was no. Sherman was in the bathroom with Delmont. Rappe walked back through 1220, where Arbuckle, Blake, and Prevost were situated, and entered room 1219 to use its bathroom.

Shortly thereafter, just before 3 PM, when Mae Taube was due to return, Roscoe Arbuckle entered 1219, the bedroom he shared with Fred Fishback. When he closed the door leading to 1220, the music faded. He locked the door.

{2}

JOURNEYS: 1887–1908

The cinema is little more than a fad. . . . What audiences really want to see is flesh and blood on the stage.

—Charlie Chaplin, January 1914

Fittingly, the account of his birth, too, contains a dubious legend, one long accepted as fact. Roscoe Arbuckle purportedly weighed sixteen pounds at delivery. His alleged heft, more than twice that of the average newborn, is likely a story spawned later to support his larger-than-life persona. Arbuckle's supposedly prodigious entrance into this world is sometimes presented as if it nearly killed his mother and left her in frail health until it did indeed eventually finish her—twelve years later! Legends breed legends.

This much is true: Roscoe Conkling* Arbuckle was born March 24, 1887, in a farmhouse near Smith Centre, Kansas, to parents William and Mary, both of whom were likely thirty-eight. He was the youngest of five children; a sixth child died at birth. His oldest sister Lola Belle (seventeen at his birth) married and moved out when Roscoe was an infant. His other siblings were Nora (sixteen); Arthur (eleven), who was already helping his father in the fields; and William Harrison (eight), known as Harry.

* It's likely he was named after Republican senator Roscoe Conkling (1829–88).

Both William and Mary had grown up in farming families in rural Indiana before marrying in 1867. They and their first four children left the Hoosier State in 1880. Like over a half-million other pioneers before them, they were searching for opportunities in the wide spaces of the West. The Arbuckles staked out a farming homestead just outside the recently formed township of Smith Centre in north-central Kansas, fifteen miles from the Nebraska border. Smith Centre fulfilled the needs of a county measuring nine hundred square miles that had exploded from sixty-six people in 1870 to nearly fourteen thousand ten years later. The town in 1883 had nineteen stores and three hotels.* Nearly every building was new. Nearly everyone had only just arrived.

Life proved harsh on the Great Plains. Farmers there cultivated wheat at a time when plows and reapers were pulled by horses and much work was done by hand. Children old enough to swing a sickle or tie a bushel were put to work from sunup to sundown. Because lumber was scarce, families huddled in earthen huts, always at the mercy of the elements. The Arbuckle home was later described as "a sod house of the most primitive kind." Though in later life he would romanticize his Kansas birthplace, Roscoe Arbuckle resided there for only his first year and a half and thus remembered only the tales of his family. And there was little to romanticize; his father was frequently drunk and abusive. In the autumn of 1888, the family sold their farm and farming equipment and headed west again.

After traveling more than eleven hundred miles by horse-drawn wagon, the Arbuckles arrived in Santa Ana, California, thirty miles southeast of Los Angeles. Incorporated in 1887 during a California real estate boom, Santa Ana became the county seat of Orange County around the time the Arbuckles settled there in 1889. Its population had blossomed to nearly four thousand and businesses were thriving because the town was a key stop on the new Santa Fe Railroad "Surf Line" connecting Los Angeles to San Diego. Tracks for horse-drawn streetcars bifurcated

* There were no saloons. In 1881 Kansas became the first state to prohibit the sale of alcoholic beverages.

the dirt streets. Buildings as tall as four stories with ornate frontispieces seemed to sprout overnight from the dust, monuments to optimism. The Arbuckles bought a double house. They crowded into the front half of the bottom floor and rented out the remainder of that floor and all of the second to boarders.

Almost as quickly as they had settled, William Arbuckle wandered again, heading to Northern California in search of more lucrative business opportunities. Later, Arthur and Harry went to work for him. It is unknown what emotional effect the departure of her husband had on Mary, a devout Baptist, but Roscoe later said he never felt loved as a child. Financially, William's absence surely had an impact on the son he left behind: the youngest Arbuckle entered the workforce at age five, running errands for storekeepers. Schoolmates would remember him wheeling around a little red wagon, delivering to families the clothes washed by his mother.

He spent much time alone. His father remained out of the picture for most of his childhood. Like his brothers, his sister Nora left home in the early years after the family moved to Santa Ana. And his oldest sister, Lola, died as a young adult. He was, in essence, the only child of a single mother. Much of the time that other children used for building friendships with peers, the youngest Arbuckle spent performing errands for his mother or employed by shopkeepers.

Still, others would recall him gathering with friends to play marbles in a dirt street. In a photo of him at age eight, he looks much as he would as an adult. His head is nearly round, cheeks plump, chestnut hair parted from the left. Teasing children bestowed on him the dreaded title of overweight kids everywhere: "Fatty." He hated it. The verbal torment he endured for his weight caused him to withdraw further.

Santa Ana had one schoolhouse, which Roscoe Arbuckle seldom attended after the second grade. Instead, he sneaked into vaudeville theaters, watching the practiced precision, smelling the greasepaint, hearing the applause, and fantasizing that he too could revel in such adoration, that he too could escape into a make-believe world of costumes and songs, backdrops and pratfalls. Adults looked down on vagabond actors performing in a train stop like Santa Ana, but the idea of playing for pay had great cachet to a lonely and curious child.

"My stage career was thrust upon me in the twinkling of an eye," Arbuckle recalled. The purveyor of this life-changing opportunity was a Northern California performer named Frank Bacon. Before turning to acting in his midtwenties, Bacon had been a sheepherder, a newspaper publisher, and a failed political candidate. In the final four years before his death in 1922 at age fifty-eight, he was probably America's most popular stage actor—star and cowriter of the Broadway smash *Lightnin'*. His obituary would be splashed on the front pages of New York's papers. In between, he was a character actor with his own stock company based in San Jose. The *New York Herald* noted, "For years and years he barnstormed from town to town with a cheap repertoire company and ate meals cooked by his wife over an oil stove. It was hard living." It is estimated he played a thousand parts through the years, many of them rustic types, owing to his large frame and inelegant features.

In 1895, near the beginning of those "hard living" years, the Frank Bacon Stock Company arrived in Santa Ana to stage their comedy and musical revue *Turned Up* in the Grand Opera House. A local child was cast for a small role, but he failed to show for the final rehearsal just hours before the opening. On that September day, a chubby eight-year-old lurked in the shadows when Frank Bacon turned to him.

The child role was that of an African American. As black roles then were nearly always played by white actors in exaggerated makeup, Arbuckle's acting debut was to be performed in blackface—but because he wore knickerbockers but was barefoot and sockless, Bacon told him to run home and retrieve black stockings to cover his calves and feet. The boy could not show up at his mother's door when he was supposed to be in school. He began to cry. So greasepaint was used to blacken not only Arbuckle's face but his lower legs and feet as well. That evening he stepped onto the stage bathed in the theater's new electric carbon arc lights, feeling the eyes of paying spectators upon him.

He received fifty cents a week for three weeks of shows and told his overworked mother he'd earned it by sweeping store floors. Meanwhile, the women in Bacon's company fawned over the cherubic child in their midst. He was stagestruck. At eight years old, Roscoe Arbuckle caught the acting bug.

His mother eventually discovered his secret, and he overcame her religious objections—a child performing with decadent adult actors!—and convinced her that acting was a lucrative supplement to selling newspapers in the streets or hawking food on the electric trains. After all, he was her only child in a home bereft of an adult male, and money was always scarce. Over the next four years, he took most of Santa Ana's child acting roles, including accomplice to a hypnotist and a psychic, as well as his first drag performance.

Offstage, he remained shy around other kids because of his pudginess, but he was better than most at athletics despite it. For recreation, he favored swimming, at which he became proficient. On Sundays, he sang with his mother in the church choir. Though as an adult he would be irreligious, the public performances and voice-tuning practice of singing hymns aided his initial career. Nevertheless, it appeared at the time that he would grow up to be just another anonymous adult who happened, as a child, to have acted the stooge for charlatans and filled out the background of theater productions long since forgotten.

As the manager of a boarding house, Mary Arbuckle devoted most of her time to the struggling business and little to her child. Nevertheless, the youngest Arbuckle was dependent on one person, the one who had not left him—and then he lost her. Roscoe Arbuckle was twelve years old when his mother died at age fifty in 1899. His need for maternal love would carry over into adulthood, when his first wife was a nurturing presence and he developed a strong bond with his first mother-in-law.

After his mother's death, he stayed for several weeks in Santa Ana with his sister Nora, her much older husband, Walter St. John, and their then-five-year-old son Alfred, who would grow up to be a ubiquitous supporting actor in his uncle's movies. Then Arbuckle was sent north to live with the father who had abandoned him. William Arbuckle owned a small hotel in Watsonville, a town of thirty-five hundred on California's central coast. On the lonely 360-mile train ride, the boy knew not what to expect when he arrived. Though he would eventually make other gut-wrenching journeys from Southern to Northern California, this was his first.

As instructed, when the train stopped at the Watsonville station he stayed in his seat until he was ushered off. Sitting forlornly on a bench at the station with his cardboard suitcase, he waited for his father. Hours later, a railroad worker took pity on the sad and frightened 180-pound boy and ushered him to William Arbuckle's hotel a few blocks away, where the boy learned that his father had sold the establishment and moved away. He was all alone in a strange town. He had two dollars and fifty cents. The desk clerk arranged for him to eat with the hotel staff and gave him a small room off the dining hall. In return for odd jobs, he would earn room and board.

He was enrolled at the local school, though as was his habit, he rarely attended. Encouraged by the hotel's dining hall singer, who believed the boy had a beautiful singing voice, Arbuckle sang for tips from guests when other hotel chores were scarce. He also practiced juggling and pratfalls. Entering an amateur contest at the local theater, he sang two songs, and then, uncertain of what to do when the audience demanded an encore, he improvised, dancing, rolling, and leaping about the stage, much to the amusement of all. This was the first time he experienced the beguiling feeling of making an audience laugh on his own, and it may also have been when he realized his fatness—the cause of so much distress when among other kids—could be an advantage. Admiring his fearless athleticism and self-effacing good humor, spectators rooted for the blubbery, baby-faced boy. Not wanting the laughs and applause to die, he continued until the giant hook (an amateur-night staple) reached for him from offstage. Dodging it, he somersaulted into the orchestra pit. He won first prize: five dollars. Soon he was an amateur-night regular.

Stories vary regarding how William Arbuckle returned to his son's life. Shortly after Mary's death, the family patriarch wed another woman named Mary, a widow who went by "Mollie" and had six children of her own. They would have two additional children together, in 1900 and 1903, the last when Mollie was forty-four. Before the arrival of the final two, the 1900 census listed eleven family members at the Arbuckles' rented farmhouse in Santa Clara—including thirteen-year-old Roscoe C., who found himself in the regular presence of his father for the first time since he was an infant.

Located forty-five miles south of San Francisco, the future high-tech capital of Santa Clara was then devoted to citrus farming. Again Arbuckle was teased for his weight, a torment compounded by his father's insistence he wear overalls and ragged shoes. One Santa Clara resident remembered, "Whenever a baseball went over the fence or out of the lot, the other lads put up a cry of 'Go get it, Fatty,' and with kicks and punches, sent the big boy on his way after the ball. He always was punched and kicked by the other boys." Again he seldom attended school. Instead, he fished and swam in a nearby pond. He toiled on the farm, as did his father and brother Harry. He cleaned a saloon. And he served coffee and donuts at the restaurant in the hotel his father bought. These years would inform his future film characters, as he later played lazy country bumpkins in overalls and lowly laborers, including hotel and restaurant workers.

Arbuckle still pursued show business, which then extended to not just shilling for medicine shows and traveling hypnotists but also dancing jigs or belly-flopping onto hard saloon floors for beer and cigarettes. In his early teen years, he again sang in amateur shows, this time at the Victory Theatre in nearby San Jose. The stage was a means to overwhelm his shyness, to replace isolation with an audience, and to find the love—if conveyed only in cheers and applause—that he didn't feel at home.

"He was aggravatingly lazy as a boy. Neither his father's cuffings nor my pleadings could cure it," his stepmother remembered. "Roscoe didn't seem to fit in anywhere." She spoke openly about what a loveless, frequently terrifying home it was for her stepson: "His father used to beat him—and he often deserved it." In a horrifying glimpse at the brutality, she claimed she saved the boy's life once when "his father was choking him and beating his head against a tree." When the adolescent Arbuckle was fortunate, his alcoholic father would only insult him for his excess weight and not draw his belt or his fists. Still, the sting of words—including William's contention that someone else must have fathered Roscoe—lingered far into adulthood. The abused boy longed for an escape.

In 1903 Arbuckle received an offer from theater owners Sid and David Grauman. Father David and teenage son Sid had migrated to Canada's Yukon Territory in 1898 during the Klondike Gold Rush. There they staked a gold claim but found greater fortune staging vaudeville shows and boxing matches for the miners. In San Francisco two years later, the Graumans bought a downtown store, moved in eight hundred chairs, and christened the Unique Theatre, a vaudeville house.* In February 1903 they opened a Unique Theatre in San Jose. They had heard Arbuckle sing at the Victory, and they soon enticed him to perform at the new Unique, singing illustrated songs for $17.50 weekly.

Illustrated songs were precursors to music videos. A singer performed onstage accompanied by either a pianist or a record while a series of slides combining photography and painting were projected on a screen, illustrating the lyrics. Offering two advantages over early motion pictures—(painted) color and verbal sound—they were popular in the early twentieth century, running between vaudeville acts or movies, buying time for the changing of stage backdrops or film reels. Audiences often sang along, and just as music videos would boost CD sales eighty years later, illustrated songs fueled sheet music sales. And for Arbuckle, performing these numbers in several vaudeville shows daily allowed him to hone his baritone voice.

It's likely that Arbuckle was also being exposed to early motion pictures. Between their first public projections in 1895 and the rise of nick-

* The Unique has a unique history. Sophie Tucker and Al Jolson performed there, and it screened the West Coast premiere of *The Great Train Robbery* (1903). The 1906 earthquake destroyed it, but for two years until they opened another theater, the Graumans screened movies in a tent in the lot where the Unique had stood.

elodeons in 1905, movies were seen primarily in vaudeville shows. Typically, they were prizefights, travelogues, or gag reels lasting as little as a minute. Their novelty waned rapidly, so "flickers" were wedged into the middle of bills with dancing girls, jugglers, comedians, and illustrated-song singers like Arbuckle, just another diversion in the theatrical lineup. But as the young performer witnessed the impact of such transformational inventions during his early years—not just motion pictures but also electric lights, telephones, phonographs, and automobiles—he developed a curiousity about technology that he retained throughout his life.

Next, the Graumans purchased San Francisco's Portola Café, which featured singing waiters. They offered the headwaiter/soloist position to Arbuckle. Thus, in 1904 the seventeen-year-old escaped his father's reach and moved to the West Coast's cosmopolis, a vibrant seaport and rapidly expanding city of over 350,000 inhabitants from around the globe. San Francisco was a mélange of unknown languages and streetcar bells, horses and motorcars, and foghorns from ships in the bay. Singing to the city's moneyed crowd, he was generously tipped for his tunes. He worked late into the night and slept away many daylight hours. Nocturnally, the City by the Bay was lit in electric and gas lights and cast in deep shadows and dense fog. An aristocrat might slip him a fiver for a song at the Portola, and a knave might steal it from him at knifepoint in a Tenderloin alley.

On March 21, 1904, the Hotel St. Francis opened its doors. A line of horse carriages and primitive automobiles stretched for blocks, as the city's elite, dressed in tuxedos and gowns, waited to tour the brightly lit Grand Dame of Union Square. Perhaps, in the ensuing months, Arbuckle first strode the palatial lobby of the city's newest attraction. If so, he would have marveled at the artwork, including an enormous painting of nearby Mount Tamalpais, purchased for $5,000 and hung behind the front desk. (The hotel's art was ruined by the earthquake's fire two years later and replaced before the 1907 reopening by newly acquired paintings and the lobby's celebrated Magneta grandfather clock.) Whether he entered or not, he surely noted its twin towers, each twelve stories tall. That's where the rich and famous stayed.

In the same year he moved to San Francisco, Arbuckle's baritone impressed another ambitious theater impresario, Alexander Pantages. A Greek immigrant who ran away to the sea at age nine, Pantages had been a sailor, boxer, Panama Canal digger, and gold prospector before entering the theater business in first the Yukon Territory and then Seattle. "Alexander the Great" would, in just a few years, build an empire of vaudeville and motion picture theaters, but when he and Arbuckle met he had but two, both in Seattle. He also had a vaudeville troupe traveling the West Coast, which, at Pantages's invitation, Arbuckle joined.

Teenage Arbuckle was a star singer on the Pantages circuit, performing with the troupe in theaters big and small from Phoenix to Seattle, spending much of his time in railroad cars. Unlike most other Americans then, who never ventured far from their places of birth, in his first eighteen years Roscoe Arbuckle had seen mountains and metropolises, the bleakest deserts and the densest forests. He had lived on farms as well as in the largest city west of St. Louis. He had traveled a thousand miles from his hometown of Santa Ana. He made an impressive fifty dollars weekly. He answered fan letters, greeted admirers, signed autographs.

While doing a stint in a Portland, Oregon, theater in 1905, he agreed to join two burlesque comedians, Leon "Rubberlegs" Errol and Pete Gerald, during their run across the upper West. It was a gig that, despite halving his pay, allowed him to branch out from illustrated songs to sing numbers untethered to a slide show—and to try his hand at comedy.

He said it was Errol "who persuaded me that I had a voice, ability, and that I would make a good actor." Errol also "taught me several valuable things like how to fall all over the place without making myself a candidate for a hospital." Practicing stunts, dancing soft-shoe, mastering comedic timing, personifying characters in costumes and self-applied makeup—this was Arbuckle's education, Errol was his teacher, and stages were his schools. Other than his dodging the hook at an amateur show, there is no remembrance of Arbuckle being a funny youth. To the contrary, he was reserved, only coming out of his shell when he sang. But at eighteen, he began to develop the skills of a comedian.

In Butte, Montana, a boisterous copper-mining town known for its vast district of bordellos, saloons, and gambling halls, the trio performed with a blonde singer of large proportions and dubious character who was popular with the overwhelmingly male audiences. A liberal drinker, she often missed her entrances, and one evening when she could not be found, a new woman appeared onstage, dressed in the female singer's white gown and sporting a blonde wig, singing "The Last Rose of Summer" in a falsetto. It was Arbuckle. The audience loved it, and even more so when the enraged female singer showed up and chased him around the stage.

The upper West circuit, known in vaudeville as the "death trail" because of the long distances between venues, was not lucrative, so Leon Errol accepted a better offer.* Arbuckle attempted to fill Errol's role with Gerald but floundered. He was not yet a skilled comedian. Gerald found a new partner, and Arbuckle returned to the dying medium of illustrated songs, earning enough for a seat on a train back to San Francisco. There, at 5:12 AM on the morning of April 18, 1906, he was awoken by a tremendous earthquake. Fires, caused by ruptured gas mains, burned for another four days and nights.

Arbuckle turned again to Alexander Pantages, who booked him as a singer in the prospecting town of Vancouver, British Columbia. When that engagement folded, he joined a stock company performing classic plays for appreciative audiences in Alaska. Heavy costumes guarded the actors against the chill of drafty theaters, just as beards and bearskin coats did for most in attendance. At the end of the year and the beginning of the next, he was in a burlesque revue in Seattle, singing solo and in choruses and doing two comedy roles per show. His rotation of characters included Jasper the Janitor, Little Willie Wilkinson, and Private Roundhouse, as he continued to refine his comedic abilities.

Twenty-year-old Roscoe Arbuckle returned to San Francisco in February 1908. He had traveled far over the previous four years, and from

---

* After a lengthy run with the Ziegfeld Follies, Errol achieved moderate fame as a comedic film actor, appearing in more than 160 mostly short movies from 1921 to his death in 1951.

boy to man, but he ultimately ended up where he started, no wealthier nor better established and still alone. There is no remembrance of him having had a girlfriend before that point, and there was little time for relationships to develop on the road. Life as a vagabond vaudevillian in the red-light districts of mining and ranching towns had grown wearisome. He wanted to stick somewhere long enough to establish his singing career. After auditioning, he was signed to sing with the Elwood Tabloid Musical Comedy Company when it moved south that June to the new Byde-A-Wyle Theatre across the street from Long Beach's Virginia Hotel, a favorite getaway destination for the region's elite and only seventeen miles from Santa Ana. Arbuckle was returning to Southern California as a featured performer at a first-rate venue.

In romantic comedies the term "meet cute" applies to the contrived ways the male and female leads meet, such as one insulting the other on a train before realizing they're both headed to the same workplace. One day, while returning to Long Beach from a sightseeing trip in Los Angeles, Arbuckle noticed a young woman seated across from him on the electric train. He offered up a smile to the auburn-haired, blue-eyed girl, who was barely five feet tall and one hundred pounds. She refused it. When her suitcase began to slip in the luggage rack above her, he pushed it back, again bidding for her attention.

"Please don't touch my suitcase," she told him. "I don't like blonds or fat men. I can manage for myself."

"Sorry," he said. "Gee, I'm sorry." He moved to another seat.

"I don't know what got into me," the woman later recalled. "Actually, I was attracted to him, but I couldn't let myself be picked up, could I?" Of his appearance, she remembered: "He was heavy but handsome. Oh, God, he looked like he had been scrubbed to death. He had a complexion any woman in the world would die to have. His hair was so blond. And he was dressed meticulously, white trousers, white shoes, blue coat, and a straw hat." Self-conscious about his excess weight, Arbuckle remained a meticulous dresser throughout his life.

The young woman was Minta Durfee. Her family, living near downtown Los Angeles, was representative of the city's working class. Just before the movies came, Los Angeles was a city of manufacturing and oil production, an "open shop" enclave as envisioned by a few business titans. Charles "Buck" Durfee was a railroad brakeman. His wife, Flora, was a seamstress. They had six children, the fourth of whom, Araminta, was born October 1, 1889. Known as Minta, she was seventeen and the stagestruck veteran of only school theater productions when a family friend put her in the chorus of a play at Los Angeles' Burbank Theatre. Afterward, she secured a chorus job with the Elwood Company in a new show at the Byde-A-Wyle. On a June day, preparing to stay in the Virginia Hotel with the rest of the company, she and her bulging suitcase boarded an electric train headed south to her new job in Long Beach. On the way, she deflected the attentions of the blond fat man.

Durfee saw Arbuckle again at the first rehearsal, but when he laughed at her outrage after being called a "dame" by her employer, he only validated her initial reservations. It was during the show's first performance, when Arbuckle's baritone voice and soft-shoe dancing enchanted the crowd, that he began to enchant her too.

The show ran twice daily. After each second show, some company members drank or danced, but Arbuckle and Durfee strolled the boardwalk beside the beach. Enamored of his singing, she encouraged him to try for bigger billings and venues. He had his own suggestion—that they sing a duet in the Byde-A-Wyle program. Holding hands at center stage, the round young man with the mellifluous voice and the waif beside him sang "Let Me Call You Sweetheart" to each other.

Fifty years later, Durfee wrote:

> His ability to do everything naturally, humorously, artistically, and with ease, made me realize he was a genius. His [effect] on audiences, his poise, lack of vanity and jealousy amazed me. I was overwhelmed by his personality and talent. He was all artist on stage, but off the stage he was the big boy who played leapfrog on the beach, swam like a champion, shot billiards to perfection, and while he did so, drank huge pitchers of cold buttermilk.

The show folded at the end of July, and Durfee planned to spend time with her family in Los Angeles before returning to chorus lines. After the final performance, Arbuckle and Durfee walked to the end of a pier, standing hand in hand, the inky waves shimmering with moonlight. He professed his love; she professed hers. It was the first romantic relationship for either of them.

To Arbuckle, if two people were in love they should wed. "Will you marry me?" he asked.

When she was noncommittal, he scooped her up and dangled her over the dark Pacific, threatening to cast her in if she said no. It was the gesture of a child, bullying playfully to hide his insecurities. She said yes. He subsequently asked her father for her hand in marriage.

Six weeks after meeting, on August 5, 1908, the couple married in the Byde-A-Wyle. Their union was turned into a for-profit, "special, once-in-a-lifetime" attraction by the theater company. Accompanied by a twelve-piece orchestra, Arbuckle sang "An Old Sweetheart of Mine" while a picture of him and his bride was projected onto a screen. The audience applauded him for five minutes. It may have seemed fantastical to twenty-one-year-old Arbuckle: marrying an eighteen-year-old girl he barely knew onstage before a paying audience, but by then the often-awkward young man was most comfortable bathed in klieg lights with all eyes upon him. Perhaps to him, turning his own wedding into another performance was a means of making such an extraordinary event feel more ordinary and not less.

Their scheduled honeymoon was replaced by a one-month run with a show in the farm town of San Bernardino, sixty miles east of Los Angeles. Durfee was bedridden with pleurisy. Arbuckle sang illustrated songs. As the newlyweds lived together in close quarters, Durfee (who kept her maiden name for stage purposes) was still getting to know the man she had married so soon after meeting him. Privately, he was sometimes shy and sometimes brooding but other times romantic or playful. He could be racked by insecurities and doubt, and yet he was supremely confident when singing. Onstage or off, he was happiest when he was performing.

{3}

VIRGINIA

Because the truth about art *is* the company it keeps with the slightly askew, and the real stunt of the beautiful is not to be *too* beautiful.

—Stanley Elkin, "Some Overrated Masterpieces"

Then as now the fashion and film industries worshipped at the altar of youth, so it was common for models and actresses to shave years off their ages. Today virtually every source, including her tombstone, lists her birth year as 1895, and it is commonly believed she was born in New York City, but Virginia Caroline Rapp entered this world on July 7, 1891, in Chicago.

Decimated by the great fire of 1871, Chicago rebuilt itself as a metropolis of wood and masonry but also metal. Steel skyscrapers reached ever higher beside Lake Michigan. Between the inferno and 1900, the city hosted a World's Fair, and its population exploded from 300,000 to 1.7 million, landing it second in the nation, behind only New York City. It was America's industrial heart, pulling in materials, pumping out goods. Waves of immigrants arrived from Eastern Europe, and after the Civil War a steady torrent of rural Americans migrated north in search of manufacturing, construction, and meat-packing jobs. Away from the towers of State Street, the mansions of Lake Shore Drive, and the monuments of the World's Fair, the city was a patchwork of ethnic enclaves, row after row of bleak tenement houses, brown and gray boxes squeezed together.

It is likely Virginia Rappe grew up in just such a brown or gray box. The only child of Mabel Rapp, Virginia was born out of wedlock when Mabel was either seventeen or eighteen. Virginia never knew her father,* and she initially believed her mother was her sister and that an older woman who answered to the name Caroline Rapp was her mother. Later, she believed Caroline was her grandmother. She was not—and was probably no relation.

Two days before Christmas 1892, mother Mabel made the newspapers, described as "a pretty girl of nineteen," after being locked in Chicago's Veteran's Building by a janitor. She was in the news again in 1898 when she was arrested for passing bad checks in association with "the most dangerous gang of forgers the police have dealt with for years." Mabel was a part-time chorus girl and sometimes model. For some time between 1900 and 1905, she and her daughter lived in New York City. Mabel Rapp died before her thirtieth birthday.

An orphan at eleven, Virginia lived in the Chicago household of her "grandmother," Caroline Rapp, and was also looked after by Kate Hardebeck, who would later call herself Rappe's "adopted aunt" and state that it was Mabel Rapp's deathbed wish that "auntie" look after Virginia. Friends would describe Rappe in childhood as a "rollicking schoolgirl, addicted to roller skates, short skirts, bobbed hair and athletic sports of all kinds." In addition to her athletics, she took dancing lessons, perhaps hoping to follow her late mother into choruses onstage.

In 1907, the year she turned sixteen, Virginia began her modeling career, changing her name from the pedestrian Rapp to the more exotic Rappe (pronounced "Rap-pay"). The five-foot-five teenager was entering an infant industry. London designer Lady Duff Gordon is credited with training the first couture models in 1894 and staging the first runway show in 1904. Then and until World War II, Paris and, to a lesser degree, London dominated high fashion. When Rappe first

* It was later claimed that Rappe's father was an English nobleman visiting Chicago for the World's Fair—an assertion disproved by the fact that Virginia was conceived more than two years before the 1893 exposition opened.

struck a pose, American women were only beginning to earn a steady income modeling dresses and hats at live shows, mostly in department stores, and in newspapers and magazines. Like the earliest motion picture actors, models were widely perceived as déclassé and were virtually all anonymous.

However, from nearly the start of her career, the ambitious Rappe sought publicity. A 1908 article in the *Chicago Tribune* asked in a bold headline, ARE THE ARTISTS' MODELS OF CHICAGO MORE BEAUTIFUL THAN THE FAMOUS MODELS OF PARIS? and featured two photo illustrations of Rappe. The piece, written by a man, paints the seventeen-year-old girl as both ingenuous and manipulative:

> It is predicted by the artists of the city that Virginia Rappe will be one of the world's famous models after the years have mellowed her and taken from her posing the slight touch of childish gaucherie which still remains. She is unreservedly beautiful and, young as she is, shows remarkable understanding of and sympathy for the subjects she represents.
>
> She is a simple little girl of 15 years* who looks out on the world with the clear, dewy eyes of a child just awakened from sleep. She lives at home, where she is the pet of the family, and she poses because she is extremely pretty and she "wants to." What Miss Rappe has wanted to do she generally has done. She is not spoiled; she has merely a happy faculty for making others see things in the same light in which they appear to her.

For a year beginning in September 1911, she worked at the mammoth Mandel Brothers department store in downtown Chicago, sometimes as a model but mostly as a sales clerk. Also in 1911 she entered into a pact with sisters Gladys and Ethel Sykes, each promising to never

* Even at seventeen she was shaving two years off her age. By twenty-four, four years were subtracted, and at twenty-eight it was seven.

accept a marriage proposal.* In October 1912, the three Chicagoans were living in New York City, where their beauty was "attracting considerable attention in the theaters and restaurants of the Longacre Square district" in midtown Manhattan. By then Rappe was likely a full-time model—and one of the first Americans who could state modeling as her occupation. She traveled extensively. When she appeared at fashion shows in the largest department store in Omaha, Nebraska, in September 1913, a newspaper interview noted, "Miss Rappe spends most of her time in New York when she is not touring the country to appear at style shows in big stores."

Published in newspapers throughout the country in 1913 was an article focused on Rappe's advice to young women. The suggestion of "Virginia Rappe, who as a commercial model travels over the United States and Europe at a salary of $4000" was that women avoid being stenographers ("too many of those") or waiting in line for poor-paying jobs and instead think outside the box. Specifically, she advocated working for wealthy families, doing tasks such as shopping or caring for silverware—the sort of jobs employers may not have known they could hire someone to do. "Be original—every girl can be that," Rappe concluded. Today the prospect of domestic work as a novel solution to unemployment seems quaint at best, but at a time when only 18 percent of American women were employed for wages, and when their most common jobs were seamstress, teacher, nanny, or maid, the idea of women creating their own positions and approaching employers rich enough to necessitate such positions was presumed a newsworthy strategy. Rappe followed her own advice by networking with people much wealthier than herself. It's also notable that at a time when the average annual salary for employed men and women was $1,296, Rappe claimed to make $4,000 (more than $90,000 in today's dollars).

---

* Stage actress Gladys Sykes had recently divorced Arthur Greiner, a race car driver remembered for a horrific crash in the inaugural Indianapolis 500 in 1911. The first to break her vow, she agreed to remarry him a year later.

She traveled abroad in a manner mostly reserved for the moneyed class. A front-page news story early in 1914 focused on her and a female friend returning to New York City from Europe on an ocean liner: "Girls in Pink Bloomers Mystify Ship's Passengers." Staking out the cutting edge of fashion, the pair (smiling in a photo, bloomers covered) stirred up some TMZ-style publicity for their underwear—though seen only via the "pink puffs" at their ankles.

Taking her own advice to be original, in early 1914 Rappe began designing her own line of clothing. She subsequently relocated to San Francisco, in part to market her fashions at the World's Fair, which launched on February 20, 1915. There she befriended a dancer who had married a millionaire, Sidi Spreckels, who ushered Rappe into high society.

Rappe the entrepreneur continued to use the press regularly for publicity. If she were designing fashions today, she would surely be a maven of social media. Then, she supplied a steady stream of stories about her designs to the papers. In May 1915 alone, there were four syndicated newspaper articles about her latest clothing creations, each with a photograph. In one, she is smiling in a gossamer hat of discoid lines: "The hat of the moment is the spider-web hat, and it's the creation of Miss Virginia Rappe, a young woman who has lifted fashion designing to the plane of fine art." A similar story showcases her ridiculous "monoplane hat," shaped like its namesake by "aviation enthusiast" Rappe. (She made a submarine hat too, as U-boats were much in the news.) Another features her "summer muff" and says her "artistic conceptions of fashion have made her famous as a creator of original style." Women's high fashion was adventerous then, but Rappe was exploring new territories, and the gambit kept her in the news.

The fourth story that May was headed "Here's the Tuxedo Girl, How Do You Like Her?" and in a photo Rappe wears a black tuxedo coat and skirt and white hat, smiling with hands upon her hips, as if confidently asserting women's liberation. The article states:

> Equal clothes rights with men!
>
> That's the important plank in the summer girl's clothes policy and she's already putting it in practice—behold the Tuxedo coat!

> It was Miss Virginia Rappe of Paris and Chicago, an artist whose medium is clothes, not paint nor oils nor clay—who first invaded the masculine wardrobe, carried off the Tuxedo coat idea and immediately converted it into a chic little street suit, attractive enough to wear to a tea, and practical enough for a shopping tour or an out-of-town journey.
>
> "Personality is the secret of dress," says Miss Rappe. "If women would study their individual style and their temperament as well, and dress to suit their personality American women would be the best dressed women in the world."

The next month, her "peace hat," shaped like two dove wings, scored publicity. A month earlier, a German U-boat had sunk the British steamship *Lusitania*, and among the 1,198 deaths were 128 Americans. The cry among many Americans to join the Great War was thunderous when Rappe publicly cast her lot with the pacifists:

> "The women of America want world peace," said Miss Rappe today. "We should express our peace sentiments in our clothes. If we believe in peace why wear military jackets and soldier caps. Clothes influence our minds. I believe that if we wear the dove of peace and the beautiful American colors have a place in our scheme of dress we will soon create a strong sentiment for peace."

Here, then, is the reality of Virginia Rappe, who at twenty-four years old established herself as an entrepreneur, demonstrated creative acumen and political independence (feminism, pacifism), adeptly utilized the press, and provided career advice to her fellow women. It contrasts sharply with the jaundiced view of her that was born in the courtroom in 1921 and only grew in the decades that followed.

Though Rappe never married, she repeatedly broke her pact to never become engaged. She committed to marry at least three men, and perhaps two more. In 1910 in Chicago, she met Harry Barker, a real estate developer from Gary, Indiana. After Rappe's death, he denied having been engaged to her. However, she did wear "a man's diamond ring of his," and another witness testified that she broke off their engagement.

Her first confirmed engagement was to forty-year-old sculptor John Sample, who reportedly broke up with her. In July 1915 it was Argentine diplomat Alberto d'Aklaine, described as a "member of an old aristocratic family of Argentina." Rappe told friends he was "nice but old enough to be my grandfather." He was followed by dress designer Robert Moscovitz, who died in San Francisco in a trolley car accident.

The d'Aklaine engagement, especially, indicates that social climbing affected some of her romantic choices. At that time in San Francisco, her best friend was Sidi Spreckels, who was notorious for marrying up. As we shall see, a final Rappe engagement was claimed by one more powerful man, and if true, it was severed only by her death.

Robert Moscovitz's tragic death may have contributed to Rappe's decision to move to Los Angeles in the spring of 1916, but she was likely motivated chiefly by the same magnet that pulled thousands of beautiful young women to Hollywood annually. So-called "movie-struck girls," most still in their teens, poured into Los Angeles from all over America, seeking the sudden fame and fortune of Mary Pickford and Lillian Gish. Each may have been the cutest girl in her high school and star of the drama club too, so of course she figured the studios would leap at the chance to make her a star. All but a few were destined for an endless stampede of disheartening cattle calls. Many faced poverty and hunger. In a sense, they were following Rappe's advice to "be original," but the migration inspired alarmed editorializing in the small towns those daughters left behind. Some such editorials painted the movie community as a den of prostitution, venereal disease, and drugs.

Rappe took up residence in the Hollywood Hotel, a palatial resort in the heart of Hollywood that was home and office to actors, producers, directors, and writers—the famous, the soon-to-be, and the never-to-be. She later moved in with her "adopted aunt" Kate Hardebeck and Hardebeck's husband, Joseph, who at this point lived just off the southeastern edge of Hollywood. Prolific film star Louise Glaum was a friend.

There were likely days when Rappe felt that big-screen stardom would remain as elusive for her as it was for thousands of other movie-struck girls, most of whom were years younger than her and many of whom had acted onstage. However, because the films of the era were silent and thus void of spoken dialogue, acting acumen was of lesser importance in many roles than it would be when sound was married to pictures. Physical appearance and personal connections could be the deciding factors in casting.

Rappe's fashion design career had sputtered, but she continued to model and travel. She struck poses in an Atlanta department store in the spring of 1917. The same year, she scored her big break when she won a lead role in the feature film *Paradise Garden*. The picture is now lost, but the *Variety* review states:

> "Paradise Garden," a seven-part Metro featuring Harold Lockwood, contains numerous twists away from the conventional "vamp" ideas. . . . Virginia Rappae [*sic*] as Marcia Van Wyck and Vera Lisson as Una Habberton were opposite Lockwood, the former a mild "vamp" and hardly doing justice to a number of closeups. She possesses a dreamy pair of eyes, with the black hair of this type. It will take a number of like roles before she reaches a number of other established "vamps."

It's ironic that her first and juiciest role was that of vamp, then a new and trendy word (derived from "vampire") for a woman who uses her sex appeal to entrap and exploit men. Furthering this irony is the fact that Lockwood's character is initially infatuated with her but upon discerning her promiscuous nature grows violent and "tears her dress in the rear, leaving her practically nude down to the waist."

The following year, *Paradise Garden*'s director cast Rappe again, this time in the anti-German World War I film *Over the Rhine*. But with the signing of an armistice between Germany and the Allies on November 11, 1918, the movie was shelved. Two years later, it would be recut and released as *An Adventuress* but barely make a blip. Another two years would expire before, in 1922, it was recut again and released as *The Isle of Love* in an effort to take advantage of the recent fame of two previously unknown actors: Rudolph Valentino and the late Virginia Rappe.

Only this version survives, and it is an incoherent mess, often reaching the status of "so bad it's good": an amalgamation of bathing beauties at a beach, biplanes, a cross-dresser, a lengthy fistfight in the back of a speeding convertible, and a convoluted, contradictory plot about schemers taking over an island of pleasure that inexplicably harbors German soldiers. Cuts are jarring. Intertitles seem stolen from another awful movie. The movie does live up to its title in featuring some surprisingly risqué content, including topless women in a stage show entering and exiting a pool.

Rappe is nearly as revealing when she steps out of the same pool dressed only in a sheer, sleeveless gown. Her role as Valentino's love interest is stretched out via repeating shots of them together in an automobile. Introduced with "Just about the neatest of all the fair femininity on the Isle is VANETTE," Rappe is first seen lounging on a sofa with one leg up, dressed elaborately, smiling slyly, and casually smoking—the very vision of emancipated womanhood, including a flapper's hairstyle.

The factor that most impacted Rappe's acting career was her relationship with director Henry Lehrman. Born in the Austro-Hungarian Empire in 1881, Lehrman had immigrated to America from Vienna in the final days of 1906, and in 1909 he began working at the Biograph movie studio in New York City. According to legend, the thickly accented immigrant told pioneering director D. W. Griffith he was an agent with France's Pathé, then the world's largest film production company, and when the ruse was debunked, Lehrman was christened "Pathe."* He appeared as a bit player in Griffith's films before collaborating on Biograph comedies with actor/writer/director Mack Sennett. When Sen-

* If the nickname was derisive, Lehrman rolled with the punch. When he moonlighted for another company in 1912, he directed under the name "Henry Pathé."

nett left Biograph in 1912 to form Keystone Studios in Los Angeles, Lehrman joined him.

Comedy movies then were one reel, lasting ten to twelve minutes, and they were churned out with great rapidity. Lehrman directed at least twenty-eight in 1913, overseeing such greats as Mabel Normand, Ford Sterling, Charlie Chaplin, and Roscoe Arbuckle, and he earned a second nickname, "Suicide," for pushing actors to do dangerous stunts. He formed his own production company, L-KO (Lehrman-KnockOut) and made better-than-average comedy shorts, then moved over to the Fox Film Corporation to head up its comedy division. Off the lot, he spent lavishly on luxury automobiles, and the dapper bachelor was a regular fixture in nightclubs.

In late 1918 Rappe began a romantic relationship with Lehrman. By January 1920 she was listed as "boarder" at his Hollywood residence, along with a twenty-four-year old maid. (Rappe's occupation was "actress." Her mother was from her namesake state of Virginia; father from New York. Benjamin Button–style, her age was twenty-two.) She was by then living the high life in Hollywood, complete with her own limousine driver and personal trainer. Dating the head of a production company had another perk. Lehrman cast Rappe in at least four films, all comedy shorts. The first, the 1919 Fox production *His Musical Sneeze*, starred Lloyd "Ham" Hamilton, then a comedic star on the rise.

After more than two years with Fox, Lehrman struck out on his own again in early 1919, forming Henry Lehrman Productions and constructing his own $200,000 studio near Hollywood. His old friend Roscoe Arbuckle rented space there to film.* In a peculiar newspaper article from September 1919, the company announced the signing of Rappe, labeling her "one of the wealthiest and most beautiful young women of western America" and the "richest girl of stage or screen." The announce-

* When the press mistakenly called the studio a Lehrman-Arbuckle partnership, Lehrman released a terse statement saying Arbuckle had merely leased space to make movies. Later, when the two were decidedly not friends, Arbuckle said his renting from Lehrman "was the only way I could get back money he owed me."

ment identified her as both an "heiress" and "the owner of more than 800 acres of the richest oil lands of Texas," with her "wealth computed in the millions." The story was bunk, likely devised by Rappe or Lehrman to garner publicity, but the fiction points to Rappe's high aspirations.

Henry Lehrman Productions' first movie, 1920's *A Twilight Baby*, again starred Lloyd Hamilton and featured Rappe in a supporting role. Publicizing it, Rappe returned to her advice formula, this time serving up old-fashioned moralizing delivered while she was living out of wedlock with her employer. This lengthy headline and subhead screamed from a newspaper on March 4, 1920:

> Back to Quakerland! "Nix of Lounge Lizards and Jazz Babies," Says Virginia Rappe, Praising "Less Society" Manors Communities Seeking To Put A Sensible Damper On Midnight Larks, "Seven-Dates-A-Week" And Other Health-Robbers Of Young Girls Have A Hearty Endorsement From Virginia Rappe, Plucked From Dazzling California Society By Henry Lehrman And Who Will Be Seen In "A Twilight Baby," One Of The 3 Ring Jazzy Circus Features At The Dome Theater. She Has A Way Of Curtailing Mothers' Fears.

The worldly Rappe offered cautions about Jazz Age partying and concluded, "Maybe it wouldn't hurt any of us to be more Quakerfied." Whether any Quakers attended *A Twilight Baby* is unknown. Rappe, though, certainly enjoyed Jazz Age dancing; she won prizes for such at a Santa Monica resort popular with the Hollywood crowd. Trial testimony later placed her at several Hollywood parties during this time.

Invoices drowned Henry Lehrman Productions before it was truly established, and Lloyd Hamilton fled the sinking ship. Rappe acted in two more Lehrman productions without him, *The Punch of the Irish* and the unfortunately titled *A Game Lady*. But by the time the latter film was released, less than two months before Labor Day 1921, Lehrman had lost his studio and his house. Debts would burden him for years. Perhaps coincidentally, his two-and-a-half-year relationship with Rappe also faltered. He signed on to direct four films in Fort Lee, New Jersey, moving, alone, to New York City in the spring of 1921.

Rappe moved back in with the Hardebecks, and she paid Kate Hardebeck twenty-five dollars weekly for housekeeping duties (or perhaps not, for Hardebeck later made a claim against Rappe's estate for over $1,000 in unpaid labor). She probably hoped to rekindle the romance with Lehrman eventually. She seldom went out socializing. "Her chief delight was in tramping over the hills around Hollywood with her dog," Hardebeck stated.

On July 7, 1921, Rappe turned thirty, a pivotal age, especially for a model/actress cognizant of the relentless march of time.* Billie Ritchie, who acted in at least sixty motion pictures, all of them for Lehrman, including *A Twilight Baby*, died the day before and was buried the day after, likely clouding Rappe's birthday with a melancholy pall.†

She had other reasons for glum introspection. Her designing and modeling careers were stalled, and after a promising film debut in 1917, four years later she had failed to establish herself as a marketable movie star. Judging only by the scant evidence that survives, she was not a particularly gifted screen performer, and her acting reputation within the industry may have been harmed by her relationship with Lehrman and the resultant perception that she was not earning her plum roles via talent. After at least three engagements and one lengthy cohabiting relationship, she remained unmarried. The great financial success she sought, which friends like the upwardly mobile Sidi Spreckels and celebrated screen vamp Louise Glaum enjoyed, had eluded her. Perhaps as she treked over the Hollywood hills, alone with her dog and her thoughts, this innovator who preached "be original" was planning the next phase of her life.

---

* It's almost certain Rappe did not celebrate the date as the big three-oh. She may not have known her true age.

† His *Variety* obituary perpetuated the myth that Richie died due to lingering injuries after being attacked by ostriches while filming a "Suicide" Lehrman production, but his death certificate lists the cause as stomach cancer.

As August came to a close, a low-level movie publicist named Alfred Semnacher, whose marriage was ending, asked Rappe if she wanted to ride with him to her former home of San Francisco. (Semnacher would later claim he had known Rappe for "about five years" but only well for the previous six weeks, during which time he had tried to place her in one movie role.) Rappe said yes. Like Semnacher, she was in need of a vacation. A woman named Maude Delmont, whom Rappe had never met, would be joining them.

They left early on Saturday, September 3, traveling in Semnacher's automobile on the future Highway 99 up through Bakersfield, passing herds of sheep and cattle, orange groves and lettuce farms. They had sandwiches and coffee in vacuum bottles, packed by Kate Hardebeck. Delmont later claimed she brought a pint of whiskey along for the trip and had six drinks on the way; her two travelmates did not partake.

They stopped in the town of Selma, south of Fresno, where Delmont solicited subscriptions for a labor journal, her current job, and they spent the night at a ranch where a friend of Delmont's lived. Rappe sent a card to Hardebeck, saying she was having a "very pleasant time." At 1:30 PM the next day, the trio from Los Angeles headed to San Francisco. They checked into the Palace Hotel at 9:30 PM the evening before Labor Day.

At 11:30 the following morning, while eating breakfast with the others in the hotel restaurant, Rappe was paged and received a message from Fred Fishback, a movie director she knew. He was at the nearby Hotel St. Francis with actor Lowell Sherman and the man who made the whole world laugh, Roscoe "Fatty" Arbuckle. The three men had a suite of interconnected rooms on the top floor, including a room for lounging and drinking and dancing. Would she care to join them?

{4}

SANITARIUM

> San Francisco can support both comic and tragic conclusions because the city is geographically *in extremis*, a metaphor for the farthest-flung possibility, a metaphor for the end of the line.
>
> —Richard Rodriguez, "Late Victorians"

When the morphine wore off around midnight the morning after Labor Day, Virginia Rappe awoke in the dark, screaming in agony again. A light came on, illuminating that woman again, Semnacher's friend Maude Delmont. Rappe lay in a single bed in room 1227 of the Hotel St. Francis. She did not know where she was or why that woman was near. There was only the pain, relentless, merciless, like a sword run through her abdomen. Doubled over, writhing in the sweaty sheets, she wailed.

The groggy Delmont summoned the hotel's house physician, Dr. Arthur Beardslee, to return to room 1227. He was the second doctor to examine Rappe, and as he had five hours earlier, he injected Rappe with morphine and again she fell quiet. Her pupils constricted, and her eyelids grew heavy. He checked her pulse and examined her body. Her abdomen was sensitive to his touch. The doctor left. The room was again quiet and dark.

Again, at five o'clock in the morning, the morphine wore off and Rappe was screaming. Again that woman was near. Again the doctor was summoned. Again a shot of morphine was administered. Delmont told Beardslee that Rappe had last urinated fifteen hours prior, so the doctor catheterized his patient, producing a small amount of urine, tinged with dark blood—the color indicating it was older and not from an open wound. He believed the catheterization would remedy Rappe's ailment and she would recover with sufficient rest. He left.

Frustrated with the house doctor, Delmont telephoned a physician she knew with the literary name of Dr. Melville Rumwell, and he agreed to take over the patient's care after Beardslee was discharged. In addition to his private practice, Melville was then an assistant professor of surgery at Stanford University's medical school and head of Stanford's outpatient clinic. Arriving just before nine o'clock on Tuesday morning, September 6, he examined Rappe and found no visible signs of injury, despite the sordid story Delmont told. Rappe said she did not recollect anything that had happened. She had lost consciousness while in 1219 with Arbuckle, and when she woke she was in agony. She continued to feel pain from her lower abdomen to her chest. Rumwell's diagnosis was alcoholism (in this case, meaning poisoning by alcohol), and he left without administering any more treatment than hot compresses on her midsection. In his professional opinion, she did not seem in dire health.

The morning of Tuesday, September 6, Arbuckle spoke with Al Semnacher, and both men surmised that Virginia Rappe was merely ill from downing too much alcohol. After noon, Arbuckle picked up the $611.13 tab for all three interconnected rooms and room 1227, where Rappe then lay. Then he, Fishback, and Sherman checked out of the St. Francis.

Arbuckle drove Fishback and Sherman to pier 7 on San Francisco Bay, and the three men boarded the steamship *Harvard*. The vessel, after being employed for troop transport during World War I, had just completed its first month of West Coast service, traveling two roundtrips weekly between Los Angeles and San Francisco, alternating with its sister ship, the *Yale*. Arbuckle's Pierce-Arrow was also on board for the fourteen-hour journey. The white steamer set off at 4:00 PM.

On board, Fishback spotted a friend, who introduced him and Arbuckle to a young woman and her mother. Twenty-one-year-old Doris Deane was just beginning an acting career. That evening, at Arbuckle's invitation, she and her mother joined the Hollywood men for dinner in the stateroom. Doris was charmed by the famous Fatty, thirteen years her elder. He was enamored with the young brunette. Before the ship docked in the port of Los Angeles the following morning, they made arrangements to go out together on Saturday evening. It was a date Roscoe Arbuckle would not keep.

As she lay in the bed in room 1227, a sequence of three nurses administered to Virgina Rappe: Jean Jameson, Vera Cumberland, Martha Hamilton. Each encountered a patient who was sometimes hysterical with pain, sometimes calmly offering up her health history. The nurses generally blamed alcohol at a time when the home-brewed and counterfeit hooch of Prohibition was responsible for much abdominal pain. Their treatment was catheterizations, enemas, and hot compresses.

On Thursday, September 8, Dr. Rumwell returned to check on his patient. He found her in no better condition, and he suspected a severe kidney infection and possible venereal disease. At around noon, he had her admitted to the sanitarium of Dr. W. Francis Wakefield, who specialized in obstetrics and gynecology. Maude Delmont and Nurse Jameson rode with Rappe in the black, hearse-like ambulance. The fact that Rappe was admitted there and not to a hospital was subsequently questioned, but Wakefield sanitarium was the closest medical facility (located just six blocks from the St. Francis), Rumwell had staff privileges there, and it was common then for even those with serious maladies to be treated outside of hospitals. Wakefield, which specialized in high-risk births, had two operating rooms as well as the staff and equipment to treat emergency patients.

The greater question is why Virginia Rappe was left to suffer in a hotel room for three days, her severe pain deadened with morphine or merely comforted with a hot towel, despite being (cursorily) examined by three doctors and three nurses and despite the appearance of blood in her urine. (The first doctor was Dr. Olav Kaarboe, called on the evening of September 5 when Dr. Beardslee was at first unavailable. His diagnosis: too much to drink.) If she had been properly treated during this time, it's likely the public would never have learned about a Labor Day party at the Hotel St. Francis, and the remainder of the lives of Virginia Rappe and Roscoe Arbuckle would have been very different.

Arbuckle returned to his Los Angeles home on the morning of Wednesday, September 7. His mansion was in the heart of the city's prestigious West Adams district, just southwest of downtown. A capacious garage on the premises housed his six luxury automobiles. He had a secretary/housekeeper, a butler, a maid, a gardener, a cook, and a chauffeur. Upon Arbuckle's arrival, the butler likely carried in his luggage. He was greeted by his three dogs, including Luke, his world-famous pit bull terrier.

He checked in with his manager, Lou Anger. His feature *Gasoline Gus* was a huge hit, and *Crazy to Marry* was about to go into wider release. Two additional films, *Skirt Shy* and *Freight Prepaid*, had wrapped and were being readied for theaters.

The next day, he met on the Paramount lot with the director of all four previous films, James Cruze, and they watched the final editing of *Freight Prepaid* and sketched ideas for *The Melancholy Spirit*, a comedy about a drunken ghost in which Cruze was planning to direct Arbuckle next. The actor suggested the young woman he had just made a date with, Doris Deane, for a role in *The Melancholy Spirit*, and Cruze and Arbuckle agreed to meet with her the following week. Arbuckle telephoned her with the good news. But like their scheduled date, this meeting would have to be canceled. He would not appear in *The Melancholy Spirit*, which was released the following January while he was spending his days in a San Francisco courtroom and was indeed melancholy.*

* Retitled *One Glorious Day* and directed by Cruze, it starred legendary humorist Will Rogers in the role intended for Arbuckle.

As the night of Thursday, September 8, bled into Friday morning, Arbuckle dreamed in the ornate, oversized bed in his master bedroom, where the walls and draperies were orchid and green and the furniture was hand-painted to match. Luke likely slept nearby. But Arbuckle was otherwise alone in the bedroom of his West Adams mansion, filled with every luxurious furnishing and decoration he could cram into it. The house, like the cars, and the one car in particular, was a testament to excess—or so it would soon seem.

At Wakefield sanitarium on the afternoon of September 8, Dr. Rumwell examined Virginia Rappe again. He believed her condition was the result of alcoholism and a resulting kidney lesion and infection. He arranged for the application of a Murphy drip to replenish her electrolytes rectally and for morphine injections every four hours.

At around 9:30 PM, the doctor returned to find Rappe's condition had rapidly deteriorated. Her pain was acute, her lower abdomen extended, her pulse elevated. He called in Dr. Emmet Rixford, a professor of surgery at Stanford University, vice president of the American Surgical Association, and one of the foremost medical professionals on the West Coast. After his examination, Rixford agreed with Rumwell's new diagnosis: peritonitis, an inflammation of the peritoneum—the abdominal lining and cavity. The likely cause was an infection created by a ruptured fallopian tube or bladder. A third doctor, George W. Reid, concurred. They believed that in her present, severely weakened condition, Rappe would not survive surgery. She was administered antibiotics in an attempt to fight off the infection.

Rappe instructed Maude Delmont to telephone her San Francisco friend Sidi Spreckels. Likely at Rappe's request, Delmont asked Spreckels to telegram Henry Lehrman in New York and inform him of his former domestic partner's dire health. Delmont also telegrammed Kate Hardebeck with the bad news. Spreckels came to Rappe's side on Friday morning. The former model's skin was pallid and clammy, her eyes sunken, her lips parched. She was so weakened, in and out of consciousness, that Spreckels was uncertain her old friend recognized her.

"Oh, to think I led such a quiet life, and to think I would get into such a party," Rappe allegedly said.

When Spreckels returned later with a telegrammed response from Lehrman, the patient had slipped into a coma. Spreckels telephoned Pastor James Gordon of the nearby First Congregational Church. He came immediately, dropped to his knees in the room, and prayed for the comatose woman's recovery and spiritual peace, punctuated with "Thy will be done." At 1:30 PM on September 9, 1921, left alone in a room at Wakefield sanitarium, Virginia Rappe died.

{5}

HOLLYWOOD: 1909–12

> Last night I was in the Kingdom of Shadows. If you only knew how strange it is to be there. It is a world without sound, without color. . . . It is not life but its shadow, it is not motion but its soundless spectre. . . . It seems as though it carries a warning, fraught with a vague but sinister meaning that makes your heart grow faint.
>
> —Maxim Gorky, after viewing a movie in 1896

There was no bolt of lightning striking a kite, no apple falling to earth. The development of moving pictures was more like a lacework of waterways, some of which trailed off while others fed the rivers that reached the sea. The film projector's antecedent was the sublimely named magic lantern, which dates to the seventeenth century and featured images painted on glass slides and projected via oil lanterns. In the 1830s, devices simulated motion by arranging a series of images in a spinning circle, and in subsequent decades this concept of revolving images was married to lantern projection. French science teacher Émile Reynaud hand-painted small panes of glass, each image slightly different from the one before, joined them with a perforated metal strip, and hand-cranked the panes through a lantern projector, magnifying the mini-paintings onto a screen. On October 28, 1892, he presented the first publicly viewed animated motion pictures. His Paris revue of three cartoons proved immensely popular and ran until 1900.

Reynaud's cartoons first screened in the midst of a race on both sides of the Atlantic to do the same with photographs. In 1889 Englishman William Friese-Greene created a camera capable of taking ten photos per second on strips of perforated celluloid film. That same year, Thomas Edison assigned his company's photographer, W. K. L. Dickson, to head a team tasked with creating a machine for viewing moving photos. Edison's Kinetoscope, unveiled in 1893, established the principles of modern projectors. But it wasn't a projector. Films were watched via a magnifying glass while peering into a peep-show-style box. Kinetoscope parlors opened in 1894, but they were a novelty that peaked and waned rapidly. The public was soon ready for the next big thing.

The intercontinental race for a photo-film projector finished in a near three-way tie in 1895. Contenders included the Cinématographe, invented by France's Lumière brothers and used for the first public screening (March 22); the Eidoloscope, the creation of the by-then-independent Dickson and another former Edison employee, Eugene Lauste, which was used for the first commercial screening (May 20); and the Phantoscope, invented by Charles Jenkins and Thomas Armat and used for a series of commercial screenings (September). The Jenkins/Armat partnership soon dissolved and Armat went to Thomas Edison, who purchased the rights to the Phantoscope, renamed it the Vitascope, and played the role he knew best: inventor, claiming the innovation as his own. On April 23, 1896, the American motion picture industry had its official coming-out party when a Vitascope projected movies onto a screen at Koster and Bial's Music Hall in New York City. The series of one-minute flicks played between vaudeville acts and included a shot of waves breaking, which caused the audience to recoil for fear of getting drenched.

Edison, the American Mutoscope Company (launched by Dickson and later renamed Biograph), and American Vitagraph were the initial "Big Three" studios, producing most of the earliest American movies. Each peddled its own projector and churned out a stream of artless films that it sold to vaudeville theaters. Audiences quickly tired of seeing vignettes or mere action. After all, with their flickering shades of gray, two dimensions, and lack of sound, movies were delivering less than spectators received from stage performances.

It was the development of "story films" such as *The Life of an American Fireman* and the phenomenally successful *The Great Train Robbery* (both 1903), both directed by Edwin Porter for Edison, that brought movies into the modern era. Audiences flocked to theaters to watch actual tales told on film, and nickelodeons began sprouting up where stores once were. For five cents, you got flat floors, 199 unfastened chairs (200 would be subject to ordinances), and a continuously repeating program of silent shorts accompanied by piano or organ music. Such theaters catered to the working class who could not afford tickets to a play.

In 1908 the Big Three formed a trust to squash competitors who wouldn't purchase their licensed cameras and projectors. (Initially, Kodak was a signatory and sold its film stock exclusively to trust companies, but it rescinded this exclusivity in 1911.) One policy was to present no on-screen credits, thus suppressing the salaries of nameless talent. Instead, movies were marketed on the strength of each company's reputation. The first movie star was world famous but known only as "the Biograph Girl." Directing, writing, or acting in motion pictures was considered a routine chore, and it paid accordingly.

The earliest film studios were in the New York metropolitan area, or in one case, Philadelphia, and two cases, Chicago. But this presented a quandary. At a time when the sun was a crucial component of even indoor lighting (via glass ceilings), the short, drab days of winter made it difficult to keep to production schedules, and the potential for inclement weather made exterior shooting impractical. Some studios wintered in Cuba, and in 1908 Jacksonville, Florida, emerged as "the World's Winter Film Capital," a title it kept for years afterward. However, Jacksonville had already, nearly unnoticed, gained a rival for the title from another city in another temperate coastal area, this one on the opposite side of what then seemed a much wider continent.

By the spring of 1909, newly married and barely twenty-two, Roscoe Arbuckle had traveled all around the American West, but he had never been east of the Kansas farm where he was born. It was therefore fortuitous that the movie industry came to him.

Started by former magician and minstrel show operator William Selig, the Selig Polyscope Company was one of the two aforementioned Chicago studios. It shot mostly slapstick comedies, travelogues, and industrial footage. In the winter of 1907, Selig director Francis Boggs and a small crew had journeyed west. Though the interiors were filmed in Chicago (with a different cast), they shot exterior scenes for *The Count of Monte Cristo* at a beach near San Diego and on a roof in downtown Los Angeles, earning incorrect renown as the first fictional film with footage shot on the West Coast. (The actual first was *A Daring Hold-Up in Southern California*, shot for Biograph in 1906.) Boggs moved to Los Angeles in March 1909 and set up an outdoor studio for Selig in the drying yards behind a downtown laundry. The third movie Boggs shot there was *Ben's Kid*, a western that featured comic relief by a young actor named Roscoe Arbuckle.*

At the time, Arbuckle and Minta Durfee were living with her family, and local vaudeville bookings had dried up. The newlywed husband was anxious to prove he could provide, even if it meant the star singer was reduced to doing mime work in the debased medium of flickers. At Selig, he earned the going rate of five dollars daily, a pittance when compared to future Hollywood salaries but acceptable (the equivalent of about $125 today) for what surely seemed an easy effort compared to a day of performances onstage.

By Arbuckle's second film, *Mrs. Jones' Birthday*, he was starring. He played a husband who keeps comically breaking the presents he buys for his wife. The *New York Dramatic Mirror* noted, "The Jones of the picture is a fat fellow, a new face in picture pantomime, and the earnestness of his work adds greatly to its value. There are times when he plays to the camera, but there are other actors more experienced than he in this line of work who do the same thing."

---

* *Ben's Kid* is now lost, as are the five additional films Arbuckle made for Selig.

He did not tell his wife where the daily five dollars came from, but following a tip, one morning Durfee and her mother took the next streetcar after his to find Arbuckle in a red satin shirt and a cowboy hat with a guitar, playing to a hand-cranked box camera. "My God! They're making a motion picture!" Durfee exclaimed, as if catching her husband in flagrante delicto.

Seeing them, a furious Arbuckle shouted, "Go home! Go home!" Later, his mother-in-law asked him why he had hidden his work, and he answered, "Because I didn't want Minty to know or to come down there. I'm afraid they will ask her to work. They need people, but I'm not going to permit her to work there. It isn't show business. I'm ashamed of this kind of work, but we need the money." He later said of film acting in those early years, "Then, there was nobody breaking in. Everyone was doing as I did—sneaking in."

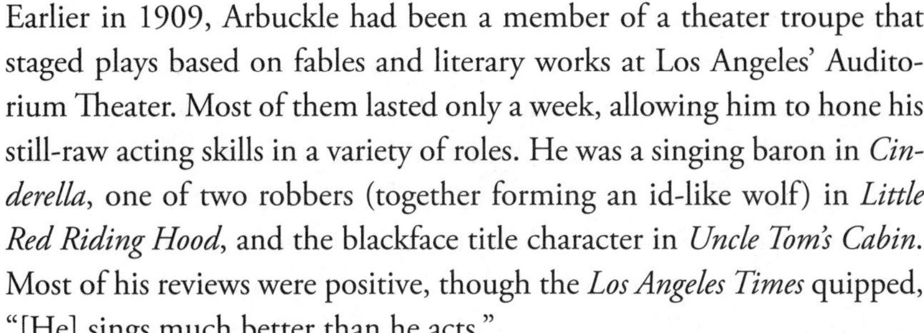

Earlier in 1909, Arbuckle had been a member of a theater troupe that staged plays based on fables and literary works at Los Angeles' Auditorium Theater. Most of them lasted only a week, allowing him to hone his still-raw acting skills in a variety of roles. He was a singing baron in *Cinderella*, one of two robbers (together forming an id-like wolf) in *Little Red Riding Hood*, and the blackface title character in *Uncle Tom's Cabin*. Most of his reviews were positive, though the *Los Angeles Times* quipped, "[He] sings much better than he acts."

Also in the Auditorium company with Arbuckle was Walter Reed, a veteran vaudevillian who highlighted his Irishness in his comedy. The two men decided to form a partnership. This was a second chance for Arbuckle after failing to deliver the laughs when he paired up with Pete Gerald three years prior. With more practice, he was by then growing confident in his comedy.

In May 1909 Reed and Arbuckle were booked into the Orpheum Theater in Bisbee, Arizona (three years before statehood), just ten miles from the Mexican border. With gold, silver, and copper discovered in abundance in the Mule Mountains that surrounded it, Bisbee had blossomed into one of the liveliest of the mining boomtowns. In the early

1900s the residents numbered over twenty thousand, mostly men, and when not shoveling ore, those men wanted to forget about shoveling ore. Drinking, gambling, and whoring were the most popular pursuits. The notorious Brewery Gulch contained a sinner's row of some fifty saloons, bordellos, and opium dens that never closed. Bisbee was the West at its wildest.

It was no place for a lady, so Arbuckle's wife stayed in Los Angeles. But her mother admonished her, "You wanted him, you married him, and you'll go where he goes." Durfee boarded a train heading east and moved into a Bisbee boarding house with her husband. She became a principal member of the Reed & Arbuckle company, acting and singing, sometimes in duets with her husband. The company changed its musical comedies every few days, staging such plays as *King Slodo* (described as an "Oriental burleque [*sic*] operetta"), *A Tip on the Derby*, and the minstrel *Way Down South*, with Arbuckle as Uncle Rastus.

Like a Las Vegas entertainer booked at a casino for an extended run, Reed & Arbuckle made the Orpheum its venue for most of 1909. There the performers ingratiated themselves with the mining executives living up high in the exclusive "Quality Hill" houses. Arbuckle sang solo at an Elks Club funeral, he and Reed serenaded and boxed three comical rounds (declared a draw) at an Eagles Club affair, and the entire company sang at a country club "dinner and smoker."* Other times they bonded with the miners who lived in the valley in crowded barracks. Reed was the timekeeper and Arbuckle the play-by-play announcer at an Orpheum wrestling match attended by seven hundred "enthusiastic followers of the game" in which the Swedish champ defeated California's best, the Big Indian. Arbuckle was a fixture in Brewery Gulch saloons, much to Durfee's consternation, and they both regularly visited the new Warren Ballpark, where the Bisbee Muckers baseball team played. Arbuckle guest umpired one game. After another game, the press noted, "Roscoe Arbuckle and the rest of the Orpheum bunch were again on

* The other entertainment that evening was for gambling purposes: a wrestling match that ended in a draw, a cane spree (one-on-one fight for a walking cane) that ended in a draw, and a duel between a dog and a badger in which the dog was victorious. If that's the entertainment at your country club, what are your saloons like?

hand making things lively in rooter's row, especially the ladies. Arbuckle gave a free eccentric dance act when his hopes ran high in the seventh. None of the thespians ever miss a game and are among the loyalist [*sic*] of the loyal legion."

Other than a stint in northern Mexico performing for American miners, the Reed & Arbuckle company remained in Bisbee for eight months. After their final, standing-room-only performance on December 27, the *Bisbee Daily Review* wrote, "At the close of the performance, members of the entire company lined up across the stage and sang 'Auld Lang Syne' as a fitting climax to their long, successful engagement here. The company left yesterday for Clifton, and Bisbee will now be a 'sure enough' lonesome town during the intervals between road shows." Clifton was another mining boomtown, also in the Arizona Territory. The Reed & Arbuckle tour of the Southwest wound down.

By the spring of 1910, Walter Reed was back in Bisbee. Arbuckle and Durfee were back in Los Angeles and living with her parents again. Arbuckle organized his own vaudeville company, writing, producing, and starring; Durfee had supporting roles. They played the Princess Theatre in downtown Los Angeles, cranking out three shows daily (3:00, 7:45, 9:15), seven days a week, changing the content weekly. The brutal schedule persisted from late April to mid-July, and the shows earned positive reviews. A newsman later recalled:

> I remember [Arbuckle] when he was a third-rate comedian playing down at a cheap little burlesque house on Main Street. He used to come climbing and blowing onto the old Main street car after the show was over. I remember how it used to embarrass him, yet sort of please his vanity, to be looked at by the people on the late car. He had about as much chance, then, of being rich and famous as he had of being turned into a little baby lamb with a pink ribbon around his neck.

At the end of his Princess Theatre run, worn down by the manic pace of producing and performing in twenty-one vaudeville shows weekly, Arbuckle decided to focus solely on his acting. He did his fourth Selig movie in the fall of 1910, *The Sanitarium*, of which *Variety* wrote, "It may have been slammed together in the night." And he joined the Burbank Theatre stock company, acting in dramas and musical comedies.

At home, Arbuckle and his wife were sharing space not only with Durfee's parents but also with her seventeen-year-old sister, Marie; her thirteen-year-old brother, Paul; and a thirty-five-year-old male lodger. But Arbuckle was content with the arrangement. He grew especially fond of his mother-in-law and brother-in-law. Flora was more fostering of him than the mother he had lost when he was twelve. Paul was the younger sibling he'd never had.

He played baseball and tag with Paul and other kids, or they pitched corncobs at tin cans and other makeshift targets. Durfee remembered, "Roscoe's swinging off the street car was always a 'come on' for the kids in the neighborhood. They would yell, run and jump on him. We always had studying for the next week's role and song to do, but watching him tumbling on the grass, throwing a baseball or playing marbles made you know he had very little fun in childhood." In contrast to an early life filled with abuse and neglect in which he entered the workforce young, the adult Arbuckle found the childhood he had desired: a loving mother and father, and siblings and friends who wanted nothing more than to play with him. The man-child he was when frolicking with the neighborhood kids would have a great influence on his big-screen persona.

Around the same time, the industry that would make Arbuckle famous was also beginning to coalesce into a now-familiar form. In 1910 the Selig Polyscope Company established the first permanent movie studio in Los Angeles. With nearly 320,000 residents, the city was then in the midst of a population explosion. Having tripled its numbers over the past decade, it would nearly double them over the next decade, and much of the growth between 1910 and 1920 would be due to the industry and glamour of film production.

In addition to its mild weather, Southern California provided movie producers with a landscape appropriate for virtually any story: deserts, forests, mountains, lakes, and ocean, from endless vistas of undeveloped chaparral to a rapidly industrializing metropolis. Los Angeles was also a nonunion town, flush with new laborers eager for any job; the craftsmen necessary for constructing stages, sets, costumes, and, ultimately, movies, pocketed as little as half as much as they did in New York. Land, too, was cheap. Soon every American movie studio of note would establish its base in or around Los Angeles, while former East Coast giants like Edison went bust.

After Selig, the second film company to set up a permanent base in Los Angeles was Nestor, which relocated from New Jersey in October 1911.* The studio opened up shop in a region of Los Angeles known as Hollywood. Named in 1887 in a quest to boost land sales and incorporated in 1903, Hollywood had been annexed by the city in 1910. When Nestor opened up shop there, it was a landscape of orange and lemon trees, dotted with the occasional plantation-style residence. A trolley car track traversed the middle of the dirt boulevard. No one would have suspected then that this sleepy community of citrus farmers would soon become a worldwide synonym for moviemaking.

The launch was ominous. On the day Nestor's studio opened, the film industry suffered its first major tragedy when over at Selig Polyscope, a caretaker burst into a meeting between William Selig and his director Francis Boggs. (Selig had only arrived from Chicago the night before.) Brandishing a revolver, the caretaker fired five times, hitting Boggs twice and Selig once. Forty-one-year-old filmmaking pioneer Francis Boggs died on his way to the hospital. Selig survived the incident. The murderer was quickly captured, but he offered no explanation then and no sensible motivation at the trial before spending his remaining twenty-six years in prison. Thus, the genesis of Arbuckle's cinematic career is also linked to a tragic death of mysterious circumstances, this one occurring on the day Hollywood as we know it was born.

---

* Arbuckle would later act in Nestor comedies, over the course of four weeks in 1913 just before joining Keystone, but the titles of those lost films are unknown.

Arbuckle and his wife joined the traveling troupe of Ferris Hartman, a veteran vaudeville performer and producer whose name was synonymous on the West Coast with first-rate revues. A new show opened every Sunday, sometimes without a rehearsal. Arbuckle won star billing, typically singing two solo songs, performing in two dance numbers, and acting in two scenes. Despite his size, he was a lithe dancer; he was the everyman with surprising talents. Advertisements for a stop in San Jose boasted, "Special Appearance of Roscoe Arbuckle, San Jose's favorite." It's unknown if he visted his father while he was in the area, but the younger Arbuckle seems to have repudiated his abusive parent after leaving home at seventeen.

On a train to Sacramento in September 1911, Durfee experienced cramps. She soon discovered she was pregnant, but her and her husband's ecstasy was short-lived before she suffered a miscarriage. They were devastated. Arbuckle blamed himself, as he reflexively did when bad things happened to those around him. Afterward, Durfee stayed in Sacramento for a week alone to convalesce while the tour moved on to Denver. They were young. They were certain they would have other opportunities to be parents.

When the company reached Chicago, it was the furthest east Arbuckle had ever been and his first visit to America's second-largest market. Contrary to the legend that Chicago was Arbuckle's Waterloo, Hartman's troupe had a critically and commercially successful run there. Afterward, the Arbuckles returned to Los Angeles before heading to the Bay Area again for Hartman's next production. In the summer of 1912 a review of an Oakland performance noted "a nice little chap named Roscoe Arbuckle" and effused, "He is a positive scream, one of the funniest fat farceurs that has caused chortlings for many a month." Once again, he was being discovered—though now it was his comedy and not his singing that earned praise. After years of practicing, he was as comfortable delivering a pratfall or punch line as he was belting out songs.

Though only twenty-five, Arbuckle had worked in theater for a decade, singing, dancing, joking, and acting for his supper, and he must have thought true fame and fortune would always elude him. Whether on the road—sleeping in hotels and rooming houses and train cars—or living in his wife's parents' house, employment was forever fickle, always at risk of being terminated without notice. He seemed destined to be a theatrical lifer, mostly eking by but sometimes not, and always addicted to the same bright lights and greasepaint and applause that had first hooked him when he was a boy looking for a place to belong.

The new offer from Ferris Hartman was stunning on two accounts. First, it was an opportunity for the Arbuckles to see exotic places to which few Americans ventured. Second, Arbuckle was the headliner, and the entire Caucasian American cast would, at times, be playing Asians before Asian audiences in Asia. In fact, Hartman himself had been shocked by the offer, made by a Manila-based American tycoon, to take his company on a tour of the Orient; perpetually in debt, Hartman had to scramble to assemble the necessary cast, costumes, props, and scripts. The troupe of forty-three singer-actors, dancers, musicians, and stagehands set sail on August 12, 1912, on a Pacific Mail steamship headed west. It was a protracted voyage over seven thousand miles of ocean. One room was occupied by the Arbuckles.

Durfee later remembered their excitement in the journey's early days: "Roscoe and I made it a habit to stand together at the rail late at night, staring at the running sea. We were extremely close at those moments, closer perhaps than at any other times in our lives. We were happy, truly happy."

They docked in Honolulu. Hawaii was then a US territory with a governor and an abdicated queen. At the premiere performance, Queen Lili'uokalani—herself a songwriter, musician, and singer—was coaxed from her royal box to center stage, where she gracefully performed a native dance. During their three-week stay on Oahu, Hartman said, he and his troupe were "serenaded by bands and royally entertained." Arbuckle, always an avid swimmer, swam in the surf, sometimes with Olympic swimming gold medalist Duke Kahanamoku.

Hartman's company sailed next to Japan, performing in Yokohama and then Tokyo. Though Japan was racing forward with electric streetcars and gasoline automobiles, rickshaws dominated on many streets. The Japanese often stared at Arbuckle, for a man of large girth was presumed to have equally great wealth. The company performed Hartman's old favorite, Gilbert and Sullivan's *The Mikado*. The all-white cast were made up to look Japanese, with Arbuckle as the title character (*mikado* means "emperor"). It was a hit.

In Shanghai, which was then the "Paris of the East" with a melange of cultures and American and British districts, members of Hartman's company were surrounded by begging children in the street. The contrast was stark between the impoverished majority in the new Republic of China and the native and foreign aristocracy who attended the performances. Reviews complimented Arbuckle in blackface as "a quaint old negro servant" and in a love scene with his wife.

There was more romance between the Arbuckles onstage than off. Memories of the "extremely close" moments on the voyage over had dissipated. Months living in strange cities far away from Durfee's family had taken their toll. Frequently after a show, Arbuckle drank with others in the company, then returned intoxicated to Durfee and complained about his insufficient salary as the show's star. He argued with her and shouted about how much better things would be had they stayed in California. If the voyage there had been their marriage's best of times, his drunken fits in the Far East were some of its worst.

The tour rolled on to two westernized cities: Hong Kong and Manila. The company remained in the Philippines for six weeks, Christmas included, and Arbuckle contracted a throat infection, probably initiated by his late-night carousing. He later all but confirmed this when he blamed it on an incident in which he "barked at a dog who barked at me." Three weeks of shows had to be canceled, causing his popularity with the company to plummet. This, in turn, compounded his insecurities and gloominess. Above all, he wanted to be liked by his coworkers, and his drinking was largely motivated by his desire to fit in with them.

The final performances were in China again, Tientsin and Peking. On January 31, 1913, Hartman's troupe boarded a ship headed east.

When the ship docked in San Francisco twenty-five days later, the Arbuckles had been away from their home country for six months. The couple spent time sightseeing in Northern California, repairing a marriage that had been frayed by Arbuckle's temper tantrums and brooding in China and the Philippines. Then they took a train south. Having traveled further than most Americans then or now, across the Pacific and through the Orient, they had many stories to tell, but the ride south to Los Angeles was bittersweet. Their luggage was loaded with exotic gifts for Durfee's family, but the money for their train fare was borrowed. The Far East tour had provided an order and purpose to their careers, and Arbuckle had been the star—a role that had at times gone to his head. But they were poorer for it. And now they were unemployed.

{6}

POSTMORTEM

California State Board of Health
Bureau of Vital Statistics
Standard Certificate of Death
Wakefield Hospital

Dr. William Ophüls, the fifty-year-old, German-born and German-schooled dean of medicine at Stanford University and one of the country's foremost experts on pathology and bacteriology, received a telephone call from his Stanford colleague Dr. Melville Rumwell with the message that a woman had just died from an apparent case of peritonitis.

Full Name: *Virginia Rappe*
Female White Single
Occupation: *Motion Picture Actress*

In the presence of Dr. Rumwell and nurse Grace Halston, the goateed Dr. Ophüls peered through his wire-rim glasses, examining the exterior of the corpse on a table in a white-walled operating room at Wakefield sanitarium. (The facilities did not have an autopsy room.) He checked Virgina Rappe's face, scalp, and neck, the front and back of her torso, her arms and hands, legs and feet, her genitalia. He found no evidence of a sexual assault. He noted two bruises on her upper right arm and two on her thighs. He poked and prodded her bloated abdomen.

Birthplace: *No Record*
Name of Father: *No Record*
Birthplace of Father: *No Record*
Maiden Name of Mother: *No Record*
Birthplace of Mother: *No Record*

A block was placed under her back to raise her chest. Wielding a scalpel, the doctor or the attending nurse made a deep incision from Rappe's pubic bone to her sternum, slicing through the abdominal wall but being careful not to incise the organs beneath. Absent blood pressure, there was little bleeding, but body fluid leaked from her open abdomen. Without an autopsy table to collect such fluid, it likely fell to the floor and into a drain there. Two further incisions, as deep as the rib cage, were made from the sternum to each shoulder, curving under her breasts. Together the three cuts formed a giant Y on the front of the dead woman's torso.

Date of birth: *1895*
Age: *About 25*

Three large flaps having been rendered—one on either side and one above—the skin, muscle, and soft tissue were pulled back. The ribs were cut away with a saw and shears.

Then Virginia Rappe was truly naked. Revealed in the bright light of the examination room was the dark world inside us all, the intricate patchwork of glistening purple, red, brown, and beige. These were the organs that circulated her blood, distributed oxygen and removed carbon dioxide, digested her food and drink, eliminated waste. The model/designer/actress/daughter/"niece"/lover/friend known as Virginia Rappe was then reduced to the parts that had worked for thirty years to keep her living and the part that stopped working first.

Date of death: *September 9th, 1921*
And that death occurred on the date stated above at: *1:30 PM*

Dr. Ophüls examined the organs, searching for abnormalities. Blood had congested in Rappe's lower abdomen, though he did not yet know the source of the bleeding. He likely removed the intestines. They appeared normal and virtually empty. The pericardial sac was cut open, revealing her heart inside, purplish and veiny. Arteries were flayed and parted to search for clots. He may have taken a heart-tissue sample and drawn blood from a heart chamber for further testing. Each of her spongy lungs was sliced like a loaf of bread and prodded with his gloved hands as he felt for areas of pneumonia or other abnormalities. The lower lobes of one were congested, likely the effect of a common virus. Though stained brown and black, for Rappe was a smoker, her lungs were functional.

Length of residence at place of death: *4 days*
If nonresident, give city or town and state: *Los Angeles, Calif.*

The peritoneum was inflamed, the thin membrane having been stretched outward. Dr. Ophüls prodded the liver and kidneys. The stomach, pancreas, duodenum, and spleen were treated similarly. Whenever asked, the nurse handed him a scalpel, a large knife, scissors, or forceps. Dr. Rumwell observed and assisted Dr. Ophüls as Rappe's parts and pieces were inventoried and inspected. The two doctors inspected the ovaries, fallopian tubes, uterus, rectum, and bladder, removing each.

Did an operation precede death? *No*
Was there an autopsy? *Yes*

Beneath the penetrating light in a room at Wakefield sanitarium, Dr. Ophüls, Dr. Rumwell, and Nurse Halston stared at the pinkish-red bladder, the ball of smooth muscle that had collected urine secreted from Virginia Rappe's kidneys. It was unusually small. As suspected, this was the organ that had failed first. There before them was the proof: in an inflamed area of the bladder's outer wall was a hole, about an eighth of an inch in diameter. With a scalpel handed to him by Nurse Halston, Dr. Ophüls made an incision beside the tear. The two doctors could then see inside the organ to a small clot of blood. There was a tear in the bladder's inner wall, about three-quarters of an inch long, that corresponded to the outer hole. It was later described by Ophüls as "a clean break." Dr. W. Francis Wakefield was also called into the room to examine the bladder. There was no doubt. This, then, was the flaw in her mortal flesh that had led, four agonizing days later, to Virginia Rappe's demise.

> The cause of death was as follows: *Rupture of the bladder*
> Contributory: *Acute peritonitis*
> Signed: *W. Ophüls*
> *Sept. 10, 1921**

A second autopsy was performed on the day of Rappe's death, beginning at 8:15 PM, this one by Dr. Shelby Strange, autopsy surgeon of the San Francisco coroner's office. He too examined Virginia Rappe's five-foot-five, 140-pound body. He noted eleven bruises (right upper arm, torso, legs) as well as a small puncture mark on her left arm, likely from a hypodermic needle used during her time at the sanitarium. Photographs were taken. The bladder and what Dr. Strange later called "the female organs" had been removed, but Dr. Ophüls brought them to Dr. Strange in specimen jars. Viewing through a microscope, Dr. Strange noticed a chronic inflamation in the tissue of the ruptured bladder. He sent the stomach to the city chemist for further analysis.

Barring any indication from the chemist of poisoning, his conclusion was the same as Dr. Ophüls's, but he reversed the cause and contributory factors. Cause of death: acute peritonitis resulting from rupture of the bladder. Owing to the extreme rarity of spontaneously rupturing bladders, Strange came to a logical conclusion—one coroners now would concur with. As he later testified, he believed that the tear in Virginia Rappe's bladder was caused by "some external force."

* Though the death certificate was signed on the tenth, the autopsy occurred on the ninth.

{7}

RISE: 1913–14

> Overnight the obscure and somewhat disreputable movie performers found themselves propelled to adulation, fame and fortune. They were the new royalty, the Golden People.
>
> —Kenneth Anger, *Hollywood Babylon*

They called it the "Fun Factory," and he called himself the "King of Comedy." Together they invented or perfected the tropes of cinematic slapstick: car chases, foot chases, custard pies to the kisser, incompetent policemen, frantic pacing, and gravity-defying feats. They propagated a working-class aesthetic that appealed to nickelodeon audiences, including millions of recent immigrants who needed not be English-literate to laugh at the universal language of buffoonish authorities and pratfalls. They spawned technical innovations in editing, stunts, and set design, and over a mere five-year run incubated some of the greatest acting talents of the silent era, including Charlie Chaplin, Ford Sterling, Mabel Normand, Harry Langdon, Chester Conklin, Charley Chase, Harold Lloyd, Gloria Swanson—and Roscoe Arbuckle.

The Fun Factory was Keystone Studios, and the King of Comedy was its chief operating officer, Mack Sennett. Born Michael Sinnott in 1880 to Irish immigrants, he was raised in rural Quebec, where his father was the town blacksmith. When he was seventeen, his family moved to Connecticut; they subsequently relocated to Massachusetts, where he worked as a boilermaker for a year and in a pulp mill for several. Dissatisfied with manual labor and inspired by a vaudeville show, he took singing lessons and in 1902 moved to New York City.

In his own perhaps apocryphal remembrance, he ventured to Broadway to audition at the Metropolitan Opera House for a celebrated theatrical impresario, who declared, "But let's be practical about you. If you won't go home, young man, the best way for you to start is this: go down to the Bowery and start in burlesque." Thus, the legend goes, Sennett's introduction to show business laid bare the divide between the leisure class (Broadway) and the working class (Bowery), which became a prominent theme of his films and fueled his lingering resentment toward the producers of "highbrow" entertainment.

Of the Bowery burlesque houses where he was soon performing, Sennett said, "The round, fat girls in nothing much doing their bumps and grinds, the German-dialect comedians, and especially the cops and tramps with their bed slats and bladders appealed to me as being funny people. Their approach to life was earthy and understandable. They whaled the daylights out of pretension. They made fun of themselves and the human race. They reduced convention, dogma, stuffed shirts, and Authority to nonsense, and then blossomed into pandemonium. . . . As a thoroughly accredited representative of the Common Man . . . I thought all this was delightful."

After struggling to eke out a living in theater, in 1908 Sennett turned to moving pictures. He found a job as an actor for Biograph, which was headquartered in a converted Manhattan mansion. Sennett joined the company around the same time as a writer/actor named David Wark Griffith. Within months, D. W. Griffith was Biograph's head director, and many of his films featured Sennett; the director thought the burly, dark-eyed Irish Canadian had a memorable appearance and used him in mostly oafish bit parts like "gypsy" and "peddler." The Canadian and the Kentuckian shared a passion for walking, and while strolling Manhattan's streets, the former absorbed all he could from the latter about the infant art of moving pictures. Of Griffith, Sennett said, "He was my day school, my adult education program, my university."

Cinema's first great filmmaker, D. W. Griffith was humor-deficient, as were most of his movies. It was Sennett who began directing and writing Biograph's comedies in late 1910. If Griffith was his university, the otherwise barely educated Sennett earned a graduate degree in comedy on his own, reading comedic short stories and plays and all he could about directing theatrical comedy. Via trial and error, he deduced the timing necessary for generating laughs in two dimensions without sound.

In July 1912, having helmed more than one hundred shorts for Biograph but frustrated with the meager financial rewards and eager for more autonomy, Sennett broke away from the studio, accepting an offer to run a new comedic film company for Charles Baumann and Adam Kessel. The budding producers had been poaching Biograph talent for the previous two years, and when Sennett partnered with them, he brought along not only Virginia Rappe's future boyfriend Henry Lehrman but also his own girlfriend, actress Mabel Normand, as well as actor Ford Sterling. Baumann and Kessel supplied $2,500 in seed money, and as equal partners with Sennett, they launched Keystone Pictures Studio, which shot a handful of movies in New York and New Jersey before Sennett, Sterling, Normand, and Lehrman headed west.

Keystone opened up shop in a former horse ranch east of Hollywood, in a part of Los Angeles that is now Silver Lake but was then called Edendale. Expanding by both buying and constructing a hodgepodge of buildings, it became the Fun Factory, a plant devoted to churning out comedies as efficiently as Ford assembled Model Ts. "Overnight our place was busting its seams with idiotics. Anything went, and every fool thing you might think of under the influence of hashish or a hangover went big. We were awash with pretty women, clowns, and storytellers who couldn't write. We made a million dollars so fast my fingers ached from trying to count." So said Sennett in his 1954 autobiography, embracing and enlarging the mythos of Keystone as the studio that rewrote the rules of comedy by subverting conventions on-screen as well as off.

Keystone's dubious press releases presented it as a madhouse and its employees as the instigators and/or victims of chaos: a script editor worked on a pile of logs; Sennett and actor Fred Mace were chased through a park by a bear; Ford Sterling was nearly turned to dust in an exploding taxicab. The industry press greeted the stream of "shocking but true" stories with some skepticism but promulgated them nonetheless. Keystone even shot "behind-the-scenes" films, imbuing its casting calls and productions with slapstick antics.

There was at least one true eccentric at Keystone. Mack Sennett reveled in his persona as the original Beverly Hillbilly. He wore a Panama hat with the crown cut out, believing sunshine on his prematurely gray and perpetually chaotic hair would stave off baldness. He rode on horseback around the lot every morning. For "health," he breakfasted on raw radishes and onions and downed whiskey shots. Stains from the tobacco he chewed colored his ill-fitting suits. He had a gargantuan marble and silver bathtub installed in his office on the top floor of the lot's tallest building, and while bathing daily, he surveyed his employees down below and gave orders, drafted letters, and held story and business conferences. After each lengthy bath, his flesh was kneaded by a Turkish ex-wrestler.

There were few motion picture conventions in the infant industry, and the lack of sound was the greatest liberator. Constricted by neither dialogue nor microphones, most of Keystone's stories were improvised after sketching out threadbare plots, and all of Southern California was the studio's backlot. Its filmmakers shot performers amid public events big and small, from the World's Fair to a bakery fire. The lake, streets, and houses near the studio appeared in movie after movie. Sennett's greatest innovation was speed—the accelerated editing pace of chase scenes and fights, the breakneck repetition that drew giggles into guffaws. Presaging the animated shorts of later decades, the films' violence often escalated to crashes through walls, fired bullets, and exploded bombs, and yet the victim always rose again with no greater damage than a blackened face and a frown. Critics dismissed the movies as vulgar, and yet that vulgarity—as with vaudeville and burlesque—appealed to the average moviegoer. Keystone comedies embraced a contorted logic all their own. They were live-action cartoons for adults.

Watching the early Keystone flicks today, their weaknesses are as apparent as their strengths. Plots are vaporous and repeatedly recycled. Acting can veer into wild pantomime. Racial and ethnic stereotypes abound. Much screen time is merely filler before the next round of mayhem. Still, you wait for the infectious moment when the uppity heiress lands in the lake or the Keystone Kops give chase in cars, bicycles, and shoes but can't quite catch the crook. Or when, again and again, a fat man falls.

In early April 1913 Roscoe Arbuckle got off the trolley car wearing his best white suit and strolled onto the bustling Keystone studio lot in Edendale. He met Mabel Normand, he met Mack Sennett, and he was hired for a salary of three dollars per day—40 percent less than he'd made for his film debut four years prior. The popularity of movies was rising in 1913, however, and Arbuckle likely felt motion pictures could provide greater long-term financial security than vaudeville.

Other histories say that Arbuckle's nephew Al St. John followed his uncle to Keystone, but the opposite is true. On the heels of an acrobatic vaudeville career, in which his specialty was bicycle tricks, the gawky, loose-limbed St. John had begun doing bit parts for Keystone the previous January. The nineteen-year-old likely introduced Uncle Roscoe, just six and a half years his senior, to Sennett. St. John, Henry Lehrman, and Sennett himself all acted in Arbuckle's first Keystone film, *Murphy's I.O.U.*, released on April 17, 1913.

Sennett called Keystone "a university of nonsense where, if an actor or actress had any personality at all, that personality developed in full blossom without inhibition." Still, he was initially oblivious to Arbuckle's skills. The new arrival was relegated to background roles—until another Keystone trailblazer intervened.

If Mack Sennett was the King of Comedy, Mabel Normand was the Queen. Born into poverty in 1893 in New York City, she was an accomplished swimmer and diver as a teen and labored in a garment factory before taking up modeling and working as a bit player at Biograph. There she met Mack Sennett. For greater opportunities, she moved to Vitagraph, where she usually played a mischievous comic character named Betty, but Sennett encouraged her to return to Biograph. By August 1911 she was back in the fold, acting first in D. W. Griffith's dramas and then almost exclusively as the star of Sennett comedies. She was a dark-haired, doe-eyed pixie with a coy smile, and the camera loved her. So did the man behind it.

Contentious romantic relationships between directors and actresses are now a Hollywood cliché, but Mack and Mabel were the first and set the template.* He was a gray-haired bear in ill-fitting clothes who never shed his rural Canadian sensibility; she was short and slender, fashionable, almost fourteen years younger, a native New Yorker. But they shared a contagious sense of humor, dedication to their developing crafts, and a laissez-faire attitude toward many of life's concerns.

By the time Sennett left Biograph to launch Keystone, Normand was a minor star, and she moved to the opposite coast with the promise of $125 weekly. Her fearless physicality dominated early Keystone comedies like *Mabel's Lovers*, released in November 1912, the first of numerous films with her name in the title.

The emergence of Mabel Normand was something of a one-woman revolution. Before her and for some time after, comediennes were deemed grotesques who tarnished the traditional norms of womanhood. They were typically overweight or otherwise unattractive, if they were represented at all. Comedy was mostly man's work—even if that man wore a dress. A *Moving Picture World* editorial of December 1912 professed, "Woman is rarely ridiculed in comedy. It does not please the better class to see her held up to scorn."

"Madcap Mabel," as she was known, was both ridiculed and ridiculing. She was also petite and pretty. She battled the male villain and

* Their tumultuous love story was adapted into the 1974 Broadway musical *Mack & Mabel*.

rescued her male rescuers. She did her own death-defying stunts. She played laborers, as in *Mabel's Dramatic Career* (dramatic career: maid) and *Mabel's Busy Day* (busy day: hot dog vending), and her persona was ideal for a studio whose principal audience was the working class. The sort of man who toiled all day in a factory thought she was an attainable beauty, and the sort of woman who, as Normand had, toiled all day as a seamstress revered her. In 1914 the readers of *Photoplay* would vote her their favorite film personality. She was also one of the first female movie directors.

Normand craved excitement. She bought a luxury sports car and a sixty-foot yacht used for deep-sea fishing and party trips to Catalina Island. She learned to fly an airplane. She won dance contests, ocean swimming contests, and horse races, and she entered cyclecar races. She purchased a summerhouse in a California forest where she and her friends fished and hunted. Her adventurous exploits were regularly reported in the press, but there was never any mention of a boyfriend. Instead, a notice in August 1914 would clarify that, despite reports, she had not recently married "the director general" of Keystone. Presumably, she was as emancipated as her strongest characters, one of the first to live the Hollywood lifestyle, with no greater concern than which car to drive and how fast to go.

It was Normand who prevailed on Mack Sennett to cast Arbuckle in larger roles, convincing her boyfriend that the fat man was funny. In *Peeping Pete*, one of the six movies Arbuckle appeared in in June 1913, he plays a housewife whose husband (Sennett) spies on his neighbor's more attractive spouse.* Normand coached Arbuckle to ignore the noisy, cranking camera and play to the invisible audience. He excelled, and as summer wore on he blossomed into her costar, supplanting Ford Sterling, and his salary was bumped to the standard five dollars per day.

* *Peeping Pete* was released on June 23, 1913, with *A Bandit*; they are the oldest surviving Arbuckle movies.

The pairing of newcomer Arbuckle with the studio's lead actress was a calculated maneuver. In 1913 Keystone's chief competition was cinema's first comedy duo, John Bunny and Flora Finch. Between 1911 and 1914 they would star in over 160 Vitagraph comedies, popularly known as "Bunnyfinches." They were as incongruous a pair as Mack and Mabel: Bunny was short and fat with a bulbous nose and jolly demeanor, resembling an obese gnome. Finch was skinny, stork-like, with an elongated neck and beaklike nose. Together playing wife and husband, they looked like the number 10, and the physical contrast was inherent in their comedy. So when Sennett, who had previously acted with Finch, teamed up Arbuckle—fair-haired, five foot eight, rotund—with Mabel Normand—raven-haired, five foot one, dainty—he hoped to duplicate the success of Vitagraph's duo.

In July Normand and Arbuckle shot *A Noise from the Deep*, playing lovers who fake Normand's drowning so they can elope. The pair supposedly improvised a gag that spawned a thousand repetitions when Normand hurled a custard pie from a catering table into Arbuckle's face.* In fact, the first pie toss occurred in Keystone's *That Ragtime Band*, released two months earlier. Regardless, the splat of pies would become a regular component of slapstick, and no one was more adept at throwing them than Arbuckle. The ambidextrous actor sometimes accurately hurled two pies in opposite directions simultaneously.

In movies, Arbuckle's athletic ability could finally be put to good use: running, leaping, swimming, climbing. He was fearless with stunts and became expert at taking falls and absorbing and throwing blows. Comedic acting had not come naturally to him—he had originally struggled with it onstage—but now he practiced playing to the invisible viewers, following Normand's advice. Because big screens could exaggerate expressions, he discovered that less could be more. He learned how to virtually "wink" at the audience via the camera lens, bringing viewers

* Custard tended to break up in flight, and it faded into the background when shot in monochrome, so later pies consisted of blackberries and whipped cream—a concoction local bakeries readily learned to devise.

in as his confidants, whereas others, including Ford Sterling, were forever hamming it up, virtually "shouting."

Arbuckle acted in at least thirty-six movies in 1913, the year in which he went from a background player to a headliner and his screen persona took shape. There were a lot of opportunities for the public to get to know him. His name was secondary; people recognized his round face and portly body on the street and at the beach and in the saloon. They had spent joyful time with Fatty before encountering Arbuckle. He was one of the first to experience this—one of the first to be recognizable on sight and beloved too, wherever he went, for his moving image was traveling before him like a goodwill ambassador.

Movie fame was different. Pharaohs, emperors, and prophets were famous millennia ago, as were presidents, authors, and stage actors in the decades before moving pictures, but their names were better known than their visages. Early newspaper and magazine "photographs" were engraved reproductions, losing verisimilitude. If you saw a celebrity alone in public void of any trappings of his fame, you would have passed by without pausing.

Not only did motion pictures accurately capture performers, they captured them in movement—smiling, laughing, frowning, striding. Stars were glimpsed inside kitchens and bedrooms and parlors, in something resembling ordinary life—and yet bigger, projected in shades of gray onto a screen, sometimes in close-ups so you could note the slightest twitch, the briefest narrowing of the eyes, the precise alignment of their teeth. Movie fame was an artificial familiarity, but familiarity nonetheless.

Roscoe Arbuckle would be much wealthier later—more famous and, later still, infamous. He would own a mansion and possessions fit for a mansion, and he would employ servants to care for it all. But the best times came just before that, when he could see it coming. He was going to make it. Out of all the vaudevillians, out of all the actors in the young medium of moving pictures, out of everyone who strode through Keystone's Edendale gates, out of even those with caps and clubs who appeared then as Keystone Kops (what were their names?), Roscoe "Fatty" Arbuckle was going to make it. His dreams were going to come true.

The first true "Fatty" film, *Fatty's Day Off*, was released in September 1913, pairing him with Normand again and tossing in a Kops chase. In title credits, he was Roscoe "Fatty" Arbuckle. The nickname he'd hated as a kid was destined to stick to him as an adult, and he accepted it as a business practice but never otherwise adopted it. Friends called him Roscoe, with the exception of Normand, who affectionately nicknamed him "Big Otto," after an elephant in the large public zoo William Selig had recently opened in conjunction with his movie studio.

Fatty's Day Off also featured a twenty-three-year-old actress making her big-screen debut: Minta Durfee. Arbuckle's wife later remembered this as a momentous time in their marriage. They were working together and with his nephew Al St. John. They were making new friends in the new movie industry and living in the city they thought of as home. They developed an especially close friendship with Normand. With his growing fame, Arbuckle's salary rose—to $200 per week by the end of 1913.

One movie presaged troubles to come. In *Fatty Joins the Force*, Fatty reluctantly saves the police commissioner's daughter and is given a job as a cop. He's harassed by kids, one of whom hits him in the face with a pie. After jumping in a lake to wash, the kids steal his clothes, and his fellow cops assume he drowned. Afterward, he falls about in his underwear, and a hysterical woman tells policemen, "There's a wild man at large." Fatty is arrested, and the film ends with him in a jail cell, disgraced, sobbing, pleading to the heavens.

While a minor Arbuckle movie, *Fatty Joins the Force* nonetheless illuminates the emerging Fatty persona: cowardly (shoved into rescuing the commissioner's daughter by his girlfriend), childlike in his simple outlook, surprisingly spry (a fall after an inadvertent punch turns into a prolonged backflip) but a clumsy chaser prone to stumbles and falls, generally genial but capable of sudden bursts of rage, a schemer whose plans will go awry. It's easy to grasp his appeal to children, for most of his characters possess the personalities of bratty ten-year-old boys, and yet

Fatty's adult motivations—sex, money, occupational success—make him a boylike brat adults could laugh at too.

But Arbuckle was eager to take on a different role: that of director. Seeing how others segued from acting to calling the shots—Mabel Normand directed her first movie in 1913—Arbuckle wanted to do the same. Many of the Fatty films were directed by Henry Lehrman, about whom Arbuckle later said, "All my mechanical knowledge of pictures I learned under the direction of Lehrman." When Lehrman and Ford Sterling left Keystone in February 1914, Arbuckle, who had already supplanted Sterling as the studio's go-to male lead, filled Lehrman's void in the director's chair. Arbuckle—forever curious about technology—supposedly dismantled and reassembled a film camera one night before his directing debut to better understand the essential moviemaking tool. But by the time he first called "Action!" there was another rising star at Keystone.

In a Keystone dressing room, he modeled crepe under his nose until he found the truncated moustache he liked. He slipped on a pair of Arbuckle's pants, losing his legs in the excess fabric. Arbuckle and others, playing cards nearby, laughed. The snug coat may have belonged to Normand, one of the few performers at the studio notably smaller than the English newcomer. The bowler hat he perched atop his dome was Arbuckle's but had originally been Durfee's father's. The clownishly large shoes were Sterling's and had smacked the Edendale streets during Keystone Kops chases. With the addition of a bamboo cane, Charlie Chaplin began to shuffle about, scoring laughs from his coworkers as he pantomimed an impoverished bumbler in ill-fitting clothes struggling to maintain his dignity. The Little Tramp was born.

The character formed in January 1914 but originated in Chaplin's youth, an upbringing worthy of the adjective "Dickensian." When, in Victorian London, his mentally unstable mother was institutionalized, he lived in a workhouse and rural orphanage and with his alcoholic father, who died when Charlie was twelve. He toured Great Britain with a professional dance troupe as a child and spent most of his teenage years playing child characters on England's stages. As he neared age twenty in 1908, he joined the troupe of former acrobat Fred Karno, who was to stage comedy what Mack Sennett would be to movie slapstick. Karno's rehearsal space was even called "the Fun Factory," and there his troupe drilled gags until every gesture was precisely timed. Discovering that pathos and slapstick were a potent mix, Chaplin fleshed out his comedic characters. He practiced a measured rhythm and developed an avidity for perfection.

In 1912 the Fred Karno Company Chaplin was winding down a tour of North America when Sennett and Normand (both still at Biograph) attended a performance. The following spring Sennett told his Keystone partners in New York to find him the English chap in Karno's show, named something like "Chapman" or "Champion." Chaplin signed to Keystone for $150 per week—three times his peak salary with Karno and a substantial investment in an actor yet to appear in a single celluloid frame. In his 1964 autobiography, Chaplin wrote: "I was not terribly enthusiastic about the Keystone type of comedy, but I realized their publicity value. A year at that racket, and I could return to vaudeville an international star."

After fulfilling his obligations to Karno, Chaplin reported to Keystone in December 1913. He was twenty-four and boyish, five foot five and slight, humble and shy—and he was tossed into the assembly line of a second Fun Factory, this one predicated on breaking the rules he had learned at the first. Comedy was fast, emotions were broadly expressed, and rewriting and rehearsals were luxuries the breakneck schedule could not accomodate. "I'm too shy, and I feel uncomfortable around here. I feel lost. I'm in a foreign country, and I don't know anyone," he told Durfee. He starred as a shifty swindler in his film debut, *Making a Living*, which pitted him against the soon-to-depart Lehrman, who also directed. They clashed offscreen as well, when the slow-working newcomer resisted the standard Keystone pace.

Soon thereafter, the Little Tramp made his first appearance, complete with Arbuckle's pants and hat. The character registered with the studio's target audience, for here was a poor man the poor could laugh at. In *A Film Johnnie*, the Tramp is a movie fan who sneaks into a studio. Actors play themselves, including Arbuckle. The bashful Tramp compliments Fatty, even nervously patting his protruding gut, and Fatty hands him a coin before striding away. The Tramp subsequently bumbles onto a set and infuriates a director, and we can now see *A Film Johnnie* as an in-joke about Chaplin's difficulties fitting in at Keystone.

Unlike others at the studio, however, Arbuckle did not resent the peculiar English newcomer nor view him as a threat. Arbuckle was not prone to jealousies; he was much more likely to focus on his own perceived faults. In addition, he was receptive to Chaplin's slower comedic pace, as he himself often lobbied for a greater variety of humor styles in Keystone movies. Finally, Chaplin shared a strong working relationship with Minta Durfee, who frequently acted opposite him; to her husband, this reflected well on the Englishman.

Including two cameos, Arbuckle was in six films with Chaplin in 1914. In *The Masquerader*, written and directed by Chaplin, they play film acting rivals, and in its best scene they torment each other in a dressing room via precisely timed gags. In contrast, in *The Rounders*, which Chaplin also wrote and directed, they play neighbors who, thrust together after drunkenly annoying their wives, go out to continue drinking. They create a ruckus in a posh café, and in a very dark ending, are destined to drown in a rowboat. That peculiar final shot of them asleep side by side and slipping underwater was the last cinematic image of these two comedy giants together.

At the end of 1914, Charlie Chaplin's Keystone contract expired. The Essanay Film Manufacturing Company was a minor studio looking to go major, and it offered him $1,250 weekly and a $10,000 bonus. This was more than Mack Sennett paid himself, and his counteroffer didn't come close. With that, the Little Tramp shuffled away.

There was one more reason why Arbuckle felt no ill will toward the ascendant Charlie Chaplin: his own celebrity, fortune, and creative control were also rising rapidly throughout 1914. When Arbuckle began directing in March, Sennett gave him his own comedy unit, which included Durfee and St. John, and he helmed thirty-one of the fifty films he is known to have acted in that year. He typically worked from 8 AM to 6 PM six days per week. Uncredited, Arbuckle also wrote many storylines, sketching out plots, routines, and stunts. He set comedies in the Old West, an amusement park, cities, farms, a seaside resort, a hot-air balloon, an Indian reservation. Unlike others, he repeatedly delivered finished films on schedule.

Durfee remembered a reward for her husband's punctuality:

> Mr. Sennett asked Roscoe, Mabel, and I to go with him to the famous old Van Nuys Hotel [in downtown Los Angeles], whose cuisine was considered some of the finest in America. And Mr. Sennett *loved* to eat. So finally, before dinner was clear over he handed Roscoe a check, and he said, "This is yours, big boy, because we now have got the release, and we owe it to you because you've kept the reels going," and he handed us a thousand dollar check. And of course neither one of us had ever had one of those in our lifetime.

Nine of Arbuckle's fifty movies in 1914 featured "Fatty" in the title, so that just as moviegoers were turning out to see Chaplin pictures, they were turning out to see Fatty pictures too.* Most featured St. John as some sort of lecher, Durfee as the love interest, and Arbuckle as an ignoble character who bumbles into trouble. Chases, fights, falls, and humiliation ensue.

"Nobody Love a Fat Man?" was the provocative title adorning a magazine profile of Arbuckle in June 1914, the sentiment tempered via the punctuation. Arbuckle joshed back and forth with the interviewer about his weight, his attractiveness to female fans, being confused for

---

* Some movies then were released under multiple titles. So *Fatty Again* might be *Fatty the Fourflusher* a week later at a theater across town.

actor Macklyn Arbuckle,* and the proficiency of the Keystone baseball team, of which he was a member. Of his acting, he joked, "But outside of falling on my ear, being surrounded by snakes, chased by bears, and made to do forty-five foot dives off the long wharf at Santa Monica, my work has been rather uneventful." In truth, Arbuckle loved his work, and he practiced and experimented to improve both his comedic acting and his film directing.

The organist begins to play, the projector flickers, and the light streaming overhead transmits the title card:

Mack Sennett Comedies
Presents
Roscoe Arbuckle
In
"Fatty's Magic Pants"

Outside a boarding house, Fatty and Durfee learn about a benefit dance. Charley Chase returns to the same house and discovers the couple dancing about on the walk. Chase, who is carrying a tuxedo, informs Fatty that he can't get into the dance without formal wear. Durfee decides to go with Chase. Trying to steal the suit, Fatty decks Chase, and then Durfee decks Fatty. The two woozy men fight.

Later, after his mother beats him instead of lending him fifty cents, Fatty steals Chase's tux off a clothesline. The extended shot showcases Arbuckle's growing directing acumen: The clothesline is strung across a courtyard as wide as the film frame from Chase's open window on one side to Fatty's on the opposite. Peeking in from the edge of the frame,

* Macklyn Arbuckle (no known relation to Roscoe) was a Broadway star. His most famous stage role was Sheriff "Slim" Hoover in *The Round Up*, and it was as this character that he uttered, "Nobody loves a fat man." Roscoe Arbuckle eventually starred in the same role and made the line his own.

Fatty pulls the clothes to himself while in the background a third window is open, heightening suspense.

He is decked out in the tight tux as he attends the benefit with Durfee, and the movie's highlight is his ludicrous heel-kicking dance. Chase sneaks in and unravels the stolen pants, leaving the embarrassed Fatty in his underwear. Chase then fires a barrage of bullets at Fatty, hitting him with all the effect of slaps. Fatty leaps out a window and to a street where a cop, noting his state of undress, places a barrel around him and beats him with a club. The final image is of Chase and Durfee laughing at crying Fatty as the clubbing cop herds him to jail.

The End

Unlike Chaplin's Little Tramp, we have scant sympathy for the title character of *Fatty's Magic Pants*, for he is insincere, cruel, lazy, and corrupt. Upon greeting him, Chase offers his hand, and after they shake, Fatty's smile melts into a scoff. A minute later, Fatty distracts Chase and coldcocks him with a board wrapped in a newspaper, only to then laugh heartily at his rival laid out on the ground. Though he resorts to stealing the formal wear, he doesn't appear impoverished; his only legitimate effort to attain a tux is begging his mother for money. The punishment for his minor thievery—public humiliation, dodging and absorbing bullets, police brutality, jail—does not fit his crime, but we have no qualms about enjoying Fatty's downfall.

This man-child is not *that* bad, so we smile at his innocence when he naively gives a hatcheck man not just his hat and cane but also his shoes, and we revel in his joy when, among high society, he dances about in unbridled ecstasy. But he's not that *good* either, a grown-up delinquent, and so, like his girlfriend and his girlfriend's new boyfriend, in the end we laugh as Fatty cries.

In 1914 Arbuckle and his wife rented a large house near the beach in tony Santa Monica. After years of traveling, they were happy to be rooted to one place. They lived there with their pit bull, Luke, a gift to Durfee from Keystone director Wilfred Lucas (the canine's namesake) after Durfee performed a dangerous stunt. They employed a Japanese servant, Oki, who lived in the guest house. Arbuckle often stayed up late, plotting out gags, stunts, and camera angles, smoking and drinking.

The couple, who had been broke the year before, spent their lavish paychecks soon after receiving them on extravagances befitting movie stars: she on designer clothes and perfumes and he on expensive jewelry for her and—something he had coveted for years—his first automobile: a secondhand Stevens-Duryea Model C-Six touring car. His love of cars bound him to race car driver Barney Oldfield, co-owner of the Oldfield-Kipper Tavern in downtown Los Angeles—a trendy refuge for male sports and movie celebrities, including Arbuckle. It was also an interest he shared with Mabel Normand.

The close friendship Normand shared with Arbuckle and Durfee provided her respite from her boyfriend. Sennett wrote, "Mabel and I were engaged and unengaged more than twenty times, I suppose, and once or twice we set a date. But things being like they were around Hollywood, she would hear stories about me and I would hear stories about her, and our affair was a series of fractures and refractures." Perhaps to heal fractures and certainly as a relief from the grueling shooting schedules, Normand spent most Sundays with Minty and Big Otto, often with Durfee's family, eating meals cooked by Durfee's mother.

Arbuckle also swam in the Pacific with Normand nearly every Sunday. Durfee remembered:

> So one Sunday morning they came back, and instead of the two of them getting out of the water immediately and coming up on the sand, there was something going on. . . . Well, what it was, as they were swimming back from the Venice pier, up came a dolphin, and instead of Mabel being frightened like anybody would, because none of us knew anything about dolphins in those days, she just put her arm over the neck of this dolphin, and he swam right along with them. And do you know, every Sunday, for nearly a year, he

came and swam with them, down and back, until one day they came back and then he disappeared, and they never saw him again.

Though Durfee was content merely to observe Arbuckle and Normand's aquatic adventures, she and her husband often partook in the local nightlife together. Recalled Durfee: "If either of us went anywhere in the evening, the other always went along. I was brought up in the belief—they call it old-fashioned now—that a wife's place was to suit herself to her husband's wishes, and to go where he wanted to go. . . . Perhaps we made a mistake by being so much together. It is the safest thing for married couples to take an occasional vacation from each other. I know that now, but you couldn't make me believe it then."

One can picture Roscoe Arbuckle and Minta Durfee as 1914 came to a close, him twenty-seven, her twenty-five, walking near the sea as they had six years before when they fell in love. Santa Monica's amusement center had burned down two years prior, but they could see the palatial auditorium and the schooner-shaped Cabrillo Ship Café at the Abbot Kinney Pier in neighboring Venice, the signpost for his Sunday swims. They talked about their future. Their marriage was sometimes strained; his drinking could darken his mood and breed arguments. But unlike Normand and Sennett, they *had* a marriage, and unlike in their first years together—mostly spent in strange towns and cities in the West and Far East—they now had the comfort of financial security and a permanent home with family and friends nearby. The sun spilled into the ocean. Then and there when everything was building, it seemed it could never end.

{8}

THE NEXT WEEKEND

> DETAIN ARBUCKLE
> Fat Comedian in Trouble As Girl Dies from Orgy
> SAN FRANCISCO, Sept. 10—Roscoe "Fatty" Arbuckle, motion picture actor, is to be "held in custody" pending the action of the police investigation of the death of Miss Virginia Rappe, motion picture actress, following a party in Arbuckle's room in the St. Francis Hotel, acting Captain of Detectives Michael Griffith [*sic*] announced today.

The giant DETAIN ARBUCKLE banner and its subheading were the spin of the *Evening News* editors in San Jose, Arbuckle's former hometown. Earlier on that Saturday, the *Los Angeles Examiner* shouted, ACTRESS DIES AFTER HOTEL FILM PARTY. The *San Francisco Chronicle* ran with the similar GIRL DEAD AFTER WILD PARTY IN HOTEL, while its rival, the *San Francisco Examiner*, alleged a crime with S.F. BOOZE PARTY KILLS YOUNG ACTRESS. As details developed throughout the day, the *San Francisco Bulletin* went for the jugular: GET ROSCOE IS DEATHBED PLEA. Others were more cautious. The *New York Times* chose ROSCOE ARBUCKLE FACES AN INQUIRY ON WOMAN'S DEATH, the *Los Angeles Times* the obscure MYSTERY DEATH TAKES ACTRESS, the *Pittsburgh Press* the optimistic "FATTY" ARBUCKLE TO HELP CLEAR ACTRESS' DEATH. But sensationalism would win out before the weekend was through.

According to the *Evening News*, the police had received two different accounts of Rappe's death. The first was "an affidavit given Detective Griffith Kennedy by Miss Alice Blake, actress"—one of the chorus girls at the party. The second was "a statement said to have been telephoned them from Los Angeles by Roscoe Arbuckle, motion picture comedian, which denied portions of Miss Blake's affidavit."

From Blake's affidavit: "About half an hour later Mrs. Delmont tried to get into the room, but the door was locked. She banged on the door and Arbuckle came out. As he opened the door we heard Miss Rappe moaning and crying 'I am dying, I am dying.' Arbuckle came out and sat down and said to us, 'Go in and get her dressed and take her back to the Palace. She makes too much noise.'"

From Arbuckle's statement: "We sat around and had some drinks and pretty soon Miss Rappe became hysterical and complained she could not breathe and began to tear her clothes off. . . . At no time was I alone with Miss Rappe. There were half a dozen people in the room all the time."

Picture a spy with multiple enemies who is courting allies and underworld connections he can never truly trust, endeavoring to attain a secret code—by any means, bit by bit—before his enemies get it first. Newspaper journalism in 1921, particularly the crime beat when the crime was worthy of daily eight-column headlines, was a devious sort of warfare. When the Arbuckle/Rappe story broke, there were five general-interest daily newspapers in Los Angeles and as many in San Francisco. In New York City, there were fourteen. Except for those owned by the same company, they were rabid competitors, segmented by Democratic, Republican, or Socialist party politics and also by the relish with which they pursued the more sordid criminal stories. There were morning papers, evening papers, and to disseminate the results of the day's final horse races, late editions. When the news warranted it, extra editions were published; there could be multiple extras throughout a day, each with a new headline on a new development, each rushing to beat competitors to the crowded stands. Today we think of the print press as a staid medium caught flat-footed when a whirlwind of events kicks up, but newspapers in 1921 were closer to today's twenty-four-hour cable news networks and the Internet's plethora of news sites and political blogs: rapid responses, strong opinions, factional politics, relentless competition.

With radio still in its infancy and no general-interest newsmagazines, newspapers were the *only* news medium of note in September 1921.* Newspaper editors, columnists, and publishers were celebrities, the equivalent of television commentators today, and none were bigger than publishing tycoon William Randolph Hearst, who had a nationwide media empire of twenty-four newspapers. His Los Angeles and San Francisco *Examiner*s shared information on the fast-developing Arbuckle story, and they reveled in the salacious.

The news industry had recently begun a trend toward greater sensationalism, and this development would be greatly accelerated by the Arbuckle case—to Arbuckle's detriment. In part, the transformation was the result of competing wire services. The United Press Associations (later UPI) was formed in 1907 to take on the Associated Press. Hearst formed the more sensationalistic International News Service in 1909 and spun off the morning-edition Universal Service in 1917. Thus, by the time of the Arbuckle trial, papers around the world could use content from multiple wire services as well as the content of other papers (transmitted via leased wires). Each wire service vied for greater sales largely by promulgating stories that could run with startling headlines.

Another factor in the shift was the rapid success of New York City's *Daily News*, launched in June 1919. America's first modern tabloid adopted the subheading "New York's Picture Newspaper," and its emphasis on photos, scant text, and provocative headlines appealed to the same working-class immigrants who had long been Arbuckle's core audience. Lured in by bold headings and the bark of newsboys, many such workers

* While there were scattered radio stations then, the medium as we know it today was born in 1922 with a major wave of proliferation. *Time*, America's first general-interest weekly newsmagazine, was launched in 1923.

scooped up a copy to graze on the subway going to or from their jobs. At its one-year anniversary, the *Daily News* had over a hundred thousand readers, and a year after that, as Arbuckle's arrest loomed, the number had blossomed to nearly four hundred thousand, spurring imitators.*

To meet the growing demand for headline-worthy provocation, crime reporters (colloquially called "hot crime men") got into police headquarters, jails, hospital rooms, coroner's offices, morgues, and law offices. They had paid sources everywhere; their newspaper expense accounts allowed them to outbid the police for details. Frequently, they arrived at a crime scene before the cops, and they followed leads that took them to the doors of witnesses, suspects, and victims, often before detectives could make an official inquiry. They weren't merely ambulance chasers; they were also ambulance leaders. Sometimes they even detained suspects and obtained confessions. As A. J. Liebling wrote, "In making 'arrests,' the reporters, who had shiny badges and pistol permits, usually represented themselves as detectives, but when printing the story their papers invariably said they had 'made the arrest as citizens.'" They shared tips with police, defense attorneys, and prosecutors, and they paid those officials to throw their competitors off the trail. Especially in New York City, where the print competition was fiercest, the police tailed the best newsmen just as reporters tailed the best detectives, and each might wear a disguise recognizable to only those with whom they had a working relationship.

Less scrupulous reporters might make up a story or report one of dubious veracity. (Six days after the Rappe story broke, the *Los Angeles Evening Record* would report, per anonymous sources, that members of a "Hollywood dope ring" made up of minor actors and other studio employees planned to kill Arbuckle, because the negative light shining on their industry since his arrest hurt their "dope peddling." Logic be damned.) When a newspaper devoted its resources to a story, it would include not just twenty-five-dollar-per-week hot crime men but also freelancers paid by the column inch who received bonuses for cover stories.

---

* By 1924 its circulation of 750,000 would make it the best-read (or best-browsed) newspaper in America.

On September 10, the feeding frenzy began.

Los Angeles Times reporter Warden Woolard beat the police to Roscoe Arbuckle's Los Angeles mansion on Friday evening, September 9, and informed the comedic superstar of Virginia Rappe's death hours earlier. The movie star told the reporter that Rappe had grown ill at his hotel party but he knew of no injuries that could have caused her death. "After Miss Rappe had a couple of drinks she became hysterical, and I called the hotel physician and the manager," he said. He denied having hurt her. "This is assuming serious proportions," he said.

"Yes, it is," Woolard agreed.

Around that time, a reporter for the *San Francisco Chronicle* called. Arbuckle lied, saying "there were no closed or locked doors" to room 1219. Futher, he implied that Rappe "threw her fit in the presence of everyone" in 1220 before being moved to 1219.

Arbuckle telephoned Joseph Schenck, the executive of his production company, who called for a midnight meeting with the unofficial suspect and the three potential witnesses then in Los Angeles: Arbuckle's suitemates, Lowell Sherman and Fred Fishback, and Virginia Rappe's friend Al Semnacher. The location: Sid Grauman's office at Grauman's Million Dollar Theatre.

On his way there, Semnacher stopped at the home of Kate and Joseph Hardebeck. "His face was grave. Something terrible had happened. And I knew before he spoke that my Virginia had died," Kate Hardebeck stated later.

In addition to the unofficial suspect and the three potential witnesses, the Million Dollar Theatre meeting likely included Sid Grauman and Arbuckle's manager, Lou Anger. The men discussed Rappe's death. "We all thought it was very unfortunate, and we could not understand it," Semnacher later testified. As a friend of Rappe's and no friend of Arbuckle's, Semnacher was the group's outsider. Did the men coordinate a strategy, agreeing on what the witnesses would and would not say to the press and authorities? It seems likely this was the reason for the meeting. Was the promise of money or movie career advancement made to Semnacher for his cooperation? Possibly.

From Grauman's office, Arbuckle telephoned a San Francisco detective and offered his outline of events, including the falsehood that he was never alone with Rappe. He also asserted that those saying he bore responsibility for her death were motivated by "ill feelings" toward him. He was told to report to the San Francisco Hall of Justice. He then tracked down his attorney, Milton Cohen, who was out of town. Cohen called his partner Frank Dominguez, who agreed to represent Arbuckle in San Francisco.

After the meeting, Arbuckle told his actress friend Viola Dana he had to return to San Francisco but couldn't say why, adding, "For God's sake, don't die on me."

Around 3 AM on the morning of September 10, Arbuckle's Pierce-Arrow headed north again, its owner behind the wheel. Along for the ride were Lou Anger, Frank Dominguez, and Joe Bordeaux, a bit player on both sides of the camera during Fatty productions and a steadfastly loyal friend whom the movie star could depend on (he called Arbuckle "chief"). Witnesses Fred Fishback, Lowell Sherman, and Al Semnacher headed north in Fishback's car. The two groups stopped at a diner in Bakersfield for breakfast.

The press pounced on the story throughout that Saturday, and "Fatty's car" was easy to track. When it stopped in Fresno, Arbuckle was quoted as saying he had never met Rappe before Monday. "She had a few drinks, and then it became necessary to call a physician and to have her removed," he said, leaving out virtually everything. The same article listed Rappe's age as twenty-three and quoted San Francisco's night captain of detectives, Michael Griffin: "No charges will be placed against [Arbuckle], but he will be detained until after the inquest." The Pierce-Arrow reached Oakland at 7 PM, and, waiting there for a ferry to San Francisco, a weary Arbuckle made a more diplomatic statement to the press, no doubt at attorney Dominguez's behest: "I am coming here to do all I can with the investigation of the case." At the ferry dock, he bought a newspaper from a newsboy while Dominguez made a phone call.

"They're saying some rotten things about you, Fatty, but I'm for you," the newsboy offered.

"Thanks, son, I'm glad to know it," Arbuckle replied as he scanned the paper's account of the St. Francis party.

"I don't know why they are saying these things. I wasn't with Miss Rappe alone at all," Arbuckle offered up for the press at the ferry. "There was someone else in the room during the entire affair. These tales of me dragging her into another room are false. She had two or three drinks and became hysterical. We did everything we could to revive her."

Arbuckle clammed up when Dominguez returned to the car. Born into one of California's original Spanish families, Frank Dominguez resembled an older version of Arbuckle, every bit as rotund but with white hair rimming his bald head. Regarded as one of the premier attorneys in Los Angeles, he had the wealth and celebrity friends to show for it. He enlisted Charles Brennan, an experienced lawyer who knew San Francisco's authorities and reporters. Brennan met Arbuckle and Dominguez outside San Francisco's Palace Hotel. So did police detectives. And so did the press, firing a barrage of questions that went mostly unanswered.

Ushered by the detectives, Brennan accompanied Arbuckle and Dominguez when, at 8:30 that Saturday evening, they pushed past reporters and photographers and climbed the steps to the San Francisco Hall of Justice. In case the worst happened and Arbuckle was charged with manslaughter, Brennan carried in a briefcase $5,000 in hundred-dollar bills, more than enough for any bail. But all were confident the spectacular show of wealth would be unnecessary.

Arbuckle released a statement regarding the events in room 1219. In it he contradicted his previous quote by saying, "[I] have known Miss Rappe for the last five years." (He would later claim he was initially misquoted.) He otherwise reiterated his previous recollection of events: After "a few drinks," Rappe became hysterical and complained of difficulty breathing and began ripping off her clothes. Two "girls" disrobed her and placed her in a tub. When that failed to help, he called the hotel manager. "I was at no time alone with Miss Rappe."

He and his attorneys were ushered into room 17, where assistant district attorneys Milton U'Ren and Isadore Golden informed them they had sworn affidavits from witnesses Alice Blake, Zey Prevost, and Maude Delmont, all claiming Arbuckle had assaulted Rappe and was responsible for her death. Dominguez had instructed his client to admit to only Prohibition violations and not answer the assistant DAs and detectives. It's unlikely the movie star could have talked his way out of arrest, not in San Francisco with the rabid press just outside the door, but as the interrogation progressed, the assistant DAs grew angered by Arbuckle's stoicism. Sworn witnesses had said one thing; Arbuckle said nothing. He was as silent as his movies.

"Roscoe Arbuckle will not even admit that his name is Roscoe Arbuckle," Dominguez declared.

After three fruitless hours, Arbuckle was allowed to leave room 17. He consulted with Dominguez while the assistant district attorneys conferenced. Shortly thereafter, just before midnight, Roscoe Arbuckle was arrested for the murder of Virginia Rappe.

Murder.

The charge: violating section 189 of the California Penal Code, which defines first-degree murder to include a killing "which is committed in the perpetration of, or attempt to perpetrate . . . rape." There would be no bail, as it was forbidden for a murder charge in California.

Murder.

There was his life before the arrest and his life after. From that moment on, nothing would be the same.

In the hallway, reporters crowded him, demanding a statement, but the stunned movie star offered none. Photographers fired off boxlike cameras while holding up trays of magnesium flash powder that ignited with bursts of light and smoke, like bombs exploding, over the hats of shouting, jostling men. When photographers asked Arbuckle to smile, he replied, "Not on an occasion of this sort."

He is unsmiling in his mug shots, which label him inmate number 32052. His bow tie is woefully uneven. His weight was 266 pounds; his height was 5'8⅜"; occupation "actor," hair "medium chestnut," eyes "blue," complexion "ruddy." Two distinguishing marks were noted: a scar at the root of his nose and another on the fourth finger of his right hand.

Arbuckle made no postarrest statement, but Captain of Detectives Duncan Matheson said, "This woman without a doubt died as a result of an attack by Arbuckle. That makes it first degree murder without a doubt. We don't feel that a man like 'Fatty' Arbuckle can pull stuff like this in San Francisco and get away with it." A man like "Fatty" Arbuckle was any nouveau riche partier from Los Angeles. In statements, both Assistant DA U'Ren and Chief of Police Daniel O'Brien noted Arbuckle's refusal to answer the charges against him.*

The top floor of the Hall of Justice was the jail, and its "felon's row" was a long corridor lined with cells. Cell 12 was Roscoe Arbuckle's new home. It was six by six with three walls of solid steel and a fourth of steel bars. The ceiling, too, was bars of steel. There were three wooden bunks stacked vertically, a wooden bench, and a washstand. As he stood just inside the door, void of the wallet he had given his lawyers, he asked for some of his money, and a jailer said, "You don't need money in here."

"Are you going to give me a partner in here?" Arbuckle asked.

"Do you want one?" the jailer replied.

"No, I guess I'll sleep better alone."

The door swung shut and locked. Arbuckle rigged up a way to hang his overcoat and jacket. Eventually, when all was dark and quiet but for stirring and snoring in the neighboring cells, Roscoe Arbuckle was alone in the dark under a blanket on a wooden bunk. Unable to sleep, he sat up several times to smoke cigarettes. He was not a religious man, but many an agnostic in his position would hedge his bet. If, as he lay there then,

* O'Brien did not share Matheson's antagonism toward Hollywood, as he and Mayor James Rolph frequently greeted film royalty. O'Brien's son, George, became a movie star, best remembered for his lead role in *Sunrise* (1927).

he gazed upward in prayer, he may have seen, in the gloom above his cell's bars but below the black abyss of the jail's ceiling, a walkway and, staring down at him, a guard with a gun.

In churches across the nation that Sunday morning, preachers condemned the alleged murderer. Fatty Arbuckle had long been a Hollywood archetype on-screen—the unruly, not-so-innocent man/boy—and now he came to symbolize Hollywood offscreen: a Gomorrah unrestrained by adherence to Christian morality. "The shame of it all," preached Reverend John Snape of Oakland's First Baptist Church, "is that good people like you in this congregation make possible the continuance of such a man before the public."

The first cancellation of an Arbuckle film had occurred in San Francisco on Saturday as its star was returning to the city: *Crazy to Marry* was pulled from two theaters. Before Sunday was through, San Francisco theater owners joined together to ban Fatty movies throughout the city. Also on Sunday, *Gasoline Gus* was pulled from the Million Dollar Theatre in downtown Los Angeles—the very theater in which Arbuckle had met with witnesses and advisers at midnight the day before. What's more, owner Sid Grauman and his father had known the star for years, having cultivated the teenage Arbuckle's singing career, and the Million Dollar Theatre was where Arbuckle had been scheduled to promote the film on Labor Day. The swiftness with which Grauman pulled *Gasoline Gus*, a popular movie with only one day of its run remaining, sent shockwaves through Hollywood.*

Here was proof that the studios' worst fear was coming true. The public outrage had only just begun, and already it was shrinking box office grosses. The fear was greatest at Paramount Pictures. Its biggest star was now an accused murderer. Paramount had released two of his films

* Grauman offered no comment for pulling *Gasoline Gus*. He likely feared the midnight meeting would tarnish him and his theater, and thus he hoped to diminish criticism.

over the previous month. It had two in the can. It had four in development. Panic reigned.

Still, the most prominent member of the motion picture community came forward to support his friend on that first Sunday. Vacationing in his native London, Charlie Chaplin averred, "There's nothing like that in his makeup. On the coast, Fatty is popular with everybody, and I hope he will be proved innocent."

Upon waking, Arbuckle had no toiletries. Soap, a towel, and a comb were lent to him by a fellow inmate—a recent prison escapee who claimed to know witness Zey Prevost. The two men walked the corridor together, talking. "I'm through with booze. Forever. No more," Arbuckle was heard to say.

Residents of the San Francisco City Jail with the financial wherewithal could order food from outside, thus Arbuckle's Sunday morning breakfast of eggs, toast, and coffee came courtesy of a nearby restaurant. The prison barber shaved him. Then the most famous resident ever locked in the San Francisco City Jail held a sort of meet and greet with his new neighbors. Chatting with the other accused felons, he answered their questions and accepted their sympathy. "He's a regular guy," one noted.

Throughout that Sunday, investigators took depositions from witnesses and searched for any available evidence. In one of the case's strangest developments, Los Angeles police, acting on instructions from their San Francisco counterparts, went to the Hollywood home of Al Semnacher and there took possession of a woman's silk shirt (missing three of five buttons) and a woman's tattered silk undergarments. They had been worn by Virginia Rappe at the party one week prior. Semnacher said he found them on the floor of room 1219 and took them to dust his automobile. Rappe's outer garments—the jade skirt and blouse she had made herself and the white Panama hat with the jade band—were in a closet in a Hotel St. Francis guest room occupied by Rappe's other travel companion, Maude Delmont.

On Sunday evening, Arbuckle met with his attorneys, then including his usual lawyer, Milton Cohen. Subsequently, the movie star asked for better accommodations but was denied, for there was only one sort of room on felon's row: small and bleak. Telling a jailer "It's too lonesome alone," he was allowed a cellmate, and he selected Fred Martin, described in the press as "a laborer accused of contributing to the delinquency of a minor." The man who made the whole world laugh told others in his cellblock: "I've heard often of 'Blue Sunday,' but until today I never knew what it meant." In retrospect, Blue Sunday was but a repose before Black Monday.

{9}

MUDDLE: 1915–16

A film is a ribbon of dreams.
—Orson Welles

It was like a magical spell—seated in the dark staring up at life projected bigger than life, cowboys and swashbucklers and a little tramp, a sinking ocean liner, a patchwork girl, and the assassination of President Lincoln. The first American feature-length films had screened in 1912. Lasting approximately an hour, they commanded two or three times the nickel admission of shorts and won greater prestige. Beginning in February 1915, *The Birth of a Nation*, a motion picture that lasted more than three hours, reined in more viewers than any other film of the silent era. Frequently banned and legally challenged, *everyone* knew about it, and seemingly *everyone* had an opinion.*

* In a conglomeration that seems to sum up the weaknesses and strengths of America at the time, *The Birth of a Nation* is a racist paean to the Confederacy, an epic propaganda piece, a work of inventiveness that rewrote the language of cinema, and a monumental business gamble that struck it rich like no motion picture before and few since. Made independent of the studios for a record-smashing $112,000 and initially commanding a ticket price of two dollars when most admissions were no more than fifteen cents, estimates of its unprecedented box office gross vary from $18 million to $60 million (a span of about $400 million to $1.4 billion in today's dollars).

As movie running times grew, feature-length films before and after *The Birth of a Nation* migrated from nickelodeons to larger venues with larger ticket prices, including converted playhouses and what were called movie palaces, with velvet curtains and pseudoclassical names.* In the best movie houses, full orchestras played and choruses sang. (Composers wrote scores, and the sheet music was distributed with the celluloid prints.) Shades of gray were replaced with tinted color: amber for daylight scenes and blue for night scenes; lavender for scenes of passion, green for danger, red for fury.† No longer was the audience made up almost exclusively of the working class. By 1915 everyone was enchanted.

Movie stars were no longer just famous faces, familiar in their on-screen personas but otherwise anonymous. Audiences knew their names and hungered for details about their personal lives. The original nameless celebrity, the Biograph Girl, had been the first to break out, when the company that became Universal Pictures lured her to sign with them in 1910 and masterfully marketed her name, Florence Lawrence, via advertisements and pioneering personal appearance tours.‡ She soon had company. Beginning in 1914 MARY PICKFORD was splayed boldly across theater marquees above the titles of her films. Pickford was the first movie superstar. Hollywood went into the fame business, and the young studios looked for ways to promote not just their movies but their performers as well.

Studio publicity worked hand in hand with a new presence in the industry: movie fan magazines. The first such publications, *Motion Pic-*

---

* The first American movie palace was the Strand Theatre on Broadway in New York City. Constructed for over $1 million, it had a seating capacity near three thousand when it opened in 1914.

† Two different colorization techniques were employed: tinting (coloring the entire frame) and toning (coloring just the black areas). Tinting and toning were even used simultaneously for a two-color effect. At its peak in 1920, colorization would be used in 80 to 90 percent of all movies.

‡ Lawrence acted in approximately three hundred films and also invented the automobile turn signal and brake signal (both in 1914; neither was patented). She committed suicide in 1938.

ture Story and *Photoplay*, had been launched in 1911, but they were mostly filled with movie-based short stories until *Photoplay* reinvented itself in early 1915 with a focus on the offscreen lives of actors.* *Photoplay* was the first true celebrity magazine, and it ushered a larger female audience into movie theaters. Before 1915 was done, thirteen additional magazines emphasizing Hollywood fame were launched.

An article in the August 1915 edition of *Photoplay*, "Heavyweight Athletics," covered the eating habits of Roscoe Arbuckle. His ideal dinner: "Martini or Bronx, crabmeat cocktail, dozen raw oysters, thin soup, stuffed celery parisienne, cold artichokes with mayonnaise, fried salmon steak or sand dabs, hungarian goulash with homemade noodles, roast turkey with dressing and cranberry sauce, fresh asparagus, green peas, stewed corn, fresh pastry, Roquefort cheese with toasted crackers, large cup of coffee." This and similar "athletic" feats of calorie consumption were surely exaggerated; Arbuckle had an average appetite.

But the celebrity press, intertwined with Keystone publicity, presented a portrait of Arbuckle more in line with the role he played onscreen: that of a man with unchecked and outsized appetites. To that end, they also exaggerated his weight, athletic ability, and gambling habits, and implied a seemingly unquenchable thirst for alcohol. In the same *Photoplay* article, Arbuckle shared an admonition: "Do not drink more than six steins of beer during the course of the meal."

Eleven floors below room 1219, six years and six months before the fateful Labor Day, Roscoe Arbuckle sat on a plush chair beneath a rococo ceiling in the palatial lobby of the Hotel St. Francis, drinking a highball.

---

* In what seems an odd dichotomy today, in addition to its gossip pages and celebrity profiles, *Photoplay*, which sported the subtitle "The Aristocrat of Motion Picture Magazines," set high standards for film criticism and scholarship during the silent era. It published work by the likes of Robert E. Sherwood and H. L. Mencken, and in 1920, it launched the first significant annual movie award.

While much of the world in April 1915 was embroiled in World War I, San Francisco was staging a World's Fair, ostensibly to celebrate the completion of the Panama Canal the previous August but primarily to advertise the city's recovery from the 1906 earthquake. The same World's Fair that attracted an ambitious model and fashion designer named Virginia Rappe also brought Roscoe Arbuckle. The Keystone cast and crew were there to shoot two movies, both directed by Arbuckle and starring him and Mabel Normand. As they waited out the rain, Arbuckle, Normand, another Keystone actress, and Keystone moneyman Adam Kessel sat in the St. Francis lobby for an interview with Flickerings from Film Land columnist Kitty Kelly.

While dramatic feature films were the rage, Kessel explained the Keystone formula for comedy shorts: attract children and their parents will follow. "I cater to the kids," Arbuckle said, before explaining how a famous operatic concerto waited twenty minutes to meet him because her eight children "are so crazy about these Keystone pictures. I really felt much complimented." Still, the column's prevailing image is Arbuckle "blinking unconcernedly at his highball." It is likely this cocktail consumption was encouraged by Kessel. If his image demanded such indulgences, the star would oblige.

With the departure of Chaplin, Arbuckle and Normand were the top box office draws at Keystone. Sennett returned to the "Bunnyfinch" formula, pairing them as husband and wife and highlighting the twosome in titles such as *Mabel and Fatty's Wash Day*, *Fatty and Mabel's Simple Life*, and *Mabel and Fatty's Married Life*. These sound like anything but must-see cinema, but their coupling meant childish playfulness and slapstick shenanigans within an adult plot. Audiences loved them.

Both Keystone stars were making $500 weekly, but Arbuckle was nursing some discontent. Sennett had offered the upstart Chaplin $750 a week to renew his contract, only to watch him defect to Essanay for even more. And the studio head had paid Broadway star Marie Dressler, a big-screen rookie, $2,500 weekly to headline *Tillie's Punctured Romance*, cinema's first feature-length comedy.* The 1914 production had been directed by Sennett and featured, with one exception, the entire Keystone company at the time, including Chaplin, Normand, Al St. John, and Minta Durfee. The exception was Arbuckle. According to legend, the full-figured Dressler insisted Keystone's rotund star not appear onscreen for fear he would upstage her. Arbuckle was feeling underpaid and underappreciated.

Arbuckle's pay was spent as quickly as he got it. "Roscoe bought me a Rolls Royce, the first one in Hollywood with a genuine silver radiator," Durfee remembered. "And jewels, my darling, like you've never seen. He was the most generous man on earth. I never knew a man as generous as he was, not only to me but to everybody. He couldn't say no to anyone. Roscoe used to give me all the money he didn't spend himself. My dear, I've sat with thousands and thousands of dollars in my purse. Roscoe always said, 'I'll make it, darlin', and you spend it.'"

At least others in his Santa Monica home were bringing home star salaries as well. In addition to his wife, their dog was making many times more than most working stiffs. Pit bull Luke's cinematic debut came in January 1915, and since celebrities were manufactured overnight at the Fun Factory, two months later he was headlining in *Fatty's Faithful Fido*, stealing scenes and pulling off stunts, some involving ladder climbing, for which the canine had a preternatural proficiency. Luke would appear in ten Fatty movies over five years, and whether the two were sharing a sandwich, drinking from the same garden hose, or snuggling in straw, the affection between Fatty and his dog registers in scene after scene. Theirs was a love story, on- and offscreen.

Critics at highbrow publications might have scorned such silliness, but those who worked in the film industry rarely shared this dismissive

* Wanting in on the greater prestige and higher ticket prices of feature-length films, Sennett sold partners Kessel and Baumann on the expensive and risky proposition by promising to land a Broadway star as the lead. *Tillie's Punctured Romance* was a success, launching Dressler's big-screen career and propelling Chaplin to his Essanay paydays. But when Dressler successfully sued the studio over her promised share of profits, Keystone's planned second feature was scrapped. The studio never made another feature-length film.

view of slapstick. When even the most serious dramas required broad pantomime and exaggerated emotions to overcome muteness, a rotund comedian in drag absorbing a custard pie garnered the respect of fellow big-screen actors and directors. Arbuckle was invited to join the prestigious Photoplayers' Club, the initial social organization of the motion picture industry. He and Durfee were among the nearly two thousand who attended the club's 1915 Valentine's Day ball, and he was a semiregular at its Wednesday dinners.

Arbuckle acted in twenty short films in the first seven months of 1915, directing or codirecting fifteen of them. Most paired him with Normand, and many featured his familial stock company: Durfee, St. John, and Luke. However, none of the preceding performers appeared in *Miss Fatty's Seaside Lovers*. Arbuckle plays a woman who is pursued by three men, one of whom is twenty-two-year-old virtual unknown Harold Lloyd.* Nor are others from his stock company in *Fatty's Tintype Tangle*, which ups the violence to such heights it plays like a parody of Keystone comedies. A jealous husband has two six-shooters that function as sixty-shooters, and every bullet seems to connect with Fatty's flesh but causes no lasting consequence. Only a point-blank shot to Fatty's chest fells him, but he rises unbloodied and unpained to run the shooter's hand through a meat grinder. Afterward, in perhaps his greatest stunt, Fatty shimmies up a telephone pole and scampers about on the suspended wires.

With the breakneck filming schedule and the fact that Arbuckle and Durfee were together at work as well as home, the couple's marriage grew strained. "We were both busy, and busy people are often nervous and irritable," Durfee remembered. "Two busy people in a family frequently clash, not because of any dislike, but simply because they get on each other's nerves, and neither one, because of the continual strain of work, has the time to acquire sufficient calmness to meet the other's needs."

---

* After a few supporting roles at Keystone, Lloyd left to headline in comedy shorts for Hal Roach's new studio, a Keystone rival. In the 1920s Lloyd starred in such classic features as *Safety Last!* and *The Freshman*.

Another time she said, "He wasn't a man who could say, 'I'm sorry.' And that hurt me in some of the disagreements we had before and after the trials. We'd have an argument, and the next day he'd make up for it by buying me a diamond ring or a necklace or just some little present. But all he had to do was say, 'I'm sorry.' He never did."

> Mabel Normand Fighting Death
> Los Angeles, Sept. 20
> While medical science waged a desperate battle for her life, Mabel Normand, famous film star and comedy queen, was unconscious and rapidly sinking today. Her physician, Dr. O. M. Justice, early today stated that the chance for her recovery was slight.

By the summer of 1915, Sennett and Normand's tumultuous relationship had stretched to more than four years, and it remained unacknowledged in the press. In June 1915, they finally, but privately, became engaged. In mid-September, the relationship ended with a crash. According to Minta Durfee's account, an actress phoned Normand and told her to go to Sennett's place immediately. She knocked on his door and he opened it in his underwear. She recognized a woman in a negligee trying to hide behind a sofa: twenty-three-year-old Mae Busch, who had arrived in Los Angeles early that year and by summer was headlining in Keystone movies. Busch hurled a vase, which met the tender flesh of Normand's forehead. Sennett tried to quell the crimson flow, but Normand pushed him away and staggered out the door.

Arbuckle and Durfee were in chaise lounges on the porch of their Santa Monica house when, as Durfee remembered, "we heard what we thought was an animal suffering. Then we saw the door of the taxi open, and there was the driver carrying Mabel, who was cradled in his arms, up to our porch. There was blood all over Mabel's face and hair. It was streaming down her neck and all over her body. Naturally, we paid the driver a little something, and Roscoe gave him something extra, hoping he would keep this a secret."

Normand was discreetly checked into a hospital. More than a week later, a cover story appeared in newspapers:

> It was learned yesterday that Miss Normand was injured during the staging of a wedding scene at the Keystone studio. It was a typical wedding, which means there was considerable "rough stuff." Roscoe Arbuckle, the heavyweight comedian, was the bridegroom and Miss Normand the bride. . . . There was a general bombardment of old shoes and rice after the ceremony, and some enthusiastic celebrator hurled a boot at the bridal couple. Arbuckle dodged the boot, and it struck Miss Normand on the head.

Normand playing a bride adds a bitter irony to the lie the studio propagated. For years, Keystone had been generating a stream of publicity about Normand's dangerous exploits. In recent weeks, she had supposedly killed a rattlesnake, stopped a studio burglar with a well-thrown medicine ball, bested twenty others in a five-mile ocean swim race, and fended off an octopus attached to her leg. But this time, Normand went off script, perhaps purposely giving a less credible explanation, when she told *Photoplay* the following April, "Roscoe sat on my head by mistake. I was unconscious for twelve days and laid up for three months. Don't talk to me about being killed—I've been through it."

Mabel Normand acted in only one other film in 1915, but *Fatty and Mabel Adrift*, written and directed by Arbuckle, is the duo's definitive collaboration, and it was a huge financial success. The usual elements are there—Fatty and Mabel as newlyweds, Al St. John as villain, Luke the dog as hero—but they occupy an ambitious disaster plot, as the newlyweds are cast on the ocean in their barely floating house. The convincing aquatic effects are carried off with a bigger-than-usual budget; shooting took place in a studio water tank and the Pacific Ocean. Arbuckle's advancement as a director is evident in his creative flourishes, as when his shadow kisses sleeping Normand and when he and Normand appear framed by hearts (linked via Cupid's fired arrow) and the heart frame of jealous St. John crumbles. It's the sort of delightful whimsy the movies forgot how to do nearly a century ago.

Before the end of 1915 Roscoe Arbuckle had made extended stays in the territories of Alaska, Arizona, Hawaii, and the Philippines; he had worked in Mexico and Canada; he was the rare American who had traveled to the Far East, visiting storied metropolises in Japan and China. And yet he had never been east of Chicago. Despite his eighteen years in vaudeville, he had never set foot in the center of American theater, never visited the nucleus of American media, never experienced the city he would come to love, the city he would—for extended periods—call home, the city where he would die.

When the train ended its journey in Grand Central Station, New York, New York, on the next-to-last day of 1915, a Keystone company of a dozen departed, including Arbuckle, Durfee, Normand, and St. John. Also in the group was Ferris Hartman, with whom the Arbuckles had toured the Orient. Arbuckle had given him the job of assistant director—a gracious gesture, as Hartman had fallen on hard times.* The company, there to make movies in nearby New Jersey, was met at the bustling station by executives of the Triangle Film Corporation, formed in July to finance, distribute, and exhibit the movies produced by three Hollywood heavyweights: D. W. Griffith, Thomas Ince (noted for his westerns), and Mack Sennett. A crowd of stunned fans swarmed as the Keystone group strolled across the concourse.

New York City in late 1915 was home to over five million residents, many of them recent European immigrants. The city was experiencing its adolescent growth spurt; while Europe was immersed in the hor-

* Hartman subsequently directed a few movies (most starring Al St. John), but attempts to resurrect his theatrical career proved unsuccessful. In 1931, at age seventy, he starved to death in a San Francisco hotel room.

rors of trench warfare, New York City was asserting itself as the world's de facto capital. And the Keystone group stayed in the center of it, on Broadway in Times Square at the Hotel Claridge. Chauffeur-driven limousines were at their beck and call. On their second night in Manhattan, New Year's Eve, they attended the Broadway musical *Peter Rabbit in Dreamland* as guests of the *New York Globe*, and the two thousand in attendance applauded them.

For Arbuckle and Durfee, the stay at the Claridge was short. On one of the company's first nights there, a drunken, belligerent Arbuckle tried to make the kitchen staff cook him a meal at 3 AM. When they wouldn't, he yelled, "Then I'll find a hotel that does!" He did—the Cumberland, a few blocks away, which provided them a larger suite and constant care. In recalling the incident, Durfee affixed a rare insult: "Roscoe knew he was good for publicity and the [Cumberland] manager knew it. Roscoe also knew that money could buy anything. Except good manners."

Filming occurred not in Manhattan but just across the Hudson in Fort Lee, New Jersey. Edison and other New York behemoths had begun shooting in Fort Lee in 1907, and independent studios had sprouted up there, building the facilities and buying the equipment to shoot, edit, and process film. By 1916 it was "Hollywood East." Triangle leased studio space there.

The main reason for the cross-country trip was to court publicity from the New York media. During Keystone's first New Jersey production, a *Picture-Play* magazine writer spent a day on the set and interviewed the stars for what became a lengthy feature article, "Behind the Scenes with Fatty and Mabel," which provided an intimate look at Arbuckle and Normand at work. The reporter is driven, wildly, to the Fort Lee studio by Normand:

> The studio was bristling with activity. Roscoe Arbuckle, the elephantine author-actor-director, was superintending the construction of a set, aided by Ferris Hartman, his co-worker, and a dozen prop men; Elgin Lessley, the intrepid camera man, who has the reputation of turning out the clearest films of any Keystone crank

turner, was loading his magazines. A dozen rough and ready comedians were practicing falls down a stairway. The heavyweight director turned and saw us.

"Oh, Miss Normand, get ready for the hall scenes please."

"Very well, Roscoe and—very good!"

The dainty little comedienne going to her dressing room, I strolled over to the busy throng and exchanged greetings with Arbuckle.

"How are you getting along with your new picture?" I asked.

"Slow, but sure," was the reply. "It's a new theme, and I want to go at it easily. I'm not trying to be a 'high brow,' or anything like that, but I am going to cut an awful lot of the slapstick out hereafter. If any one gets kicked, or pie thrown in his face, there's going to be a reason for it."

"How about that staircase?" I queried. "That looks as though something exciting was going to happen."

"Oh, nothing much," he answered.

"St. John and I are going to fall down it, but that's about all. Here, I'll show you," and I snapped the picture as he did.

"Oh, it's great to be a comedian—if there's a hospital handy!"

As the day's shoot got under way, the *Picture-Play* reporter marveled at the surreality of the experience (a pistol shot rang out, and Arbuckle said, "Oh that's only St. John shooting apples off Joe Bordeaux's head. I'm going to pull that stunt in my next film!") and at the Keystone players' ability to take falls and absorb blows without complaint (bit parts in New Jersey were played by new recruits, and they were shell-shocked by the repetition of violence, including St. John bloodying an extra's nose with a kick). Arbuckle credited his coworkers with helping him talk through story ideas: "I certainly have a clever crowd working with me. Mabel alone, is good for a dozen new suggestions in every picture. And the others aren't far behind. I take advice from everyone. It's a wise man who realizes that there are others who know as much, if not more than he does himself."

The lasting images of the article are Arbuckle falling off the bannister—once face-first—in take after take, and in another scene, cracking heads with an actor while searching for a button, and again doing it repeatedly despite the pain.

"How many times do you take the same scene?" the reporter asked.

"Till I can't do any better," Arbuckle replied, as one assistant straightened his bow tie and another combed his hair. "Often I use 10 or 15 thousand feet of film for a two reel production. . . . Generally, I take a month or more to produce a picture that runs less than thirty minutes on screen."

The movie Arbuckle, Normand, and company were making that January day was *He Did and He Didn't*, an odd but compelling departure for the team. How odd? The alternate title was *Love and Lobsters*, and in a sequence near the end, jealous Fatty shoves the man he suspects of cheating with his wife out a window and strangles his wife (Normand) to death before he's shot dead. Spoiler alert: it's a nightmare, brought on by consuming bad shellfish.

Arbuckle went on to write, direct, and star in a total of seven movies in Fort Lee. But only one more featured Mabel Normand. She left Keystone, but Sennett—who himself wanted to get free of his New York partners—offered his ex her own independent production company, complete with facilities in Los Angeles. Wanting to focus on dramedy feature films, she accepted. Rehearsals began in June for her feature *Mickey*. That summer, Normand gave a "burial party" aboard her yacht. Inside a casket was a slapstick. As a funeral dirge played, "Madcap Mabel" offered her final good-byes to her old friend, and the casket was committed to the sea.

Minta Durfee returned to Los Angeles as well, to act in *Mickey* and be with her mourning family; her father had died. Her husband stayed behind to shoot his last three films in Fort Lee. These pictures featured twenty-year-old Alice Lake, a five-foot-two brunette, a former dancer and native New Yorker. She resembled a younger and more spirited version of Durfee, the woman she was replacing on-screen—and may have already been replacing offscreen.

"What's the worst thing that can happen to an actor?" a journalist asked.

"To arrive," Arbuckle replied.

"I thought that was what they all desired more than anything else."

"They do," Arbuckle said, "but the trouble is, once they arrive, there isn't much to do but to leave again. When they are coming up, the public applauds and says, 'That chap is coming along—doing better every day.' But once the actor is heralded as an absolute arrival, the public begins to criticize and pick flaws and expect him to better his own standard, and it is a tremendous strain. He's simply forced to keep ahead of the public's opinion and to spring something newer and better every season. The man or woman who can survive an 'arrival' is a star of the greatest magnitude."

"The world has Chaplinitis. . . . Any form of expressing Chaplin is what the public wants. . . . Once in every century or so a man is born who is able to color and influence the world. . . . A little Englishman, quiet, unassuming but surcharged with dynamite is flinching the world right now." So *Motion Picture Magazine* had stated in July 1915. At Essanay in 1915, Charlie Chaplin spawned fourteen films, including his seminal *The Tramp*, and his vagabond persona took hold of the public imagination like none before or since. Syndicated comic strips let readers follow the Little Tramp's adventures daily. All manner of Little Tramp merchandise flooded stores. Wearing the wardrobe and mimicking the mannerisms of the beloved character became so ubiquitous that movie theaters sponsored "Charlie Chaplin nights" wherein whole audiences were packed with Tramps.

Chaplin the employee proved to be as vagabond as his character. He left Essanay, as he had Keystone, after one year. In February 1916 the onetime resident of a London poorhouse signed with Mutual Film Corporation for a record $10,000 weekly and a $150,000 bonus. In return he had to make one comedy short per month for twelve months—an obligation he took eighteen months to fulfill.* As "Chaplinitis" spread unabated, and as its namesake signed a deal worth $670,000 in a year, Roscoe Arbuckle—who had been, three years prior, Chaplin's more celebrated costar—was still at Keystone with an annual salary of $26,000.

In 1916, of filmdom's four biggest stars, Charlie Chaplin relied on the business acumen of his older half-brother Syd, while the other three—Mary Pickford, Douglas Fairbanks, and Arbuckle—negotiated their own contracts. Talent agents had played supporting roles in the theatrical business since the 1890s, but they wouldn't take hold in the film industry until the late 1920s. Here, Arbuckle would be a trailblazer. In Los Angeles he may never have encountered an agent, but in New York he shook hands with Max Hart, the leading vaudeville talent rep. Hart specialized in elevating his clients—including Eddie Cantor, W. C. Fields, and Will Rogers—to Broadway. Arbuckle had retained his love for the stage while his singing voice was silenced by cinema, and Hart may have promised him Broadway stardom as great as his Hollywood fame. As for Hollywood fortune, the agent secured Arbuckle a contract with Metro Pictures worth $200,000 annually, which also brought along Durfee and St. John.

But before Arbuckle could make the move, fate intervened in the short, portly personage of Lou Anger. Touring with his songstress wife, Anger had been a minor vaudeville comedian for a decade. As late as February 1916, he was performing onstage at a military benefit in New York City, but he was searching for a career change, and he had a connection to the film industry he was eager to exploit. Promising a better deal than Hart's, Anger enticed Arbuckle to attend a clandestine meeting in Atlantic City. There the Keystone star met thirty-seven-year-old Joseph Schenck.

* At the end of that contract, he would sign to make eight movies with First National Pictures Inc. for $1 million and a $75,000 signing bonus.

Born in Russia in 1878, Schenck was fourteen when he immigrated to New York City with his family. He and his younger brother Nicholas operated a beer concession stand in an amusement park, offering free vaudeville performances to keep their thirsty patrons near the suds. In 1910 they purchased controlling interest in the Palisades Amusement Park in New Jersey, a small, crude dump that the Schenck brothers popularized by adding better attractions. The man who advanced their financing was Marcus Loew, then the owner of a chain of vaudeville theaters and nickelodeons. Consequently, when their park began turning a profit, the brothers also invested in the fledgling movie business, buying and operating nickelodeons in partnership with Loew and financing low-budget movies, some of which were distributed by Paramount.* By 1916 Joseph Schenck was looking for a route to the Hollywood big time.

Founded in 1914, Paramount Pictures was the first nationwide distributor of feature films. Previously, features were leased to regions or screened in rented theaters, but Paramount cultivated its own coast-to-coast theater network. Of the production companies whose movies were distributed by Paramount, the most prominent were Famous Players Film Company, run by Adolph Zukor, and the Jesse L. Lasky Feature Play Company, run by its namesake. In May 1916 half of Paramount's stock was acquired by Zukor and Lasky. Lasky became Paramount's vice president and primary creative force, and in 1917 Zukor would take over as president and begin to consolidate production, distribution, and exhibition into one increasingly powerful entity.

From the studio's earliest days, when Lasky's company raided Broadway talent, Paramount was noted for its prestige feature films (many directed by Cecil B. DeMille), and it launched a protracted quest to lock up Hollywood's major stars. The first to sign was Mary Pickford, in 1914. Zukor and Lasky tried to entice Chaplin, but his price was bid up too high. In the summer of 1916, they turned to the second-biggest comedy star: Roscoe Arbuckle.

---

* Loew subsequently owned a vast empire of movie palaces as well as a major Hollywood studio, MGM. Nicholas Schenck became Loew's chief lieutenant in 1919 and, following Loew's death in 1927, rose to president of MGM and ran the studio during its glory years (1927–55).

Schenck proposed that a company be formed to produce Arbuckle's movies, which would then be distributed by Paramount. Arbuckle would get script and cast control and a salary of $5,000 weekly plus 10 percent of profits. Schenck would head the company and pocket 20 percent of Arbuckle's take, plus a share of the company's profits. Lou Anger would function as Arbuckle's agent and pocket 10 percent of Arbuckle's remaining $4,000 weekly take. Therefore, Arbuckle's annual base salary, minus Schenck and Anger's shares, would be $187,200—over seven times what he was making at Keystone and, with profits, potentially much more lucrative than the Metro deal Max Hart had negotiated for him. It was an enticing mix for an actor: the big money, the autonomy of his own production company, the prestige of Paramount's distribution. He accepted, reneging on his deal with Hart.* The signing bonus was a Rolls-Royce Silver Ghost touring car.

After at least 122 films over three years, Arbuckle's career at Keystone was over. Mack Sennett's immediate reaction is unknown, but in his 1954 autobiography he gave his onetime superstar the cold shoulder. He mentions the "notorious" Arbuckle's arrival at Keystone and, twenty pages later, the "scandal" that harmed the film industry five years after "Roscoe had left me," but the man who was the focus of that scandal is relegated to barely more than 1 of 284 pages. In contrast, Chaplin, who bolted after one year and thirty-six films, gets a chapter entitled "Poetry in Slapstick," and the book is nearly a paean to Normand. The best Sennett could do in Arbuckle's defense was "It is hard to believe that Roscoe Arbuckle, the butt of our jokes and comedies at the studio, was as evil as some people say he was." Three years after leaving Keystone, Arbuckle grumbled, "To this day, I guess [Sennett] doesn't think I'm funny."†

Minta Durfee was dismayed by her husband's Paramount deal, which he did not tell her about until he returned to Santa Monica in August.

---

* Schenck paid Hart $20,000 to release Arbuckle from his contract.

† Sennett himself gave up all rights to the Keystone brand name and its movies in June 1917 in exchange for ownership of the facilities and the contractual obligations of most of the remaining stars. Only a few additional "Keystone" comedies were produced, and they were pale imitations. Sennett formed the Mack Sennett Comedies Corporation and continued producing comedy shorts at the same pace and of the same sort he always had.

He had kept her in the dark regarding the biggest decision of his—and her—career. Fifty-three years later, she said: "I was greatly upset at how quickly Roscoe had succumbed to the ruthlessness of a Joe Schenck. Joe was all about money, and Roscoe suddenly was all about money to the extent that in cutting ties with Max Hart, he was ruining Al's [Al St. John's] chance and my chance of earning a living." Arbuckle told her he would get her something, meaning a studio deal, of which Durfee recalls: "But I knew there wouldn't be *something*. I knew it was the beginning of the end of us."

The press in 1916 covered the stories the studios wanted covered when the studios wanted them covered. News of Arbuckle's leaving Keystone didn't break until September, and it was subsequently reported that the name of his production company would be the Comique Film Corporation. (*Comique* is French for "comic." Arbuckle pronounced it "Cumeeky.") There was no mention of Paramount. On December 13 a Santa Monica city commission meeting addressed the establishment of Arbuckle's "moving picture concern" there. It was never built.

In the weeks after he returned to Santa Monica, a skin infection near Arbuckle's left knee had grown inflamed. It likely began as an insect bite scratched repeatedly, but by Labor Day weekend it was much more than an annoyance. His knee was severely swollen, and he could barely walk because of the extreme pain. Durfee called neighbor Hobart Bosworth, a pioneering film actor and director. Despite his condition, Arbuckle vetoed a hospital visit, for fear it would engender negative publicity and jeopardize his new contract. Durfee and Bosworth telephoned doctors and eventually spoke to a hospital intern who agreed to make a discreet house call.

Diagnosis: a carbuncle from *Staphylococcus aureus* was endangering his leg, and if it spread through his bloodstream, it could be fatal. The intern injected Arbuckle with morphine and incised the carbuncle. The incision was kept open to further drain the pus, and Arbuckle was given a morphine prescription to offset the pain. And thus one of the movie industry's first superstars became one of its first drug addicts.

In the last decades of the nineteenth century and first decade and a half of the twentieth, morphine was sold as an over-the-counter pain reliever, as was its related opiate, heroin, and as was cocaine. Reputable pharmaceutical companies sold kits that contained vials of drugs and hypodermic syringes and needles, allowing customers to self-administer their fixes, and doctors and pharmacists recommended such drugs for even minor ailments. It was estimated in 1911 that one in every four hundred Americans was addicted to an opiate. In 1915 a federal law restricted the sale of opiates and cocaine, effectively making them illegal to sell or buy without a prescription. Doctors, however, still readily prescribed the kits. Old habits died hard.

The intern gave Arbuckle subsequent morphine injections when he returned to inspect the open wound and lengthen the incision, but because the painkiller was to be administered every few hours, the movie star injected the drug when the intern could not. Arbuckle sat in the living room, dressed in a gown, his legs propped on another plush chair. The needle penetrated his cephalic vein in the crook of his left arm. The plunger retreated, suctioning his blood—a little red cloud—into the clear morphine solution in the glass syringe. This ritual assured him there was nothing between him and it. Then the plunger slid, and the opiates flowed through him.

Morphine works fast, racing through the bloodstream from the injection site to the brain. Around thirty seconds after injecting it, Arbuckle felt a pleasant rush, a tingly sensation that passed within a couple minutes. His skin may have itched, his cheeks may have flushed. Morphine mimics the effects of endorphins, though in much greater quantities, binding with receptor sites in the brain and central nervous system and blocking the transmission of pain signals. He was soon drowsy, his muscles numbed, his body heavy. The pain dissipated, replaced with a warm, gratifying sensation. As the effect continued, he was stranded on the precipice of slumber, seeming to sleep but capable of hearing and, if he parted his heavy lids to reveal his constricted pupils, seeing. The morphine's effects peaked at around forty-five to sixty minutes but kept him drowsy and numbed for four to six hours. Even those who were near seemed distant. His wife was there, and the housekeepers, sometimes the medic, sometimes Hobart Bosworth or Lou Anger. What they said, sometimes directly to him, was lost in the haze. Words tumbled and sank. Images melted away.

Eventually, regrettably, the fog rose. Noises jarred. Light hurt. The pain reasserted itself. He craved the needle and his next fix.

Morphine reduces motility in the intestinal tract, thus severe constipation is a common side effect. Others include a loss of appetite, dry mouth, and respiratory depression. Tolerance grows rapidly, so doses must increase to remain effective. As days blurred, the man known as Fatty shed pounds. He no longer wanted to eat. All he cared about came in a syringe.

His leg was horrid. The open wound was not healing. When the intern determined that amputation was the most prudent course, Durfee contacted Bosworth, who called a friend, Dr. Maurice Kahn. The doctor diagnosed Arbuckle's morphine addiction and enrolled him in the Kaspare Cohn Hospital near Hollywood. There his leg was saved.

The science of drug addiction was inchoate. Methadone did not yet exist, and weaning addicts onto less addictive drugs was problematic because of the scant research. Morphine had been used for alcohol addiction. Cocaine had been used for morphine addiction. Then came the "nonaddictive" cure-all: heroin. By the time Arbuckle was a morphine addict, the most prudent course was the most daunting: abrupt cessation.

If he was to kick his jones for opiates, he had to do it cold turkey, locked in a padded cell in a hospital. Officially, he was not there. Officially, he was home in Santa Monica, playing with Luke, swimming in the bay, romancing his wife, and drinking—of course. Keystone publicity and the subservient movie industry press had portrayed him as borderline alcoholic, but drugs, though legal without a prescription just two years prior, were viewed as degenerate—a vice of the lowest class.

Within a few hours, the first withdrawal symptoms began: watery eyes, diarrhea, runny nose, perspiration. Whereas the opiates brought on a rush of euphoria, he now suffered its opposite. He was restless, irritated, sad, anxious, and all the while craving the needle. As the hours crawled, the initial symptoms worsened, joined by involuntary twitching and kicking, hot and cold flashes, muscle and bone aches, and intestinal cramping. He screamed and moaned, maybe for hours on end. He was unable to sleep, unable to eat, unable to ease the revolt of his body and mind. His blood pressure increased, his temperature rose, his breathing labored. He was nauseous.

On the second day, all symptoms worsened until they were seemingly unbearable. His vomiting, diarrhea, and urination were involuntary, and when there was nothing more to eliminate, his twitching flesh kept endeavoring to wring every drop from him. He lay in the fetal position, shaking uncontrollably, racked by pain that permeated every fiber of him. He cried but had no tears. The withdrawal symptoms peaked two to four days after his last morphine injection and—mercifully, finally—subsided in eight to twelve days.

From his first morphine injection to the day he returned home from the hospital, the man known as Fatty lost over eighty pounds, dropping from 275 to 193. His clothes draped him; so did his skin. His eyes seemed to have retreated into his skull, the contours of which were then eerily visible. Unable to walk or even stand on his left leg, he was propelled via wheelchair. He had never been so effectively disguised onstage or on-screen. Even in drag or blackface, he had been more himself than he was without his fat. It was perhaps advantageous that few could have recognized him and inquired why and how. Roscoe Arbuckle was a specter of his former, famous self. Then, uncertain if he would ever again walk with ease, void of the body that brought him celebrity and wealth, he knew how quickly and cruelly it could all end. He thought, then, that he knew the worst of it.

{10}

INDICTMENT

Plan to Send Arbuckle to Death on Gallows
—*Los Angeles Times*, September 12, 1921, front page

When on Monday morning, September 12, 1921, reporters entered cell 12 of the San Francisco City Jail, they found Arbuckle seated at a table eating breakfast with his new friend Fred Martin. The movie star was nattily attired; his cellmate was dressed in the "rough clothes of a laborer." The boiled eggs, toast with marmalade, and coffee had again been delivered from a local restaurant. Other prisoners had congregated to watch the celebrity and his envied cellmate eat, but guards ordered them away. Now the newsmen tried to score a juicy quote from Arbuckle.

"Nothing I could say now would do any good," Arbuckle replied. "My attorneys have asked me to remain silent at present. What I have to say will be said in my own defense later. Everything I have said in the past while I was on my way up here seems to have been distorted and made to appear against me. I am not as black as I have been painted, and when I go into court the public will have a different opinion of me. You can easily see that a man in my position should remain silent at this time, because words are liable to be twisted into a meaning other than you intended."

The jail's barber had shaved him the day before, but after breakfast Arbuckle sent for a presumably more skilled razor-and-shears technician from outside the jail. That man shaved both the movie star and his cellmate. Arbuckle got a massage. Just after nine o'clock, the inmates lined up for roll call.

"Roscoe Arbuckle, murder," a jailer shouted.

"Yes, sir."

"Step out of line."

With his hands in his trouser pockets, Arbuckle slouched over to the line of inmates awaiting their turns in court.

Fatty Marshals Influence and Wealth in Defense As Bitter Struggle Impends

—*Denver Post*, September 12, 1921, front page

The district attorney of San Francisco had been out of town the weekend the Arbuckle case broke, but on the following Monday, Matthew Brady took the reins from his underlings. Born in San Francisco in 1875, Brady had been a lawyer in private practice there before securing appointments to the Civil Service Commission and then the police court bench. He narrowly defeated a scandal-tainted incumbent to become the city's DA, taking office in January 1920 and positioning himself as a reformer, eager to resuscitate his office's reputation. It was speculated that he craved the San Francisco mayoralty or California governorship.

The forty-six-year-old, silver-haired Brady assessed the quality of his case. Though there were sworn affidavits from Alice Blake, Zey Prevost, Maude Delmont, and nurse Vera Cumberland, the first two were showgirls who had willingly come to a booze party held by men they had only just met, and the last had only secondhand knowledge of the events in Arbuckle's suite. Brady decided that Maude Delmont, the apparently selfless woman who had befriended Rappe in her final days, was his strongest witness.

Delmont alleged that Arbuckle had lured a cautious Rappe to the party with the promise of "something big" for her film career, only to have Rappe reject his "proposition." Newspapers made much of her allegation that Arbuckle "dragged" Rappe into 1219. But her less incendiary affidavit read as follows:

> Miss Rappe went into the bathroom off Room 1219, leaving the rest of the party in Room 1220, and when she came out Arbuckle took hold of her and said, "I have been trying to get you for five years." After he took hold of her and made this remark he then closed and locked the door of Room 1219, leading into Room 1220, leaving the rest of the party in Room 1220.
>
> I felt anxious about Miss Rappe. When she did not return to our party I became very anxious about her. I called to her several times [but received] no answer, then kicked against the door with the heel of my shoe at least a dozen times during the next hour. When I told her what I had done afterwards she said she must have been unconscious immediately after he locked the door, otherwise she must have heard me.
>
> After an hour's wait, I became alarmed, took down the receiver to the telephone and called for help from the office. Mr. Boyle, the assistant manager, came up. When Arbuckle heard our conversation he opened the door, standing in his pajamas, wet with perspiration, and had Miss Rappe's Panama hat on his head.
>
> The bed where she lay was saturated wet and she was semiconscious and tearing her clothes. She tore the cuffs off her white silk [shirt]waist and threw them on the floor, screaming: "He did it, I know he did it. I have been hurt, I am dying." This was said in the presence of Arbuckle.

She further told of Rappe's pains in her neck, left leg, and, especially, abdomen, and of "monkey bites" on Rappe's neck and big marks on her right arm and left leg. Early on Tuesday morning, the severely pained Rappe allegedly told her: "Maude, Roscoe should be at my bedside every minute and see how I am suffering from what he did to me." But Delmont's affidavit was riddled with crucial falsehoods. For example, she did not see Arbuckle and Rappe go into 1219, and they were not in the room for anything remotely as long as an hour.

Riding the courthouse elevator on the morning of September 12, Delmont begged, "Oh, please don't make me face Arbuckle. I don't ever want to lay eyes on him again." But she subsequently steeled herself: "If I have to do it, I will. I will try to nerve myself to the ordeal, but it will be terrible." The defendant was not in the courtroom shortly after 11 AM when Delmont stood beside DA Brady and swore under oath to the accuracy of her previously transcribed account. After the short formality, she nearly fainted to the floor. Hysterical, she was led from the courtroom.

When a dejected Arbuckle appeared in court with his attorneys at 11:30 AM, he was greeted by an explosion of camera flashes and chatter from the mostly male observers who packed the gallery, standing and clamoring for a better view. Accused men awaiting their turns in court pressed against the steel grating of the prisoner's dock. Called to the bench, Arbuckle approached, hands clasped, face twitching. Grimly, he heard a clerk read Delmont's complaint.

Subsequently, Brady told the press, "I desire to state that I will spare no effort to punish the perpetrator of this atrocious crime, although I know I will be opposed by the cleverest lawyers and the greatest influence which money can purchase."

ARBUCKLE DANCES WHILE GIRL IS DYING, JOYOUS FROLIC AMID DEATH TRAGEDY

—*SAN FRANCISCO CALL AND POST*, SEPTEMBER 12, 1921, FRONT PAGE

In New York City, Henry Lehrman had received the news about his old friend and former coworker Arbuckle and his former domestic partner Rappe. From his apartment in midtown Manhattan, he fired off a vituperative statement:

> From information I received from San Francisco, I believe Arbuckle is guilty. For his sake, I wish that he will receive full measure of justice so there will be no other crime necessary. You know what the death of Virginia means to me. I will not attempt to express it. She died game, like a real woman, her last words being to punish Arbuckle, that he outraged her and she begged the nurse not to tell this, as she did not want me to know. . . . Would I kill Arbuckle? Yes. I feel just as would any other man with red blood in his veins. I will not deny that I have said I would kill him if we were to meet. I hope the law will punish him and that he will receive full justice for the crime.
>
> Arbuckle is the result of ignorance and too much money. He was originally a bar boy, although he has been in the chorus and done other things. I directed him for a year and a half, and I had to warn him to keep out of the women's dressing rooms. There are some people who are a disgrace to the film business. They get enormous salaries and have not sufficient balance to keep right. They are the kind who resort to cocaine and opium and who participate in orgies that are of the lowest character. They should be driven out of the picture business. I am no saint, but I have never attended one of their parties. Virginia's friends were decent people, and I know she would not have associated with anyone she knew to be vile.

Surprisingly, Lehrman claimed that at the time of her death, he and Rappe were engaged to be married. His malicious attack on Arbuckle was a sensation, and with it the prolific and accomplished director, producer, writer, and actor achieved his greatest fame.

Many Cancel Movies Made by Arbuckle

—*Tulsa Daily World*, September 13, 1921, page 7

With great rapidity, the films of Roscoe Arbuckle were banned throughout the country—by theater organizations, by theater chains, by censorship boards, by police commissions. In other instances, individual theater owners followed Sid Grauman's lead and instituted banishments themselves. In Jersey City the commissioner of public safety contacted every theater owner, inquiring about Arbuckle's movies. Every theater had withdrawn them. "I know of no legal method to prevent the showing of Arbuckle features," the commissioner said, "but I think it would be common decency on the part of motion picture theater owners not to show the pictures until Arbuckle is cleared of the charges." At some theaters that persisted, temporarily, to disregard "common decency," protests were launched, marquee billboards were defaced, and lobby posters were torn down.

Conversely, a demand grew for films in which Virginia Rappe appeared. In death, she was given the star billing on marquees she never received in life.

ARBUCKLE, THE BEAST

—*OXNARD DAILY COURIER* (OXNARD, CALIFORNIA),
SEPTEMBER 12, 1921, FRONT PAGE

The coroner's inquest into the death of Virginia Rappe was moved forward three times and ten days to stay ahead of the grand jury, which was scheduled to convene the evening of Monday, September 12. So at 2 PM that Monday, in an office of the county morgue (also located in the all-purpose Hall of Justice), the inquest began. A coroner's inquest has one goal: to determine the manner of a death. In San Francisco in 1921, a jury of citizens sat in judgment and could ask questions of witnesses, though most questioning was done by the attorneys and the coroner. The proceeding commenced with a heated argument between Assistant DA Milton U'Ren and defense attorney Frank Dominguez.

The prosecution argued that they were still gathering information and wanted to delay Maude Delmont's testimony so she could first be heard by the grand jury, away from the ears of defense attorneys and reporters. Fearful of her being coached, the defense demanded to question their chief accuser. "We want the full facts placed before the people, and we want it done today at this inquest," Dominguez said. The prosecutor retorted that Arbuckle's silence was not contributing to such transparency.

Overseeing the proceedings, San Francisco coroner Dr. Thomas B. W. Leland took offense at the implication that a coroner's inquest was unworthy of key evidence, but after deliberation he delayed Delmont's testimony and ordered the defense to bring her to the stand the next morning.

The first witness was Hotel St. Francis assistant manager Harry Boyle, who testified to being called to 1219, carrying Rappe to 1227 with Arbuckle, and calling Dr. Olav Kaarboe—the second witness. Dr. Melville Rumwell and Dr. William Ophüls spoke of performing the first postmortem examination, and they bolstered the defense by proclaiming that they saw no evidence of violence other than the lacerated bladder. To the assertion that theirs was an illegal autopsy performed by private citizens, Rumwell claimed he called the coroner's office and learned Leland was out of town and could not be reached. Quizzed about the cause of Rappe's torn bladder, Rumwell ruled out a puncture created by a catheter and a spontaneous rupture caused by overdistention. After Drs. Emmet Rixford and George Reid spoke about their consultations with Rumwell in the sanitarium prior to Rappe's death, the proceedings adjourned for the day. The press reported that Arbuckle was "an almost unnoticed figure at the inquest."

ARBUCKLE MAY HANG FOR MURDER

—*EVENING REPUBLICAN* (MITCHELL, SOUTH DAKOTA),
SEPTEMBER 12, 1921, FRONT PAGE

Pressed for comments, most in the film industry steered clear of opinions on Arbuckle's guilt or innocence and served up "this is unfortunate" banalities. Those at Paramount said nothing publicly.

Alice Lake emphasized her friend's compassion: "He was always doing kind things, and he certainly was always one of the first to help at benefits for poor people and other unfortunate ones." Buster Keaton was unequivocal in his support: "I don't believe he is guilty. I never saw him pull any such parties. . . . I think it is wrong to ruin a man before he is even heard."

From his office in New York, Joseph Schenck was equally stalwart, and he went on the offensive against prosecutor Brady: "Arbuckle is a great big, good-natured, lovable sort of chap, and I think that he is not guilty of the charges that certain California public officials seeking notoriety are trying to hang on him."

But the Los Angeles Athletic Club, home away from home to the city's elite (and, previously, the literal home of Mack Sennett and Charlie Chaplin), held an emergency meeting and voted Arbuckle out. The club president said, "I have little to say regarding the action except it was the unanimous belief of the directors that such a step should be taken. We do not want that kind of men in the club for we do not care to associate with that class."

FATTY ARBUCKLE, MOVIE COMEDIAN, BATTLES FOR LIFE

—*CHRONICLE-TELEGRAM* (ELYRIA, OHIO), SEPTEMBER 12, 1921, FRONT PAGE

When the grand jury hearing commenced at 7:30 PM on Monday, a throng of reporters and other observers crowded the hallway and pressed as near to the closed doors as guards would permit. Over the remaining hours of the evening and into the next morning, witnesses, flanked by police officers, were brought in and out to much commotion and a barrage of camera-powder flashes.

A grand jury room is void of reporters, observers, defense attorneys, the defendant (unless testifying), or a judge. Questioning is done by the prosecutors and jurors, and the sole mission of the jurors is to determine if there is sufficient evidence for a trial.

The first witness was Maude Delmont, who was questioned for more than an hour and later brought back for an additional fifteen minutes. When she emerged from the closed doors, she was leaning heavily on a policewoman and said to be ill "due to the shock induced by the death of her friend." Subsequently, Al Semnacher, Zey Prevost, and Drs. Rumwell, Ophüls, and Rixford testified, as did the surgeon from the coroner's office who performed Rappe's second autopsy, Dr. Shelby Strange.

Two floors above in cell 12, Arbuckle was sitting nervously on the edge of his bed when guards approached shortly before 1 AM. He was wanted in the grand jury room. He dressed hastily. A reporter described him trudging to the courtroom, flanked by guards: "He looked nervous, his comedy face was gloomier than that of a tragedian, and beads of perspiration sparkled on his brow." Inside, the jury foreman asked Arbuckle to give his account of the events in question. His answer: "My attorneys have advised me to say nothing at this time." He was in the courtroom for three minutes before he was led back to his cell by a phalanx of guards.

After the prosecutors were excluded from the room, the jury deliberated for nearly an hour. At around 2 AM, the foreman announced the jury had decided against voting on the matter and instead wished to give "District Attorney Brady more time in which to secure certain information which we desire." Brady addressed the press, contending the case had not been weakened by the grand jury's equivocation.

He then made an announcement that would scream in Tuesday's headlines: "We have sent Miss Zey Prevon* home under [police] sur-

---

* Sadie Reiss, a.k.a. Zey Prevost, also answered to Zey Prevon, an earlier stage name. In either case, the press frequently butchered it. There were more than two dozen unique misspellings of her name in print.

veillance. The girl changed her story completely before the grand jury. Whether or not we shall arrest her and charge her with perjury depends on further developments. I am convinced that undue influence and pressure has been brought to bear on her and other witnesses, one of whom, Alice Blake, has mysteriously disappeared from her home in Berkeley. We have been unable to find her."

HIS FAMOUS SMILE IS GONE
—*LOS ANGELES EVENING HERALD*, SEPTEMBER 12, 1921, PAGE 4

It is hard to fathom today how pervasive the newspaper coverage was that first week. The tsunami of ink was greatest in San Francisco and Los Angeles, but if a newspaper covered any national events, it likely splashed ARBUCKLE or FATTY prominently across front pages. From Seattle to Miami, in big cities and small towns, the Arbuckle case was the overriding news story, just as it was, in a melange of languages, in cities across the Atlantic and Pacific—oceans Arbuckle and his movies had traveled.

The tidal wave reached its zenith on Tuesday, September 13, when the *San Francisco Examiner* printed seventeen stories related to the case and the *San Francisco Chronicle* and *Los Angeles Times* each published sixteen. There was much fast-breaking news that day, with both the coroner's inquest and the grand jury hearing in progress, new evidence and witnesses introduced, and charges of perjury, missing witnesses, and "undue influence and pressure." But it wasn't enough to merely cover the legal proceedings. After all, your competition was printing Brady's statement the same as you were. You had to ferret out what the others didn't have.

That Tuesday an interview with Arbuckle's housekeeper ("Roscoe is just a big, good-natured boy") was newsworthy, as was the fact that the inmate in the cell *next to his*, a convicted murderer, would soon be returning to Maryland, where he had escaped from prison (ARBUCKLE WILL LOSE NEIGHBOR IN JAIL). Another headline stated, GRAVE OF ARBUCKLE'S MOTHER IS NEGLECTED and explained that the wooden slab marking Mary Arbuckle's final resting place in a Santa Ana cemetery was so faded it was unreadable and "overrun with grass and weeds." (Arbuckle had repeatedly paid for its upkeep.) Minta Durfee made her first public statement on Tuesday, and effusively supportive comments by Arbuckle's sister Nora were widely published ("He has the kindest, tenderest heart in the world") as was his brother Harry's "no comment" the next day (under the misleading heading BROTHER IS NEUTRAL). Housekeeper, neighbor, mother, wife, sister, brother—what next?

> BULLDOG MOURNS FOR ARBUCKLE
> Faithful Pet Waiting at Door for Return of Comedian
> Fatty Arbuckle has one sincere mourner, one mourner whose love and faith no reports can shake. That mourner is Luke, Fatty's old bulldog. Luke usually goes with Fatty on his long trips, but the comedian didn't take him to San Francisco with him.
>
> This is the longest time that the comedian and Luke have been separated. And out at Fatty's house, Luke sits, disconsolate at the door, waiting for the familiar step and the well-known voice. He doesn't eat. He waits.
>
> Whatever befalls Fatty, Luke will not forget.

Apparently, with Arbuckle away then for only one day longer than he had been the week before, Luke had gone on a solidarity food strike. If true, he had surely been reading the newspapers.

It's always easier to create news than find it.

A headline promised OTHER ILLEGAL ACTS CHARGED TO FILM STAR and then suggested that Arbuckle may have attended Hollywood "drink and drug orgies." Another header asserted, SECOND GIRL ESCAPES FATE OF MISS RAPPE, but dealt with Lowell Sherman luring a model into his room after Rappe was moved to 1227. An article in a Flagstaff newspaper was headlined FATTY ARBUCKLE TREATS WIFE ROUGH IN ARIZONA and alleged that, twelve years prior, not only did he beat Durfee, blackening both of her eyes, but he also abandoned her penniless at the train stop in Benson, Arizona, where she was rescued by the good citizens of Bisbee.

The one source listed for this was "word received here today."* Words could convey anything.

In fact, the very words "Virginia Rappe" seemed to denote a heinous felony: Virgin Rape. It was the sort of on-the-nose name no Hollywood screenwriter would dare pen, but it was exploited by newspaper editors in headlines that referred to the "Rappe Girl" or "Rappe Tragedy." Most newspapers then had policies against even printing the word *rape* (*assault* was the popular euphemism), which imbued the name Rappe with even more power.

Many of the same papers that shunned *rape* freely printed *orgy*. The word, unstated by the police or prosecutors, had first appeared in bold print on September 11: Dying Girl Laid Blame on Comedian: So Charges Woman at Bedside of Orgy Victim in Statement to S.F. Police. There was soon thereafter a national orgy of "orgy" headlines. The September 5 party—originally just an informal gathering—was an "orgy," a previous Arbuckle "orgy" was referenced (more about this in chapter 15), and the prevalence of Hollywood "orgies" was documented. A headline in Tuesday's *Baltimore Sun* was typical: Arbuckle Affair No Surprise After Orgies of Film Colony. Wednesday's *San Francisco Examiner* said of Arbuckle, "Tales of his sickening orgies have spread from one coast to the other. Everybody who knows anything about him or his kind ought to know what a 'party' given by him would mean."

Most "orgy" headlines promised more salacious specificity than they delivered, but an article published in Philadelphia's *Evening Public Ledger* was a notable exception. Positioned on the page next to two large photos of Rappe and an article entitled "Arbuckle Party Drank Forty Quarts" was "Hollywood Orgies Exposed by Police," which purported to blow the lid off a group called "the Live Hundred," made up of Hollywood heavyweights including, allegedly, Arbuckle. The "orgy" best detailed was reportedly attended by witnesses in the Arbuckle case, and "the host spent $20,000 for decorations" alone. There's no telling what the host,

* Neither in her available memoir manuscript pages nor in her many interviews did Durfee ever allege her husband was physically abusive.

"a prominent male actor of the screen," dropped on this refreshment budget:

> From without, as the group sat down at the long table in the "grotto," the watchers [detectives] saw a maid push a wheeled tea tray in after extensive indulgence by all in drinks. On the tray was an assortment of needles, opium pipes, morphine, cocaine, heroin and opium. Each guest hilariously helped himself or herself to liberal doses of drugs and selected needles or pipes as the individual desire demanded.

After which a cocaine-sniffing actress announced, "I want the most beautiful man here. I am his." This was presumably the start of the orgy part of the orgy, but the detectives then pounded at the door. When it was finally opened, all evidence had been destroyed or concealed and the host had escaped.

Likewise, a headline in the *Denver Post* that Thursday reads like something from the *Onion* today: NARCOTICS NEEDLES TURNED TAME PARTY AT HOLLYWOOD INTO ASTOUNDING SUCCESS. Indeed. Suddenly, every Hollywood rumor, scandal, and peccadillo was dragged into the morning light in the morning paper. A short United Press story, which ran on the front pages of numerous newspapers on Monday, linked Rappe's death with six other Hollywood "scandals," including Charlie Chaplin's divorce on grounds of cruelty, that previous Arbuckle "orgy"—described as a "girl and wine revel"—and the accidental death by poisoning of actress Olive Thomas, who in September 1920 mistakenly drank a solution of mercury bichloride.*

A September 13 editorial in the *Los Angeles Times* was equivocal on Arbuckle's guilt in the Rappe case but nonetheless offered:

* A haunting snippet of newsreel footage features three promising movie actresses seated together. Presumably, they were friends. On one side is Olive Thomas; on the other is Edna Purviance (Charlie Chaplin's leading lady). In the middle is Virginia Rappe, who died exactly one year after Thomas's fatal poisoning.

> For three or four years the smart set in the movies has been traveling at a furious pace. Their marital infidelities have clogged the pages of the divorce records. They have taken supreme delight in flinging their money from the windows. However moderate might be the pictures they produced, in real life the machine was always running in the high. Now one of the fastest of the furious set has driven his machine into the ditch. . . . The Times trusts that the example will prove a salutary warning to others who have been going at a similar pace; for Arbuckle is not the only cinema star who has given mixed parties at which the host received the guests clad only in bath robe and pajamas.

The constant drumbeat about the Labor Day "orgy" attended by those in and around the movie industry, the linkage of it with other such "orgies" and "scandals," and a rash of moralistic editorials all painted Hollywood as Babylon. This rocked the movie industry and had censorious repercussions for decades to come.

But the greatest impact that first week was to Arbuckle's reputation. He had gone from a beloved comedy icon to, at best, a degenerate lout deserving of universal condemnation, and, at worst, a rapist and murderer deserving of the gallows. His physique, previously a signifier of joie de vivre, suddenly symbolized carnality and unbridled impulsiveness. On Tuesday the *Denver Post* printed a front-page artist's illustration of a pitiful Arbuckle behind bars in which he seemed twice as heavy as his 266 pounds and twice as old as his thirty-four years. The next day, the same paper published an article entitled "Arbuckle's Fat Is to Blame for His Trouble, Declares Famous Psycho-Analyst," wherein the psychoanalyst proclaimed that "the hundred too many pounds rolling over the film comedian's body is so much moral weakness and potential crime." That reads nearly complimentary next to a *Dayton Daily News* editorial: "Arbuckle is a gross, common, bestial, drunken individual, and it is perfectly apparent that he has never deserved the patronage he has received. This is not his first escapade. Filled up with liquor, his low bestiality asserts itself in treating a woman like a grizzly bear would a calf."

Whereas before, Arbuckle had been revered as the working-class vaudevillian whose wealth came via talent and long hours of labor, he was now portrayed as a lucky-to-be-rich degenerate living outside society's norms. Envy clearly fueled some of the reaction. An editorial in the *Atlanta Constitution* entitled "Ruined by Wealth" averred, "Arbuckle, made suddenly famous because his grotesque figure and comical antics before the camera was amusing to the 'moviegoing' world, accumulated money so rapidly that his most difficult problem was to spend it as fast as it came up."

Newspaper photographs of Arbuckle captured him either unsmiling and pensive, as if troubled by what he had done, or in his Fatty character—the mischievous, somewhat lecherous man-boy in the undersized bowler. In contrast, the press never tired of publishing glamour shots of smiling Rappe, frequently referred to as "the best dressed girl of the movies." Many of her photos were five or more years old and thus served to emphasize her youth and vitality. Photo montages with titles like "Once in Happy Repose" and "Beautiful, Laughing Virginia Rappe in Film Scenes" grabbed attention. Sometimes lurking nearby would be a dour or ridiculous shot of Arbuckle. Sometimes the photo of one would overlap the other, as if he was interrupting her carefree life. Plastered across the front page of Thursday's *San Francisco Examiner* was a spiderweb, spun via an illustrator's pen, ensnaring photographs. In the center was arachnid Arbuckle and two bottles of booze while around him was his prey, seven female guests at the Labor Day party, including Rappe. This striking image was entitled "They Walked into His Parlor," and the caption began, "Caught in the web spun lightly at an afternoon 'party' a week ago, the eight persons shown in the above photographic cartoon today find the mealies still sticking to them."

Open up the *New York American* the day before and you would have found "Hope for Fame Lured Actress to Her Death" and its assertion that "the lure of 'something better' in her motion picture career, possibly, the stardom she had craved for years but never had attained, was the snare with which Roscoe Arbuckle, charged with her murder, enticed Virginia Rappe into his net." Outside of statements from his relatives, friends, and coworkers (and the loyalty of his dog) and biographical articles that sketched his improbable rise to superstardom, the preponderance of press that first week cast Arbuckle in a negative light and often presumed his guilt. He was the spoiled movie star who knew no boundaries, forever seeking the next thrill, openly disdainful of his marriage, a gaudy beast, Fatty. Rappe was the stylish but innocent beauty lured into his lair, engaged to marry, perpetually smiling, Virgin Rape.*

Arbuckle's defense attorneys faced a seemingly unwinnable war. The prospects of even assembling an impartial jury were dim after the ceaseless barrage of vitriol from the Bay Area newspapers. On Tuesday the *San Francisco Examiner* published the following portrait of the man who, until recently, made the whole world laugh:

> But in his innermost soul, deeper than the casual eye can reach, slept the Arbuckle that Virginia Rappe knew. Sated with money, contemptuous of success from years of familiarity with its constant presence, bored by life's decency, scornful of straight roads, disdainful of what men call honor, bathing his decadent soul in every fountain of viciousness which lines the by-roads of life, on his shoulders the mantle of lawlessness, on his head the Grape leaves of Bacchus.

"Roscoe Arbuckle is just a great big, lovable, pleasure-loving, overgrown boy whose success and prosperity have been a little too much for him, but he is not guilty of the hideous charge made against him in San Francisco." So said the ever-supportive Minta Durfee in New York City on Tuesday while preparing for a five-day train trip to San Francisco. She had been vacationing on Martha's Vineyard with her mother and had not learned of her estranged husband's arrest until she received a telegram from her sister on Sunday night. The next day, mother and daughter returned to Manhattan to find reporters had staked out the lobby of Durfee's midtown apartment building.

* Her age was invariably given as twenty-five. She was thirty on September 5, 1921, just four years younger than Arbuckle.

By Tuesday Durfee was ready to talk. "I am going to him because I think it is my duty to be near him. I want to help him in any way I can." Speculation was swirling about the Arbuckle marriage; that day, the *New York Times* reported the "rumor" that the couple had recently separated. Durfee, who suddenly preferred the name "Mrs. Arbuckle," clarified: "Five years ago we agreed to disagree and I received a separation maintenance. . . . A reconciliation? That depends on whether I find that my place is with him and whether he finds that he is ready to return to the life we led when we were married, when I was his inspiration. All I know now is that I am going to a friend who needs every bit of help he can get."

As ordered, star witness Mrs. Bambina Maude Delmont took the stand at the coroner's inquest on Tuesday morning. She wore black, like a mourner—or a villain. The press described her as a "beauty specialist." In a photo of her from that day, her head is tilted slightly, chin up, as if in defiance, black hat over her graying black hair. Gray eyes glare from under weary lids; a dim frown tugs downward the corners of her thin, closed lips. Despite this rigid appearance, she was described as "an exceedingly nervous witness" who took frequent drinks of water. Perhaps this was due to Arbuckle's presence nearby; he stared at her throughout her testimony, averting his gaze only to whisper to an attorney.

Delmont recounted a tale that mostly clung to her affidavit and previous statements—but with a few crucial modifications, principally that Arbuckle did not take hold of Rappe nor drag her into the room. Her account was punctuated by Rappe saying, "I am hurt! I am dying! He did it!" with *he* being Arbuckle. "Right from the start," Delmont testified, "Virginia accused Roscoe—she always called him that—but she didn't want anyone to tell Lehrman about it." Thus, Delmont served up the crucial accusation from Rappe's lips and placed Arbuckle there to hear the dying woman and not deny it.

Still, her account was erratic. Coroner Leland frequently cautioned her to "consider your statements well." "Maybe I was leading you," he said once after a question and affirmative answer. "Sometimes people go to sleep and just say 'yes.'"

Bizarrely, Delmont replied, "I'm not asleep, for I had a little hypodermic before I came here and I'm all right." What drug was in that hypodermic is unknown.

As for why she was wearing a pair of Lowell Sherman's pajamas at the Labor Day party, she said she had grown warm from dancing. And as for her Prohibition violation, she seemed to revel in it, confessing to drinking from her own pint of whiskey on the Saturday ride from Los Angeles. (Though consuming liquor in one's own home or a private residence in which one was an invited guest was not illegal, transporting liquor was.) When the coroner asked her what she did after the doctor came to 1219, she replied, "Oh, the [hotel] detective, he was very nice; he and I went back and drank all the gin and orange juice." She claimed Rappe had had three orange blossoms, and of Rappe's accused murderer she said, "It impressed me that Arbuckle was more intoxicated than anyone else in the party. He was just a little gone. He showed it in his eyes and by being very talkative. He was not staggering or anything of that sort." But Delmont was likely not an astute judge of anyone else's state of mind on that previous Monday, having, by her own admission under oath, consumed "eight or ten" whiskeys at the party.

The coroner asked, "How do you know what happened if you had so many drinks of whiskey?"

Delmont replied, "My memory is always good."

Nurses Jean Jameson and Vera Cumberland were two presumably impartial witnesses who had heard from the ill Rappe in the days before her death. Each testified in ways that aided the defense, with the former testifying that Rappe claimed she "had been suffering for six weeks with internal trouble" and the latter saying, "The patient admitted to me that her relations with Arbuckle in the room had not been proper." Both corroborated one element of Delmont's testimony, recalling that Rappe had expressed anxiety about Henry Lehrman hearing of the events in 1219, indicating that she still had strong feelings for him. Their inquest testimony barely registered in the press.

Al Semnacher explained that he had not been at the party during the events in question and only returned around the time the assistant manager was called. When he next saw Rappe on the bed, she was naked. According to him, she was not much of a drinker ("I have seen her take one or two drinks and get dizzy"), and he reiterated his odd reasoning for taking her torn clothing, which was introduced as evidence: "I thought the shirtwaist would make a nice dust cloth for my machine [car]." When he visited Rappe on the day after Labor Day, she supposedly told him, "Roscoe hurt me." Salesman Ira Fortlouis, having been asked to leave the party before Rappe grew ill, proved not much of a witness.

Because Alice Blake and Zey Prevost still had yet to testify, the jury could not deliberate, and the coroner once again chastised the prosecution. The DA's office assured the coroner the two women would testify the next day. Once again, Roscoe Arbuckle was led toward cell 12, ignoring the barrage of reporters' questions and the smoky explosions of cameras.

Some of those reporters captured the confrontation when Semnacher stopped to say good-bye to Delmont. She asked why he hadn't brought Rappe's "aunt" to the proceedings from Los Angeles, and he replied that he was not aware Kate Hardebeck was without money, and he had left for San Francisco in the middle of the night.

Growing excited, Delmont asked, "Well, what am I going to do about my bills at the St. Francis? They come to about $250."

"I'm sure I don't know," Semnacher replied.

"Well, if you were a man you'd pay them. And what am I going to do about my baggage?"

"Why, Maude, you know the only baggage you have is in that little handbag you're holding."

Enraged, Delmont shrieked and swung the bag with all her force at Semnacher's face, missing.* "You dirty dog! Get out of here!" she screamed as she was subdued by policemen.

---

* Semnacher claimed Delmont said, "I am still holding the bag," to which he replied, "The only bag you are holding is that little bag in your hand." Commence swinging.

Leaving the room, Semnacher remarked, "Why should I pay her bills? I'm under no obligations to her."

Subsequently, and presumably at her request, Henry Lehrman wired Delmont money to cover her stay at the St. Francis.

Also on Tuesday, Arbuckle was taken to a Prohibition office, where officials had opened an investigation the day before to determine who supplied the alcohol for the Labor Day party. He was questioned for nearly an hour but denied knowledge of any alcohol in his room, despite the discovery of two whiskey bottles in 1219's wastebasket after the party. His repeated answer to repeated questions about the booze was "Never had any."

District Attorney Brady's strategy was evolving. He knew after her coroner's inquest testimony that Maude Delmont was unlikely to fend off many blows under cross-examination in a criminal trial. Thus, two previously unknown chorus girls who dreamed of show business success and answered to stage names grew in importance. If Zey Prevost and Alice Blake—friends with no one at the party except each other—could back up Delmont's version of events, then Brady believed a murder conviction was likely. The problem was that Prevost refused to tell the grand jury what she had told detectives on one occasion and prosecutors on another: that Rappe had said, "I'm dying. I'm dying. He killed me." She claimed she'd been frightened and confused when questioned before.

Accompanied by her mother, Prevost was escorted to the Hall of Justice by police. Meanwhile, Blake was brought in by a family friend who claimed she had gone into hiding to save her wealthy Oakland family from embarrassment. Separately, prosecutors endeavored to get both showgirls to sign statements to back up Delmont's charge that Rappe said, in Arbuckle's presence, "He did it"—a less precise accusation than "He killed me." Both eventually did. Prevost's new recollection: "He hurt me, he hurt me. I am dying. I am dying. I am dying."

Brady called the grand jury to session again at 8 PM on Tuesday and produced three witnesses: Zey Prevost, Alice Blake, and Grace Halston, the nurse at the first autopsy. The chorus girls backed up Delmont's version of events, though they still vacillated on specifics. Crucially, the grand jury had heard Prevost give a different account the day before, so it is unclear how much this "makeup" reappearance helped the prosecution.

The grand jury's decision came in Wednesday's first hours. In the death of Virginia Rappe, Roscoe Arbuckle should be indicted for involuntary manslaughter—a killing committed without malice aforethought. (A manslaughter conviction had a maximum penalty of ten years imprisonment.) However, Brady still had Delmont's first-degree murder complaint ready to proceed in police court, and he was hopeful the coroner's inquest would bolster it by recommending a murder trial.

In the morning in cell 12, Arbuckle was getting dressed when he heard the news from a guard that he had been indicted for manslaughter by the grand jury. He made no remark but told his cellmate Martin he had not slept well. His and Martin's restaurant breakfast was delivered, as was Arbuckle's usual stack of letters and telegrams.

"I protest in the name of this state against these girls being called. For them to testify will be detrimental to the case of the state." So said Matthew Brady at Wednesday morning's coroner's inquest. The girls were Blake and Prevost, by then household names, and Brady did not want the defense to have a record of their inquest testimony, revealing possible discrepancies. "I repeat that there are but two people who know exactly what took place in that hotel room. One of them is dead. The body of Virginia Rappe, lying in the morgue, cannot speak. The other one is Roscoe Arbuckle, and he is in this room. Call him if you want the facts."

Dominguez lifted his rotund form from his seat at the counsel's table in order to forcefully assert that Arbuckle was within his rights not to testify. Coroner Leland deliberated with the jury in his chamber and announced that they did not need to hear from Blake and Prevost. In conclusion, Drs. Strange and Ophüls testified again about their autopsies. Ophüls stated that only violence of "some force" could have created Rappe's bladder rupture. Asked to elaborate on a violent cause, he replied, "Finger pressure."

The coroner's inquest jury began deliberating at noon. As they filed out, Arbuckle tried to light a cigarette, but his shaking hands betrayed him. When the jury returned a decision three and a half hours later, it suggested not just a cause of death but also a means of preventing similar deaths. Leaning forward as the verdict was read by the coroner, Arbuckle trembled slightly at the mention, twice, of his name. After briefly stating the particulars, the verdict read:

> Said rupture was caused by the application of some force which, from the evidence submitted, we believe was applied by one Roscoe Arbuckle, and the undersigned jurors, therefore, charge the said Roscoe Arbuckle with the crime of manslaughter.* We recommend that the District Attorney of the City and County of San Francisco, in conjunction with the Grand Jury, the Chief of Police and the Federal Prohibition officials, take steps to prevent a recurrence of affairs similar to the one in which this young woman lost her life, so that San Francisco shall not be made the rendezvous of the debauchee and the gangster.

That last sentence reads as if it were penned by a group, born nine months earlier, that regularly railed against the dangers facing the women of San Francisco. In the first hours of Thanksgiving Day 1920, a gang of at least eight young men drugged and sexually assaulted two teenage girls in a shack on Howard Street. The case was huge news in the Bay Area,

* One dissenting juror, Ben Boas, wrote the following: "I, the undersigned juror, find that the said Virginia Rappe came to her death from peritonitis caused by a ruptured bladder. Said rupture was caused by the application of some force, and from the evidence submitted I am unable to determine who was responsible for the application of said force."

perpetuated when three additional young women made other gang rape charges. Understandably, headlines like Girl, 20, Sobs Recital of Attack by 19 fostered outrage and fueled a fear that the streets of the city were teeming with packs of rampaging males. On December 13, 1920, more than seventy-five San Francisco women's clubs sent representatives to a meeting, and the Women's Vigilant Committee was formed. The name drew purposeful parallels to the male vigilante groups of the 1850s that meted out frontier justice in San Francisco to ward off Gold Rush criminality.

Curbing vice was one stated goal of the WVC. Another was the support of females—victims, witnesses, and family members—at trials. On the Wednesday that the grand jury's indictment and the recommendation of the coroner's inquest were handed down, the WVC held a meeting about the Arbuckle case. It was attended by two hundred members and appointed a committee of twenty women to bolster female witnesses. Club president Dr. Mariana Bertola (a physician at an Oakland women's college) said the Arbuckle case "is no better than the Howard Street gangsters case in many of its particulars. Nor should the ones responsible for it be shown here leniency." Another WVC member said, "We are not going to stand for these orgies with their inevitably terrible results, whether their scene be a shack on Howard Street or a gilded caravansary in rich man's row."

Women's clubs had blossomed in the early twentieth century, and many had worked to pass the Eighteenth (Prohibition) and Nineteenth (women's suffrage) Amendments. The latter was ratified on August 18, 1920, four months before the Women's Vigilant Committee was formed, and politicians were then eagerly courting the large new bloc of female voters. On Thursday Bertola met with District Attorney Brady and made arrangements for WVC members to monitor Arbuckle court proceedings. The WVC was the most prominent of several women's clubs to side with the prosecution and encourage a hard line from Brady, whose employment depended on the vagaries of voters. The front-page subheading of the *Los Angeles Times* article about the Bertola/Brady meeting read "Women After Arbuckle."

While Arbuckle was locked behind iron bars in cell 12 of the city jail, his $34,000 customized, purple-blue Pierce-Arrow was parked in an alley behind the Hall of Justice. Visited daily by throngs of curious viewers, it was the city's newest tourist attraction. (Prohibition officials were threatening to seize it, if they could prove it had been used to transport alcohol.) In Los Angeles, residents came to gaze at Arbuckle's West Adams mansion.

Arbuckle's net worth at the time was estimated at between $500,000 and $1 million. The press made much of his extravagant free-spending ways, estimating he had spent $100,000 on automobiles (approximately $1.3 million in today's dollars) and thousands more on just "having a good time." The amount he could obtain via liquid assets was around $200,000.

On Monday a furniture company had filed a lien, claiming Arbuckle owed $6,500 for twenty-five pieces of furniture. On Wednesday an interior decorator filed an attachment against all known Arbuckle property, claiming the jailed actor owed $11,400 for decorating his house and grounds. The superstar had made purchases on credit because retailers and contractors offered him such deals to win his implied endorsement, but now that his name hurt their reputations more than it helped, they were calling in the debts. He had managed his money unwisely. The man with the million-dollar contract had much less than he should have, and his outrageously expensive legal team was quickly depleting it.

Try as it might, that legal team could not spring Arbuckle out of jail. The grand jury's manslaughter indictment was presented on Thursday, bail was set at $5,000, and Arbuckle's team handed over a cashier's check in exchange for their client's freedom. But their client spent another night in jail, awaiting a hearing on the murder charge in police court on Friday morning. It seemed a mere formality that it would be dismissed in favor of the manslaughter charge endorsed by both the grand jury and the coroner's inquest. The defense team was so confident of their client's imminent release, they booked a car for him on the Saturday train to Los Angeles.

District Attorney Brady held a long, private conference on Thursday with Police Chief O'Brien and Captain of Detectives Matheson. In addition to pressure from the women's clubs, Brady received a telegram from Henry Lehrman, released to the public:

> For the sake of God and justice to men, don't let justice be cheated. It brought tears of rage to my eyes when I read your speech that influence and wealth are brought into play to bar justice. I cried because you told the truth in spite of the pressure of gold to stifle it. You are convinced from the facts and I from knowledge that Arbuckle killed Virginia Rappe. Now, don't let them cheat justice, for God's sake, for he is guilty. I held court with the facts in my conscience and convicted him.

An enormous crowd overwhelmed the Hall of Justice on Friday morning in hopes of viewing Arbuckle's arraignment. Thousands thronged before the building's entrance and on both sides of the street. A so-called "army of special police" was enlisted to keep order in and out of the building. Per an agreement between Brady and the women's clubs, the event was held in a women's court; such venues forbade male spectators so women could more openly testify in rape and other emotionally sensitive cases. (The restriction did not apply to court personnel, attorney staffs, or reporters.) The 156 seats reserved for spectators were occupied by vigilant women, most dressed in mournful black, including a cadre from the WVC. Fortified with sandwiches, they were seated hours before proceedings began while the courtroom's doors were locked against the throngs outside.

To the disappointment of those crowding the halls, Arbuckle was brought from his cell to Police Judge Sylvain Lazarus's chamber via an inside corridor. He remained there with his attorneys and Lou Anger as other cases were adjudicated, one of which featured Joyce "Dollie" Clark, a showgirl who pleaded guilty to obtaining goods under false pretenses for charging a hat purchase to another woman. In an odd coincidence, Clark had been a guest at the Labor Day party but arrived after Rappe fell ill.

The clerk read, "The next case is number five on the continued list, your honor: the State of California against Roscoe Arbuckle, murder." And the courtroom fell into a hushed silence. Vigilant women craned their necks as the accused strode into the room and stood before the judge, shifting nervously and never acknowledging the female spectators.

With Brady's confident pronouncement—"The people are ready to proceed on the murder charges"—a hum of gasps and murmurs spread and rose. Arbuckle glared at the floor and bit his lip.

In a decision that, according to him, came just before Friday's arraignment, Brady ignored the grand jury's manslaughter complaint and the manslaughter recommendation from the coroner's inquest and instead proceeded on the original murder charge. Whether because of pressure from the voting public (especially the new women's bloc), fealty to Rappe's honor, his own competitive pride, or some combination thereof, Brady would not be moved. Arbuckle was stunned, as was his defense team. The DA was ready to begin the preliminary hearing without delay.

Defense attorney Dominguez asked for a continuance of twelve days. Brady countered with six. Judge Lazarus decided on the latter, setting a court date for the following Thursday, September 22, at 1 PM. At the conclusion of the give-and-take between Dominguez and Brady, the DA said, "We want to be courteous to everyone, even if they do come from Los Angeles." Feminine observers applauded the barbed witticism.

Afterward, Brady issued a written statement:

> The District Attorney's office, from the time that the facts became known, has always been firmly of the opinion that the correct charge involved in the Arbuckle case was murder. . . . It is the sole province of the trial jury to determine, after the evidence has been taken, in the event it should find the defendant guilty, whether the verdict should be one of murder, manslaughter or any other crime comprehended in the charge, and also to fix the degree thereof.

And thus Arbuckle remained a resident of the San Francisco City Jail. Deflated, he was ushered away from the photographers and the vigilant women and back into the judge's chamber. There he nervously smoked a cigarette and spoke with his attorneys before guards accompanied him again to cell 12, where he was to stay, indefinitely.

"On the beautiful face there is a peaceful expression and the lips are smiling with unearthly knowledge." So read a newspaper account, describing Virginia Rappe, lying in repose in a parlor in the Halsted & Company funeral home in San Francisco. As thousands of mourners (virtually all of whom knew her only from recent newspaper accounts) milled past on Thursday, September 15, she was dressed in "slumbering robes" of silver cloth and cream-colored silks and "veilings that a bride could wear." The room was infused with the aroma of roses, chrysanthemums, and funeral wreaths—some compliments of Rappe's old friend Sidi Spreckels, most from strangers, many with cards identifying the sender as a sympathetic mother. Maude Delmont attended and collapsed in anguish.

The impressive display of one thousand pink lilies was from Henry Lehrman. Gold letters said, To My Brave Sweetheart, From Henry. Lehrman was assuming the bills, and via telegram he told the undertaker to whisper "Henry loves you" in Rappe's ear before closing the casket lid. Per Lehrman's wired instructions, late on Friday night, Virginia Rappe, encased in her metal casket, was loaded onto a Southern Pacific train bound from San Francisco to Los Angeles. She would travel the same journey she made five years earlier, then in search of fame and fortune in Hollywood.

{11}

GLORY: 1917-18

> To come upon the Hollywood of those days is like taking off for the moon, landing there and finding it inhabited by all the people we always thought and hoped people would be.
>
> —Adela Rogers St. Johns, *Love, Laughter and Tears*

Paramount had a plan for promoting its newest star. The studio would put him on a train in a private car and send him from the Pacific to the Atlantic on a twenty-three-stop tour, meeting with local exhibitors at banquets and heralding his future with Paramount Pictures. There were problems. When the February 17, 1917, departure date arrived, Arbuckle's left leg was still debilitated, and he loped about with a cane. He still battled pain with painkillers. And having lost eighty pounds during his convalescence, the recovering morphine addict beloved as Fatty remained notably undersized.

The shill must go on. The sendoff party was held on a Friday evening at the Hotel Alexandria in downtown Los Angeles and attended by Hollywood's elite. Seated on the dais were Paramount execs Jesse Lasky and Adolph Zukor. The Los Angeles district attorney served as toastmaster. A giant red banner shouted in yellow letters: He's Worth His Weight in Laughs. When the guest of honor entered—illuminated by a spotlight, serenaded by an orchestra, exalted by a standing ovation—he was supported by his wife, Minta Durfee, on one side and his manager, Lou

Anger, on the other. By then they were the two primary and competing influences in his life.

Durfee was Arbuckle's motherly nurturer. After his later arrest, many of her references to him would infantilize him ("*Roscoe Arbuckle is just a great big, lovable, pleasure-loving, overgrown boy*"), as if to say such a naive innocent could never have done what he was accused of. Because Durfee was more careful about money matters, she'd often served as his de facto business manager as well—until Lou Anger came along. Anger was six years older than Arbuckle, a fellow comedian, and they shared vaudeville pasts and a love of baseball. He positioned himself as Arbuckle's jocular compatriot and confidant—a big brother. This trip would determine which influence—mother or brother—won out.

The morning after the banquet, Arbuckle boarded the private train car along with Anger, Durfee, her sister and her sister's husband, good friend Joe Bordeaux, a masseur, and a doctor. The train went initially to San Francisco and then wove eastward, stopping in places both small (Milford, Utah) and large (Chicago). An ad in a Salt Lake City newspaper featured a giant cartoon Fatty riding atop a train with people, animals, and the sun cheering him on: "Boys and Girls, join the parade behind the brass band and escort the King of Funmakers to his hotel." Durfee remembered: "At night, there was always a banquet. Zukor or Joe Schenck or Lasky would make the usual talk about how happy they were to be in whatever town they were in, list some of the upcoming [Paramount] films, and introduce Roscoe. Roscoe would only thank the people for attending, but they laughed as if he had just told them a lot of jokes."

Arbuckle told an incredulous Chicago reporter of his recent hospital stay and weight loss, and his short stay in the Windy City provoked a mention of his injury and a reference to his libidinous big-screen reputation:

> Arbuckle had a carbuncle on his knee. The farthest he walked, while in Chicago, was from the train to the street, where an Elgin Six was

> waiting for him.* Ordinarily, "Fatty" likes the lady admirers, but, in this case, his wife was with him, so he could do nothing else than place his foot on the accelerator and shoot through the dense crowds as fast as the speed ordinance would allow.

He was "chairman of the reception" at a free screening of Paramount's *Snow White* in Pittsburgh one day and guest of honor at a Motion Picture Machine Operators Union ball in Washington, DC, the next. Between a parade for him at the Philadelphia train station and a ritzy banquet that evening, he placed a wreath on the Liberty Bell. As the trip progressed, the daily public luncheons and dinners, during which Fatty was expected to eat heartily, packed the trademark pounds back on.† Boston was the last stop on the tour, where on the evening of March 6, dinner was served at the regal Copley Plaza Hotel. Zukor, Lasky, Marcus Loew, and the Massachusetts attorney general were among the notables in attendance when Arbuckle was enthusiastically received by more than 125 of Paramount's New England exhibitors.

That was the official reception party. There was also an unofficial afterparty—and what a party! In the early hours of March 7, several prominent members of the Arbuckle reception attended an event in nearby Woburn, Massachusetts. The location was Mishawum Manor, a brothel. Hush money kept the criminal facts of that late night quiet for over four years. But they would scream out on July 11, 1921, less than two months before Labor Day. Thus, the notorious Mishawum "chicken and champagne orgy" will be addressed when our story turns to the summer of 1921.

Later on March 7, the Arbuckle entourage took a train to New York City, where the Arbuckles moved back into a suite at the Cumberland

---

* Automobile fanatic Arbuckle had the Elgin Six touring car delivered from the Elgin Motor Car Corporation, located in suburban Chicago. He had his own such car in Los Angeles.

† What Fatty ate remained a press preoccupation. A Philadelphia newspaper published "Breakfast a la Arbuckle," the menu of the first meal the movie star consumed on his day in Philly: fruit, cereal, steak and potatoes, six eggs on toast, three cups of coffee, butter and rolls.

Hotel. Arbuckle regained lost leg strength. And as he began planning comedy shorts for his new production company that did not include his wife, the bonds of his marriage grew weaker. Durfee would always blame Lou Anger for forcing her out of her husband's film plans, effectively ending her acting career and severing her marriage beyond repair. She was right on one count: by 1917 the Arbuckles' marriage, which had begun with a for-profit wedding, had been reduced to principally a business arrangement.

Lou Anger may have hastened the end of that arrangement, but the romantic relationship had been troubled for years. Arbuckle liked drinking with the guys and wild nights on the town; Durfee liked reading books and quiet nights at home. They argued. In private, fueled by alcohol, his insecurities could boil over into a rage. And by Durfee's accounts, her pained husband had not been able to perform sexually on the cross-country tour. She recounted one rampage after he failed at sexual intercourse in which he threw dresser drawers and ripped a telephone free of the wall. "I'm a star! I'm not supposed to be married! I can't be hampered by a wife!" he yelled at her, before kicking a table, cutting his leg. He subsequently locked himself in the bathroom, remorseful and embarrassed. "I never heard a man cry so hard in my life," Durfee said. "It was terrible."

Arbuckle had probably been unfaithful, most likely with Alice Lake and with others as well. He had married young, with little experience in romance, when he was a poor and virtually unknown singer in stage shows. Eight and a half years later he was one of the most famous men in the world, wealthy and soon to be much wealthier, and he was a film director capable of launching the careers of beautiful young actresses. As Durfee, his loyal supporter, recalled him saying, "*I'm a star! I'm not supposed to be married!*" He wanted to experience all that the movie star lifestyle entailed.

March 24 marked Arbuckle's thirtieth birthday, and Durfee bought him memberships in the Friars Club and the Lambs Club, exclusive all-male New York City theatrical societies. Soon thereafter, he moved into the Friars' new Manhattan clubhouse (dubbed the "Monastery"), claiming the massages and baths there were ideal for his recovery. A little over eight and a half years after it began, the Arbuckle marriage ended in all but title. Durfee moved into a Manhattan apartment with her sister and brother-in-law.

Years later, trying to bolster her husband's reputation after his arrest, Durfee offered a judicious view of the marriage breakup (which again infantalized her husband), but nevertheless she pointed to fissures that had likely grown over years: "Well, if he can be stubborn, so can I. Probably our separation was as much my fault as it was his. We began to clash a little, probably over some very unimportant things. He wouldn't admit that he was wrong, and neither would I. He is like a boy; he wants to be coaxed; and as for myself, I cannot force myself on anyone, least of all a man, if I have the slightest feeling that I may not be welcome. So we simply got on one another's nerves, and it never got properly straightened out."

In 1917 divorce was a scandal sure to harm Arbuckle's image, and at a crucial turn in his career. Durfee signed a separation agreement that paid her $500 weekly (about $9,000 in today's dollars) while he and she privately lived apart. And thus, finally, there was a price for their business arangement.

Mickey, the troubled production of troubled Mabel Normand, would not be released until August 1918, but it was well reviewed and popular, and Durfee had a plum supporting role. In 1919 Durfee starred in a series of two-reel comedies for Truat Film Corporation, a small New York company. Few noticed. She slipped from public view, only to emerge again in September 1921, defending the husband from whom she had been separated for four and a half years.

One door closed and another opened. In the same month that Arbuckle's marriage effectively ended, his strongest friendship began.

Joseph Keaton was born October 4, 1895, as his parents passed through tiny Piqua, Kansas, in the employ of a traveling medicine show. The story of his early years grew more in the telling than Arbuckle's own:

A cyclone blew away the town where he was born. When not yet two, on "a pretty strenuous day," he lost his finger in a clothes wringer, his head was split open by a brick he had tossed, and he was sucked out of his bedroom window by another pesky tornado and deposited a block away. He called the trifecta of torment "superb conditioning for my career." And the nickname that his career would make famous was given to him by Harry Houdini; after the tot fell down a flight of stairs but suffered no consequences, the great magician noted, "That was a buster."

Little in the previous paragraph about Buster Keaton's toddlerhood is true. Houdini was a family friend, but if we can believe the original version of the story told by Keaton's father, another entertainer bestowed the name upon the boy after just such a youthful tumble. And while a too-curious infant Buster did shred his right index finger in a clothes wringer (a doctor then amputated it at the first joint), the tale of misfortune was embellished to further the legend of the indestructible child.

Keaton began his stage career at an even younger age than Arbuckle. His parents, Joe and Myra, moved with their son to New York City in 1899, and against all odds, they began to establish Joe's acrobatic table act in vaudeville theaters. (Myra played the coronet and sometimes dodged Joe's kicks and table twirls.) In Delaware in October 1900, Joe placed his five-year-old son onstage as a miniature observer. Soon Buster was garnering laughs, and thus the Two Keatons became the Three Keatons, the act focusing on the father's doomed attempts to control his rambunctious son. When Buster repeatedly interrupted Dad's monologue, Joe tossed him about the stage and into the orchestra pit. Slapstick child abuse caused the audience to recoil and squirm, but then laugh and applaud when Buster reappeared unhurt—only to be punished again.

Joe realized the biggest laughs came when a pratfall went unacknowledged, so he coached his son not to smile or grimace no matter how funny or painful the gag. Buster's stone-faced persona was thus born just a few years after he was. "The Man with a Table" and the show's unique, pint-sized participant, "the Little Boy Who Can't Be Damaged," grew in reputation and profitability. A 1901 story in the *New York Clipper* said of Buster, "The tiny comedian is perfectly at ease in his work, natural, finished and artistic."

Buster always claimed he enjoyed the professional roughhousing and learned early how to break his falls, rarely suffering more than the sorts of abrasions earned in child's play. But New York's child labor laws restricted young performers, and the Keatons played cat-and-mouse games with enforcement agents for years before incurring a two-year ban from New York theaters in 1907. On October 4, 1909, an ad in *Variety* announced Buster's sixteenth birthday and his legal return to the stage. He was actually fourteen, but regardless, he had grown too big to be easily hurled about. The act had evolved. Father and son traded blows as physical equals, and Buster parodied popular songs and other acts on the bill.

Over subsequent years, resentments and grievances between father and son grew, accelerated by Joe's fondness for alcohol. Sometimes the onstage violence was as real as it appeared. The Three Keatons stayed together until January 1917, but by then twenty-one-year-old Buster was exhausted by the thrice-daily performance schedule and weary of his father.

He signed with Max Hart, who secured a role for him in Broadway's *The Passing Show*. Keaton's relationship with Hart was as brief as Arbuckle's—and was ended by the same man. In mid-March, in the midst of rehearsals for the stage production, Keaton was striding through Times Square when he ran into Lou Anger, with whom he had shared vaudeville bills. Now Anger was segueing into movies as the manager of Roscoe Arbuckle, who was starting production on his new company's first motion picture. The manager invited the vaudevillian to stop by the set the next morning.

Joseph Schenck's Colony Studio occupied a warehouse on East Forty-Eighth Street. On the morning Buster Keaton paid a visit, the Norma Talmadge Film Corporation was on the first floor, making another opulent drama starring its eponymous star, who was also Schenck's wife.* On the top floor, beneath a glass roof, the Comique Film Corporation was shooting in a re-creation of a general store. There, as the bustling crew set up the next shot, director and star Roscoe Arbuckle was going over gags for a slapstick scene with Al St. John and actors playing store customers. Arbuckle was dressed in the costume that had become nearly as recognizable as Chaplin's: plaid shirt, suspenders, pants worn too high, and, balanced precariously atop his head and angling slightly left, a bowler, several sizes too small.

Arbuckle was familiar with the Keatons' act, and he invited the visitor to join the on-screen mayhem. Keaton hesitated. Though he had grown up sharing vaudeville bills with moving pictures and later sat in the dark, mesmerized, watching *Tillie's Punctured Romance* four times and *The Birth of a Nation* thrice, his father considered film acting beneath a theatrical performer. Perhaps the desire to break fully free of his father influenced his decision to join the scene after a bit more coaxing. Mostly, he was eager to experience firsthand the art of performing for a camera lens.

Dressed in overalls and a straw hat, Keaton plays a customer who examines brooms and effortlessly kicks one up off the floor with a maneuver worthy of a soccer star. Buying a bucket of molasses from butcher Fatty, Keaton's foot sticks in a puddle of the goo, and he's knocked free and out of the store by Fatty. Arbuckle could easily throw the five-foot-five, 140-pound Keaton about. "Between one thing and another," Keaton recalled, "I would say that my long career as a human mop proved most useful from the start of my work as a movie actor."

Like Arbuckle, Keaton was fascinated by mechanical inventions. "Roscoe—none of us who knew him personally ever called him Fatty—took the camera apart for me so I would understand how it worked and what it could do. He showed me how film was developed, cut, and

* When Schenck met Talmadge in August 1916, she was starring in movies for Triangle, and the hammer-faced thirty-seven-year-old Schenck was smitten by the comely twenty-three-year-old brunette. He promptly set up her film company, and two months after meeting, they were married.

then spliced together." Keaton was hooked. "Everything about the new business I found exciting and fascinating." That included the secretary, another Talmadge sister, Natalie, whom he met that first day and would marry five years later.

The next morning, Keaton told Hart he was withdrawing from *The Passing Show* to pursue movie acting with Arbuckle.* Twice foiled by Lou Anger, Hart tore up their contract—presumably for another fee. When Keaton later arrived on the Colony Studio set, Arbuckle looked up and said, "You're late." One of the most fruitful pairings in cinema history had begun.

Their first film together was *The Butcher Boy*, which like most Comique two-reelers was a tale in two halves (each lasting ten to twelve minutes): the first in the general store, the latter in a girl's boarding school with both Arbuckle and St. John dressed in drag. Keaton's three-and-a-half-minute segment is the highlight, culminating in a flour fight among Arbuckle, St. John, and Keaton. In comparison to what followed, *The Butcher Boy* is a tepid retread of Keystone absurdity. But *The Butcher Boy* was Arbuckle's first movie in over nine months; accustomed to getting a new Fatty flick about every two weeks, Fatty's audience had been on a severe diet. Paramount's publicity machine generated a buzz, some newspaper ads were as big as those for feature films, and it was well reviewed and well attended.

By this point, Al St. John had developed a niche for himself as the villain in Arbuckle's movies, a role he played in all five of the initial Comique shorts and most of those that followed. Usually, he was a psychopathic rube endeavoring to steal Fatty's girl. When the camera began rolling on *The Butcher Boy*, Arbuckle's nephew was twenty-three and married and had appeared in nearly a hundred movies. St. John was never leading-man material; Uncle Roscoe referred to his "gross contour" and "supremely terrible face." Still, it was mostly stagecraft that imparted his distinctive creepiness. Teeth were blackened to look lost. Makeup ghoulishly accen-

---

* Keaton claimed he had never discussed pay with Arbuckle and was surprised to find only $40 in his first weekly pay envelope. This climbed to $75 weekly six weeks later and "not long after that" to $125 weekly.

tuated his cheekbones and darkened his lips, giving him a skeletal mien; he typically wore the clothing of a country bumpkin; and he flung his gangly form about on rubbery legs and mugged for the camera with bug-eyed grimaces or goblin grins. He was an actor of broad strokes but one whom the audience came to accept immediately as an amoral foil, and he was an acrobatic athlete who performed his own superb stunts. It is difficult to imagine Arbuckle's oeuvre without Al St. John.

Four more shorts followed *The Butcher Boy* over the next six months, and working with Keaton, Arbuckle's artistry grew substantially. In an extended scene in *The Rough House*, Fatty lazily fights a fire in his burning bed with one cup of water at a time, and then he wrangles with a garden hose as if it's an out-of-control fire hose. This is the sort of surreal comedy in which Keaton would later specialize in his own movies. In a throwaway bit, Fatty makes two rolls dance as Charlie Chaplin would, to great fame, in *The Gold Rush* eight years later.

His Wedding Night is likely the first movie featuring a same-sex marriage ceremony, as Fatty nearly weds, by mistake, Keaton, who had earlier donned a wedding dress. The movie contains a scene in which Fatty kisses a woman while she is knocked out. It was just one of numerous cinematic moments in which the licentious Fatty behaves unscrupulously toward females. Frequently his libido is raging, his morals are lax, and his shame is nonexistent. Remembrances of such on-screen behavior would help the public form a rapid opinion in September 1921.

There's more of the same in *Oh Doctor!* with Arbuckle as the salaciously named Dr. Fatty Holepoke, who brazenly tries to cheat on his wife. Keaton plays Arbuckle's abused son, but with each blow from his father, the son seems mortally injured and cries uproariously, lampooning his previous employment. Arbuckle also references his past, donning a Keystone Kop costume and even a Chaplinesque moustache.

The fifth and final film Arbuckle and Keaton made in New York in 1917 was shot on location.

Joseph M. Schenck
Presents

ROSCOE "FATTY" ARBUCKLE
in
CONEY ISLAND

The opening shots are of Coney Island's Luna Park and its Mardi Gras parade. (As was the practice at Keystone as well, Arbuckle filmed an actual event that would have been prohibitively expensive to stage.) At the beach, following Luke's lead, Fatty not only digs in the sand but buries himself and then escapes his shrewish wife (Agnes Neilson). In the park, Keaton attempts to rescue his lost date (Alice Mann) after she's stolen away by Al St. John—a turn of events that leaves "Old Stone Face" crying. After Fatty facilitates St. John's arrest, Keaton's date winds up with Fatty instead, and, after a wild water ride, the two enter a bathhouse.

When Fatty tries to rent a bathing suit, the man behind the counter says, "Can't fit you. Hire a tent." Fatty steals a fat woman's bathing suit, and he breaks cinema's fourth wall when he sees the camera about to capture him naked and tells it to shoot him from the chest up. The camera obliges.* At the beach, Keaton and Mann reunite, while Fatty and St. John fight in the ocean. Cops are called. Thrown in the same jail cell, Fatty and St. John restart their battle but knock out the cops. Escaping, Fatty locks up his wife. Outside, he and St. John swear: "RESOLVED: That women were the cause of our trouble. From now on we cut them out. We stand one for all and all for one." Their resolution remains in effect only until two women pass by.

THE END

Written by Arbuckle, *Coney Island* has a caustic view of romantic relationships. Fatty brazenly cheats on his wife, a woman leaves her date for first one man (who can better provide for her) and then another, and the perpetually prurient St. John pursues every female (and a cross-dressing Fatty) without regard to their availability. Only Keaton's char-

* Arbuckle debuted this gag three years earlier in *The Knockout*.

acter remains righteous. When he sees Mann in the leotard she wears under her swimsuit, he faints, but Fatty ogles and grins. Keaton wins Mann back, but the final image is of St. John and Fatty on the prowl again. Earlier, a fortune-telling machine promises Fatty an answer to the question "When will I marry and have a happy home?" The married Fatty receives a card that reads, "There ain't no such animal."

In the spring and summer of 1917, Arbuckle was newly "single," newly wealthy, and living a bachelor and moneyed lifestyle in New York City. As desired, he got to experience all that a movie star life entailed. And he had a new best friend in Buster Keaton. Unlike his cinematic persona, Keaton was quick to smile and laugh offscreen; he and Arbuckle shared a similar irreverent sense of humor, including a love of practical jokes. They also shared a fascination with cars and trains. Though the two men worked long hours at the studio or on location, they spent their evenings on the town, dressed impeccably and traveling in Arbuckle's Rolls-Royce.

They were regulars at Reisenweber's. A veritable department store of dining and entertainment nestled in Manhattan's Columbus Circle, Reisenweber's occupied half a block and was four stories tall with a rooftop garden lounge and a dozen dining rooms. It employed a workforce of one thousand and could hold five thousand diners and spectators. Its tropical-themed Hawaiian Room featured hula dancers, while its lavish Paradise was a ballroom that showcased a cabaret revue and imposed the city's first cover charge (twenty-five cents). When Reisenweber's 400 Club opened in January 1917, it booked the Original Dixieland Jazz Band, which promptly became *the* band to see in *the* venue to be seen in, thus helping popularize a new music known as jazz. At 400, Roscoe Arbuckle danced to such songs as "Livery Stable Blues," "Darktown Strutters' Ball," and "Tiger Rag." He was front and center at the inception of the Jazz Age.*

* Reisenweber's, which originated as a tavern in 1856, was not around for most of that age. A prime target for Prohibition raids, it closed in 1922.

Some weekends, Arbuckle and Keaton attended Gatsby-like parties at the waterfront estate of Joe Schenck and Norma Talmadge in Bayside, Queens. There they sailed on Long Island Sound, ate the steaks Schenck barbecued, drank champagne (Arbuckle drank for both, as Keaton was a teetotaler then), played croquet, and conversed with various business tycoons and celebrities, almost always including composer Irving Berlin, a childhood friend of Schenck's.

Arbuckle appeared at public events, sometimes for charity, sometimes for profit. In May, at the Motion Picture Charity Ball—a benefit for the Red Cross attended by "at least 5000 people," including "almost every prominent film actor and actress in New York"—he had the honor of leading the grand march and punctuated it with a bit of comical dancing. The weekend after the ball, he traveled three hundred miles with seventy-five others on a private train to attend opening night of a minor league baseball game in Portland, Maine. The Duffs were owned by Hiram Abrams, a Portland native who was then president of Paramount.*

America had entered World War I on April 6, 1917, and in June the draft was instituted for all men aged twenty-one to thirty-one. That month, Comique purchased nearly $50,000 in loans to support America's efforts, and Arbuckle declared that he was "in doubt as to his practical usefulness on the 'firing line.'" He did, however, joke that he would "be very efficient when it came to stopping bullets or providing a human fortification behind which my entire company could hide." On June 5 both he and Keaton registered for the draft, as required. Keaton listed his employer as "Roscoe Arbuckle"; Arbuckle wrote "Comique Film Corp." Question 12 read: "Do you claim an exemption from draft (specify grounds)?" Keaton, who was missing most of his trigger finger, left it blank. Arbuckle wrote "yes" but specified no grounds.

In August Arbuckle sold his Rolls-Royce, which had become a familiar sight in midtown Manhattan, to Hiram Abrams, and he purchased his first Pierce-Arrow. Three months later, he bought his manager, Lou

---

* He was soon replaced by Adolph Zukor, who had installed Abrams as a figurehead the previous July but grew dismayed when Abrams treated his title as more than honorary.

Anger, a surprise gift: a new Cadillac. Minta Durfee said, "Roscoe was a poor boy, abandoned as a kid by his father, who was an alcoholic. So I guess he had to make up for his impoverished childhood. He spent money wildly. He was the first star to have the entourage."

That entourage was a group of men, mostly employed in the film industry but less famous and wealthy than Arbuckle. Included in it were Buster Keaton, Lou Anger, and Joe Bordeaux, but members could change from night to night and from nightclub to nightclub. "Roscoe loves company," Anger stated. Durfee said, "He likes nothing better than to get a crowd of men together and sing and laugh and enjoy themselves like a crowd of college boys." In effect, Arbuckle created the family he'd never had. And it was *his* family. He called the shots; he picked up the tabs; he led and they followed. At thirty he was enjoying an extended adolescence.

Some of the money wildly spent went toward new suits, hats, and shoes. Arbuckle was a clotheshorse, for as he said, "There's nothing in the world so repulsive as a fat man who isn't well-dressed." But he had the funds for fancy clothes, his generous gifts for coworkers and friends, and his entourage's nights of food and drink at Reisenweber's and other hot spots. His weekly income, minus Schenck and Anger's shares and Durfee's $500 and not counting his share of box office profits, was $3,100, which was slightly more than twice the average *annual* household income in America at the time. Arbuckle was acquiring money to match his fame and establishing himself as the archetypal Hollywood celebrity.

Directing, cowriting, and starring in two-reelers churned out at a pace of one every six to seven weeks, Arbuckle grew ever more meticulous about his craft, and his craft was, foremost, the production of laughs. He was a student of humor, analyzing how and why jokes and gags did or didn't work. An article noted, "Mr. Arbuckle has probably the most complete joke library in the world. . . . Every joke that appears in the weekly and monthly publications is clipped and placed on Mr. Arbuckle's desk and then classified in the library." As he matured as a comedic filmmaker, he grew less dependent on slapstick and stunts and was able to garner laughs in other ways, such as heightened absurdity, macabre shocks, intertitle wisecracks, and parodies of silent film tropes.

In May and July of 1917, he did two interviews that provided insights into his filmmaking processes and philosophy.

Improvisation: "I make up my own plays. I don't write them. I make them up as I go along. I have a general idea in my head when we begin, but I don't have a written scenario or even a synopsis. I try out every scene I can think of, working out the business by actually rehearsing it. And all the time I'm rehearsing out there I'm trying to devise funny little twists that will get a laugh."

Acting: "I never try to divert attention from the situation to myself. If you feel a scene slipping, let it slip. If you are rehearsing, do it over again, even if it is seventy times seven, and only when you know that you have it right get out your camera."

Production: "How long do you think it takes to make a picture that you'll laugh at—maybe—for half an hour? It takes me a solid month, and it costs $40,000 in cash."

Editing: "By the time I'm through I have about 15,000 feet of film—and all I need is 2,000 feet. I've got to skim the cream off that milk. I go over all the films and pick out the best scenes. Then is the time I write the story. I make out the scenario from the scenes I intend to use."

Comedy: "I refuse to try to make people laugh at my bulk. Personally, I cannot believe that a battleship is a bit funnier than a canoe, but some people do not feel that way about it. There are persons who think it is excruciatingly funny because I weigh 300 pounds. Of course, I cannot keep them from laughing at me, but I refuse to sanction it.

"A situation must be funny enough to play itself once it is properly placed, and no amount of grimaces or slapstick comedy will make it humorous if it isn't."

"I know one thing. I'd a heap rather make people laugh than make 'em cry. It's a darned sight harder to do. Sometimes I think I've picked out the worst job in sight. If you don't believe me, try to be funny for thirty solid minutes yourself. After that you'll want to be a villain or a vampire just by way of a little relaxation."

Arbuckle had spent a winter filming in the New York area two years earlier. That was enough of that. In October 1917, as the days grew shorter and colder, he and his company relocated to Southern California in rapidly populating Long Beach, where he had performed and married more than nine years prior. Two brothers, Herbert and Elwood Horkheimer, had purchased Edison's small Long Beach studio in 1912 and started expanding. By the time Arbuckle and company arrived, Balboa Studio occupied twenty buildings on eight acres in downtown Long Beach, six blocks from the ocean. The studio was noted for its modern facilities and technical innovations, including the largest glass-enclosed stage on the West Coast. With as many as ten companies shooting simultaneously, Balboa in 1917 was Long Beach's largest employer and tourist attraction, and luring Arbuckle there and away from Hollywood was its biggest coup.

Arbuckle rented a house on the ocean about a mile from the studio, sharing it with former vaudevillian Herbert Warren, then working as Comique's editor, Warren's wife, and Luke the dog. Keaton rented an apartment with his parents. Witnessing his son's rapid rise in movies, Joe Keaton had changed his opinion of the medium, and he acted in the three initial Comique pictures shot at Balboa.

The first of these, *A Country Hero*, is the only Arbuckle and Keaton movie now lost, but it exemplified Arbuckle's greater emphasis on elaborate settings and Keaton's focus on technology-themed comedy. A scene in which a train crashes into two cars ballooned the budget, and a rural town, dubbed "Jazzville," was constructed on the Balboa lot. The town's name captured the hot new music, while according to dubious Comique publicity, the town itself was an exact reproduction of Arbuckle's birthplace of Smith Centre, Kansas.

Having grown accustomed to New York City nightlife, Arbuckle sought out the same in and around Los Angeles. He and his entourage were almost certain to encounter fellow movie royalty at Al Levy's Tavern in still-somnolent Hollywood, the Cabrillo Ship Café off the Venice pier, and Cafe Nat Goodwin on the Santa Monica pier. A typical Tuesday night began with dinner at the tony Hotel Alexandria downtown, moved to ringside seats for the professional boxing matches at Jack Doyle's two-thousand-seat arena in nearby Vernon, and ended with dancing and (more) drinking at the Vernon Country Club, where waiters drew lots to serve Arbuckle because of his stream of generous tips.

The entourage expanded as the night progressed. Casual acquaintances and even strangers learned they could be friends with Fatty by the end of a late night if they joined his group along the way. And, as always, the movie star picked up every bill. Celebrity journalist Louella Parsons said of him and his entourage: "Some men might resent such a thing as putting them in the easy-mark class, but it is one of the nice things about Roscoe Arbuckle that he is like a big boy in wanting to share with his friends the good things which have come his way."

Comique's next Balboa film, *Out West,* was Arbuckle's first western and a spoof of the genre. We can see his continuing advancement as a director when the men chasing him atop a speeding train are captured beautifully in a long-shot silhouette. Both Arbuckle and Keaton were fans of macabre humor, and much of the comedy in *Out West* is dark. Keaton's saloon-keeper character casually shoots a card cheat in the back multiple times, kicks the dead man through a door in the saloon floor, drops a corset onto the corpse, dons his hat for a one-second blessing, and slams the door shut. So much for no blow or bullet inflicting damage in slapstick comedies. Part of the way *Out West* spoofed early westerns was by exaggerating their violence.

As Arbuckle continued to innovate within the medium of filmed pantomime, Comique comedies grew increasingly surreal. *The Bell Boy* contains a random but excellent scene involving a mysterious man with a long beard who desires the services of a barber. Fatty the bellboy uses scissors, a razor, and hats to turn the customer into a dead ringer for first General Grant, then Abraham Lincoln, and then Germany's Kaiser Wilhelm. *Moonshine* features a shot wherein forty-five men come out of a Model T and another of a blown-up cabin reassembling itself. This was the sort of magical humor only motion pictures could provide. There's much of it in *The Cook*, as chef Fatty instantly prepares foods and beverages that he then flips across the kitchen for waiter Keaton to effortlessly catch without spilling a drop—even as both are dancing "Egyptian-style" in a spoof of Theda Bara's title role in *Cleopatra* (Fatty wears a risqué costume he makes out of pots and pans).

The height of Arbuckle's surrealism was *Good Night Nurse*. It opens with drunken Fatty in a torrential rainstorm as people literally blow by him. Fatty rips the skirt off the woman he's trying to help, and she promptly high-kicks him in the face (she's Keaton); and he helps a fellow drunk get home by sticking stamps to his face and draping him over a mailbox. Other ingenious bits include Arbuckle in drag and Keaton bashfully flirting in a hallway and an orderly in a hall catching two items tossed out of an operating room: a saw and a human leg. *Motion Picture Magazine* complained, "It borders over much of the vulgar. The parading of a man in a supposedly blood-splattered physician's apron is not at all our idea of a comedy situation." But it's this macabre humor that makes *Good Night Nurse* feel surprisingly modern today.

Many of the biggest laughs in these shorts came via intertitles. These were generally written after filming, and with a slower production schedule than at Keystone, Comique's titles were markedly improved. Sometimes they functioned as a comical commentary track. In *Moonshine*, the fourth wall is demolished when, after the moonshiner's daughter leaps into Fatty's arms, Fatty tells her father, "Look, this is only a two-reeler. We don't have time to build up to love scenes." The father replies, "In that case go ahead, it's your movie." One can picture Arbuckle and company at an editing session noting how truncated the romance is and deciding to insert the lines that make them laugh the loudest with no concern about the story.

The short films Arbuckle made with Keaton are the best of his career, and in part this is because of his generosity as an actor and director. Whereas other comedic stars would have felt threatened, Arbuckle welcomed Keaton's ability to generate laughs, and he gave his friend the space and time to improvise. The teaming of the rotund and expressive Arbuckle with the slight and reserved Keaton was inspired, and in movies like *The Cook* they feel like equals, though only one name appears above the title. Arbuckle also encouraged Keaton's contributions to writing, directing, and editing, and Keaton served as Arbuckle's de facto assistant director. Keaton said in his autobiography:

> The longer I worked with Roscoe the more I liked him. I respected without reservations his work both as an actor and a comedy director. He took falls no other man at his weight ever attempted, [and] had a wonderful mind for action gags, which he could devise on the spot. Roscoe loved the world and the whole world loved him in those days. His popularity as a performer was increasing so rapidly that he soon ranked second only to Charlie Chaplin. Arbuckle was that rarity, a truly jolly fat man. He had no meanness, malice, or jealousy in him. Everything seemed to amuse and delight him. . . . I could not have found a better-natured man to teach me the movie business, or a more knowledgeable one.

The war in Europe was still raging, and by mid-1918 America would be sending ten thousand soldiers per day "over there." Arbuckle said his excessive weight kept him out of uniform. Instead, he used his celebrity and wealth to support the war effort. He performed at military and Red Cross benefits, "adopted" an army company, and let some American and Canadian military personnel, back from the front, visit him on his Balboa Studio set. In January 1918 he and his Comique troupe performed gratis vaudeville shows at Southern California army camps.

War bonds were the primary means for those at home to support the military. In New York City in April 1918, Arbuckle was one of five "kings of the movies" (the other four were studio executives) who pledged to purchase $50,000 in bonds. In May he was the surprise participant in a Long Beach war bond parade, waving an American flag and mobbed by children. In movies financed by the American and Canadian governments, he proclaimed the benefits of each country's bonds. And as a longtime smoker, he made it his cause to ensure that soldiers were not denied their nicotine fix. His contributions to the *New York Sun* Tobacco Fund helped them ship cigarettes to the front, and every time he bought a carton of cigarettes for himself he dropped another into one of the receptacles on the Balboa studio grounds,* which were there "to gather in smokes for the boys in France." The *Los Angeles Times* article that focused on the latter practice was entitled, simply, "Patriotic Arbuckle."

Buster Keaton did not merely support the soldiers. He was one, drafted into the army in July 1918. The night before he departed for Camp Kearney, near San Diego, Comique threw him a farewell dinner at the Jewel City Cafe in Seal Beach.† An impromptu vaudeville and minstrel show featured Arbuckle and Al St. John. When Keaton's outfit shipped to New York three weeks later, Arbuckle, St. John, and Lou Anger journeyed to Camp Kearney to see their friend off.

While stationed at a New York base awaiting a ship, Keaton was visited by Natalie Talmadge in a chauffeured limousine. That day, spent dining and dancing at Long Island's finest establishments, was the genesis of the Keaton/Talmadge romance. Stationed in Amiens, France, Keaton saw no combat, but it was cold and frequently rainy, and he slept on the ground or on equally dirty floors and developed an ear infection that permanently impaired his hearing. When the Germans agreed to a cease-fire on November 11, 1918, the war on the Western Front was over, but Keaton's service was not. He was transferred to a town near Bourdeaux, and there the movie star organized entertainment for anxious soldiers awaiting ships to carry them home. He remained in southwest France, performing for his fellow doughboys, even as his audience was continuously shipping back to America.

---

* The last film shot at Balboa Studio was *The Cook*, made in June 1918. The Horkheimer brothers' production company had declared bankruptcy that April. The studio facilities were demolished in 1925. Hollywood won.

† The café was popular then with movie stars working or staying in Long Beach, including Charlie Chaplin, Theda Bara, and Douglas Fairbanks. Long Beach was dry while neighboring Seal Beach was not.

In its 1918 "Analytical Review of the Year's Acting," *Photoplay* said:

> Roscoe Arbuckle shares comedy honors this year with Chaplin—though no comedian, it must be admitted, even approaches Chaplin in personal variety and appeal. But Arbuckle's material—his own make—has, in the main, been consistently funny and human. He has surrounded himself with good people. He has made good productions. He has kept moving.

He kept moving in Keaton's absence, enlisting a Comique gag writer, the Italian-born Mario Bianchi, to step in front of the camera, acting under the name Monty Banks. (Banks became a prolific comedic actor and director.) After completing *Camping Out*, his second movie without Keaton, Arbuckle spent two weeks at the end of 1918 in San Francisco, seeking more nightlife than Los Angeles could provide.

The press did not note the peculiar absence of his wife on the trip, nor did they mention a different female companion—though it is probable Arbuckle did not sleep alone on a two-week holiday sojourn. He was subsequently romantically linked to Alice Lake (as was Keaton). She called him "Arbie."* Actress Viola Dana, who dated Keaton, claimed the Arbuckle/Lake relationship was off and on for three years, but it stayed out of the fan magazines because Arbuckle remained married.

The press was mindful of Arbuckle's privacy, but his audience could be more demanding. When out in public, Arbuckle was frequently mobbed by fans. Around the time the war came to an end, *Photoplay* said:

> The people adored "Fatty," I soon discovered—young and old. They felt that somehow he was a rock to cling to, a prop against the

---

* *Camping Out* was the last movie Lake made with Arbuckle. In 1919 she acted for Keystone before signing a deal with Metro that made her a minor star.

shadows that are falling all too heavily these days of stress. He represented the way of escape—he and his merry-making crew—the defiance that we humans must hurl at woe; in a way he typified the happy, serious spirit of the American: the ability to see the funny side of anything, however seemingly tragic.

{12}

PRELIMINARIES

. . . that abominable and voluptuous act known as reading the paper.
—Marcel Proust, "Filial Sentiments of a Parricide"

An angry mob of 150 men and boys spilled into the movie theater in Thermopolis, Wyoming. Cowboys pointed their six-shooters at the screen and fired, riddling the jolly image of Roscoe Arbuckle with holes. Then they stormed the projection room, ripping the latest Fatty movie from the spools and carrying it into the street, where they set the nitrate ablaze. Wyoming Mob Shoots Up Fatty, screamed the front page of a newspaper that same day, September 18, 1921.

The next day, the story made front pages from coast to coast. Few editors could resist such a tale of frontier justice, the good guys riding in with guns blazing to save society from America's greatest villain. The perfect story. Print it, page 1. Except it was a lie, concocted by the theater's manager to drum up publicity. Four days later, a brief retraction was buried in middle pages, if it ran at all.

Adolph Zukor wrote to William Hearst, who was not just a newspaper tycoon but also the owner of a movie production company, asking him to tone down his papers' reportage of the Arbuckle case. "Will do best I can," Hearst replied curtly but then continued, "It is difficult to keep news out of a newspaper. I agree that certain kinds of publicity [are] detrimental to moving pictures but the people who get into the courts and coroners are responsible. The newspapers are no more responsible than the courts." The coverage did not change.

Iron walls. Iron bars. Wooden bunks. Wooden bench. Washstand. Beginning his second week of captivity, Roscoe Arbuckle sat in cell 12 on the top floor of the San Francisco Hall of Justice. He chatted with cellmate Fred Martin and others on felon's row. He read his letters and telegrams.* He smoked. He worried.

On Saturday the seventeenth of September, he'd been arraigned for manslaughter—a formality since District Attorney Brady was proceeding with the murder charge. The next morning, Arbuckle requested that the city newspapers be brought to him, and he read news of the outside world for the first time in over a week. He was visited by his brothers, Arthur (living in San Francisco) and Harry (living in Fresno). For twenty minutes, they sat on a bench. The conversation was unheard, but the famous brother was seen smiling broadly. Perhaps they recounted tales of their deceased parents, of their boarding house in Santa Ana, of their older sisters Lola (deceased) and Nora (living in Los Angeles), of the brief times long ago when they were together under the same roof and a happy family.

District Attorney Brady and Assistant DAs U'Ren and Golden entered the twelfth-floor suite of the Hotel St. Francis on Sunday, accompanied by their principal witnesses: Maude Delmont, Alice Blake, and Zey Prevost. The three women were instructed to arrange the furniture in 1219, 1220, and 1221 as it was on Labor Day. The rooms had been cleaned by a maid and, only two days prior, searched for fingerprints. Now Brady wanted to approximate the conditions of the party. In 1219 he examined

* Though the majority of the mail was supportive, Durfee later said, "Some of the mail that came to us was unbelievable. There were threats against Roscoe's life and against mine. Some wrote and said that Roscoe had torn down the moral fiber of the country, that he was a monster, that he deserved to hang."

marks on the wall and on the small table between the two beds. He listened, in 1220, to the volume of voices in 1219 behind a closed door. He said he was there "to get the lay of the land."

"Fatty Stands Before Nation with Leering Grin While His Hands Drip Blood" was the title of a sermon delivered that same Sunday by John Roach Straton, one of the country's foremost evangelists, and widely excerpted in newspapers. Needless to say, it presumed no innocence for the leering grinner with bloody hands. Instead, the sermon averred, "Lured by lust and fueled by liquor, we find him turned into a raging beast, more heartless and brutal than a tiger of the jungle could have been." Prominent evangelist Robert Shuler stated, "He has assaulted public decency and morality. He has betrayed the thousands of little children who laughed at his antics. He has defied chastity and mocked virtue." They were just two of the many preachers who condemned Arbuckle that Sunday and for many Sundays thereafter. From America's pulpits, the movie star was typically presumed guilty of murder. At best, he was a married man in a hotel room cavorting with showgirls, openly consuming alcohol, and pursuing extramarital sex.

There was one notable exception to the homiletic assaults, and it was delivered by America's premier Protestant preacher, Billy Sunday, whose daughter-in-law Mae Taube had been at the Labor Day party. "I feel sorry for 'Fatty' Arbuckle and do not see how any court in the land could convict the fallen idol for murder or manslaughter," Sunday began. He blamed liquor for Rappe's death and called for greater funding of Prohibition enforcement. "The girl died, but I believe her death was caused by an accident and not by Roscoe Arbuckle." He concluded with a cautionary note, invoking an image of Babylon that would later become pervasive. In so doing, he previewed what would eventually be a key defense strategy: tarnishing the victim. "The party of Arbuckle's was just a case of a modern Belshazzar entertaining. 'Fatty' fell for whiskey and wild women."

Virginia Rappe appeared angelic, shrouded in white silk and adorned with white roses. She lay in her silver casket in the Strother and Dayton funeral parlor on Hollywood Boulevard as thousands milled past for six hours on Sunday.* Among the assortment of bright flora was a bouquet of roses from Maude Delmont with a note that read, "To Virginia: You know I love you as though you were my sister." As at the San Francisco visitation three days earlier, there was an overwhelming display of lilies from Henry Lehrman to his "brave sweetheart," though, in an era before commercial airline travel, Lehrman himself remained in New York City.

On Monday morning at Rappe's funeral, Strother and Dayton's chapel was filled two hours early with curious strangers, mostly women. The police were enlisted to clear the pews and lock the doors. Afterward, only intimate friends of the deceased were admitted, and police kept at bay the growing throng on Hollywood Boulevard. Among those attending were actress Mildred Harris (Charlie Chaplin's teenage ex-wife), Al Semnacher, and Rappe's "adopted aunt and uncle," Kate and Joseph Hardebeck. The services there and at the burial site were conducted by the rector of Hollywood's St. Thomas Church. There was no eulogy.

The six pallbearers were a who's who of Hollywood then and after: directors Al Herman, David Kirkland, and future Oscar winner Norman Taurog (Taurog was a friend of Lehrman's who oversaw Lehrman's requests for the funeral and burial); actor Frank Coleman, who performed in three movies with Rappe; comedic actor/director/writer Larry Semon, who achieved great popularity in the early 1920s; and actor Oliver Hardy, recently Semon's villain of choice, who, with Stan Laurel, went on to form one of cinema's most beloved comedy duos. They carried Rappe in her flower-shrouded coffin through the parted crowd and to the white hearse parked on the boulevard. Followed by a procession of automobiles, the hearse traveled only a mile to Hollywood Memorial Park (now Hollywood Forever Cemetery). Surrounding streets were clogged with Model Ts, as were lanes inside the cemetery gates. The throng that scurried over graves and clustered around the burial site was

* The count varies from over three thousand to eight thousand.

estimated at fifteen hundred. The plot was Lehrman's (his secretary had been buried there two years prior), and it was just four blocks from the home Rappe had shared with the Hardebecks after coming to Hollywood five years prior. There, after a brief ceremony, on the nineteenth day of September 1921, on a gentle slope beside a lily pond, Virginia Rappe was laid to rest.

Frank Dominguez was in Los Angeles as well, digging dirt on the primary prosecution witness, Maude Delmont. Delmont herself remained in San Francisco. From her bed in her room at the Plaza Hotel—where she was cared for by a nurse and guarded by a policewoman—she told the press on Monday, "I'm ready for the defense anytime. All I have to do at the trial is to tell the truth. And all the 'Fatty' Arbuckles and Frank Dominguezes in the world won't be able to shake me. Virginia Rappe was a good girl. Any suggestion to the contrary is a lie and a defamation."

In an earlier interview, she had admitted her testimony at the coroner's inquest was weak and sometimes wrong, blaming it on illness and the medication—presumably self-administered with the "hypodermic" she referenced at the time. She said she planned to alter her testimony for the manslaughter trial to shore up her story and "greatly benefit the prosecution's case."

Also on Monday, Minta Durfee and her mother, Flora Durfee, arrived at the San Francisco Hall of Justice. So Arbuckle's legal team could coach them not to speak to the press, their train had been met by Milton Cohen and Charles Brennan in Sacramento, after which a boilerplate statement from Durfee about her estranged husband's innocence was released. In the visitor's pen of the city jail, Arbuckle embraced his wife. With her mother and his brother Arthur, they talked for thirty minutes.

From a newspaper story on Tuesday, September 20:

> Ada Gillifillian, sixteen years old, a farmer's daughter, was found in a straw stack eighteen miles from home [in southwest Iowa]. She had been without food and water for three days.
>
> "Fatty" Arbuckle was her film favorite and she had pictures of him in her room. She said her mother whipped her when she refused to take them down, so she ran away. When found in a semi-conscious condition she had a picture of Arbuckle clasped tightly to her chest.

On Tuesday the San Francisco grand jury took up two new questions. First, was the initial autopsy of Rappe illegal? The accused, Dr. Melville Rumwell, testified. Second, did the defense tamper with a prosecution witness? This stemmed from an allegation that party guest Joyce "Dollie" Clark, fresh off her hat-pilfering conviction, had said, "There is money in this Arbuckle case, and I am going to get some of it." She and two men (one described as a "man-about-town and sportsman," the other "president of the Italian-American Oil Company") allegedly plotted to collect this money from the defense by suggesting that Clark could impeach the testimony of her friend Zey Prevost. The two men had visited Milton Cohen and asked what Clark should say under oath. Cohen's reply: "Tell the truth." The grand jury took no action on either matter.

The following day, at DA Brady's request, a Los Angeles grand jury questioned Al Semnacher about something he had not previously shared. Semnacher said that the morning following the Labor Day party, Arbuckle claimed he had "forcibly applied a piece of ice to Miss Rappe's body." Coverage of this development varied greatly. On the hysterical end was this screaming headline: Declares Arbuckle Told of Using Foreign Substance in Attack on Miss Rappe. And thus a meme was born.

In San Francisco on Wednesday, Brady investigated Semnacher's story further by questioning Fred Fishback and Ira Fortlouis. Lowell Sherman was subpoenaed while on a train bound for New York City. A process server, a detective, and reporters waited for him at Grand Central Station only to learn he had given them the slip by exiting the train at an earlier stop and leaving in an automobile driven by a red-headed woman.* After he was located the next day in his Manhattan apartment, he gave a statement to the New York DA regarding Rappe and the party that essentially supported the defense, and he agreed to return to San Francisco, where the preliminary hearing on Arbuckle's murder charge was beginning. He never did. He later gave a deposition swearing that Arbuckle was never alone in a room with Rappe—a definitive (and false) declaration that ultimately clashed with the strategies both of the prosecution and the defense. Meanwhile, he acted in Broadway plays, keeping a continent between himself and the courtrooms.†

On Wednesday, eleven days after his arrest, Paramount invoked a nonperformance clause to halt payments to Arbuckle. The next day, Universal became the first studio to institute a morality clause in contracts, permitting the stoppage of salaries to "actors or actresses who forfeit the respect of the public." Universal's attorneys stated that although the studio had no relationship with the accused murderer, the clause was "a direct result of the Arbuckle case in San Francisco."

Thursday, September 22, was the first day of the preliminary hearing, which would determine whether the state had sufficient evidence to bring Arbuckle to trial for murder. That day, an editorial in the *San Francisco Bulletin* was syndicated throughout the country. It harked back to the infamous gang rape case that gave rise to the Women's Vigilant

* Grateful for a local angle on the nation's biggest story, New York newspapers attacked the minor subplot of Sherman's march. Hence, even the hair color of the driver of a car in which Sherman was the passenger was widely reported (subsequently, he claimed she was his wife).

† Sherman's ploy worked to minimize his connection to the scandal, and his cinematic career subsequently thrived. He transitioned to directing with the sound era, and he was helming the pioneering color feature *Becky Sharp* when he died of pneumonia in 1934 at forty-six.

Committee, and telegraphed the difficulty that lay ahead in seating an impartial jury:

> The drunken orgy at the St. Francis will be probed as thoroughly as was that in the Howard Street shack. . . . It was the merest chance that the Howard Street girls escaped with their lives, but had they died as a result of their ordeal their murderers would still have been less fiendish than the monster that perpetrated the foul crime in the St. Francis Hotel. . . . From the details at hand, the attack appears to have been savage without qualification. A veritable giant, one that has been described as a mountain of lecherous flesh, hurled himself upon a frail woman and fought with her after the manner of a mad elephant. But for that final avalanche of lard, the woman might have saved at least her life, for she seems to have struggled until the last vestige of her clothing had been torn to tatters. . . .
>
> We know that a fiendish crime has been committed and that one of the principals in that crime is a man suddenly raised from obscurity and a difficulty in earning his living into the spotlight of the world and an affluence greater than many kings. Petted by the public and showered with riches, he lost all sense of decency and came to the belief that he was above the moral code and could write whatever code he chose. He lived a law unto himself, flaunting his new found wealth and spending it with all recklessness of immoral and bestial ignorance. Like the most brutal of the feudal barons, he believed that he could command whatever was necessary to satisfy his savage passions.

Women began showing up at the Hall of Justice at 8 AM, for a preliminary hearing that was not set to begin for another five hours. Said the *Los Angeles Times* of the gathering storm, "Men are being excluded everywhere, shoved forcibly out through thick ranks of women, laughed at, snickered at, jeered at. It is a 'no man's land.'" Hundreds of women, many dressed in their Sunday best and fortified with box lunches, crowded hallways and stairways outside the women's court of Judge Sylvain Lazarus—the same room and judge as at the arraignment one week prior.

A phalanx of policemen cleared the courtroom at noon, much to the consternation of those seated. They reopened the doors a half hour later. As the DA instructed, eighteen seats in the front row were occupied by members of the Women's Vigilant Committee. After all the courtroom seats filled up, five hundred women remained in the hall. With great difficulty, policemen parted that sea of womanhood to make way for the defendant, his wife, his mother-in-law, and his defense team.

Judge Lazarus would decide whether the murder charge could proceed. Before he ruled, both the prosecution and the defense could call witnesses, introduce physical evidence, and cross-examine. With Assistant DA U'Ren questioning, the prosecution called three witnesses the first day: Dr. Shelby Strange, Dr. William Ophüls, and nurse Grace Halston. They testified to the ruptured bladder, the newness of the injury, and the injury's probable cause (Ophüls: "some force from outside"). Photographs of bruises on Rappe's limbs were placed into evidence. Dominguez offered no cross-examination.

The next day, Al Semnacher was the only witness. It was up to him to tell the tale of the Labor Day party, but he relinquished details of drinking and cavorting so reluctantly the prosecution declared him a hostile witness. The session finished after three contentious hours, with Semnacher still on the stand and yet to explode his bombshell. It went off the following day. That's when the crowded courtroom of mostly concerned mothers heard more than they bargained for, and all the vague stories about ice or a foreign substance forcibly applied suddenly came into focus.

Assistant DA Golden asked Semnacher about what he had heard the morning after the party: "Did Arbuckle say anything at that time about a piece of ice?"

"He did," Semnacher replied.

"What did he say?"

"He told us that he had placed a piece of ice on Miss Rappe."

"On?" Golden asked.

"No," said Semnacher.

"Well?"

Semnacher's response was not printed in newspapers. He said Arbuckle claimed to have placed the ice *in* Virginia Rappe. A collective gasp rose in the courtroom as the meaning was inferred. Red-faced Arbuckle stared at his fidgeting fingers. Behind him, Durfee also looked downward, fussing with a long stream of amber beads draped about her neck. She summoned strength and patted her husband on his shoulder with her tan-gloved hand.

Golden pressed on: "Exactly what did Arbuckle say?"

Semnacher glanced about the room of mostly women staring back at him. "I don't want to say his words."

"I insist," said Golden. "They are important."

When Semnacher hesitated again, Golden told him to whisper it to the court reporter. He did. This was then written on a note, which was passed to the prosecution and defense.

Arbuckle allegedly said he had placed the ice in Rappe's "snatch"—her vagina.

Semnacher conveyed the word only to the stenographer and never again uttered it in court. However, Golden had no such compunctions about saying "snatch" in mixed company, again and again, wielding it like a knife, stabbing it at his hostile witness, slashing it at Arbuckle's reputation, as if to say any man who could cavalierly use such a crude profanity about a woman as she lay dying in a room nearby was capable of anything—including rape and murder.

The United Press correspondent described the testimony as follows, and his version was syndicated widely: "[Arbuckle's] time in court today was only ninety minutes, but he heard Al Semnacher, his friend, and Miss Rappe's former manager, charge that when Virginia was lying nude on one of Arbuckle's twin beds, the big baby-faced comedian had tortured her indescribably." Semnacher was not Arbuckle's friend and not really Rappe's manager; more important, the ice incident was presented in court not as torture but as a very coarse joke by a heartless celebrity. Under Golden's questioning, Semnacher indicated that Arbuckle made no explanation for inserting ice into Rappe's vagina, but that when he mentioned it at least some of the listeners laughed. (Semnacher refused to pinpoint any man in particular as having done so, however, including himself.) But the United Press account of his testimony spawned front-page headlines such as WITNESS TESTIFIES ARBUCKLE CONFESSED HE TORTURED ACTRESS.

When Golden finished his questioning, Dominguez got Semnacher to admit he had never witnessed any improper conduct by Arbuckle toward any of the women present at the Labor Day party. Semnacher agreed that Arbuckle acted as a gentleman on that day, at which point Golden interjected, questioning whether the "snatch" remark was gentlemanly. Dominguez strenuously objected—sustained—but the damage was done, and calling the defendant a gentleman would not undo it. Undoing it required a charge capable of equal or greater destruction.

Dominguez's attack began at the next court session. First, he livened up what should have been the pedestrian questioning of hotel doctor Arthur Beardslee by asking him if on his visits to room 1227, where Rappe lay ill and Maude Delmont watched over her, Delmont was "under the influence of alcohol or morphine" or if he ever saw her "taking a white powder." Objections thundered.

It was merely a warm-up for the full frontal assault on Semnacher, who was called back to the stand that afternoon. Dominguez succeeded in establishing that Semnacher was not Rappe's manager, despite that occupation being his synonym in the press (he claimed he had been misquoted) and that he had known her well for only six weeks. More important, Dominguez got him to admit Arbuckle may have said he placed the ice "on" Rappe's "snatch" and not "in" it. Dominguez was less successful in establishing anything untoward about Semnacher occupying a Palace Hotel room connected to the room of Delmont and Rappe.

And then the defense attorney got down to business, first with a few minor shots at Delmont's character that Semnacher successfully volleyed, then with the introduction of a new name: Earl Lynn, a minor movie actor. Delmont had supposedly tried to extort money from Lynn's father in exchange for her keeping private her sexual relationship with Lynn and her resulting pregnancy. Golden objected, and Judge Lazarus ruled that the defense should not go beyond the murder case at hand.

Dominguez explained the relevance: "If we can, we will show that Semnacher, in conversation with Mrs. Delmont and someone else, plotted that Virginia Rappe's torn clothing should be taken to Los Angeles, there to extort blackmail from Arbuckle. If we can show that Semnacher was aware of circumstances that we expect to show connecting Mrs. Delmont and Earl Lynn, of Los Angeles, we will then establish the intimate relations existing between Semnacher and Mrs. Delmont. We will show, moreover, that Earl Lynn is not the only individual to be mentioned in this connection."

Judge Lazarus declared, "I am not going to try the character of every witness appearing here."

But it was too late for Al Semnacher. At his own request, the question of his conspiring to blackmail Arbuckle was promptly brought before the grand jury. He testified as the only witness. The grand jury took no action. Afterward, Semnacher told reporters he was bringing a civil suit against Dominguez for defamation of character.

The question of why Rappe's torn shirt and undergarments were found in the possession of Semnacher has never been satisfactorily answered. *Car dusting?* At the preliminary hearing, he said his original intent was "joshing" Rappe but he later kept them to clean his car. (He never used them for this purpose.) It is possible that after Rappe's injury, Semnacher and Delmont (who had Rappe's outer clothing) saw the possibility of enlisting Rappe in a conspiracy to blackmail Arbuckle with the promise they would keep events out of the press and unreported to the police. The clothes could have been used as possible evidence of an assault. If this was a scheme, it collapsed with Rappe's death and the resulting criminal investigation.

Bambina Maude Delmont's role as countervailing force to Roscoe Arbuckle was then coming into focus—avenging angel if one presumed his guilt, conspiring con artist if one presumed he was wrongly accused. This is what is known about her life before September 1921.

She was born in New Mexico in 1882, to Mr. and Mrs. Winfield Scott, both from Indiana. She had a younger sister. At some point prior to 1910, she got married to a man named Delmont. But by the time of the 1910 census, she was divorced and a guest at a New York City hotel; no occupation was given.

On November 27, 1912, she remarried in Los Angeles. The groom was John C. Hopper, a Canadian farmer and ex-soldier. They separated on March 1, 1914, and Delmont was granted an interlocutory divorce decree on grounds of nonsupport.

Reporters in September 1921 dug for dirt about her past but found little. A wire story stated that she lived for a time in Wichita, Kansas, under an assumed name. The *Los Angeles Times* reported that in 1919, authorities asked her to leave Catalina Island: "She conducted a beauty parlor in the dance pavilion. She left without contesting the official warning. Her baggage was held some time on the island until certain debts were paid, island officials say."

The 1920 census had found her renting a home in Los Angeles with her sister, a nurse. She reported her occupation as "corsetier." Presumably, she co-owned a corset-making business with her next-door neighbor, a divorced forty-one-year-old mother who shared the same unusual occupation.

On February 26, 1921, she married again, wedding Cassius Clay Woods, a publicist, in Madera, California. Both were thirty-eight and residents of Los Angeles. Both were listed as divorced.

September 27 was the fifth and final day of testimony in the preliminary hearing. Blake and Prevost testified, both recalling, with minor variations, that after Rappe moaned "I'm dying," Arbuckle told her to be quiet or "I'll throw you out the window." Prevost confirmed parts of the ice story. According to her, Arbuckle said to Rappe regarding his application of ice, "That'll bring you to"—which might indicate that he intended it as a remedy, though the line could also be interpreted as a crude joke.

The prosecution then called a surprise witness, a stout and nervous woman in a blue dress named Josephine Keza. Keza was a maid at the Hotel St. Francis. She explained in heavily accented English that on Labor Day she had been in the twelfth-floor hallway when she heard a woman scream behind the door to 1219 and then say, "No, no, oh my God!" A man's voice followed: "Shut up!" On cross-examination, Dominguez tried to trip up her remembrance but made little headway.

Afterward, the state rested.

The defense was stunned, as were Arbuckle and, just behind him, Durfee. Dominguez leapt to his feet. "Do you mean to say that the prosecution in this case is not going to call Mrs. Maude Delmont to the stand? She is the principal witness; she swore to the complaint. In the interest of truth and justice, I appeal to you, Mr. District Attorney, not to deny this defense the right of cross-examining this witness."

"Put her on the stand yourself," Brady said.

"She is your witness," Dominguez insisted. "I have no desire to be held responsible for her testimony. I appeal to you in the interest of fair play and justice to put her on the stand. I never knew of a case in the jurisprudence of California where a complaining witness has not been placed on the stand. I know you do not want to put her on the stand. And I'll tell you, the only reason you will not call her is because you know that the moment you give me the opportunity to cross-examine her, I'll impeach every word of her testimony."

Judge Lazarus also expressed surprise at the failure to bring Delmont before the court. "You are traveling very close to a line which might necessitate me dismissing these proceedings," he warned Brady.

But she was not called. And then the defense rested without calling a single witness. Court adjourned.

The following afternoon, September 28, the judge was ready to deliver his decision. But first, he said, "the court will indulge in a little discussion." He blamed the Hotel St. Francis and all of society for allowing "this orgy" to occur. He said, "It is of such common occurrence that it was given no attention until something happened, until the climax made it notorious."

As for the prosecution's case, he said Arbuckle's action with the ice was very regrettable but had no connection with murder. "Some of the witnesses were absolutely worthless, especially Semnacher, who occupied two days' time. The only witness in the entire case who gave any direct testimony bearing on the guilt or innocence of Arbuckle was the nervous chambermaid, Josephine Keza." And yet he also dismissed the voices Keza overheard as, perhaps, adults shifting the boundaries of consensual sex. He concluded: "The question for me to decide from the merest outline of evidence, this skeletonized description of what occurred in those apartments on Labor Day, is whether I am justified in holding the defendant for murder. And I don't think I am justified in sending him to trial on this grievous charge under the circumstances. Therefore, I hold him for trial on the charge of manslaughter."

The courtroom of mostly female observers erupted in applause. Arbuckle embraced his wife and hugged and kissed his mother-in-law. When court was adjourned, a dozen women rushed forward to shake the hand of Roscoe "Fatty" Arbuckle, and he accepted congratulations without a smile but with watery eyes. As he and his wife and mother-in-law were ushered into the judge's chamber, Durfee began to collapse, and her husband held her up and quieted her with great affection. Women observers cooed. His mother-in-law smoothed back his hair.

The defense's $5,000 cashier's check submitted thirteen days prior for bail on the grand jury's manslaughter complaint was finally accepted. Arbuckle was a free man, if perhaps only temporarily. He returned to what had been his residence for the last eighteen days, cell 12 on felon's row, and said good-bye to Fred Martin and others. He stuffed his clothing into a suitcase as newspaper photographers crowded the cell, snapping photos with flashes of fiery light.

A photographer suggested, "Roll a cigarette with one hand when we take the next snap."

"I can't," the man accused of manslaughter answered. "It's the other Arbuckle that does that."

When he left the Hall of Justice with his family and his lawyers and his lackeys, women lining both sides of the street cheered him.

That evening Brady released a statement declaring that if Arbuckle "were unknown and unimportant, he would have been held for murder." It is, though, much more likely that an unknown man would never have been charged with murder. The evidence for murder was weak, and a grand jury and coroner's inquest had already favored manslaughter.

The movie star, his wife, and his mother-in-law spent that night and most of the next day at his brother Arthur's house in San Francisco. Thursday night at the train depot, he was stopped by women well-wishers, some of whom gave him flowers. Aboard the train headed south, the conductor, porters, and many passengers congratulated him. He quietly said thanks without smiling. Congratulations were awkward for a man out on bail charged with manslaughter.

The next morning when the train arrived at the Los Angeles station, a large crowd of friends and curious spectators had gathered. A woman stood on a suitcase to loudly denounce Arbuckle, and some agreed with her, but many more in the crowd supported him. Several young women kissed him. A rumor that the homecoming was as staged as a movie scene was hotly denied.

What should be made of the fact that many women reacted positively to the lesser charge for Arbuckle? The *New York Times* published an editorial questioning it entitled "Some Problems for the Psychologists." Here, then, some psychoanalysis.

Just as his celebrity spawned the tsunami of negative press, it also aided him. Some fans could never shake the impression of him created by his projected image. They felt they knew Fatty—he was coarse and capable of petty crimes and cartoonish violence, but no one got hurt for long. He was no rapist, no murderer. One crying woman who waited in a hall outside the courtroom for three hours to see him but still missed him as he passed by said, "I've only seen him on the screen, and I wanted to see him in real life." There may have been more women like her in the Hall of Justice than vigilant mothers.

As for the vigilant mothers, there is no tally of how many, if any, cheered or otherwise approved of the decision. However, one stated purpose of the Women's Vigilant Committee was to monitor proceedings to make certain justice was served, so perhaps many of those who observed the preliminary hearing agreed with Justice Lazarus that the case for trying Arbuckle for murder had not been made.*

Another factor was the daily presence of Minta Durfee and her mother. The estranged wife, herself a movie celebrity, had traveled across the country to stand by her man. And the mother-in-law, then sixty-four and as matronly as any of the vigilant women, was standing by him too. In a women's court where all the attorneys were male, where the judge was male, where most reporters were male, and where all the amateur observers were female, the presence of two other females visibly supporting Arbuckle and proclaiming his innocence spoke volumes. The newspapers reported Durfee's reactions as closely as Arbuckle's. Her photos ran regularly during the preliminary hearing, highlighting her choice of dress and necklace and hat, crowding out photos of that other fashion maven, Virginia Rappe.

Durfee's presence was so valuable in bolstering Arbuckle's eviscerated image, it was speculated that Paramount paid her way to San Francisco and picked up her expenses. She always denied it. But another form of leverage was probably in play. Durfee later wrote of her "tense trip to Los Angeles, to a home that I had never seen, where if Roscoe desired to do so my separate maintenance could be cut off for all time." The fear of losing her $500 weekly payments from Arbuckle almost certainly factored into her decision to support him so publicly.

---

* There was a mild backlash against the Women's Vigilant Committee. During the preliminary hearing, a controversial editorial in the *Los Angeles Times* entitled "Feasting and Vigilance" criticized the WVC's members for turning court proceedings into theater, for heartily dining at the Palace Hotel before the first day of the preliminary hearing, and for picnicking and applying makeup in the courtroom. It also questioned why the WVC's presence was necessary for a fair trial. This editorial, which itself fueled a backlash in Northern California, reflected the ongoing rivalry between Los Angeles and San Francisco.

That Friday night, his first back in his West Adams mansion in three weeks, Roscoe Arbuckle was the guest of honor at a homecoming party. Limousines pulled up outside, delivering movie industry friends. There, behind closed doors, Arbuckle smiled. He shook hands and accepted congratulations. "He has seen fair-weather friends fall away from him, and he has learned the value of his true friends," Durfee said. It was the last day of September and his first party since the one on Labor Day, but this time no alcohol was served. "Half the people there whispered and tiptoed around, and the others laughed too loud," Buster Keaton remembered. "What could you say to the poor bastard?"

{13}

BLISS: 1919-20

I sometimes wonder if the world will ever seem as carefree and exciting a place as it did to us in Hollywood during 1919 and the early twenties. We were all young, the air in Southern California was like wine. Our business was also young and growing like nothing ever seen before.

—Buster Keaton

It was in June 1919 when—among his daily deluge of autograph requests, unsolicited story suggestions, pleas for donations, and fawning praise from around the globe—Roscoe Arbuckle received a letter signed with a number:

Dear Mr. Arbuckle,
I have just been sentenced to twelve years in this prison for burglary and now that my head is shaved and I've got the stripes on, I don't think they were joking. I used to drive a taxi cab in New York and you occasionally rode with me. It is only a step from driving a taxi to second story work and my foot slipped.

I told all the boys here in this prison that I knew you and they asked me to write and invite you to come down here and entertain us some evening. Please come, Mr. Arbuckle. Anything you do will be appreciated because it is very dull here.

Subsequently, Arbuckle, accompanied by Lou Anger and a few Comique players and escorted by armed guards, strode through the gates of a California penitentiary. From the stage in the main hall, he told old vaudeville jokes, and after three rousing ovations, he greeted individual members of his captive audience.

As indicated by this anecdote, as well as his financial and moral support of the troops during World War I, Arbuckle was charitable with his time and money. In fact, he went further than most of his fellow movie stars. Louella Parsons recounted how benevolent he was to individuals behind the scenes. She mentioned an instance involving "a certain little girl whom Fatty had given his friendship and advice." Two and a half years before a very different image of Fatty took hold, Parsons wrote, "To those who think the Arbuckle life is one round of continual pleasure, it might be well to hear how he went out of his way to befriend this girl when things looked black for her. I shall like him always for that, though he modestly refused to admit he had done more than any other man would do when I spoke to him of this young woman."

By mid-1919 Arbuckle was in a position to be particularly generous. Just a few months earlier, he'd signed a deal worth $3 million.

The inmates took over the asylum. The seed had been planted the previous year, when Charlie Chaplin, Douglas Fairbanks, Mary Pickford, and William S. Hart were together promoting war bonds. With their power and popularity, why couldn't they oversee the distribution of their own films, thus maintaining creative control and ownership from the first spark of an idea until the final print was projected? D. W. Griffith joined them, and as negotiations progressed, the press dubbed the quintet the "Big Five." Hart eventually bowed out, but on February 5, 1919, Chaplin, Fairbanks, Pickford, and Griffith launched United Artists. With neither contract players nor acres of stages, UA was an affront to the increasingly powerful studio system. It was a "studio"—a film exchange incorporating four independent production companies—run by artists to distribute their own art. Only three UA films were released in

1919, and none were Chaplin's (due to contractual obligations to First National Pictures, he would not make his UA debut for another four years). Nevertheless, the news of United Artists' formation rocked the industry—including Arbuckle's employer, Paramount, which was by then the premier Hollywood company.

UA was launched, in part, by former Paramount president Hiram Abrams, who became the new company's managing director. Fairbanks and Pickford had only recently declined to re-sign at Paramount. That left Arbuckle as the studio's brightest star. Fortuitously for him, his contract was expiring. Rumors swirled in early 1919 that the "Big Five" would become six (or remain five, when discussions with Hart fell through), with Arbuckle joining his friends Chaplin, Fairbanks, and Pickford. It would be a major coup for Abrams, with whom Arbuckle had maintained a friendship, to pull the strongest remaining pillar away from Paramount. Negotiations ensued.

But on February 21 Arbuckle met Adolph Zukor in Kansas City, Missouri, where the superstar signed a three-year Paramount contract reportedly worth $1 million annually.* "Anyhow, you can see by this contract that the big one decided not to take in the big five," Arbuckle quipped. The big contract for the "big one" accomplished its immediate intention, stirring up nationwide publicity for Paramount and its star: $1,000,000 A YEAR FOR MOVIE "FATTY," screamed one front page, and similar $1 million or $3 million headlines appeared throughout the country. Arbuckle set out on another Paramount promotional tour, two years after his initial contract victory lap, traveling by train to New York City, Washington, DC, and New Orleans. "With all the stars I have had Mr. Arbuckle is the least tempermental and the most appreciative," Zukor effused.

During a brief stay in Manhattan, Arbuckle met opera legend Enrico Caruso (Arbuckle was a fan). He also hung out with Louella Parsons; the celebrity gossip pioneer was present in a smoky Manhattan screen-

---

* In fact, the contract paid Arbuckle $3 million for twenty-four movies. In addition, Lou Anger and Comique president Joseph Schenck took their shares of Arbuckle's pay.

ing room with Arbuckle, Zukor, Schenck, and others as actresses were considered for Arbuckle's love interest in future Comique comedies. Parsons accompanied the men to Sherry's, a French restaurant popular with high society. There, over oysters, chicken, and cocktails, Arbuckle revealed that if he were not an actor/director/writer, he would like to be a surgeon. For entertainment and enlightenment, he frequently witnessed a doctor friend operating in the Los Angeles county hospital. "I have watched Doc take out so many appendices, I believe I could do it myself," he mused. "It is a pretty sight to see Doc work." Several times, Charlie Chaplin accompanied him, and the world's two greatest comedic actors spent evenings peering inside human bodies.

Also in the month of February, an article entitled "On the Advantages of Embonpoint" appeared in *Photo-Play Journal* under Arbuckle's name. It contended:

> [A fat man] is regarded as harmless and innocent just because he looks so solid and easy-going. He may be harboring the most malicious thoughts, but he is disarmed by his own fat. Nobody suspects him. . . . A fat man makes a comfortable person to have around the house. His lap is a favorite perch for young and beautiful debutantes and sub-debs. They call him Uncle and punch him in the solar-plexus and generally kid him along. What fat man could fail to be happy under such circumstances?

When a sub-deb was not perched upon his lap, and when he was not gazing at an appendectomy or betting on a boxing match or buying yet another round for friends and hangers-on, Arbuckle continued to make movies without his best friend, Buster Keaton, who was still serving Uncle Sam. All told, Arbuckle made six shorts while Keaton was in the army.

In the first years of the twentieth century, the West Adams district near downtown was the most exclusive area in Los Angeles. Its Victorian mansions housed Southern California's titans of industry. The home at 649 West Adams Boulevard was built in 1905 for US Navy officer Randolph Huntington Miner and his socialite wife, who furnished the twenty rooms with treasures from their foreign travels. The drawing room alone could accommodate two hundred guests. The house was constructed in the Tudor revival style, with a gabled roof, stained glass windows, and exterior walls of red brick on the ground floor and a second floor decorated with half-timbering that formed branch-like trusses near the roof. It was as if a European country estate had been transported into the heart of a city born yesterday. The image was not just old money but medieval money—a salient point to Hollywood's nouveau riche.

The first movie star to live there was the original vamp, Theda Bara, who rented it from the Miners in 1917 when they headed to France and Bara's fame and fortune were soaring. Bara was born Theodosia Goodman in Cincinnati, but Fox publicized her as an Egyptian-born occultist with an affinity for snakes and raw meat, and the Jewish star's new name was supposedly an anagram of "Arab Death." She played along, in part by filling the mansion's elegant rooms with sarcophagi, crystal balls, and other exotica. Her home was portrayed in the press as a sort of proto–Addams Family dwelling, one you had best be wary of. When Bara's contract with Fox lapsed near the end of 1919, she retired. By then, she had left West Adams.

Meanwhile, Comique's productions had moved from Long Beach to a studio in Edendale, next door to Keystone. Arbuckle was in need of a home nearer his workplace, and Joe Schenck encouraged him to live in a house worthy of a millionaire celebrity. He moved in to the West Adams house, also renting from the Miners. He ordered the removal of Bara's ghoulish or feminine decor and began decorating to match his own ostentatious tastes—befitting, so he thought, a wealthy movie star. A tongue-in-cheek article in the *Los Angeles Times* wondered if the refinements of such a house—its Japanese meditation garden and koi pond, for instance—and the bourgeois neighborhood would cause Arbuckle to forsake the "shimmey at Vernon," "wild, rude games of poker," and the Tuesday-night fights in favor of drinking "tea with his little finger crooked daintily." The article concluded with the assertion that "Theda Bara's astral mind" was leading Arbuckle to Ibsen and Oscar Wilde.

Arbuckle was indeed behaving like a man possessed, but his preoccupation was an old one and not especially genteel. With haste, he was stocking the walled shelves in the basement of his new abode with a collection of alcohol that grew to legendary proportions: gin, scotch, rye, rum, wine. This was his doomsday shelter, meant to protect him against the coming ravages of Prohibition. It's unlikely his regular parties, which typically lasted until dawn, significantly depleted his stockpile—but not for lack of trying.

The rapid rise in the popularity of movies over the fist two decades of the twentieth century coincided with the similar ascension of baseball. Grander stadiums—including Wrigley Field and Fenway Park—opened, and such players as Honus Wagner, Walter Johnson, Ty Cobb, and Babe Ruth garnered headlines and pulled in an ever-expanding fan base. Arbuckle was one such fan. He had played the game as a youngster and on Keystone's team, and he had regularly attended games, whether on the vaudeville circuit or in Southern California.

Until the late 1950s, baseball teams traveled via train, and by train, the West Coast was days away from eastern cities. That's why in 1919, there were sixteen major league teams but none farther west than St. Louis. The West Coast had the Pacific Coast League. Unaffiliated with major league clubs, the PCL for the first half of the twentieth century was, in effect, a shadow major league, and it nurtured such legends as Joe DiMaggio and Ted Williams. Until 1958, when the Dodgers moved to Los Angeles and the Giants to San Francisco, the PCL was the big league for baseball fans in California.

Thus, it was huge news when on May 5, 1919, Arbuckle bought controlling interest in the PCL's Vernon Tigers and installed himself as president. Since their inception in 1909, the Tigers had been unprofitable. Their location was not ideal for family entertainment. Vernon, home of the aforementioned boxing arena and nightclub, was Los Angeles' adult playground, and the ballpark was located adjacent to Doyle's Bar, billed as "the longest bar in the world," with thirty-seven bartenders working thirty-seven cash registers and space to serve more than a thousand patrons.

After Arbuckle's purchase, Lou Anger, whose wife was the sister-in-law of the team's ace pitcher, became the Tigers' general manager, despite having no previous baseball experience. Arbuckle professed, "I'm just going into it for the sport of the thing and nothing else." He later said he "just bought them to please Anger" and all he did was "sign checks."

Still, as the first celebrity owner of a sports franchise, he received a windfall of publicity. Game reports referred to the Tigers as "Fatty's Team." He appeared in team photos and on the covers of game programs. He even had his own baseball card (dressed in the Tigers' uniform, he is biting into a baseball).* He was the biggest attraction at any game. A May 16 story noted, "San Francisco won a ball game for itself, 8 to 5, when Vernon got back on the losing end. Yet President Fatty Arbuckle is no less a hero. Even in the hour of defeat, fond mothers stood at the exit and pointed out this great man to their children." At another May game, he, Al St. John, and Buster Keaton, fresh from his military stint, performed in Tigers uniforms, pitching and hitting with plaster-of-Paris bats and balls that, when ball met bat, exploded to the delight of the crowd. By August the press had nicknamed the Tigers the "Custard Pies" in a nod to Fatty's Keystone roots.

On August 8 Arbuckle and his entourage—including Anger and Keaton—headed by train to San Francisco for several games pitting the Tigers against the San Francisco Seals and the Oakland Oaks. The actors performed baseball sketches before record crowds of thirty thousand. San Francisco nights were spent at parties in Arbuckle's honor and drinking and dancing at the Tait-Zinkand Cafe. One night began at Tait's by the bay and ended, sometime in the morning, at Tait's downtown. Arbuckle presumably stayed at the Hotel St. Francis, which soon thereafter began

* In 2011 an Arbuckle 1919 baseball card sold at auction for $5,288.

touting him in its advertising. As always, he picked up the bill for everyone. He estimated ahead of time the trip would cost him about $2,000 (about $26,000 in today's dollars).

On October 5 the Tigers won their first-ever Pacific Coast League title, edging past their chief rival, the Los Angeles Angels, by sweeping a doubleheader on the series' final day. But, in the year of the Chicago Black Sox scandal, the Tigers' championship was blighted by its own gambling infraction. Allegedly, opposing players were bribed to throw games in Vernon's favor. Five players were expelled from the PCL. Arbuckle was not implicated, but the publicity for "Fatty's Team" had gone from good to bad. Owning a team had required more time and money than he had bargained for, and when he should have been celebrated as the president of the league champions, his name was instead sullied via its association with cheating. He sold the Vernon Tigers less than seven months after purchasing them.*

Corporal Buster Keaton had not left France until more than three months after the armistice that ended World War I. Suffering a hearing impairment, he convalesced in a military hospital in New York and at another in Baltimore. After being discharged from the army on April 29, he returned to Los Angeles, where he again acted opposite his best friend, Roscoe Arbuckle.

Comique's acting roster had changed over the previous nine months. Molly Malone was in. Alice Lake was out. Jackie Coogan was in.† Al St. John would soon be out. *Back Stage*, the first movie Keaton made upon returning, was St. John's last with Comique. Arbuckle's nephew signed

* The Tigers won the PCL title again in 1920, without controversy. But without Arbuckle and without alcohol (Prohibition had begun), attendance plummeted. Before the 1926 season, the team was sold, moved to San Francisco, and renamed the Mission Reds.

† A former vaudeville dancer, Coogan had a truncated film acting career before going into producing. His son, also known as Jackie Coogan, achieved greater fame, first as an actor (he played the titular role in Chaplin's *The Kid*), then as the namesake of the Coogan Bill, which financially protects child actors. The junior Coogan fondly remembered playing with Arbuckle in the summer of 1919.

with Paramount before moving to Fox, where he was the prolific star and director of slapstick shorts.

The three shorts Arbuckle and Keaton made in 1919 each have bursts of brilliance. *Back Stage* has a stunt in which the front of a house falls toward Fatty but misses him as the open window passes over him.* *The Hayseed* presents Fatty at his most likeable in a subdued, more character-driven comedy. And *The Garage*, which, like *The Hayseed*, was shot at Henry Lehrman's studio, includes some inspired gags involving the overuse of motor oil and a giant turntable for washing and drying cars.† Best of all is a bit in which Keaton hides from a cop by walking, stride for stride, in front of or behind the much-wider Fatty. There is also an in-joke wherein Fatty kisses a photo of Mabel Normand. Released in January 1920, *The Garage* marked the fourteenth and final comedy short with Arbuckle and Keaton together.

Offscreen, when not watching a Tigers game or boxing match or partying at a nightclub, Arbuckle and Keaton reveled in practical jokes. When Adolph Zukor attended a dinner party at Arbuckle's West Adams mansion with Sid Grauman, Alice Lake, and others, he was the only one not in on the joke that the clumsy butler spilling the turkey dinner was Buster Keaton, even after an "outraged" Arbuckle shattered a breakaway bottle on the butler's head. When Marcus Loew came to town, Keaton played Arbuckle's chauffeur, inflicting upon the theater magnate a horrifying ride through Los Angeles. Pretending to be gas company workers, Keaton and Arbuckle nearly tore up the pampered front lawn of actress Pauline Frederick's Beverly Hills mansion. And they convinced Vic Levy, a Belgian dressmaker who clothed the Hollywood community, that the king and queen of Belgium wished to dine at his house. At the resulting dinner, only Levy was unaware that the royal couple were actors. Keaton said, "Few of us in that whole Hollywood gang had had time to acquire an education. I suppose we were doing the things in our

---

* Keaton repeated this dangerous gag in his first short without Arbuckle, *One Week*, and, famously, in his feature *Sherlock Jr.*

† During this time, Arbuckle interacted with Virginia Rappe, as she was at Lehrman's studio filming *A Twilight Baby*.

twenties* that we would have done earlier if we'd gone to high school and college." In his autobiography, Keaton detailed these shenanigans in a chapter titled "When the World Was Ours."

Six years after Keystone's feature *Tillie's Punctured Romance*, Arbuckle had still not appeared in a movie longer than two reels. Comedy was the genre of shorts, and those shorts played prior to features on the same bills. In the fall of 1919, he was eager to transition to feature films. "I mean to have some real drama interspersed with comedy," he said. Features were beyond the scope of his current production company, so Joseph Schenck sold Arbuckle's contract from Comique to Paramount—the studio that was already paying handsomely to distribute Arbuckle's movies. Keaton would become the new solo star of Comique shorts, and Arbuckle would star in Paramount feature films written and directed by that studio's top talents.

Along with seemingly everyone else in the film industry, Roscoe Arbuckle spent the early hours of Thanksgiving 1919 at the Hotel Alexandria, dancing, drinking, and dining at the Directors Ball, then Hollywood's most glamourous annual event. Most evenings he pursued the low entertainments of boxing, gambling, and jazz dancing, but when Hollywood's formal galas occurred, he was almost always there. He was a member of the Motion Picture Directors Association and attended events of the American Society of Cinematographers. Fraternal organizations were popular then, and Arbuckle joined a Los Angeles Elks Lodge. He was not a recreational reader, the first commercial radio broadcast in Los Angeles was still two years away, and he had no children, so it was rare that he would spend an evening at home unless he was throwing a party.

Just before Christmas, he fulfilled a longtime dream by performing on a New York stage—and not just in any theater, but in the fifty-three-hundred-seat Hippodrome. He was part of a one-night all-star benefit that included singer Sophie Tucker. He subsequently spent the holiday

* Arbuckle turned thirty-two in 1919.

with his wife. They had remained on good terms, corresponding via affectionate letters and frequent long-distance telephone calls.

Brewed over decades by an alliance of puritans and Progressives, the Eighteenth Amendment went into effect at the stroke of midnight on January 17, 1920, prohibiting the manufacture, sale, or transportation of intoxicating liquors. The Volstead Act put the devil in the details of its enforcement. On the eve of Prohibition, an especially cold night in the East, the expected last-chance revelry failed to materialize. The *New York Times* noted, "Instead of passing from us in violent paroxysms, the demon rum lay down to a painless, peaceful, though lamented, by some, death." Billy Sunday had staged the demon rum's funeral in Norfolk, Virginia, the day before, complete with a twenty-foot coffin carried by twenty pallbearers. The evangelist told ten thousand "mourners": "The reign of tears is over. The slums will soon be only a memory. We will turn our prisons into factories and our jails into storehouses and corncribs. Men will walk upright now, women will smile, and children will laugh. Hell will be forever for rent." Reports of the demon's death were greatly exaggerated.

Just before Prohibition took effect, Arbuckle bought the West Adams mansion from the Miners for $250,000 (about $3 million in today's dollars). "Had to do it to save my cellar!" Arbuckle joked of the purchase and its liquor-filled basement. "The authorities won't let me move it, so I bought the whole house to protect it. Also I'm thinking of giving out to the newspapers a story that my cellar has been robbed, so if there's anybody contemplating doing this they'll lay off."

According to the census, on January 2 Arbuckle lived in the house with a thirty-seven-year-old male cook and a twenty-seven-year-old female maid. Both were Japanese immigrants. His secretary/housekeeper, butler, chauffeur, and gardener lived elsewhere. The house's other movie star, Luke the dog, was not counted in the census. Arbuckle now had three dogs. Durfee said, "He and the big St. Bernard have wonderful times. Mr. Arbuckle gets into his bathing suit, and puts a tub in the garage, and he and the dog are perfectly happy there for half a day."

He continued decorating the house in a manner he deemed befitting West Adams and its titans of industry. He imported an intricately carved front door from Spain (cost: $12,000) and bought and bought and bought: ornate mahogany paneling, gold-leafed bathtubs, crystal chandeliers, Oriental rugs, marble counters, fine-art paintings, antique china. The red lacquer dining room table with golden-clawed feet was from China. The lanai featured a Hawaiian royal chair. There was a Japanese bridge over the pond. Forever fascinated by technical gadgetry, Arbuckle had his closets and dressers wired with lights that came on when a door or drawer was opened.

As ostentatious as his house's interior was, it was overshadowed by his new car. In 1919 he'd had the mammoth skeleton and innards of a Pierce-Arrow delivered to Don Lee Coach & Body Works in Los Angeles. There twenty-five-year-old Harley Earl* performed $28,000 worth of coachwork to the luxurious $6,000 original, reshaping the hood and cowl and adding such features as a backseat mahogany cabinet, headlamps like silver soup pots, and a radiator cap monogrammed with an *A*. In April 1920 Earl completed his work, and for the next week more than ten thousand awed observers crowded into Don Lee's showroom to marvel at the $34,000 machine. The *Los Angeles Times* stated that it would take "a special squad of police" to clear traffic of stunned witnesses whenever Arbuckle's Pierce-Arrow appeared on a street.

Arbuckle continued to throw frequent house parties, ever so slowly depleting his cellar stockpile while the jazz played. There were stag parties, lawn parties, dinner parties, early morning parties. He staged a party around a dog wedding, at which Luke was the best man, so to speak. His favorite Venice and Vernon haunts had gone dry, so some weekends he journeyed to San Francisco or Tijuana. He was among the Hollywood celebrities who spent Halloween of 1920 at Tijuana's Sunset Inn. A news story said that "a 'spirited' program is assured in the Mexican village."

---

* After making his name customizing Arbuckle's car and the autos of others among Hollywood's elite, Earl designed numerous now-legendary automobiles while at General Motors from 1927 to 1959.

More than nine months into Prohibition, the quotation marks bracketing "spirited" were a knowing wink.

The painted poster features Arbuckle in a ten-gallon hat (properly sized), a leather vest, and a blue shirt. A red kerchief adorns his neck, a six-shooter is strapped to his waist, his arms are crossed, and his eyes gaze wistfully into the distance. His name is as big as the title, *The Round Up*, but "Fatty" is parenthesized and squeezed between the much larger "Roscoe" and "Arbuckle," as if a mere whisper. Although Arbuckle's first feature film includes his signature bit of rolling a cigarette with one hand and a few other minor gags (one featuring Keaton, uncredited, as a blackface Indian), it is otherwise void of comedy. It's a western romance with too many plots. *Variety* wrote, "It is evident that Fatty Arbuckle of the mammoth breeches and slapstick funnies has given away to Roscoe Arbuckle in a regular hero role, serious in personation with but a modicum of comedy for relief as behooves his corpulent build. The change has not been for the better."

It may have alienated fans of slapstick, but *The Round Up* accomplished its goal. A box office success, it established its star's bona fides as a feature film actor. The story remains tedious, but Arbuckle brings a surprising pathos to the part of Sheriff "Slim" Hoover, the role that gave him his signature line. In the end, unable to get the girl, he forlornly rests his head on a fence post, and the final intertitle reads, "Nobody loves a fat man."

Passport application of Roscoe Arbuckle:

> November 16, 1920.
> Object of visit: *business*
> Father: *dead*

William Goodrich Arbuckle had only recently died from cancer at age seventy-one. Roscoe paid his father's final medical bills, but it's unknown whether he ever saw the man again after leaving their unhappy Santa Clara home at seventeen. (His bitter stepmother claimed he "abandoned" his stepfamily when he became successful.) He did not attend the funeral.

Instead, he was in New York City, planning to board an ocean liner bound for France with friend Fred Ward, a former actor. As they awaited its departure, a rumor surfaced in *Variety* that Arbuckle would soon be marrying a former Ziegfeld Follies showgirl. Never mind that he was still married to Minta Durfee; even the showbiz press had forgotten. In Jazz Age Manhattan, Arbuckle partied so much that he literally missed the boat, and he and Ward had to take another ship five days later. Never mind that Prohibition had been the law of the land for eleven months. Addressing the marriage rumor, Arbuckle joked that he might return from France with a French wife. Never mind that he was still married; perhaps even he could forget.

Eight years after his trip across the Pacific, this was Arbuckle's maiden journey across the Atlantic. In Europe, he learned just how great his fame had grown. Motion pictures were a major American export—even more so after World War I decimated the European movie industry.

"Paris went wild over Fatty Arbuckle," *Photoplay* noted. "From the time he landed until he sailed for home, he was dined and wined and feted, for the French took him in portly person as readily as they take to his pictures." Four thousand Parisians crowded on a street just to glimpse him. Hundreds of fans and dozens of reporters followed his chauffeured car wherever he went. There were banquets and dinners and dances. Much of the official thanks given Arbuckle was for the comfort his movies had provided the French during four years of bloody conflict. He reciprocated when, at the Arc de Triomphe, he laid a bouquet on the spot where the Tomb of the Unknown Soldier would appear a few weeks later.

His trip's final nine days were in London. There, while staying at the luxurious Hotel Savoy, he hosted a dinner attended by 150 British notables. For a movie star of his magnitude, simply being in the right public places while cameras clicked and delivering ready-made quips to the swarming reporters was a function of his occupation. Roscoe "Fatty" Arbuckle's product was himself, and every day in every place was an opportunity to sell. He returned to New York City on December 22 and again spent Christmas in Manhattan with his wife, even if all had forgotten he was married.

The Round Up was the first of five feature films Arbuckle acted in in 1920, though with their greater postproduction and publicity schedules, they weren't making it to screens nearly as fast as his slapstick shorts had. Only one other was released that year. In it Arbuckle plays an unsuccessful attorney who runs for political office. In an unfortunate subplot, a woman tries to entrap Fatty and spawn a ruinous scandal. Originally released in December 1920, it was still playing in theaters ten months later when a ruinous scandal engulfed its leading man, conferring a morose irony on its title: *The Life of the Party*.

{14}

FIRST TRIAL

That's what Fatty Arbuckle said, and you know what they did to him.
— Hunter S. Thompson, *Fear and Loathing in Las Vegas*

Three weeks and three days after the death of Virginia Rappe, on October 3, 1921, the *Los Angeles Times* published a letter that began:

> Now that the wave of insanity, for it was nothing less (nor more) in regard to the Arbuckle case has passed over, it would seem that disappointment is to be the daily portion of those who, blind to the fact that no evidence is forthcoming, merely hoped for the downfall of Roscoe Arbuckle for no reason but that he was a successful screen star.

This was the sentiment of the minority, but it was growing fastest in Los Angeles, which depended so profoundly on the likes of Arbuckle for its image and a principal industry. That industry's defensive strategy is best exemplified by an October 1 editorial in *Moving Picture World*: "Enclosed in the following space is our idea what should be said by everybody in the motion picture business about the Arbuckle Case from now forth until the entire matter is settled." The remainder of the page was blank.

Arbuckle himself was no longer generating any industry. So complete was the banishment that one of his movies was pulled from a screening in Sing Sing prison and future Fatty films were banned there. The warden's reason was "the same which kept scrupulous theater men everywhere from putting on the films."

From a letter by Roscoe Arbuckle to Joseph Schenck, October 1, 1921:

> I want you to have explicit faith and confidence in me and tell Mr. Zukor to have the same. I have done no wrong, my heart is clean and my conscience is clear and when it is over I have the guts to come back and I will come back and make good. . . . I know what they [Paramount executives] have tied up in me at present and irrespective of whether we ever due [*sic*] business together again I will come out of this affair clean and vindicated so that they can realize on their tremendous investment. I am not asking for sympathy or forgiveness. I have done no wrong but I do want you and the ones financially as well as personally interested to know that I am innocent, a victim of circumstance, the only one of prominence in the party and therefore I had to be the goat.

San Francisco detectives tailed Arbuckle in Los Angeles, but they must have studied every branch and every brick on West Adams Street, for the accused who formerly rarely spent an evening in his mansion now rarely left it. "A palatial residence was to be our home for nearly a year on West Adams in the beautiful and exclusive part of Los Angeles, where we were to be veritable prisoners," Durfee later wrote. Patrolled by his own newly hired security force, Arbuckle's home was his bunker, fortified against a world that had largely turned against him. At all hours, people slowed outside to honk or hurl insults and sometimes stones.

And for the first time his wife of thirteen years was living there with him. "We slept in separate bedrooms, I think because Roscoe was self-conscious," Durfee remembered. "Neither of us wanted to speak about what actually happened in that suite at the St. Francis. And yet we both knew we couldn't avoid the issue. It was what had brought us both together and had allowed me to come home with him. We had to live together for the sake of the public. We had to show everyone that we were a loving man and wife, even though there was that long separation."

On October 7 Arbuckle was arraigned for manslaughter. Defense attorney Frank Dominguez was not present; the official story was that he had quit as chief counsel because the trial would require too much time and Arbuckle would be better served by a San Francisco attorney. However, the decision was likely made by Schenck and Zukor, who were displeased with Dominguez's strategy in the preliminary hearing, especially his failure to call Arbuckle and Maude Delmont to the stand. They felt their money-minting superstar should have been cleared and his movies returned to big screens. So Dominguez was out.

Gavin McNab was in. Not only was McNab a San Francisco native and longtime political powerhouse, but the balding, gray eminence also had experience with celebrities, having successfully represented Mary Pickford (divorce) and boxer Jack Dempsey (draft evasion) the year before. McNab brought to the case one of his law partners, Nat Schmulowitz, and another local lawyer, Joseph McInerney, was also enlisted. The dream team of five also included two holdovers from the preliminaries: Arbuckle's regular attorney from Los Angeles, Milton Cohen, and his original San Francisco lawyer, Charles Brennan. Later, Assistant DA U'Ren called them "a million-dollar array of counsel."

The same day McNab took over the case, a story emerged from Chicago that Rappe had left a daughter there. Supposedly, the father vanished before the girl was born, and Rappe moved away soon thereafter, leaving her daughter with foster parents but sending money. The story's one source should have set off alarm bells: a Chicago-based traveling salesman named John Bates, who had written to officials in Los Angeles and San Francisco to determine the value of Rappe's estate.* He estimated the daughter was eight or nine, and he claimed not to know her whereabouts but was confident he could locate her. "If [Rappe's] estate is of any value I intend to see that her daughter receives the benefit of it," Bates said. No such daughter was ever located. The abandoned daughter story was a harbinger, however; others in Chicago had more sensational tales about Rappe's teen years and young adulthood. Eager to listen, defense attorney Brennan boarded a train heading east.

Meanwhile, the state was following leads of its own. Matthew Brady journeyed to Los Angeles twice in October on fact-finding tours of Hollywood's underbelly. As the second such trip ended, the home team *Los Angeles Times* lambasted the San Francisco prosecutor with an article entitled "Ho, Hum, 'Wild Parties' Tame," which chided that the parties "where hypodermic needles were passed around pasty-face guests on a tray have resolved themselves into knitting bees. Where, oh where (in a loud despairing wail) is the reputed wickedness of Los Angeles?"

DEAD MOVIE MAN IN ARBUCKLE CASE, read a headline on October 11. Al Stein, an assistant director to Fred Fishback, died at twenty-six after a night of drinking. News coverage played up notes found in Stein's Los Angeles apartment that were made by Fishback and pertained to the Arbuckle case. In death, Stein became a potential witness and possible murder victim. But he succumbed to alcohol poisoning, a common malady during Prohibition.

The investigation of Prohibition violations at the Labor Day party continued in parallel with the inquiries in the manslaughter case. Arbuckle's was the most high-profile flaunting of the Volstead Act, and the feds were determined that it not go unpunished. On September 30

* Her estate consisted of her personal effects, $800 in a bank account, and some stocks and bonds.

Gobey's Grill, the restaurant that had provided the alcohol for the party, was raided. The manager and three other employees were arrested, but the cellar shelves where $40,000 in liquid refreshment was supposedly housed were empty. Gobey's had been tipped off. Jack Lawrence, the deliveryman who had brought the alcohol from the restaurant to the party, had vanished but was eventually located in Oregon and returned to San Francisco. He pleaded guilty to transporting alcohol and was fined $250. After being arraigned for manslaughter, Arbuckle was arrested for violation of the Volstead Act and posted $500 bail. The hearing was superseded by his manslaughter trial.

> What the microscope reveals of mute testimony from the floor and furnishings of Room 1219, the chamber where the film actress was in an hour transformed from a jovial guest to an hysterical woman with the touch of death upon her may prove as potent as the tale of any witness. Edward O. Heinrich, noted criminologist and microscopist, has for weeks been subjecting that room to the minutest expert scrutiny, and his findings, says the prosecution, will constitute the outstanding new development of the trial.
>
> —"Microscope's Evidence May Determine Arbuckle's Fate," *Evening Independent* (Massillon, Ohio), October 31, 1921, front page

Fingerprints were first admitted in an English criminal case in 1902. The first comprehensive forensic hair study was published in France in 1910. An antibody test for typing dried blood was developed in 1915. By the autumn of 1921, Edward O. Heinrich was a pioneer in such matters. Though most of his reputation as "the Wizard of Berkeley" or "America's Sherlock Holmes" was earned afterward, he was, at the time of Rappe's death, America's foremost forensic scientist. Heinrich spent his teen years working in a pharmacy, remarking later that "a drugstore is a veritable laboratory in behavioristic psychology. I learned what people do in secret." After obtaining a chemistry degree, he consulted on criminal investigations, and in 1916 he was appointed chief of police of Alameda, California. In 1919 he accepted a post as a criminal expert to the city of San Francisco (and another as a chemistry professor at Berkeley). In his lab in Oakland, he studied and practiced to gain expertise in all fields of criminal science. Just before the Arbuckle case, he investigated the August 2 kidnapping and murder of a priest and helped to prove the guilt of the man who found the body (and wanted the reward money) by connecting him, via microscopic details, to beach sand and a tent cord on or near the corpse. It remains a landmark forensics case.

Heinrich strove to find forensic evidence in the Arbuckle case. However, he did not enter room 1219 until September 16, eleven days after the Labor Day party and after a maid had cleaned it. Visiting the room on three occasions, he compared hairs found there with those from Rappe's head; he searched for fiber filaments that matched her clothing; he had 1219's doors taken to his laboratory. America's Sherlock Holmes peered through his microscope lens, searching for a clue invisible to the naked eye, a key to unlock the mystery of what happened on Labor Day at the Hotel St. Francis.

On November 12, two days before jury selection began, Arbuckle moved into what would be his home for the duration of the trial: the Palace Hotel, where Virginia Rappe had stayed nearly ten weeks earlier. "I'm certainly glad my trial starts Monday morning," he said. "You may think it's funny that I'm so eager to go before a judge and jury and take a chance of lounging in the penitentiary for ten years. But if you'd gone through what I have—the loss of friends, the shame, the stories, the rumors about me, the attitude of the American public, the sermons of the ministers, to say nothing of the loss of money—you'd be glad to get it over with, too."

Though the Nineteenth Amendment, guaranteeing women's right to vote nationwide, was ratified in 1920, women had served on juries in California since October 1911. The practice was repeatedly challenged until codified in California law in April 1917.* In November 1921 women on juries remained controversial. Traditionalists balked at members of "the fairer sex" being taken from their household duties to hear salacious testimony, being sequestered with male strangers, and passing judgment on men. Women were deemed by many men to be too emotional and irrational to decide matters of life, death, and imprisonment.

And so the possible inclusion of women on the Arbuckle jury made nationwide news. When the pool of sixty-six potential jurors included thirteen females, headlines appeared such as WOMEN MAY TRY ARBUCKLE. Still, a (male) journalist with the *San Francisco Examiner* predicted, "When the jury finally is completed, there will be no women let upon it." He was wrong. Over four days, a jury of seven men and five women was selected, along with one male alternate. While the male occupations varied from confectioner to explosives expert, four of the women were listed as "wives" and the fifth was a "spinster" (unmarried). Before opening statements, one of the male jurors admitted to having formed an opinion that Arbuckle was innocent. After he was excused, the alternate was seated in the jury box. (A new alternate was selected.) That twelfth juror and one of the five women were destined to have a profound impact on the life of Roscoe Arbuckle.

On November 18 the trial opened with an overly erudite statement by Assistant DA Leo Friedman (who replaced Isadore Golden). The defense chose to delay its opening statement until after the prosecution presented its case. First up for the state were Drs. Shelby Strange and William Ophüls, who discussed the two autopsies. The defense scored points by getting Strange to admit Rappe's bruises may have been caused after death and by getting Ophüls to say a bladder could rupture spontaneously. Another witness introduced architectural drawings of the hotel rooms.

* California was the fourth state to do so. By the end of 1921, seventeen states allowed women jurors.

On the second day, after nurse Grace Halston testified, defense counsel McNab asked Dr. Arthur Beardslee, "Did Mrs. Delmont give you what was purported to be the history of the case? What was the history she gave you?"

District Attorney Brady objected, and Judge Harold Louderback sustained the motion.

McNab pressed on: "Did Mrs. Delmont or Miss Rappe intimate to you that Mr. Arbuckle was responsible for her condition?"

"Objection!"

"Sustained."

Assistant DA Milton U'Ren labeled the questions "poison." There followed a verbal battle between the prosecution and defense. The defense was trying to insert comments by Rappe into evidence; Delmont had supposedly heard her make a statement to the hotel detective that they said absolved Arbuckle. Further, Delmont supposedly told Dr. Beardslee that Arbuckle attacked Rappe, only to have Rappe contradict her. The state called all of this hearsay.

Judge Harold Louderback was forty, a native of San Francisco, a graduate of Harvard Law, an army captain during the war. He was still in his initial year as a Superior Court judge when he was assigned the biggest celebrity criminal trial in American history. He repeatedly sustained the prosecution's objections regarding Rappe's alleged statements.

On the third day, the state called Dr. H. Edward Castle, who had briefly attended Rappe at Wakefield sanitarium, and the facility's head, Dr. W. Francis Wakefield. Both testified that Rappe was bruised before her death. Then came Zey Prevost and Alice Blake, the state's star witnesses and reluctant celebrities. After the preliminary hearing, they had been placed in protective custody in the house of a DA clerk's mother. While Blake's wealthy family eventually won her release, Prevost had spent the last seven weeks under a sort of house arrest in someone else's house. The defense made much of this, as in this retort from McNab to the prosecution: "I do not know what she was doing when she was in your private prison."

Prevost recounted how Rappe entered 1219 and "Mr. Arbuckle followed her and closed the door." According to the witness, a half hour later Maude Delmont kicked at that door several times and demanded, "Open the door. I want to speak to Virginia." Prevost stated that a red-faced Arbuckle opened the door, fumbling with his robe. He said nothing as he strolled into 1220. When Delmont and Prevost entered 1219, they found Rappe on the bed, fully clothed, moaning and writhing.

"Did she say anything at this time?" Assistant DA Friedman asked.

"Yes," Prevost replied, "she said 'I'm dying. I am going to die.' She then began tearing at her waist."

Prevost recounted that she and Delmont removed Rappe's clothing for a cold bath, after which Fred Fishback, who had just returned to the hotel suite after scouting his film location, carried Rappe back to the bed.

"After the bath, did she say anything?" Friedman asked.

"Yes, she said, 'He hurt me.'"

Thus the crucial statement that the prosecution had labored over during preliminaries had collapsed into two parts. "I'm dying" was no longer paired with "He hurt me," and the latter could be applied to Fishback carrying Rappe.

"Did the defendant say anything?" asked Friedman.

"Yes, he said, 'Aw, shut up. I'll throw her out the window if she doesn't stop yelling.'" Prevost also recounted Arbuckle applying ice to Rappe's "abdominal region" and saying, "That will make her come to."

In cross-examination, McNab highlighted the inconsistencies of Prevost's varying recollections, and he suggested that Brady had pressured Prevost to sign a statement with the words "He killed me."

Blake was a supporting player after Prevost's starring role, testifying only briefly before she was excused until the state could produce a suppressed statement she'd made to a detective.

After Kate Hardebeck testified to Rappe's good health, the state called Jesse Norgaard, a sixty-two-year-old security guard who'd worked at Henry Lehrman's studio when Arbuckle shot *The Hayseed* and *The Garage* there. He claimed that in August 1919, when he returned to the studio office to get his hat, Arbuckle asked him for the key to Rappe's dressing room, and when he refused, Arbuckle said it was for a joke and offered "a big roll of money and said he would trade it for the key." Upon hearing Norgaard state this, Arbuckle laughed so loudly the bailiff called for order.

When Blake returned to the stand the next day, her statement to a detective was introduced: Rappe said only "I'm dying" and not, as Blake remembered on the stand the day before, "I'm dying. He hurt me."

In cross-examination, McNab pounced. "Was not your memory of the incidents of the party clearer at that time than it is now?"

"Yes, sir," said Blake

McNab replied, "That's all."

Al Semnacher told of seeing Rappe pained, tearing at her clothes and claiming she was dying. He said the morning after Labor Day everyone merely thought Rappe had been drunk, and Arbuckle told the ice story. Again, in regards to the icing, Semnacher wrote but did not speak "snatch." Under cross-examination, he admitted to having seen Rappe tearing off her clothes "two or three times" when drinking on previous occasions.

After Rappe's personal trainer demonstrated the medicine ball exercises she did, illustrating her good health, the state brought back its most effective witness from the preliminary hearing: hotel maid Josephine Keza. She was much less effective this time, perhaps because the defense was better prepared. She theatrically retold her tale of a woman screaming behind the closed door to 1219 and saying "No, no, oh my God!" followed by a man commanding, "Shut up!" But Keza had supposedly been in and out of the suite throughout Labor Day, sometimes hiding in closets, other times listening at keyholes, and under cross-examination specifics melted into one debauched party. "Oh, what an afternoon!" she exclaimed to laughter, playing to the audience. The remark was stricken from the record. By her account, Rappe was, improbably, screaming off and on for two hours, and multiple men had told Rappe to shut up.*

---

* She recounted seeing Lowell Sherman sneaking out of a room with a woman, both dressed only in underwear, and another underdressed man chasing a lingerie-clad woman down the hall. Whatever her veracity, Keza at least fleshed out the "orgy" aspects of the story.

The state saved its only direct evidence for its dramatic conclusion. For Edward O. Heinrich's presentation, the door leading from 1219 to the hallway was brought into the courtroom. Heinrich explained that fingerprints on it belonged to Arbuckle and Rappe, aligned in a manner that indicated the former had pressed the latter's hand against the door, as if she was trying to leave and he prevented her exit. The state rested its case.

As at the preliminary hearing, one witness was conspicuously absent from the state's roster: Bambina Maude Delmont, or, as the press repeatedly called her, somewhat sinisterly, "the avenger." In fact, Delmont was subpoenaed for the trial, and she attended as a spectator and dined with a state witness. Later, when the state called rebuttal witnesses, a front-page headline would scream, "AVENGER" MAY TESTIFY AGAINST ARBUCKLE, and the accompanying story would say that she "hovered behind the closing scenes of the Arbuckle trial today, the one remaining mysterious figure of the case."

The avenger was destined to remain mysterious, but the reason is no mystery. The defense had spent much of its resources investigating her past, and in addition to the Earl Lynn extortion charge, they supposedly uncovered numerous instances of fraud, unpaid debts, and petty crimes. The defense was prepared to present Delmont as a con artist whose latest and greatest victim was Roscoe Arbuckle. Brady was surely wary of putting her on the stand before a hungry defense team eager to dredge up her past, especially after her poor performance at the coroner's inquest, but his decision was made easy when her past intruded on her present.

An investigation had begun in late September in Madera, California, and on the first day of testimony in the Arbuckle trial, a formal complaint was filed. Brady delayed the matter in case he needed Delmont to take the stand, though the chances of that had shrunk from slim to infinitesimal. On December 2, just after the Arbuckle trial went to the jury, Delmont would be arrested in San Francisco, charged with bigamy. After separating from John Hopper in 1914, she had never finalized their divorce before marrying Cassius Woods seven years later.* When she pleaded guilty to bigamy on December 10 and was sentenced to one year's probation, it was front-page news throughout the country. Upon her arrest, she gave her name as "Mrs. Bambina Maude Delmont Hopper." Occupation: "actress."

Much of the press coverage of the trial focused on Arbuckle's reaction to testimony. The *Los Angeles Times* repeatedly broke up the most dramatic parts of Friedman's opening statement to cut to the defendant's nervous tics:

- "Arbuckle dug into his pocket, extracted a gold pencil and began to play with it, his eyes gazing downward."
- "Arbuckle took an open letter from his pocket and began to scribble on it."
- "Arbuckle turned the envelope over and scribbled some more."
- "Arbuckle's eyes dropped and he ceased scribbling."
- "Arbuckle wrinkled his brow and squinted at Friedman."
- "Arbuckle was busily engaged tearing paper into tiny bits."

Often he was said to look disinterested, but when Prevost spoke of his applying ice to Rappe, he seemed to be purposefully distracting himself and perhaps other observers: "Arbuckle balanced his chair on two legs, leaned over and took a thumb tack from The Times' [*Los Angeles Times*'] section of the press table. . . . Arbuckle stuck his thumb with the tack, winced, and then the noon recess was declared."

If every mannerism of Arbuckle was news, so was every item of clothing worn by Minta Durfee. She and her mother sat behind the defendant, sometimes joined by his brother Arthur, and the daily outfit

* It would seem likely that Arbuckle's defense team uncovered this crime. If so, they left no fingerprints. The matter came to light when Hopper was granted an annulment of the marriage, at which time Delmont acknowledged consciously breaking the law when she married Woods.

of the estranged-yet-loyal wife demanded an exorbitant amount of news ink. On the second day of state testimony, the *San Francisco Examiner* noted, "There was but one feature of importance to yesterday's proceedings. Mrs. Minta Durfee Arbuckle wore her black velvet hat." Prevost and Blake were also covered as if models at a fashion show.

Female fashion was featured so prominently in newspapers because women were so enthralled by the case. In San Francisco, the trial was the hottest ticket (actually, a blue card) in town, and it was free. One report noted:

> Society women continue to make up the majority of spectators as the trial progresses. Seats are at a premium, and the little blue cards bearing the magic words of admission to the "scandal theater," are highly prized and sought after. The social register is not alone in seeking entrance, for there is a good sprinkling of everyday women. "I saw Fatty today," seems to be as much the topic of the drawing room as in the backyard gossip.

The trial was a chance for a Pacific Heights patrician as well as an Alameda housewife to learn all she wanted to know (and more than the newspapers could print) about Jazz Age coed booze parties and Hollywood's culture of excess.

One trial spectator specialized in the seamy side. Gouverneur Morris, the author of numerous crime stories and novels,* sat behind Arbuckle, near the two Durfees. The pulp writer was on assignment for the movie fan magazine *Screenland*, for which he would write an article sympathetic to Arbuckle that appeared in the November 1921 issue. Demonstrating how sensational even fan magazines got in the wake of the Arbuckle arrest, the next issue of *Screenland* asked on its cover, IS VIRGINIA RAPPE STILL ALIVE? Their answer was: sort of, as Rappe reportedly appeared "in a materialized form" at a seance and proclaimed Arbuckle's innocence.

---

* Gouverneur Morris was the great-grandson of the Founding Father of the same name, who is credited with writing much of the US Constitution. The younger Morris wrote the short stories "What Ho, the Cook," "You Can't Get Away with It," and "The Bride's Dead."

"The state has miserably failed to prove its case," Gavin McNab pronounced in his opening statement. Judge Louderback struck the assertion from the record and asked him to merely state what he intended to prove. Roscoe Arbuckle's innocence, McNab told the jury in many more words.

The defense's first witness was George Glennon, formerly the house detective at the St. Francis, to whom Rappe had supposedly made a statement absolving Arbuckle of guilt. The state's objection called the statement hearsay. The judge agreed, and Glennon was excused. (The defense tried and failed again another day to get Glennon on the record.) An elderly St. Francis maid, Kate Brennan, testified that she had dusted and thoroughly polished the door of room 1219 before Heinrich checked it for fingerprints.* A guest in 1218 stated that she was in her room all Labor Day and heard no screaming or moaning.

A local film producer, R. C. Harper, claimed to have been lurking in the hallway outside the twelfth-floor suite for thirty-five minutes starting at two thirty or two forty-five, during which time he heard no screaming and never saw Josephine Keza. According to his implausible story, he'd come with a business proposal for Arbuckle, a man he didn't know, only to grow bashful at the threshold and decide to linger in the hall in the hopes of ambushing the movie star instead—a plan he discarded after half an hour, all conveniently during the period most crucial to the defense's case. His testimony smacks of someone on the outskirts of the film industry attempting to ingratiate himself with those on the inside. In his closing argument, Friedman would ask of Harper, "Is it not an insult to one's intelligence to ask us to swallow a story like this?"

The next morning, by court order, the jury, judge, attorneys, and defendant briefly toured the three rooms in question on the top floor of the Hotel St. Francis. As closely as possible, the furniture and furnishings

* In the hours after the party, Arbuckle offered "girlie" (as he called Brennan) a generous tip of two dollars and fifty cents for cleaning the room. He also offered her whiskey. She refused the latter and accepted the former.

had been arranged to appear as they were on Labor Day. Arbuckle made no comment and was said to appear "thoughtful" as he strode through the interconnected rooms.

Back in court, the defense called Fred Fishback, who testified that Rappe was tearing at her clothes on a bed in 1219 when he returned to the party. "She was making a noise, but I don't know whether it was moaning or screaming or what sort of noise it was," he said. He demonstrated to the court how he lifted her to and from a cold bath, an act which may have bruised her—though it would've bruised the wrong arm. He also said that Rappe did not appear pained, an assertion the state challenged on cross-examination by introducing an unsigned statement from Fishback to the contrary. He claimed to have been misquoted. Dr. Olav Kaarboe supported Fishback by testifying that as the first doctor to examine Rappe, he too had found her unpained. Bladder expert Dr. Asa W. Collins stated that a spontaneous rupture was possible with a distended bladder, but under cross-examination he admitted such ruptures were very rare and he had never attended a patient suffering from one.

On Thanksgiving, Arbuckle, his wife, and his mother-in-law feasted on turkey stuffed with oysters at the house of his brother Arthur. The twelve jurors and one alternate walked in the cold rain to a restaurant. None of them saw a family member on that holiday. They were sequestered during the trial in rooms at the stately Hotel Manx, one block from the St. Francis. They were not allowed to read a newspaper, and their mail was inspected and, if necessary, censored. Their only diversion was the occasional group trip to a movie theater or restaurant, guarded always by four deputy sheriffs.

Three weeks earlier, Dr. Melville Rumwell had been arrested for the misdemeanor crime of performing an unauthorized autopsy on Rappe. (He was subsequently fined $500.) The day after Thanksgiving, he testified about his treatment of Rappe prior to her death. He said his patient did not recall what could have caused her injury.

Most of the other defense witnesses that day and the next broke into two categories: doctors who stated that distended bladders could spontaneously rupture and people who had previously seen Rappe in abdominal pain and/or tearing off clothing when intoxicated. In the latter group were:

- Irene Morgan, a nurse/housekeeper employed by Rappe when she lived with Henry Lehrman, who said Rappe had frequent bouts of abdominal pain and when drunk ripped off her clothes
- Minnie Neighbors, wife of a retired Los Angeles policeman, who told of seeing a pained Rappe at a hot springs spa the month before her death
- Harry Barker, who stated that he dated Rappe in Chicago from 1910 to 1915 and claimed to have seen her on several occasions "all doubled up and tearing at her clothes," but he was foggy on details*
- Florence Bates, a clerk at Mandel Brothers department store in Chicago in 1913, who said that during a two-week fashion exhibit in which Rappe was a model, she appeared pained and publicly tore off costly clothes three times
- Philo McCullough, a film actor, who told of Rappe bringing her own gin to a party at his Hollywood house and, after drinking, noisily removing her stockings and shirtwaist

The defense's emphasis on Rappe's alleged proclivity to strip in public served to tarnish her character, but other than perhaps bolstering the contention that she had a prior medical condition, it was otherwise irrelevant to Arbuckle's guilt or innocence. The state and defense agreed that

---

* Under cross-examination, Barker denied the contention that he had been engaged to Rappe and she had broken off the engagement. Three days later, Catherine Fox, a rebuttal witness for the state, would claim she witnessed Rappe breaking said engagement.

Rappe was clothed while alone with Arbuckle in 1219. Only afterward, when others were present, did she start to undress.

The defense called Edward O. Heinrich back to pummel his testimony and reputation, including a mocking jab at him for referring to himself as "Sherlock Holmes." They highlighted that Heinrich found Rappe's hairs between 1219's beds. They then called Ignatius McCarthy, former investigator with the US Department of Labor. McCarthy claimed the fingerprints on the door to 1219 were forgeries, but the state successfully challenged his credentials as a fingerprint expert, invalidating his testimony.

The defense had one final witness—the only living person who could testify from firsthand knowledge about the occurrences on Labor Day behind room 1219's locked door.

> Ten to six for acquittal. Those are the odds being offered on the outcome of the Arbuckle case. Considerable sums of money are being wagered at these odds at places in San Francisco.
>
> —"Arbuckles' [*sic*] Acquittal Looked For," *Painesville Telegraph* (Painesville, Ohio), November 28, 1921, front page

"Mr. Arbuckle, take the stand," attorney Gavin McNab said at 10:35 AM Monday, November 28, 1921. After the solemn movie star was sworn in, he squeezed into the wooden witness chair, and those who had been out in the hall conversing or smoking when Ignatius McCarthy's testimony was cut short rushed in for the feature presentation.

The grandfatherly McNab began guiding Arbuckle through the tale of how he came to be at a booze party of his own making attended by Virginia Rappe and other women (none invited by him, it was duly noted). His wife and mother-in-law smiled, and he seemed increasingly at ease as the story of a typical Prohibition party took shape. McNab then guided him out of 1220 and into 1219. Here is Arbuckle's version of what occurred in the room he shared with Fishback.*

"When I walked into 1219, I closed and locked the door, and I went straight to the bathroom and found Miss Rappe on the floor in front of the toilet, holding her stomach and moving around on the floor. She had been vomiting. I saw it in the bowl and there was the odor of it. When I opened the door [to the bathroom], the door struck her, and I had to slide in this way [*standing briefly to illustrate*], to get in, to get by her and get hold of her. Then I closed the door and picked her up. When I picked her up, I held her and she vomited again. I held her under the waist, like that [*standing briefly to illustrate*], and by the forehead, to keep her hair back off her face so she could vomit. When she finished, I put the seat down. Then I sat her down on it. She was gasping and had a hard time getting her breath. Later I asked her, 'Is there anything I can do for you?' She said, 'No, just leave me lie on the bed.' Before that I had given her two glasses of water."

He recounted how he helped her to the single bed in 1219. He lifted her feet off the floor and left her lying there as he returned to the bathroom.

"I came back into 1219 in about, well, I was there about two or three minutes, and I found Miss Rappe between the two beds rolling about on the floor and holding her stomach and crying and moaning, and I tried to pick her up, and I couldn't get hold of her. I couldn't get alongside of her to pick her up, so I pulled her into a sitting position [on his double bed]. She turned over on her left side and started to groan, and I immediately went out of 1219 to find Mrs. Delmont."

He claimed Delmont was not located right away, putting his version at odds with Prevost's version, which had Delmont kicking at 1219's door. When located, Delmont and Prevost went into 1219. Arbuckle followed. "[Rappe] was sitting on the bed, tearing her clothes; she pulled her dress up, tore her stockings; she had a black lace garter, and she tore

* McNab's questions have been eliminated here, for they merely propelled Arbuckle's story.

the lace off the garter. And Mr. Fishback came in about that time and asked the girls to stop her tearing her clothes. And I went over to her, and she was tearing the sleeve of her dress, and she had just one sleeve hanging by a few shreds—I don't know which one it was—and I said, 'All right, if you want that off, I'll take it off for you.' And I pulled it off for her. Then I went out of the room."

He returned to 1219 a short time later to find Rappe naked on the single bed. "I went in there, and Mrs. Delmont was rubbing [Rappe] with some ice. She had a lot of ice in a towel or a napkin or something and had it on the back of her neck, and she had another piece of ice and was rubbing Miss Rappe with it, massaging her. There was a piece of ice lying on Miss Rappe's body. I picked it up and said, 'What's this doing here?' [Delmont] says, 'Leave it here. I know how to take care of Virginia.' I put it back on Miss Rappe where I picked it up, and I started to cover Miss Rappe up, to pull the [bed]spread down from underneath her so I could cover her with it, and Mrs. Delmont told me to get out of the room and leave her alone, and I told Mrs. Delmont to shut up or I would throw her out of the window, and I went out of the room."

And thus Arbuckle dismissed the salacious business with the ice and, in confirming one of the more incriminating comments attributed to him, contended not that he was threatening to pitch Rappe out the twelfth-floor window but that his ire was directed instead at Delmont, the accuser who had not and would not be appearing at the trial to dispute Arbuckle's testimony. That said, because Rappe was naked at the time, Delmont ordering a man out of the room seems an appropriate response, and his remark seems unwarranted.

Arbuckle continued: "Mrs. Taube came in and telephoned for the hotel manager. I told Mrs. Delmont that the manager was coming up. Mr. Boyle, the manager, then came in. Mrs. Delmont and I put a bathrobe on Miss Rappe. We then took her around to room 1227. Mr. Boyle opened the door. I carried her part of the way. She seemed to have no life in her. I asked Mr. Boyle to boost her up in the middle. He took her out of my arms and into 1227."

McNab asked, "Was the door of 1219 [to the hallway] unlocked all day?"

"As far as I know it was," Arbuckle said. McNab also elicited from him that the window in the room was open and that he had raised the curtain himself.

"During the time you were in 1219," McNab then asked, "did you hear Miss Rappe say, 'You hurt me'?"

"No, sir, I heard nothing that could be understood."

"The next day or at any other time, did you talk with Mr. Semnacher regarding a piece of ice?"

"No, sir."

"While in 1219 with Miss Rappe, did you ever at any time place your hand over Miss Rappe's on the bedroom door?"

"No, sir."

"At any time of that day did your hand come in contact with her hand on the door?"

"No, sir."

"Have you ever had a conversation with Jesse Norgaard at a Culver City studio regarding the key to Miss Rappe's dressing room at the studio?"

"No, sir."

Then, after establishing that his client had nothing more to add, McNab, with a flourish of his hand, defiantly told the prosecution, "Cross-examine the witness."

Assistant DA Leo Friedman stood. Seated at the counsel's table, DA Brady frequently whispered strategy to Friedman as the cross-examination progressed. In answering Friedman's questions, Arbuckle again recounted early events at the party. Alcohol consumption was highlighted, including a boozy noon meal that Arbuckle called "breakfast for some, lunch for others." Then Friedman steered the accused into room 1219: "At 3:00 PM you decided to go into 1219 and get dressed. What was the first thing you did?"

"I locked the door," Arbuckle answered.

And on that cliffhanger, Judge Louderback halted the testimony for the noon recess. Dramatically, a female deputy coroner carried in a specimen jar that contained a prosecution exhibit: the ruptured bladder of Virginia Rappe.

After lunch, an animated Friedman hounded Arbuckle on the timeline of occurrences in 1219, trying to shake the defendant free of his contention that he was alone with Rappe for no more than ten minutes. Arbuckle stayed firm, eliciting his biggest laugh from observers when he answered how he knew the clock on the mantelpiece in 1220 was accurate: "Well, everything else in the hotel is pretty good. I suppose their clocks ought to be all right."

Having poked few holes in Arbuckle's tale, Friedman finished by attempting to dismantle the defense's characterization of Arbuckle as a Good Samaritan assisting the ailing Rappe: "Did you tell the hotel manager what had caused Miss Rappe's sickness?"

"No," Arbuckle replied. "How should I know what caused her sickness?"

"You didn't tell anybody you found her in the bathroom?"

"Nobody asked me," Arbuckle said.

"You didn't tell anybody you found her between the beds."

"Nobody asked me, I'm telling you."

"You never said anything to anybody except that Miss Rappe was sick?"

"Nope."

"Did you tell the doctor what caused Miss Rappe's illness?"

Arbuckle nearly rose from his seat. "No! How could I tell him what I didn't know!"

Friedman then established that Arbuckle had conveniently only told his version of what occurred in room 1219 to two people prior to that day—his lead attorneys, past and present.

The defendant spent four hours in the witness box before being excused. Some of his answers seemed false (he claimed to be unaware that Rappe, Blake, or Prevost were coming to the party), some seemed too convenient (he passed all the blame for procuring alcohol to Fishback), and some painted him as coarse or brazen (his cavalier attitude toward Rappe's nudity). But he had reframed the events in 1219 not as an assault but as an assist. Helping a sick person—and someone who was neither a relative nor a close friend—to vomit without soiling her hair would seem a grand act of altruism. There was thus a new image of Roscoe Arbuckle to compete with that of a savage beast and spoiled Hollywood playboy raping and fatally wounding an innocent beauty. It was the image of a man alone in a bathroom aiding and comforting a pained woman at her lowest.

After Arbuckle's testimony and over the prosecution's objection, the deposition of Dr. Maurice Rosenberg was read into the record. (He had been interviewed by defense attorney Brennan in Chicago.) Rosenberg stated that he treated Rappe in Chicago in 1913 for cystitis, a chronic inflamation of the bladder. After the deposition was read, the defense rested.

The next day, the state began calling rebuttal witnesses. Tellingly, they did not attempt to impeach Arbuckle's testimony. (The obvious witness to do so was Delmont, for the avenger had a very different version of what occurred in and about 1219.) Instead, they refocused on Rappe's health. Catherine Fox* of Chicago claimed to have known Rappe for twenty-two years but never knew her to be in pain or tearing her clothes or consuming alcohol. After Assistant DA U'Ren queried Fox for two hours, the defense posed but one question.

"Were you with Maude Bambina Delmont yesterday?" McNab asked her.

"Yes, I was with her all afternoon."

"That's all."

Others testified to Rappe's good physical health: the former assistant manager of the Hollywood Hotel, where Rappe had lived; a psychiatrist who had treated her; a chauffeur, a nurse, a director, a cameraman. A magazine publisher testified to hallway lurker R. C. Harper's bad reputation, though it would seem Harper's improbable testimony had accom-

* Actual name: Dot Nelson.

plished as much. Harry Boyle stated that 1219 had not been occupied since Arbuckle checked out, and Edward Heinrich returned to detail all the dust and hairs he found in 1219, thus arguing against Kate Brennan's contention that she had thoroughly cleaned the room before he entered it.

In what branched off into its own sideplot, a clerk at the hot springs where Minnie Neighbors told of seeing a pained Rappe said she did not remember Rappe, and she produced the spa's register, which lacked Rappe's name. Likewise, Kate Hardebeck returned to say her "niece" had not been away in August. Before the day was over, Brady had Neighbors arrested for felony perjury. The next day, the defense called a hot springs attendant who remembered renting a bathing cap to Rappe and speaking to Neighbors about her; they then recalled the hot springs' clerk to demonstrate that her memory of guests was fallible. Countering, the state introduced the hot springs' swimwear rental book, which lacked Rappe's name. Around and around they went.

The final witnesses in the trial were three MDs who had been appointed by the court nine days prior to microscopically examine Rappe's bladder. The panel's findings: Rappe had suffered from a lingering case of cystitis. It was a rather ambiguous diagnosis, for it failed to determine how long she had suffered or the severity of the symptoms (which can vary greatly), and none of the doctors could say with certainty that cystitis predisposed her bladder to rupture. They did dispense with a defense theory that she may have had a partial tear prior to the deadly rupture. However, the defense interpreted Rappe's prior medical condition as confirmation of the testimony about her abdominal pains and of a bladder disease that dated back, at least, to Dr. Rosenberg's diagnosis in 1913. The defense offered to go to the jury without either side giving closing arguments. The prosecution refused.

Even odder than the subplot of Minnie Neighbors is the one centered on Irene Morgan, who testified to Rappe's frequent fits of agony and proclivity for public stripping. The state had attempted to impeach her by proving she lied under oath when she claimed to have served as a Canadian military nurse in World War I. After she was recalled to the stand and grilled by the prosecution, U'Ren promised to further investigate with the threat that she faced a potential perjury charge. "If there is a case against Miss Morgan and it is no stronger than their case against Mrs. Neighbors, then they are welcome to go ahead," McNab quipped.

During closing statements, Cohen would break the shocking news that Morgan had been poisoned by "a tall, gray-haired official-looking man" she claimed to have seen in the courtroom the day before and who subsequently hounded her at a dance hall. Incredibly, she had agreed to walk about the city with him, and during that time he gave her two pieces of candy. After she ate them, she grew dizzy, and the man allegedly said, "Go to hell. You're done for. You've made others suffer; now suffer yourself." She was found unconscious in her hotel room, and the hotel physician deduced she had been poisoned with opiates. It all seemed ludicrous and suspiciously timed to avoid a perjury charge. In his closing statement, McNab would call her "a heroine, wounded in battle." Brady promised, facetiously, the entire police force would be enlisted to find the perpetrator of the alleged crime. The poisoning of Irene Morgan remains unsolved. Moral of the story: don't take candy from strangers.

"At the expiration of thirteen days, it devolves upon the people to present facts against Arbuckle. We are here to try Roscoe Arbuckle—not Roscoe Arbuckle the comedian, not Roscoe Arbuckle the hero of a thousand laughs, nor Roscoe Arbuckle the nationally known figure, but Roscoe Arbuckle the man." So began the state's closing argument, as delivered by Leo Friedman. He contrasted the story of what occurred in the twelfth-floor suite as told by prosecution witnesses—especially Prevost, who saw Arbuckle follow Rappe into 1219 and Delmont kicking at the door—with the benign story told by Arbuckle. He explained that none of the physicians who testified had ever seen a case in which injuries similar to Rappe's developed without the application of external force. He pointed to the physical evidence: Rappe's bruises and, most especially, Arbuckle's fingerprints over Rappe's on the door ("That fact alone is sufficient to say Arbuckle is guilty"). He challenged the veracity of defense witnesses.

Friedman laid out the state's version of what caused Rappe's bladder to rupture. He contended that Arbuckle followed Rappe into 1219, closed and locked the door. Rappe was standing near the bathroom. She tried to get away from him, rushing to the door that led to the hallway. He pulled her away from that door and threw her on the double bed. He then threw himself on top of her, intending to sexually assault her, but when his body met hers, her distended bladder ruptured and she passed out (the result of a sudden loss of blood pressure initiated by her bladder rupture). He then successfully revived her.

Friedman also ridiculed various theories put forward by the defense: "The theory that the rupture may have been caused by dipping the girl in a tub of cold water, a defense theory until Dr. [Franklin] Shields pulled the plug and let that theory go into the sewer. The theory that the rupture may have been caused by vomiting. Where in this entire case, other than the defendant's testimony, has been shown evidence that Miss Rappe was vomiting? The theory that falling off a bed may have caused it, contained only in the defendant's story. A theory here and a theory there with the evident purpose of confusing the minds of the jurors. Fact by fact has been brought here to refute all these theories."

Growing animated, Friedman lambasted Arbuckle, who was gazing downward, sometimes fidgeting with his tie. Seated behind her husband, Durfee held a small bouquet of violets in one hand and smelling salts in the other, and as the *Los Angeles Times* noted, "She alternated their journeys between her lap and her nostrils." Asked Friedman, "The big, kind-hearted comedian who has made the whole world laugh—did he say, 'Get a doctor for the suffering girl'? No. He said, 'Shut up, or I'll throw you out the window.' He was not content to stop at throwing her out the window. He attempted to make sport with her body by placing ice on her. This man then and there proved himself guilty of this offense. That act shows to you the mental makeup of Roscoe Arbuckle. . . . I say there was a struggle in 1219. Roscoe Arbuckle tried and succeeded in keeping her there. I leave it to you what was the purpose of his attack upon her.

The rupture that caused her death was caused by no other manner than by the assault Roscoe Arbuckle made upon her!"

Gavin McNab began the defense's closing by bolstering their allegedly poisoned witness Irene Morgan—then supposedly clinging to life—against the state's attacks upon her character ("Since Mary cradled Jesus in the manger, the name of woman has been a sacred thing"), thus placing the defense on the side of an injured woman. He noted the absence of the complaining witness: "It is not mercy that keeps Mrs. Delmont out of the case, because you witnessed the venom with which our case has been attacked." One by one, he dismissed the testimony of various prosecution witnesses. Of Semnacher's damning allegation that Arbuckle placed ice in Rappe's vagina, McNab labeled it "a collateral incident"—though in doing so he endorsed the prosecution's version of the icing.

Using clocks as props, he plotted out the timeline established by witnesses and asked when an attack could have occurred. He compared Heinrich's fingerprint evidence to a belief in witchcraft. He asked why the healthy, athletic woman presented by the prosecution could not even manage a shout if assaulted. By reading their conflicting statements and testimony, he questioned the veracity of the "imprisoned girls," Prevost and Blake, and he further argued that just as Brady had taken away their liberty he might do the same to an innocent man. He asked, really laying it on, "We sent two million men overseas to end this sort of thing forever. Why should we allow it to continue in San Francisco?"

McNab postulated that there were many ways Rappe's bladder could have ruptured before or after Arbuckle entered 1219. His strongest theories were that the trauma was caused by the strain of vomiting (though there was no evidence of her vomiting) or via a fall in the bathroom or off the bed. He summarized: "The prosecution has painted Arbuckle as a monster, yet we see him carrying Miss Rappe in his own arms to a place of comfort [room 1227]. He was in the room [1219] alone with Miss Rappe but ten minutes, and during that time there was no outcry or sound of a struggle. I gather these facts from prosecution evidence. The scientific men we produced said there were many ways in which Miss

Rappe could have suffered her fatal injury. Surely the jury must admit there were many ways also rather than the one way pointed out by the prosecution."

Concluding with Christian imagery as he began, McNab wrangled a tear from his eye, and from the eye of at least one juror: "Since Christ said 'Suffer little children to come unto me,' the instinct of little children has always gone out to good men, never to bad, and Arbuckle has been crucified here by speech but not by evidence. . . . This man who has sweetened human existence by the laughter of millions and millions of innocent children comes before you with the simple story of a frank, open-hearted, big American and submits the facts of this case to your hands."

It returned to the state to get the final word, and Milton U'Ren drew a tortured biblical parallel of his own (echoing Arbuckle ally Billy Sunday): "He came up here and the word was sent out by his friend Fishback that Fatty was in town, and the people poured into his quarters, food was spread, drinks were served, and this modern Belshazzar sat upon his throne and was surrounded by his lords and their ladies, and they went on with the music, feasting, wine, liquor, song, and dancing. The great Belshazzar saw the handwriting on the wall and quaked as it was interpreted. The modern King Belshazzar has also seen the handwriting on the wall. The king is dead and his kingdom is divided. He will never make the world laugh again."

For an hour, U'Ren summarized the state's case, placing particular emphasis on the fingerprints. He repeatedly countered McNab's evocation of innocent children, presenting Arbuckle as a deceiver of young people who hid his "rotten nature." U'Ren sneered, "Oh, if the children of America could have seen Roscoe Arbuckle put ice in the private parts of Virginia Rappe, how they and their mothers would have laughed with glee!" In conclusion: "We ask you to do your duty so that when you return to your families, you can take them to your breasts; and we ask you to do your duties so that when you take your children upon your knees that you will know that you have done what you could to protect them from this defendant and from all the other Arbuckles in the world, not existing and yet to come. And ask you to do your duty so that this man and all the Arbuckles of the world will know that the motherhood of America is not their plaything."

> It is considered a forgone conclusion that Arbuckle will be acquitted.
> —UP WIRE STORY, DECEMBER 2, 1921

With final instructions from Judge Louderback, the case went to the jury at 4:15 PM on Friday, December 2. While seven men and five women deliberated behind a closed door, Arbuckle was in the courtroom, pacing or chatting with his attorneys or the newsmen. His wife sat nervously between the comforting wives of Arthur Arbuckle and Milton Cohen. The jury broke for dinner and resumed deliberations thereafter. Several times a bailiff was called into the jury room, eliciting a flurry of whispers among observers but no verdict.

At 11:00 PM court was adjourned. Word leaked that the jurors were deadlocked eleven to one for acquittal. In fact, it was later learned that early ballots had gone nine to three for acquittal or eight to three with one abstention, but the image of a lone juror, a woman, standing firm for Arbuckle's guilt took hold over the weekend with headlines like the *San Francisco Examiner*'s WOMAN VOTES ACTOR GUILTY SAYS REPORT.

On Saturday the jury continued deliberating. The women who packed the courtroom saw Arbuckle joking with reporters, attorneys, and bailiffs, chatting with the alternate juror, smoking, eating, reading newspapers, and performing magic tricks. Hours dragged on. The jury adjourned at 10:37 PM, and Judge Louderback ordered them back at 10:00 the following morning.

Though the sequestered jury was kept away from newspapers during the trial, their names, occupations, and addresses appeared in the same papers they couldn't read, as did a group photo of them posed in the jury box. Curiously, one person hid when that photo was snapped, ducking to reveal only the top of her black hat. As the jury remained deadlocked on Saturday, that juror—Helen Hubbard, the forty-six-year-old wife of an attorney—grew internationally famous as the "lone holdout."

On Sunday morning, while the jury deliberated for its final two hours, Arbuckle played hide-and-seek with a child in the corridors. It was as if he was reverting back to a time before he was rich and famous, back eleven years to when he played daily with his brother-in-law and neighborhood kids in a Los Angeles street. At noon, nearly forty-four hours after the trial went to the jury, the jury was declared hopelessly hung. The tally of the final ballot was ten to two for acquittal. Hubbard had been joined, as she frequently was on ballots, by fifty-four-year-old candy shop owner Thomas Kilkenny, the former alternate juror who had only been seated after one of the original twelve admitted a bias toward Arbuckle's innocence.

"We had some wild times in the jury room," one of the ten said of the heated attempts to convince the stubborn two to side with them. "We felt the case had not been sufficiently proved," another said. "Some of the jurors believed that Arbuckle was innocent, others believed that not enough proof had been presented to warrant a conviction." The jury foreman, August Fritze, a sales manager, released a statement that read in part:

> The ten members of the jury who voted on the last ballot for acquittal felt that they voted on the evidence—fully considering it all. One of the two minority refused to consider the evidence from the beginning and said at the opening of the proceedings that she would cast her ballot and would not change it until hell froze over. The other was fluctuating, sometimes casting a blank ballot, sometimes voting for the defense and sometimes for the prosecution.

The fluctuating Kilkenny never spoke to the press and quickly faded into history. It was reported that he voted with Hubbard in an effort to win her confidence and thus convince her to change her vote to one for acquittal, but that seems illogical. More likely, he didn't fit the press's narrative; their arc light was aimed at the intractable Hubbard. A typical front-page headline read, WOMAN JUROR BLOCKS AGREEMENT IN TRIAL OF ROSCOE ARBUCKLE.

Hubbard granted one interview to two female reporters, one with the *San Francisco Chronicle*, the other with the *San Francisco Examiner*. Because she was married to an attorney, she expressed her surprise at being allowed to serve. She felt she did not need to read through the over thirteen hundred pages of trial transcripts nor review the evidence in the jury room, for she had heard the evidence presented firsthand. "It was the matter of fingerprints purely in the final analysis that decided me," she said. "Arbuckle failed to convince me with his story absolutely. Once on a jury I would vote my own husband guilty if I really believed him to be that in my heart, and nothing could shake me once that belief was established in my mind." She reserved her harshest criticism for Fritze and the other men on the jury, whom she accused of verbal abuse in attempting to cajole her to change her vote. "There is no place for the woman on the jury," Hubbard lamented. "Any woman is a fool to even get on one if she can possibly get out of serving. I'd rather die than go through it again. The general attitude and language of the men is offensive to a woman."*

Male editorial writers agreed with her general proposition that women should not serve on juries. The *San Francisco Chronicle* opined, "The jury was subjected to indignities which could not have failed to affront any woman. Certainly a woman's mind and body are less well equipped to withstand strains to which they are put in cases of this character." Rappe's hometown *Chicago Tribune* concurred: "It is a fair presumption that the cause of exact justice was injured by the presence of women on the Arbuckle jury. A woman might have to overcome her aversion for a man charged with immorality before she could get anywhere near the issue of whether he was guilty of manslaughter."

The Women's Vigilant Committee praised Hubbard's independence. They also chastised Arbuckle, though in a subdued tone: "Regardless of

---

* Mrs. Hubbard also told the DA's office that two men known to her husband had phoned Mr. Hubbard on the final night of deliberation and urged him to tell his sequestered wife to vote for Arbuckle's acquittal.

the guilt or innocence of this defendant, this committee wishes he had shown more humility at the end of his trial. He admitted that he had staged a drinking and dancing party."

Upon hearing of the jury's indecision, Arbuckle rolled another brown cigarette. His wife dabbed away tears. And when the date of January 9 was agreed upon for a retrial, Arbuckle lit the cigarette, inhaled, and exhaled smoke.

Assistant DA U'Ren offered his hand to McNab. "I just want to congratulate your client on his gameness."

Standing nearby, Arbuckle retorted, "I'm game because my conscience is clear, much clearer than yours, U'Ren."

Afterward, as Arbuckle and his attorneys drafted up a statement, Minta Durfee stood with her mother and friends outside the San Francisco Hall of Justice. "The poor boy," she said. "Now he'll have to go through it all again."

Arbuckle's posttrial statement read:

> While this is not a legal acquittal, through a technicality of the law, I feel it is a moral one. But for one woman on the jury of thirteen, who refused to allow her fellow jurors to discuss the evidence or to reason with her, and who would give no explanation for her attitude, my trial would have resulted in an immediate acquittal.* After the organized propaganda designed to make the securing of an impartial jury an impossibility and to prevent my obtaining a fair trial, I feel grateful for this message from the juror to the American people. This comes, too, after the jury had heard only part of

* The alternate was counted in the tally of thirteen jurors, as that man stated he would have voted for acquittal. The tally also failed to count Kilkenny with Hubbard, helping to perpetuate the image of the lone, biased female juror. This statement was released before Hubbard granted an interview, thus the remark about her lack of "explanation for her attitude."

the facts. The effect of the District Attorney succeeded in excluding from the evidence statements made by Miss Rappe to people of high character, statements completely exonerating me.

The undisputed and uncontradicted testimony established that my only connection with this sad affair was one of a merciful service, and the fact that ordinary human kindness should have brought upon me this tragedy seems a cruel wrong. I sought to bring joy and gladness and merriment into the world, and why this great misfortune should have fallen upon me is a mystery that only God can reveal. I have always rested my cause in a profound belief in divine justice and in the confidence of the great heart and fairness of the American people. I want to thank the multitudes from all over the world who have telegraphed and written me in my sorrow and expressed their utmost confidence in my innocence, and I assure them no act of mine ever has or ever shall cause them to regret their faith in me.

{15}

OVERTURE: 1921

> But yet I know them. They have forced my barriers. Fatty Arbuckle, Elmo the Mighty, Mary Pickford, Norma Talmadge, Theda Bara . . . I know them by sight. They live with me. They eat their meals beside me.
>
> —Philip Curtiss, "Is Fame Becoming Extinct?"

It was the worst of times. The shock of peace sent America's economy into a nosedive. Manufacturing had ramped up during World War I and the armed forces employed millions, but afterward factories closed and returning men flooded an overwhelmed job market. After a mild recession, a depression hit at the start of 1920 and lingered for eighteen months. The stock market gave up nearly half its value. Deflation was the most acute in American history. Unemployment peaked at nearly 12 percent.

And it was the best of times. Eight hundred fifty-four feature films were produced by Hollywood studios in 1921, more than in any other year before or since; by 1922 nearly 40 percent of Americans would go to the movies every week. They saw *The Kid*, Charlie Chaplin's first feature; *The Four Horsemen of the Apocalypse*, a box office smash that launched a tango craze and Rudolph Valentino's career; Mary Pickford playing the titular boy (and his mother) in *Little Lord Fauntleroy*; Douglas Fairbanks at his swashbuckling best in *The Three Musketeers*; Lillian Gish in

Roscoe Arbuckle and Charlie Chaplin as two drunks in a sinking rowboat at the end of *The Rounders* (1914).

Luke the dog, Arbuckle, and Mabel Normand in *Fatty and Mabel Adrift* (1916).

Left to right: Buster Keaton, Arbuckle, and Al St. John in a publicity photo for *Back Stage* (1919). Arbuckle is dressed in his best-known costume: flannel shirt, suspenders, baggy pants worn too high, undersized bowler.

Poster for *The Round Up* (1920), Arbuckle's first feature.

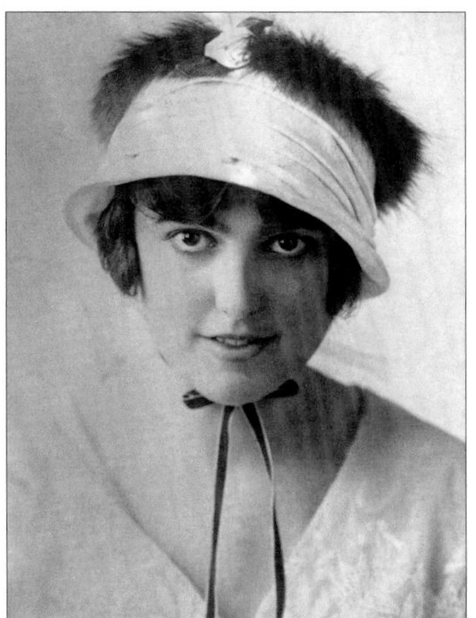

Virginia Rappe.

Rappe modeling an outfit of her own design, circa 1915.

The Hotel St. Francis. Arbuckle's suite is visible on the top floor of the leftmost wing. At the upper left corner of the facade is one window of room 1220; to its right are two windows of room 1221. Room 1219 is out of view on the left side of the building.
San Francisco History Center, San Francisco Public Library

Arbuckle's mug shots after being arrested for the murder of Virginia Rappe, just before midnight on September 10, 1921.

The preliminary hearing. Seated at the table, left to right: defense attorney Frank Dominguez, Assistant DA Milton U'Ren, and District Attorney Matthew Brady. Arbuckle is seated behind the lawyers, between U'Ren and Brady.

Arbuckle and wife Minta Durfee in court on September 28, 1921, the final day of the preliminary hearing, when the judge announced that Arbuckle would be tried for manslaughter.

Arbuckle and his defense team on November 18, 1921, the opening day of the first trial. Left to right: Nat Schmulowitz, Milton Cohen, Gavin McNab (standing), Arbuckle, Charles Brennan (standing), Joseph McInerney. *Library of Congress*

Will Hays, the man charged with cleaning up Hollywood in the aftermath of the Arbuckle scandal. *Library of Congress*

Arbuckle's second wife, Doris Deane, in 1925. *Los Angeles Public Library Photo Collection*

Arbuckle directing, circa 1931.

Arbuckle with his third wife, Addie McPhail, in 1932. *Los Angeles Public Library Photo Collection*

D. W. Griffith's last major commercial success, *Orphans of the Storm*; and a whopping five feature films from Roscoe "Fatty" Arbuckle, a tally that would have been even greater if not for a Labor Day spent in San Francisco.

The movies were where Americans went to dream together, to forget their tenement flats and bleak employment prospects. They laughed when the Little Tramp and the kid were chased by a giant policeman. They cheered when the impoverished American boy (played by a woman) learned he was to be an English lord, or when the dueling musketeer did an astonishing one-handed handspring. And they grinned when Fatty was bequeathed $5 million—with a catch.

And when they left the theater, many of them bought the latest issue of *Photoplay* or one of the other movie magazines populating newsstands. The dream continued, page by page, by the light of an oil lamp or an incandescent bulb. They were comforted by the knowledge that their favorite stars were living lives of opulence in the perpetual summertime of Southern California—the lavish paydays and parties and mansions and servants, the charity balls, high fashion, international trips, practical jokes, the blissful days of pretending. Movie stars were America's royalty, and Americans watched their royalty with rapt attention.

In late September 1921, during the depths of Arbuckle's revilement, New York society columnist O. O. McIntyre would remember a day earlier in the year when the superstar was returning from an East Coast promotional tour. The reminiscence provided a rare, PR-free portrait of Arbuckle at the apex of his fame and fortune:

> Last March I traveled on the same train with Arbuckle from New York to Los Angeles. I had never met him before. There were only about 20 people aboard and of course the comedian was the center of attention. He took a special fancy to my dog and would have the chef especially prepare pork chops for him. He struck me as a bewildered boy. Success had come too quickly. He appears more

> youthful than the photographs show. His type in our town used to live in the unpainted houses along the railroad tracks, their mothers eternally hidden away in damp kitchens. His clothes were gaudy and he wolfed his food like a starving beast.
>
> When the train stopped and we stretched our cramped limbs in the small towns of Kansas, Colorado and Arizona crowds gaped at Arbuckle, but he seemed quite unconscious of it. The most of his time was spent organizing crap games among the Negro waiters in the dining car.

Arbuckle did like his flashy suits, and he may indeed have been bewildered by his great success, though that would seem difficult for a new acquaintance to perceive. (McIntyre may have assumed it because he himself was bewildered by the immense fame and fortune of movie stars.) Still, the anecdote leaves the distinct impression of a down-to-earth celebrity who cared more about a dog and the train's waiters than the attention his fame brought. Twelve years later, McIntyre would recall that trip again, and the time he spent, silently, alone with Arbuckle on the train's observation platform while crossing an Arizona desert painted iridescent: "Under the prismatic spell of the dying splendor he sat rigid until the landscape was eclipsed by dusk. The train lights came on. He was wiping away a tear hurriedly, clumsily. . . . He loved the sunset."

> While most of us are struggling to lay a few dollars on a shelf for a rainy day, along comes a fellow who suddenly receives a gift of a million dollars. No sooner has he recovered from the shock of that surprise than another interested party offers him five million if he will spend the other kind gentleman's donation within a year and is broke at the end of that time.
>
> —From a notice for *Brewster's Millions*

> For His Uncle Samuel, He Worked for a Dollar but Sh-h-h! Fatty's a Deteck-ativ!
>
> —Newspaper advertisement for *The Dollar-a-Year Man*

> Did you ever hear of slapstick drama? Neither did we until Roscoe Arbuckle introduced it, and most successfully in his recent vehicles. He has opened up a field particularly well suited to his talent, and should win over many who have scorned his custard-pie offerings of the past.
>
> —FROM A REVIEW OF *THE TRAVELING SALESMAN*

Arbuckle made four features in the first eight months of 1921. It is oft said the last three were shot without a break, and thus he was in great need of a vacation by Labor Day weekend, but this is a falsehood perpetuated by his supporters.* *Brewster's Millions*, *The Dollar-a-Year Man*, and *The Traveling Salesman* were shot in 1920 with overlapping schedules and released in 1921. The four features produced in 1921—*Crazy to Marry*, *Gasoline Gus*, *Skirt Shy*, and *Freight Prepaid*—each had at least a three-week break between one production ending and another beginning, and three weeks had elapsed since wrapping *Freight Prepaid* when Arbuckle headed to San Francisco.

That's not to say that acting in nine five-reel feature films over twenty-one months was not an arduous schedule. It was. Chaplin made one six-reel feature and one two-reel short during the same period. But Arbuckle was neither writer nor director on any of the nine features, so his Paramount schedule was not as grueling as his workloads at Comique or Keystone when he was director, star, and (usually) writer or cowriter. "I can't sleep nights when I'm making one," he said of his previous experience directing films. "No, I'm going to let the other fellow [Chaplin] have the trouble of directing, and devote my time to thinking up original comedy touches."

Five of the final six features were directed by James Cruze; the lapsed Mormon and former snake oil salesman had launched a prolific acting and directing career in 1911. Paramount no doubt preferred the greater

* Writing of this "triple assignment" thirty-six years later, Jesse Lasky said, "It would be hard to imagine more strenuous work than making those old-fashioned lightning-paced comedies. I don't know of another star who would have submitted to such extortionate demands on his energy. But Fatty Arbuckle wasn't one to grumble. There were no temperamental displays in his repertoire. He went through the triple assignment like a whirling dervish."

output that Arbuckle, its prized attraction, generated by mostly focusing on his acting (he still consulted on writing, directing, and editing decisions). The studio was so flush with Fatty movies that *The Traveling Salesman* was not released until eleven months after production wrapped.

Though they were commercially successful, Arbuckle's features are not nearly as entertaining as his Comique shorts. Unlike Chaplin, he never found the right balance of drama and comedy to flesh out longer stories, but also unlike Chaplin, he was now dependent on the writing and directing of others. The feature-length comedy was just taking form, and thus it's likely the plotting of Arbuckle's efforts would have improved as the genre matured in the mid-1920s. He may even have made features comparable to the classics of Chaplin and Keaton—if he had gotten the chance.

So movie-mad was the public and so eager were the papers to report on the bigger-than-life Fatty that in April alone there were stories about his appearing at a Knights of Columbus charity benefit; about his merely posing for an acrobatic photo with Buster Keaton, Alice Lake, and Viola Dana; and about his writing a ten-word telegram to an actress jailed for speeding. The latter was part of a publicity coup like none before.

Reports of Arbuckle's recurrent speeding stops were a running joke in local newspapers. His luxurious automobiles weren't just for show; he drove them fast, especially on the then–sparsely traveled streets of Santa Monica. (Frequently, the policemen—astonished by his customized cars and his fame—let him go without even a warning.) But it was his friend Bebe Daniels who turned a lead foot into a cause célèbre. Though only twenty, Daniels was a film veteran. Previously the on-screen and (very young) offscreen romantic interest of Harold Lloyd, she was a fast-rising star at Paramount in 1921 when she was arrested in leisurely Orange County, California, for driving 56.5 miles per hour at a time when that was considered outrageously fast. Before the trial, Daniels taunted the judge by singing "Judge Cox Blues" at a benefit. For the March 28 jury trial, more than fifteen hundred spectators crowded the courthouse to catch a glimpse of the celebrity, who arrived in a limousine and wore a fur coat and veiled hat. She lost when Judge John Cox sentenced her to ten days in jail, but she won via the windfall of publicity.

On April 15 Daniels arrived at jail with a phalanx of luggage. The next day, a furniture store delivered a bedroom suite to her cell. Someone provided a Victrola and 150 records. Local musicians serenaded her. And guests arrived, 792 over the ten days, including numerous Hollywood celebrities (themselves earning publicity) and one new celeb, Judge Cox. Roscoe Arbuckle sent her a telegram, written for public amusement: "Dear Bebe, Houdini is in town. Can we help? Love."* Upon release, she began her next film, *The Speed Girl*, a comedic account of her ordeal. Six months before Arbuckle's arrest, the young Bebe Daniels showed how to use a trial and incarceration to her great advantage.† It was a lesson unique to her crime, though it did demonstrate how hungry the public was to view their favorite stars in three dimensions and actual size, as they were when they took an oath and testified.

In England, Arbuckle appeared in the movie-themed comic book *The Kinema Comic*, in his own weekly strip, "The Playful Pranks of Fatty Arbuckle." Strip titles hint at their slapstick plots: "A Whacking Good Stunt!" "Good 'Buoy'!" "He Felt Board!" They gave the distinctly American Fatty a stereotypically British accent. For example, in "A 'Neck'-straordinary Stunt!" after getting men to make stairs out of themselves and the sandwich boards they were wearing so he can sneak his girlfriend out of a second-floor window, Fatty says, "That's the style, my lads! That's the caper! Now, then, come along, Clara! Come forth! Trip down your sandwich-boards, and all shall be well. Cheerio!"

---

* Arbuckle was friends with Harry Houdini. The magician and escape artist had visited the set of *Back Stage*.

† In the September 1921 issue of *Vanity Fair* is a now-famous Ralph Barton caricature, "When the Five O'Clock Whistle Blows in Hollywood," which depicts filmdom's biggest stars leaving work. Charlie Chaplin, Buster Keaton, and Harold Lloyd are among the seventeen actors and actresses. Mabel Normand is missing, reflecting her fallen popularity. Bebe Daniels is present, and, as she is near the center in a dramatically striped dress, eyes are drawn to her—as well as to the giant form of Roscoe Arbuckle nearby. The caption for Daniels jokes, "Still wearing stripes after her recent imprisonment for speeding."

At home, Arbuckle continued his lavish spending; high-end consumerism was an addiction as comforting to him as mashed potatoes or gin. In addition to his tricked-out Pierce-Arrow, he filled his West Adams mansion's six-car garage with the best automobiles on the market: a Locomobile, a Rolls-Royce, a Cadillac, a Hudson, a Renault. They were painted in attention-grabbing colors. He bought more imported suits and shoes than could fit in his closets and more artwork than could hang on his many walls. He lavished expensive jewelry, perfume, and designer clothing on women. He threw extravagant parties. He bought on extended credit from merchants eager to say they'd sold to Fatty Arbuckle, a practice that later proved imprudent, and he made risky investments, which later devastated his financial security. He could never spend the money faster than it arrived, and it seemed it would arrive forever.

"Since he had made his fortune," his sister Nora said, "he had always been generous to his own people. He has done many kind things for me and my family and for my brother [Harry] in Fresno." Minta Durfee elaborated:

> I know of many cases: men who have persuaded him to give them money, girls with whom he was friendly who have actually made him a joke because it was so easy to get money away from him. . . . Ever since he was a boy—and he practically grew up with our family—Mr. Arbuckle has been careless with money. He never considered expense. Money simply meant the means of getting what he wanted, of enjoying himself, of helping other people. Incidentally, helping other people is the way a great deal of his money has gone. He has been most generous with me, ever since our separation. He has supported relatives. He has always been ready to help anyone who needed it. He has half a dozen pensioners about whom nobody but his own people know.

In public, he willingly played the clown, as was expected of him. At an American Society of Cinematographers ball, called "THE social event of the season," he stole the show. A *Photoplay* column noted:

> Roscoe Arbuckle helped lead the orchestra part of the evening and did very well, but his prize performance of the night, to my way of thinking, was the last dance, which he had with a lovely little Follies girl. The rotund comedian had had a hard day, apparently, the evening had been long—and rather wet—and Roscoe went to sleep on the floor, resting his head gently against his partner's rosy cheek and continuing to move his feet occasionally to the music.

On July 3 he was the biggest of the Hollywood stars at a charity rodeo on the expansive grounds of Pauline Frederick's Beverly Hills mansion (the same grounds he and Keaton had threatened to tear up for a practical joke). Keaton and his new bride, Natalie Talmadge, were there, as was the notorious vamp Alla Nazimova. Will Rogers and Tom Mix rode horses. *Photoplay* noted, "Roscoe Arbuckle—not being much of a horseman—nevertheless did his bit in a clever way by pretending to get caught in the middle of the ring. It took him some time to make his way out past the horses and he had the grandstand in convulsions by the time he arrived in his seat." He was forever the life of the party.

"'FATTY' NOT AT PARTY IN ROADHOUSE, read the July 13 headline in the *Los Angeles Times*, with "road-" standing in for "whore-" and Arbuckle connected with said party via his absence. The subhead read, "Lew [*sic*] Anger Says Arbuckle Did Not Go to Frolic That Caused Scandal." That scandal would, of course, be eclipsed two months later by a much greater one, but in mid-July the long-suppressed story of the Mishawum Manor "chicken and champagne orgy" of four years and four months earlier splashed onto front pages.

March 6, 1917, marked the last stop on the Paramount publicity tour celebrating Arbuckle's signing with the studio. After the dinner banquet at Boston's best hotel, where Arbuckle was the guest of honor, fifteen prominent attendees—including Jesse Lasky, Adolph Zukor, and Hiram Abrams—journeyed eleven miles north to the Mishawum Manor, a stately residence that had been converted into an upscale bordello. As he was traveling with his wife (shortly before their separation),

Arbuckle declined the invitation. Joseph Schenck also avoided the affair. The party was arranged by Abrams, Paramount's president, and overseen by Lillian Kingston, a madam who went by the name Brownie Kennedy, and it included fried chicken, fifty-two bottles of champagne (all allegedly consumed), and sixteen women (euphemistically called "actresses"). The *Providence News* reported, "The orgy was described as a drunken debauch, with much transpiring which is unfit to print." It began at midnight on March 7, and some men didn't leave until daylight. Abrams paid the bill of $1,050.

Two months later, Kingston was tried and convicted for keeping "a liquor nuisance" and a "house of ill fame," after the ill-famed house's female piano player and one of its prostitutes testified against her. She was fined one hundred dollars and sentenced to six months in prison; she appealed. Names of Paramount executives who'd attended the party appeared in Boston papers, and a story was mailed to the wife of one such exec. But that was merely the first, faint thunderclap of a potentially devastating storm. The husbands of two female participants and the father of another (a minor) hired lawyers to bring civil complaints against the film executives and press county DA Nathan Tufts to file criminal charges. Abrams hired Boston lawyer Daniel Coakley, who met with Tufts to steer the execs clear of the storm. This was accomplished via $100,000 in Paramount hush money and some company stock. Coakley made payments of between $7,000 and $16,500 to potential complainants in exchange for signed agreements stating they would not pursue the Paramount executives legally.* No charges were made, criminally or civilly, and the drunken debauch remained a New England story, quickly forgotten.†

And so it remained for four years and four months. Then, on July 11, 1921, the long-dormant tale exploded when a hearing was held in Boston to remove Tufts from office. Though none of the hush money

* Coakley admitted that between $31,000 and $32,000 was left after payments, and he said a member of his staff was paid $14,000.

† Upon appeal, Kingston pleaded guilty to the liquor charge and paid the hundred-dollar fine. The bordello charge was dismissed when the paid-off complainants refused to come forward again and it was established that Mishawum Manor was out of business.

was traced to him, that may have merely proved he was adept at covering the trail. Tufts was found in dereliction of his duty in not fully investigating potential crimes at the "orgy" and for conspiring with Coakley and with Kingston's attorney to extort the Paramount executives under the threat of indictments.* On October 1, 1921, three days after Arbuckle was released from jail on bail, the Massachusetts Supreme Court would release a ruling that removed Tufts from office.

The hush money kept Zukor, Lasky, and Abrams out of court in 1917, but in July 1921 it placed them at the heart of a widely reported legal scandal. This had three effects on the fate of Roscoe Arbuckle.

First, it primed Paramount to sever ties with him. In September 1921 Abrams was the managing director of United Artists, but Zukor and Lasky were the top executives at Paramount. The prior negative publicity resulting from their involvement in an "orgy" in a "roadhouse" compounded their distress when Paramount's biggest star was arrested for an "orgy" gone deadly. They left it to Schenck to support Arbuckle publicly while those at Paramount made no comment but suspended his contract and recast his planned movies. They wanted ticket buyers to stop associating Fatty with their studio. When the Tufts/Mishawum story broke, the press repeatedly referred to "Paramount executives." Two months later, mercifully from Zukor and Lasky's perspective, the press rarely referred to the arrested Arbuckle and Paramount together. Zukor and Lasky wanted that disassociation to continue.

Second, the story of motion picture heavyweights at an "orgy" in a "house of ill repute" whetted the public's appetite for more such tales. Hence September's orgy of orgy stories.

Finally, though the press was careful not to place Arbuckle at Mishawum Manor, the March 1917 affair was frequently described as a party in his honor. As the impeachment of Tufts stretched into October, Arbuckle was linked to two sex scandals simultaneously. What's more, the Mishawum Manor "orgy" narrative portrayed crass, outrageously wealthy visitors from Hollywood or Manhattan preying on poor, vulner-

* Coakley was disbarred on April 21, 1922.

able women and then enlisting lawyers to buy their way out of trouble. As reported, it seemed as if the movie industry big shots didn't think criminal laws or common morality applied to them, and this laid a treacherous foundation for the trials of Roscoe Arbuckle.

He was absent from Mishawum Manor. Still, was Arbuckle the sort of affluent celebrity who would willfully mistreat those occupying society's lower strata? It was a question with implications for his trials, for he had interacted in the hotel suite with chorus girls, a former corset maker, and a minor actress. The behind-the-scenes view of him on a train playing dice with the African American waiters would suggest he went out of his way to treat lowly workers as equals. In addition, he generously gave his time and money to charities. He helped friends and even some strangers in need—and friends and hangers-on who weren't in need. And he was an unusually big tipper whom waiters drew lots to serve.

But boorish behavior toward the "little people" need only express itself occasionally to indicate insensitivity. Such an occasion may have occurred in July, when Arbuckle was in Chicago shooting scenes for *Freight Prepaid* and staying downtown at the Congress Hotel. The following news story appeared seven weeks before Arbuckle's much more public arrest:

> "FATTY" ARBUCKLE $50 OUT AFTER HAVING REAL FIGHT
> Movie Funny Man Has Trouble with Bellboy and Forfeits Court Deposit
> Chicago, July 20 (Special)—Though the first reel was a riot, "Fatty" Arbuckle's latest feature, "Ouch, My Eyes," limped to a pepless finish in Police Court today. Arbuckle was to have stood trial on a disorderly charge lodged against him by Joe Greenberg, a bellboy at the Congress Hotel, who complained that "Fatty" hit him in the eye. "Fatty," it was alleged, had engaged the bellboy to do some work, but they could not agree on the wage. Words, as is the movie custom, were followed by blows. The bellboy got the worst of it, he

said. The judge heard Greenberg's story and forfeited the $50 bond put up by "Fatty" when the celebrity failed to appear.

On September 11, when every newspaper was screaming of Arbuckle's arrest for a murder in the final minutes of the day before, the *Los Angeles Examiner* published a very different version of the Congress Hotel story, which reads like a Keystone comedy come regrettably to life. The setting was the hotel's restaurant, Greenberg was recast as a waiter, and the plot revolved around Arbuckle entertaining his lunch mates by flattening one sandwich on Greenberg's head and whizzing another past his nose before smashing a platter of creamed chicken into the waiter's face in the manner of a custard pie. Outraged, Greenberg retrieved two policemen, but instead of a Kop chase, they escorted Arbuckle to the police station for booking. The conclusion remained unaltered: the movie star skipped his day in court, forfeiting fifty dollars.

In her August 8 gossip column, Louella Parsons referred to "the row [Arbuckle] had with a waiter in Chicago," thus giving some weight to the latter version, published a month later. The last account seems too outrageous, though, especially considering it occurred in a public setting but went unreported at the time. Regardless, a violent act was attributed to Arbuckle in another world-class hotel in another city. Was the incident, reported without Arbuckle's comment, an unfair representation even before the *Examiner* rewrite? Was it the result of a flair of anger for which Arbuckle felt genuine remorse, or did it reveal a superstar's contempt for the background players of his privileged life?

The preponderance of evidence suggests that Arbuckle paid an unusual amount of respect to the working class from which he came. (He had, after all, performed menial jobs in hotels himself as a youth.) At worst, whatever happened at the Congress Hotel seems akin to his drawer-throwing, table-kicking outburst with his wife in the Cumberland Hotel four years prior—a glimpse at Arbuckle's temper. Most of the time, the movie superstar was as blithe as one might expect of a man in his comfortable position, but he had never entirely shed his childhood insecurities—his feelings of unattractiveness and neglect, his need for familial love—and they could still fuel anger that would sometimes erupt.

In early August, newspaper advertisements for Omar cigarettes began appearing, depicting a hand holding a lit cigarette. A small caption read, "This is an actual photograph of Roscoe Arbuckle's hand holding an OMAR," while the slogan stated, "Good nature is evident in the way Roscoe 'Fatty' Arbuckle holds his OMAR." Omar was the American Tobacco Company's line of premium Turkish-blend cigarettes. For Arbuckle, a longtime smoker, the ads associated him with luxury—he was a glamourous movie star rather than a slapstick comic—but that association lasted little more than a month. The last Arbuckle/Omar ads ran on the weekend after Labor Day. Roscoe Arbuckle was the first American celebrity to have advertising halted on account of a scandal.

On Wednesday, August 31, three days before he headed north to San Francisco, Arbuckle was at the West Coast premiere of *The Three Musketeers*, starring his friend Douglas Fairbanks. The screening, attended by numerous Hollywood notables—including Bebe Daniels, Alla Nazimova, and Jesse Lasky—was held in downtown Los Angeles, and the audience of movie stars, moviemakers, and movie executives repeatedly broke into applause.

On September 4 the *Los Angeles Times* announced the local premiere of another film:

> "GASOLINE GUS ARBUCKLE SHOW AT GRAUMAN'S."
> Roscoe Arbuckle in "Gasoline Gus" . . . combined with several special attractions, ushers in Paramount Week in Los Angeles, beginning Monday.

Originally scheduled to appear at that opening, the star of *Gasoline Gus* had made other plans for Labor Day.

{16}

SECOND TRIAL

ARBUCKLE ABANDONS HOPE.

—*LOS ANGELES TIMES*, FEBRUARY 3, 1922, FRONT PAGE

During the month between the end of the first trial and the start of the second, Roscoe Arbuckle mostly stayed out of sight in his West Adams mansion, living with his no-longer-estranged wife. He granted an interview to the local press soon after returning from San Francisco, saying, "This case has put quite a crimp in my pocketbook. I resent the damage it has done me because I know I am innocent." He later told a reporter he was broke as a result of the first trial and his lack of income,* but he didn't mention that he'd bought Durfee a diamond-and-emerald brooch and a $1,000 jeweled purse for Christmas, both of which she would show off on the first day of the second trial. He also said he would never drink alcohol again and that he and Durfee were reunited for good: "My wife has proven that she is the one woman in the world for me, and I intend to keep her—if she'll let me; and I think she will."

Movie Weekly was sort of the *US Weekly* of the Jazz Age, with cover lines like "Confessions of a Movie Wardrobe Mistress," "What Is Hollywood Really Like?," and "The Convict Ship and the Movie Star." For its

* The press reported that the first trial cost Arbuckle $35,000 while his total loss during that period was "more than $100,000." Going by later estimates, both figures were low.

last two issues of 1921, it featured Arbuckle on both covers. First came "The True Story of My Husband" by Mrs. Minta Durfee Arbuckle, followed one week later by "Roscoe Arbuckle Tells His Own Story."

"As surely as God is above me, and I believe in Him very sincerely, I know that Roscoe Arbuckle did not do the thing for which he has been made to stand trial." So began Durfee's forty-five-hundred-word "true story" of her husband, which was surely composed by or with the defense team and intended to answer pressing questions regarding her marriage, the case, and Arbuckle's personality.

Motives for his accuser(s): "As a matter of fact, he has told me that he did complain of the actions of certain members of the party and told them that they were going too far. Perhaps that very thing aroused a spirit of revenge that was responsible for the charges made against him." She also said that with her husband's reputation for generosity and his poor money management, "it is no wonder he attracted people who were after him for what they could get, to put it bluntly."

Maude Delmont: Durfee said "Mrs. Delmont" was "really the only one to accuse Mr. Arbuckle directly" before stating how flimsy Delmont's story must be if the prosecution refused to put her on the stand.

Virginia Rappe: "The minute I saw her name in connection with the case it made me more sure than ever that my husband was being made the victim of circumstances." This was followed immediately by "I do not want to say anything against her."

His wearing pajamas at the party: "Not long before the trip to San Francisco, Mr. Arbuckle was accidentally burned with muriatic acid." She did not say where the burn was but only that he had to wear a "thick dressing" and the loose pajamas were more comfortable than other clothes. She also said the pajamas and robe covered him in thick material from ankles to neck.

His chasteness toward women: "I do want the women of the country to know that in spite of all the insinuations and ugly stories that have been circulated since this thing began, Roscoe Arbuckle is the most modest of men. . . . I never remember a single action or a single word that, by the farthest stretch of the imagination, could be called even immodest, to say nothing of vulgar or lewd." Durfee even added a morsel about their sex life: "It is an actual fact that in all the years I have been his wife, I have never seen him when he was not clothed."

Further on this theme: "All his life Arbuckle has been embarrassed by his size. He has believed that women could not like a fat man, and for that reason he has hesitated even more than might be natural about developing friendships among women. He is not the type of man who caresses a woman. If he likes a girl, he will tease her or make her presents or generally be nice to her, but he will never think of putting his hands on her. In fact, he carries it so far that it is almost an obsession."

It was a curious article, in part because she referred to her husband only once as "Roscoe" ("Roscoe has no great faults; that I know") and six times as "Roscoe Arbuckle" but a whopping twenty-four times as "Mr. Arbuckle," thus making it read more like a trial argument penned by his attorneys and less like a wife's portrait of her husband. The essay did deliver the sort of personal details about a marriage and a famous man that the readers of *Movie Weekly* doubtless coveted, but how many of those details were true is left in doubt.

In contrast, Arbuckle's three-thousand-word "own story," published the following week, focused primarily on what occurred in the twelfth-floor suite on Labor Day, and it clung to the same tale of his finding and aiding a sick Virginia Rappe that he told in court. That narrative was relayed with minimal emotion, while at other points he passionately portrayed himself as the victim of his accusers, the prosecutor, the press, and those fans who turned on him.

His accusers: "Whatever motive inspired the people who accused me, it was not knowledge that I had done the thing they said I did. It seems almost impossible to me that anyone could be so cruel and malicious as to make such terrible charges against a man without the most positive proof to support those charges, and yet that is what happened."

His wearing a bathrobe at the party: "I had arisen that morning about 11 o'clock and had put on my pajamas, bathrobe and slippers." One wonders why he would have to *put on* his pajamas upon waking; perhaps this was a simple misstatement. Nevertheless, his admission that he woke an hour before noon and continued to wear sleepwear when women arrived (because he did not anticipate those guests, he said) is a much weaker defense than his wife's acid-burn alibi, and thus is probably more truthful. As he made no mention of acid, it seems his "own story" was written without consulting Durfee's "true story."

The party's refreshments: "And by the way, the liquor which was served that afternoon was not mine."

Virginia Rappe: "All this talk of my having been infatuated with Miss Rappe or trying to 'get her' is absurd. I knew her for several years; we had worked at the same studios, and I had met her in other places, but that was absolutely all."

His marriage: "One really good thing has come out of all this trouble. It has been the means of reuniting my wife and myself after five years of separation. We are happy to be together again, and we have discovered that the things that kept us apart were very unimportant after all." By name, he referred to Durfee only once, and in that case he called her "Mrs. Arbuckle"—the surname she adopted only after his arrest.

In conclusion, he lamented his "great misfortune" in the same words he had used in his statement the day of the verdict. Arbuckle would have more to say on the subject shortly before the prosecution's opening statement in the second trial, speaking with reporters in a corridor of the San Francisco Hall of Justice: "It's not prison I'm afraid of. It's not the loss of fame or fortune. It is the loss of regard; the loss of affection, the fact that the kids may think I am guilty that hurts me. . . . Guilty? The law says a man is not guilty until he is proven so. But, my friend, let a man once be arrested and charged with a crime; let his name go broadcast in those first, cruel stories, regardless of fact, and he is branded guilty. . . . I have suffered. All I ask in repayment of the wrong done me is that the world which once loved me now withhold its judgement and give me a chance to prove before another jury that I am innocent."

Dashiell Hammett penned such hard-boiled classic novels as *The Maltese Falcon* and *The Thin Man*, but before he wrote about private eyes he was one. In January 1922 he was twenty-seven, a transplant from the East to San Francisco and nearing the end of his intermittent six years of employment with the Pinkerton National Detective Agency. The Pinkertons were hired by Arbuckle's defense team to find evidence and witnesses to aid their case, and Hammett was one such investigator.

The legendary author later recalled, "It was the day before the opening of the second absurd attempt to convict Roscoe Arbuckle of something. He came into the lobby [of the Hall of Justice]. He looked at me and I at him. His eyes were the eyes of a man who expected to be regarded as a monster but not yet inured to it. I made my gaze as contemptuous as I could. He glared at me, went on the elevator still glaring. It was amusing." Of the case itself, Hammett's conspiratorial assessment was worthy of a hard-boiled detective plot, the sort that might only be untangled by his creation Sam Spade: "The whole thing was a frame-up, arranged by some of the corrupt local newspaper boys. Arbuckle was good copy, so they set him up for a fall."

On January 11, 1922, jury selection for the second trial began in Judge Louderback's courtroom, while in a courtroom nearby, a remnant from the first trial was discarded. The perjury case against defense witness Minnie Neighbors had crept along for a month before a judge dismissed it.

Voir dire proved more difficult for the second manslaughter trial, because so many San Francisco residents had formed an opinion based on the overwhelming coverage of the initial trial. Seventy-nine potential jurors were questioned before both the defense and prosecution agreed on a panel of eleven men and one woman and two alternates (one man, one woman). The jury would again be sequestered in a hotel.

District Attorney Brady predicated the second trial on the grand jury's manslaughter indictment rather than the police court charge sworn to by Maude Delmont, hoping to sidestep criticism for not calling the avenger to the stand. The state began its case. Such familiar faces as Al Semnacher, Harry Boyle, Jesse Norgaard, Josephine Keza, Dr. W. Francis Wakefield, and Dr. Arthur Beardslee testified, reconstructing crucial events before, during, and after Labor Day.

The state's star witnesses remained showgirls Alice Blake and Zey Prevost, but neither had been a strong attestant in the first trial, and both proved hollow this time. The very definition of a reluctant witness, Blake spoke so softly in a morning session that all of her testimony was reread in the afternoon session. She recollected seeing Rappe and then Arbuckle go into 1219, Delmont demanding entrance, and Rappe saying, "He hurt me, he hurt me. I am dying," but on the imperative point of Arbuckle being in the room when Rappe made the assertion, Blake could not remember. "I don't recall" was her common, barely audible reply to numerous questions she had answered previously. A photo of her appeared in print under the heading HER MEMORY GONE with the caption "This is Alice Blake, who now, on the second trial of Fatty Arbuckle, forgets everything that happened at the famous party."

On cross-examination, McNab focused on Blake's time in protective custody, using the terms "incarcerated" and "impounded." "When did you escape?" McNab asked Blake, and, when laughter filled the courtroom, Judge Louderback ordered the bailiff to eject those responsible. "Well, what can you do when the lawyers furnish the comedy?" the bailiff replied.

Prevost was even less of an asset for the prosecution. On a day so cold in a building so poorly heated that the jurors were brought overcoats and a recess was granted because the court reporter's frigid fingers were stiff, the showgirl recanted her testimony from the first trial (as well as the grand jury and police court pretrial hearings) by stating she never heard Rappe say "He hurt me." When Assistant DA Friedman pressed her on her previous statements under oath, she answered, "I did not remember. I'm telling the truth now." To McNab, she explained that Brady's team wanted her to sign an affidavit stating that Rappe said, "I'm dying. He killed me," and when she refused she was placed in a cell and threatened with jail time before she finally signed, "He hurt me."

"I told Mr. U'Ren that I didn't remember Virginia saying anything of the kind, but that if he said that she had said it, it was all right."

District Attorney Brady asked the court to declare Prevost a hostile witness so the state could impeach her. Motion denied. The next day, the *New York Times* led with: "The case against Roscoe ('Fatty') Arbuckle seemingly went to pieces today during the examination of Miss Zey Prevost, a show girl, who had been one of the State's star witnesses." Rumors that Brady would drop the case in the wake of Prevost's testimony were denied. Instead, two days after Prevost's testimony, the state called to the stand the clerk who took Prevost's original statement. The defense objected. Sustained.

> SECOND ARBUCKLE SHOW FALLS FLAT; NOT SO WITH ACTOR
> The Roscoe Arbuckle manslaughter trial was rapidly losing its punch. Instead of the "thrill-a-minute" biggest show on earth affair which the first trial was, the big comedian's second appearance before the superior court degenerated into a heated, uninteresting battle of lawyers.
>
> Even the introduction of Virginia Rappe's riding habit Saturday failed to create interest. The crowd looked at it expectantly but seemed to recall that at the preliminary examination it didn't stop at the natty hat and trim dress, but paraded more thrilling things before the jury's and courtroom's eyes.
>
> —*MILWAUKEE JOURNAL*, JANUARY 22, 1922, FRONT PAGE

When Heinrich returned with the hallway door to room 1219 and explained the science of fingerprints, McNab again jabbed him for referencing himself as "Sherlock Holmes" and got him to admit fingerprints could be faked. Still, Heinrich insisted, "Any competent observer can tell the difference between forged and genuine prints."

Warden Woolard, the *Los Angeles Times* reporter who broke the news of Rappe's death to Arbuckle, testified that the actor denied having hurt Rappe but admitted he "pushed her down on the bed to keep her quiet" when she was in pain. Because of contradictions between Woolard's account of what Arbuckle said on September 9 (claiming he was never alone with Rappe) and Arbuckle's testimony at the first trial (claiming he assisted Rappe when they were alone together), the state had Arbuckle's entire testimony read into the record. This triggered the defense to announce it no longer needed to call Arbuckle to the stand.

The defense opened. In contrast to the first trial, in which they were unable to contradict Heinrich's testimony, this time the defense brought forth two experts: Adolph Juel and Milton Carlson. Again, the state challenged their credentials. Wrangling over Juel's expertise dragged on for an hour, despite the fact that he was employed as a fingerprint expert by the San Francisco Police Department and had testified as an expert witness in prior cases for the same district attorney's office that was now objecting to him. Eventually, both Juel and Carlson took the stand, expressing doubts that the prints on 1219's door were those of Arbuckle and Rappe.

Fred Fishback returned as a defense witness, and in cross-examination, he failed to remember certain answers he had previously given. An employee of Henry Lehrman's studio disputed Jesse Norgaard's contention that Arbuckle tried to get a key to Rappe's dressing room. Dr. Rosenberg's statement about treating Rappe in Chicago was again read, and other doctors testified that distended bladders could spontaneously rupture. As in the first trial, the defense tried unsuccessfully to get the St. Francis house detective's recollection of a conversation with Rappe into the record.

When elderly maid Kate Brennan returned to speak about thoroughly cleaning the room before Heinrich's inspections, she grew embroiled in a new legal subplot. The state petitioned to have her testimony stricken by presenting evidence that she spent 1909 to 1920 locked in an asylum because of mental illness and was never cured. The judge denied this request, but it allowed for future arguments about Brennan's mental faculties.

The defense claimed it wanted to call Irene Morgan, famous for her alleged poisoning, but had failed to locate her after three weeks of searching. It did recall Florence Bates, who retold tales of an agonized Rappe violently disrobing in a Chicago department store in 1913. New witnesses spoke of Rappe's painful past:

- Eugene Presbrey, screenwriter, said Rappe went into convulsions in the Hollywood Hotel in March 1917 after drinking two glasses of wine.

- J. M. Covington, café owner, said that Rappe and Henry Lehrman argued in his establishment in May 1918 and that after drinking liquor, the actress went outside "tearing her clothes and shrieking in pain."
- Helen Barrie testified to being at a party for "the eclipse of the moon" on April 22, 1921, at the house of a film director, and that after a few drinks "Miss Rappe threw herself down on a divan and tore at her clothing."
- Annie Portwell, resident of the Selma ranch where Semnacher, Delmont, and Rappe stopped on their journey to San Francisco, testified, "We were out riding in my car when Miss Rappe said, 'Please stop the car if you do not want me to die.' She left the car all doubled up and drank a quantity of dark-colored liquor from a gin bottle. She said it was herb tea." The bottle was introduced into evidence.

The defense called as its final witness the state's leading attack dog, Assistant DA Milton U'Ren, but the questions and answers pertained only to what U'Ren knew about the fingerprints on room 1219's door.

ARBUCKLE'S ACQUITTAL IS FREELY PREDICTED

That Roscoe (Fatty) Arbuckle will be acquitted of the manslaughter charge on which he is being tried for the second time is taken almost as a forgone conclusion in San Francisco. . . . In the opinion of most observers, the bottom fell out of the state's case when its three most important witnesses, Zey Prevost and Alice Blake, show girls, and Al Semnacher, manager of Miss Rappe, failed to remember many important details of Fatty's "gin jollification," despite the fact that they gave such testimony at the time of the first trial.

—*PITTSBURGH PRESS*, JANUARY 27, 1922, PAGE 14

The state began calling rebuttal witnesses. Two fingerprint experts affirmed that the prints on 1219's door belonged to Arbuckle and Rappe. The asylum superintendent confirmed that Kate Brennan had been an inmate. A doctor claimed that Rappe's bladder rupturing may have been unrelated to any previous condition. Kate Hardebeck said the brown liquid in the bottle was indeed tea, and she reaffirmed Rappe's "excellence of health"—a contention harmed when the defense got her to admit to Rappe's treatment by a doctor. Catherine Fox again testified to young Rappe's good health in Chicago, and five additional witnesses from Los Angeles spoke of Rappe's apparent vigor. The state called the assistant manager of Chicago's Mandel Brothers department store, who presented employment records showing that Florence Bates and Virginia Rappe were no longer working at the store when Rappe supposedly disrobed there in 1913. Recalled to the stand, Bates denied a 1910 employment application signature was hers, but the state countered with a handwriting expert who said it was.

Thus the second Arbuckle manslaughter trial sputtered to a close with wrangling over a twelve-year-old signature on a department store employment form. Even before then there were empty seats in the courtroom for a rerun of what had previously been the toughest ticket in town. The Women's Vigilant Committee was again vigilant, but in lesser numbers than before. On the final Saturday, Judge Louderback delayed the trial to conduct a wedding.

Part of the malaise was because the promise of greater scandal had dissipated. No longer did it seem likely you could hear fresh details—shocking evidence that would lead to a superstar's imprisonment. Newspapers highlighted weaknesses in the prosecution's case and predicted Arbuckle's acquittal. The defense seemed in a rush to its victory lap. It offered no counter to the state's rebuttal testimony, and, as in the first trial, it offered to present the case to the jury without any closing arguments. Again the prosecution declined, and four hours were assigned to each side for arguments.

Even if the machinations of the second Arbuckle trial had sometimes slipped off front pages, newspapers still needed to feed the public's newly stoked appetite for Hollywood scandal. On the final weekend before the case went to the jury, a large story appeared with the ungrammatical title NERO'S ORGIES RIVALED ON COAST FOLK. After first saying that the "madness" at the St. Francis party resulted in Rappe's death, it purported to tell "some of the things discovered first-hand by a recent visitor in Hollywood," including a two-day booze and gambling revel costing $10,000, "snow parties" (cocaine parties), and the following, presented under the subheading "When 'Fatty' Played Host":

> One night, some months ago, was called "Arbuckle Night" at the inn [Sunset Inn in Santa Monica, formerly Cafe Nat Goodwin]. As the Peruvian rum for which Arbuckle's cellars are famous warmed the crowd, a game of "strip" poker was called between "Fatty" and one of the men in the party. The star played a losing game from the first. His party screamed wildly when he bet his shirt on a hand and lost. Another chorus of screams went up when its removal revealed the star wearing a corset cover elaborately trimmed in lace and pink ribbons. There was another round of drinks. He lost. Then "Fatty" nonchalantly wagered his trousers. Just then the two policeman crowded in at the door and arrested him.
>
> Arbuckle paid his fine, slipped two bottles of Scotch whiskey into the policeman's pocket and carried his party off to Mountain Inn, a resort in Laurel Canyon, which the sheriff has since closed, to finish the night.
>
> Some said afterward that Arbuckle had staged the whole affair by way of entertainment, the arrest providing the thrill movie folks are constantly looking for.

In just a few days, those craving Hollywood scandal greater than PG-rated strip poker would get their wish.

Every seat in the courtroom filled as U'Ren began the state's closing argument. He attacked Arbuckle's testimony from the first trial. Of Blake and

Prevost, he said, "The defense charges that they were *processed* by the district attorney. From their attitude on the stand, they were certainly well prepared by the defense." He cut to the essence of what occurred behind the locked door to room 1219: "The ailment which the defense says resulted in Miss Virginia Rappe's death was of years' standing. It is strange that it should have reached its fatal climax while she was alone in a locked room with Arbuckle. The prosecution has blasted part of the truth out of the lips of Zey Prevost and Alice Blake. What the whole truth is, it is for you to determine. Virginia Rappe entered Arbuckle's room a well and vigorous girl. A few minutes later she was in a death agony."

U'Ren's ninety-six-minute argument was followed by a fifteen-minute recess, during which the defense team conferred. "Whatever you do is all right," Arbuckle said, rolling a cigarette as he walked away from his attorneys. The court was gaveled back into session. The defense team whispered with Arbuckle again before McNab rose and addressed the judge: "If the court please, we have decided that it is unnecessary for us to make an argument. We feel that the case is so simple that argument on it would but weary the jurors. We therefore submit it without argument."

Shocked murmurs.

The unusual strategy had the effect of cutting off the state's concluding rebuttal, for which it had surely saved its strongest arguments (and the state still had nearly two and a half hours on the clock), but it also rendered the defense mute aside from McNab's brief affirmation of confidence.

After instructions from Judge Louderback, the case went to the jury at 3:42 PM on Wednesday, February 1. Durfee sobbed as the jurors strode out. Two hours later, the jury returned to the courtroom, and participants and observers rushed back in, anticipating a verdict. Instead, the testimony of eavesdropping maid Josephine Keza was reread. At 9:30 PM the jury returned again, having requested that the judge reread his instructions to them.

"This is the end. No matter what this jury does, this is final. I'm through with this case for good," Brady told the press that evening.

The jury deliberated until 11 PM before retiring for the night. The front-page headline in the next day's *Chicago Tribune* announced, JURY QUITS FOR NIGHT, 11 TO 1 FOR ARBUCKLE.

William Desmond Taylor lay on his back on his living room floor, his left leg beneath a chair. At 7:30 AM on February 2, Henry Peavey, Taylor's African American valet/cook, arrived as usual at the house, one of eight two-story domiciles crowded around a courtyard in a fashionable district near downtown Los Angeles. Upon finding the lifeless body on the floor, Peavey shrieked, backed out of the house, and yelled for the landlord. The landlord and neighbors rushed in. When the police arrived, they failed to disperse the crowd, which obliterated evidence. A mysterious man who identified himself as a doctor but whose name remains unknown claimed without examining the body that death was due to natural causes. The general manager of Paramount removed letters and other personal items and later destroyed them. It wasn't until the coroner's deputies moved the body that a pool of blood was discovered beneath it. The postmortem tracked the deadly bullet's unusual path: entering the left, lower side of Taylor's back and traveling upward to lodge at the base of his neck on the right.

After abandoning his wife and daughter in New York City, William Desmond Taylor (an assumed name) had acted in his first film in Los Angeles in 1912 at age forty. Within a year, Taylor was directing, and he helmed approximately fifty films before enlisting in the army of his native Britain near the end of World War I. Upon returning to Los Angeles, the Englishman revived his directing career, signing with Paramount and serving as president of the Motion Picture Directors Association.

Mabel Normand was one of Taylor's closest friends and the last known person to see him on the evening of February 1, 1922. Then twenty-eight, she was still starring in romantic comedies, though her popularity had waned. Her alcohol and cocaine use could be problematic, as evidenced by her stay in a New York sanitarium in the autumn of 1920 for a "nervous breakdown." And yet the always-adventurous Normand was an inquisitive reader, studying literature and philosophy. That fateful February evening she discussed books with Taylor, and he gave her two. She was in Taylor's house from approximately 7:05 to 7:45 PM, and afterward he walked her to her limo and returned to his home.

Then forty-nine-year-old William Desmond Taylor was murdered. Robbery was ruled out when his pockets were found to contain seventy-eight dollars and various valuables. No suspect was ever arrested. The case remains unsolved, and the endlessly engaging mystery has only grown with time as the multitude of tentacled subplots extended to drug dealers, obscure phone calls, buried pasts excavated, a body in a river, a collection of keys to unknown locks, a woman's nightgown, homosexual solicitation, coded love letters from the then-seventeen-year-old movie star Mary Miles Minter to her then-forty-seven-year-old boyfriend (and director) Taylor, a woman dressed as a man, the kidnapping of Henry Peavey by reporters, and a bizarre 1964 confession. Over the decades, amateur detectives have pointed to over fifty suspects.* One of the prime suspects, Edward Sands—Taylor's former valet, who embezzled from him and robbed his house—was never located after Taylor's murder. Another, Charlotte Shelby—the threateningly overprotective mother of Mary Minter—possessed a rare gun that fired unusual bullets matching the .38 caliber slug found in Taylor. Though Normand had quarreled with Taylor and was implicated by Peavey (himself a suspect), she was cleared by the police. Nevertheless, in addition to her association with Arbuckle, the avalanche of press surrounding the Taylor murder quashed the image of Madcap Mabel and hastened her career's decline.

The greater effect of the scandalous Taylor murder was to refocus newspaper stories and outraged editorials on depraved and dangerous Hollywood. Calls for censorship increased. Front-page reports throughout February of the ever-widening mystery of Taylor's demise would

---

* Those "detectives" included Mack Sennett (himself an unlikely suspect), who devoted three chapters of his autobiography to the case, and legendary director King Vidor, who researched the mystery for a screenplay and whose notes were used for the 1986 book *A Cast of Killers*.

entangle it in the public consciousness with the Arbuckle manslaughter trials. The *San Francisco Chronicle* made the connection overt on its front page on February 3, running the banner headline WOMEN FEATURE FILM MURDER (about Normand and Minter's relationship to the Taylor murder) above ARBUCKLE JURY STILL OUT, 10 FOR ACQUITTAL, REPORT.

Arbuckle and Taylor were both employed by Paramount in 1921 and had attended the same social events for years. While the jury deliberated on February 2, Arbuckle, seated at the counsel's table, was informed by a reporter of Taylor's violent death. His eyes watered. "Taylor was the best fellow on the [Paramount] lot," he said. "He was beloved by everybody, and his loss is a shock. . . . I cannot understand why anyone would wish to murder him as he was the last man in the world to make an enemy."

Nearly two weeks later, a statement attributed to Arbuckle made a pointed statement about the Taylor case and Arbuckle's legal ordeal:

> The American public is ardent in its hero worship and quite as ruthless in destroying its idols in any walk of life. It elevates a man more quickly than any nation in the world, and casts him down more quickly—quite often on surmise or a mere hunch. It is the general inclination, when trouble happens to strike in film circles, for the thoughtless to whisper, malign and gossip and to speak with that mock sagacity of the times of "the inside dope" and "the low down." This was brought out quite forcibly in my own case and has been accentuated in the case of William Taylor. . . .
>
> Never in history, perhaps, have men and women been so quickly elevated to prominence as have the successful folk in pictures. That is because of the millions before whom they appear via the screen almost nightly. Their names become household words. Their features widely familiar. They are virtually next door neighbor to everyone in the land. The man and the woman who thus accepts as worthy of esteem this filmland neighbor should do himself or herself the moral honor of refusing to accept tattle and shoulder shrugs in place of fact—as he undoubtedly would in the case of his respected physical neighbor.

At 10:00 AM on the morning William Desmond Taylor's body was found, the jury in Roscoe Arbuckle's manslaughter case began its second day of deliberation. Shortly before noon, the jury asked for and received the trial transcript. Throughout the day, Arbuckle was seen pacing the halls outside the courtroom, smoking hand-rolled cigarettes, occasionally exchanging brief comments with reporters or speaking with his wife. In its front-page story, "Arbuckle Abandons Hope," the *Los Angeles Times* said he had given up on a verdict.

Deliberation was cut short that evening because a juror was ill. Also that evening, the avenger Maude Delmont, under probation for bigamy and presumably having legally untangled herself from her previous marriages, engaged to marry a vaudeville actor. They were in Lincoln, Nebraska, where she was said to be "attending to business matters." The engagement made front pages throughout the country.

At 11:30 AM on Friday, February 3, the jurors returned to their box and spectators scrambled to fill the seats of Judge Louderback's courtroom. Forty-four hours after getting the case, the jury was hopelessly deadlocked. The first ten ballots had been nine to three; the last four were ten to two. But reports had been wrong—the majority had not been for acquittal. Ultimately, ten of the twelve jurors voted Arbuckle guilty of manslaughter. The defendant was stunned, as were the attorneys for the defense and prosecution. A buzz of shocked mutterings filled the room. Durfee broke into tears.

The two men who voted for acquittal on all fourteen ballots, Helen Hubbards in reverse, declined to speak with reporters. Other jurors said plenty, revealing that the defense's crucial mistake was to not make a final argument. One said, "The jurors believed that the defense's failure to argue was due to fear of Prosecutor Friedman, whose argument was cut off by the defense action." Another juror: "The defense presented a very weak case. Its failure to argue the case counted greatly against it. The fact that Arbuckle did not take the stand had no effect on us." The latter may have been true in a narrow sense, but a third juror said, "From the reading of Arbuckle's testimony at the last trial, the majority of the jury believed that his story was contradictory." Of course, Arbuckle never took the stand in the second trial to answer contradictions and present himself as a believable witness. Furthermore, the defense offered no counterargument after the state highlighted Arbuckle's incongruities in its truncated closing argument.

McNab enlisted some creative accounting, focusing on the nine-to-three votes and adding the two alternate jurors, both of whom professed they would have voted for acquittal. He called it a more palatable nine-to-five loss, and he recalled the ten who voted for acquittal in the first trial. Brady wasn't buying it: "Had the majority of the jury been in favor of an acquittal, I would have asked for a dismissal. As the jury stood ten for conviction to two for acquittal, it is manifestly my duty to try this case again."

"In this life you've got to take a punch now and then," Arbuckle said, sounding like one of his put-upon characters. "I am ready to go to trial again. I feel sure that I shall be able to prove my innocence of this charge at another trial." But the punches, too hard and too many, had taken a steep toll.

{17}

THIRD TRIAL

The jury that will determine his future is not the jury that will determine whether or not he will go to jail. The jury trying him will be the public, and regardless of what the court jury hedged about by the technicalities of court procedure may do, the public will do its own judging.

—"There'll Be Two Juries," *Hollywood Daily Citizen*

Four days after the second trial, a newspaper story quoted Chicago attorney Albert Sabath, who, acting on behalf of the defense, had acquired a deposition from a "surprise witness" testifying to Virginia Rappe's past. "The vote of ten to two for conviction by the last jury," Sabath said, "ended the defense policy of shielding [Rappe]. It appears almost impossible to free Arbuckle and at the same time steer the testimony clear of the facts about Miss Rappe's condition. We must show the kind of life which she led."

From the *New York Times* of February 14, 1922:

Waited for Zeh Prevost
But Supposed Arbuckle Witness Outwitted New Orleans Police
New Orleans, La, Feb. 13—A young woman thought by police

> to be Zeh [*sic*] Prevost, the missing Arbuckle case witness, escaped from a hotel here today while detectives were waiting in the lobby for authority from San Francisco to arrest her. She is believed to have lowered herself by rope from a third-story room to a courtyard below.

The woman who called herself Zey Prevost had registered at the New Orleans hotel under a predictably peculiar name, Mrs. Zabelle Elruy, with no given address. The day before her getaway, while denying to newspaper reporters that she was Prevost, she claimed she was leaving soon for Cuba. Prevost had been held for seven weeks in a stranger's house before the first Arbuckle trial, impeached in the second trial, repeatedly lambasted and ridiculed in the press, and faced a possible perjury charge from the San Francisco district attorney. Escaping out a third-story window seemed the most rational course for "Zabelle Elruy" if it meant dodging those staked out below—the reporters but especially the policemen who would expedite her return to San Francisco for yet another Arbuckle trial. So the search for the prosecution's (faded) star witness continued, expanding to include the Caribbean.

The state doubtless believed that an earlier perjury charge, the one against Minnie Neighbors, had worked to effectively eliminate one defense witness and potentially frighten away others. So even though the charge had eventually been dismissed, they brought another. Before jury selection began in the third trial, a grand jury indicted both Neighbors and Florence Bates for perjury. Ultimately, neither woman was tried, but neither woman testified again either.

On March 16, after the questioning of fifty-one citizens, a jury of eight men and four women was seated for the third trial of Roscoe Arbuckle. Once again, Judge Louderback ordered them sequestered in a hotel. Then, soon after opening arguments began, the state tried to remove juror Edward Brown, because the grocer had twice been prosecuted for violating pure food laws and thus could be prejudiced against the district attorney. Because he had already been sworn in, Brown stayed; he eventually served as jury foreman.

The prosecution called five doctors, including Ophüls, Wakefield, and Beardslee, to discuss Rappe's condition before and after her death. But the defense was determined not to merely rerun the previous two trials for a different audience. Under cross-examination, they delved into the health of Rappe's bladder and urethra to get doctors to admit that an inflammation in the former may have caused a constricting of the latter, and that a resulting inability to urinate may have predisposed her distended bladder to rupture.

Perennial but reluctant witness Alice Blake recounted her version of events for the sixth time—including her affidavit, the grand jury, the preliminary hearing, and the two previous criminal trials. Her memory was again foggy, and under cross-examination she broke into tears. The defense scored points when Blake couldn't recall seeing Rappe and Arbuckle enter room 1219 nor Rappe subsequently saying "He hurt me." She also said Rappe and Arbuckle were in the room alone for no more than fifteen minutes.

Blake's fellow star witness Zey Prevost was located again in New Orleans and detained. Her telegram to Brady read, "If you want me to appear as witness in the Arbuckle case wire me ticket and I will come immediately." Brady wired the appropriate train fare, but Prevost claimed she was "taken sick" just before the train's departure and did not know when she would be well enough to travel. She never was—until the trial ended.

Nurse Grace Halston testified again and, after strenuous defense objections, described in detail the bruises she saw on Rappe's body. A police photographer then presented photos of the bruises. When a shot of Rappe's lifeless face was passed about the counsel's table, Arbuckle hung his head to avoid seeing it.

Friday, March 24, was Roscoe Arbuckle's thirty-fifth birthday. He spent it in Judge Louderback's courtroom listening to Prevost's previous testimony read into the record and prosecution witnesses retelling tales from earlier trials: Drs. Rumwell and Strange on Rappe's autopsies, Dr.

Castle on Rappe's medical treatment at Wakefield sanitarium, and the always crowd-pleasing hotel maid Josephine Keza, who under defense cross-examination abruptly declared, "I don't think I'll answer any more questions"—a large laugh line. Arbuckle received birthday telegrams and presents from fans and, during recesses, well-wishes from many in the courtroom. The presents included a fancy checkbook from an unknown giver. "I don't see why I should be sent a checkbook," he said. "I haven't money enough anymore even to make out one check, much less a whole book." Though it was said in jest, on Sunday ARBUCKLE IS BROKE was front-page news throughout the land.

The state continued to bring forth witnesses from the previous trials: reporter Warden Woolard, fingerprint expert Edward Heinrich, Rappe's "aunt" Kate Hardebeck, and studio security guard Jesse Norgaard. When the defense brought up Norgaard's recent arrest for escaping from a chain gang in 1918 (his original arrest was for selling alcohol to soldiers), the prosecution objected, applying the word "shyster" to opposing counsel, and when the defense replied in kind, Judge Louderback told both sides they were bordering on contempt.

As the prosecution's case followed the pattern of the second trial—if more contentious as the defense challenged the vulnerabilities of witnesses it had come to know—it may have seemed that the state was willing to rely on its nearly winning strategy of weeks earlier. But District Attorney Brady had a surprise final witness, a name not previously heard: Virginia Breig. She was the secretary at Wakefield sanitarium, and she told a story potentially devastating to Arbuckle.

Breig claimed to have visited Rappe on the day of her death. "She asked me about the amount of the bill that would be due,"* Breig said of the feeble Rappe. "She said she did not see why she should pay the bill as Arbuckle was responsible for her being there. I told her that if Arbuckle or anyone else should pay the account after she left, the money paid by her would be returned. She replied that she was not going to leave, that she was going to die. Then I asked her why she thought she was going

* It came to thirty-four dollars.

to die. It was then that she told me the details of the party." The following detail mattered most. According to Breig, the dying Rappe said, "Arbuckle took me by the arm and threw me on the bed and put his weight on me, and after that I do not know what happened." Here then was the missing piece to complete the prosecution's puzzle: a witness heard Rappe say Arbuckle committed a specific act that could have burst her bladder.

McNab pounced. He asked if Breig had telephoned Arbuckle asking him to pay Rappe's bill, with the threat that if he didn't she would tell her tale to the district attorney. Breig denied this. He asked why she had kept her story to herself until that Monday, six and a half months after Rappe's death. She said she wanted to avoid the notoriety and had been summoned to testify only two days prior. McNab moved to have Rappe's deathbed accusation, as told by Breig, stricken from the record as hearsay. Motion denied.

Maude Delmont was in Chicago, where she said that the depositions taken there "trying to blacken Virginia Rappe's character" were false. She was accompanied by an Illinois assistant state's attorney representing Brady. She said of the trials, "A great opportunity was lost in making a wonderful example of Arbuckle's case. It's not the first time he had done a thing like this, either. It makes me boil to see these attempts to defame Virginia's character and none whatever of Arbuckle's past brought up."

When the much-anticipated defamation of Rappe's character arrived, it was less than advertised. The defense did, however, win early headlines when Chicago nurse Virginia Warren stated that Rappe prematurely birthed a baby during bladder trauma in 1910. However, Warren stumbled under cross-examination when her nursing credentials were challenged. Also, like so many in this case, Warren had adopted a different name, and when pressed by the prosecution, she wasn't even certain of her real name. Most of one day was taken up with reading the depositions of Chicago medical personnel regarding the young Rappe's bladder and abdominal pains. The state later succeeded in getting one of the depositions stricken from the record when the doctor was uncertain if the girl he remembered was Rappe.

But the most inflammatory deposition was that of Josephine Rafferty (a.k.a. Josephine Roth), who was most probably the "surprise witness" to whom Albert Sabath alluded when he spoke of showing "the kind of life which [Rappe] led." Rafferty said in her deposition:

> I first saw Virginia Rappe in February 1908 in my home. I had studied medicine for three years and was a midwife. At that time Virginia Rappe [then sixteen] was about to become a mother. Between that time and 1910, Virginia Rappe was about to become a mother on four other occasions. I attended her on each occasion. The first time she was very ill. On the next three occasions, I attended her six weeks each time. The first time she was ill a baby was born. Miss Rappe throughout my attendance of her was a sufferer from bladder trouble.

Because Rafferty was not called to the stand, the state could not cross-examine her, but it would take its shots in its closing statements. Friedman treated her very name with disdain, calling her "Rafferty-Roth," and he stated that "according to her own testimony and the testimony of Mrs. Warren, [Rafferty] was conducting nothing but a house of abortion." Abortion was then illegal in Illinois. Rafferty's statement regarding "attending" Rappe on four occasions when she was "about to become a mother" was likely a euphemism for abortions.

Jesse Norgaard's character, still smarting from the defense's focus on his recent arrest, took up much of a day when a justice of the peace testified that he could speak to Norgaard's morals but not his integrity, and thus the trial veered off into a lengthy cul-de-sac as a dozen authorities and a dictionary were quoted so the prosecution and defense could attempt to define "integrity." Alas, integrity eluded both sides.

A screenwriter and two actors told tales of Rappe's inability to consume alcohol without convulsing in pain and/or tearing off her clothes. And a woman named Helen Whitehurst testified that when she and

Rappe were friends in Chicago in 1913, Rappe had suffered two similar public attacks at cafés and one at a political campaign dinner. Fred Fishback could no longer recall much of anything; FISHBACH [*sic*] LOSES MEMORY ON STAND, read a headline.* And two doctors explained why Rappe's distress indicated chronic bladder problems.

Having learned from its mistakes in the second trial, the defense called Roscoe Arbuckle to the stand at 10:45 on the morning of April 5. He was smiling as he wedged into the wooden seat. With the movie star speaking under oath for only the second time, the trial was again the toughest ticket in San Francisco, though the female audience was described as "less enthusiastic" than that at the first trial.

Arbuckle retold the tale of finding Rappe in 1219's bathroom and helping her. Asked if Rappe said anything to him, he replied, "Miss Rappe never said a word while I was in the room. She moaned and groaned." He admitted having known Rappe for years, but said he knew none of the other guests at the Labor Day party. As for Jesse Norgaard, he claimed to have never made his acquaintance. He denied having placed ice upon Rappe, and he denied having placed his hand over Rappe's on 1219's door. "I was not near that door for the whole time I was in the hotel except when Miss Rappe was carried from the room," he said, referring to his later carrying her part of the way to room 1227. Arbuckle's purple bathrobe, which the defense sarcastically referred to as "wicked"—a word stricken after the state's objection—was placed into evidence by the defense.

In its rebuttal, the state brought forth a doctor who testified that bladders could not spontaneously rupture, as well as people who claimed Rappe was healthy during various stages of her life: friends in Chicago, the Hollywood Hotel manager, a chauffeur she had employed. Kate Hardebeck said her "niece" was mostly in great health, though the state likely regretted calling her when she said Rappe had been treated for an unnamed ailment in 1921 and the doctor advised her to get an operation.

* In the wake of the scandal, Fishback began directing under the name Fred Hibbard. He died of lung cancer in 1925 at age thirty.

To Hardebeck's knowledge, Rappe was never pregnant. Again enacting a favorite strategy, Brady ordered Virginia Warren and Helen Whitehurst before a grand jury for perjuring themselves, under the presumption that others had effectively invalidated their testimony.

In surrebuttal, the defense called Rappe's former boyfriend Harry Barker, who repeated his tale of seeing Rappe pained and tearing off clothes in Chicago. A doctor, Charles Barnes, told how he operated on Rappe in Chicago in 1909 for a bladder abscess. A woman claimed to overhear Hardebeck saying Rappe had been ill, and two chauffeurs said Rappe's former driver told them Rappe had had an attack in his car.

Henry Lehrman was supposedly in San Francisco meeting with the prosecution and would perhaps take the stand to defend the honor of his "fiancée," but he never appeared in the courtroom as a witness or as a spectator. Three days before the trial ended, thirty-five-year-old Lehrman, the grieving "fiancé," announced his engagement to a nineteen-year-old Ziegfeld Follies dancer. Seventeen days later, they wed. After twenty volatile months, they divorced. It was his only marriage.*

"And that night Belshazzar, the king, was slain and the Medes and the Persians took possession of the kingdom and divided it. Roscoe Arbuckle's kingdom is ended! He has been weighed in the balances and found wanting! God has finished his kingdom!" This was not the sermon of some barnstorming preacher. It was the climactic erudition of Assistant DA Milton U'Ren in his closing statement, which was otherwise much more professorial than evangelical. U'Ren mostly focused on inconsistencies in Arbuckle's story, arguing for the unlikeliness of events behind

* Between his marriage and his divorce, Lehrman filed for bankruptcy. His directing career subsequently sputtered, resuscitated, and ended with the sound era. He died of a heart attack at sixty-five in 1946 and was buried beside Virginia Rappe in what is today Hollywood Forever Cemetery.

the locked door of 1219 happening as Arbuckle said, and pointing out that the movie star's story was kept secret until the first trial and then seemingly tailored to counter the state's witnesses. U'Ren highlighted how Rappe appeared hearty before spending time in room 1219 with Arbuckle, and he returned again to the "ice episode." "Oh, if the mothers of the children of America could have seen Roscoe Arbuckle making such sport of the poor, sick, senseless body of Virginia Rappe! The moral leper make the world laugh? Thank God, he will never make it laugh again!"

Again avoiding the errors of the second trial, the defense opted to deliver its own closing statement. First, Nat Schmulowitz reiterated at length Rappe's history of bladder illness, and he highlighted the medical testimony about bladder ruptures. Then came the emotional speech of Gavin McNab. When not quoting scripture, he reinflated the previously punctured reputations of defense witnesses and denigrated the expertise and impartiality of prosecution witnesses. Receiving the worst of it was Wakefield secretary Virginia Breig. He pointed out the absurdity of Rappe sharing her deathbed accusation with "the sordid bill collector" only to have such an accusation remain unrepeated until a third trial. Further, he accused Breig, "this creature," of trying unsuccessfully to extort the defense and then selling out to the prosecution for the cost of a hospital bill.

Blake and Prevost were "the private prison witnesses," with the former "seized and placed in a corral like a beast." In conclusion, McNab widened his argument beyond the freedom of his client: "If, through the extraordinary attention to his case, the vile, hideous, and barbarous practices that have prevailed in criminal processes in San Francisco, unknown to the public, are no longer possible, and unfortunates, that are being railroaded to the penitentiary without offense against the law, will have fair trials hereafter, then this persecution will have served a good purpose and Arbuckle will be repaid."

Countering for the state, Friedman said near the start of his statement, "Mr. McNab, who is so quick to invoke the scriptures, who so gladly calls down the Ten Commandments to his aid, forgets that there is one which reads, 'Thou shalt not kill.' He also beautifully eulogizes womanhood, then blasts and damns every woman appearing in this case, including his own witnesses." Friedman deflected the contention that the state had coached Blake and Prevost, and he belittled much of the medical testimony, saying it made no difference why Rappe's bladder was distended. He argued that Rappe was too young for multiple pregnancies in and before 1908.* And he spelled out again the state's version of what happened in room 1219 and why it was the only logical explanation. Arbuckle, he said, forced Rappe onto the bed, "threw his weight upon her, her bladder ruptured, and she passed into a state of unconsciousness. . . . We do not claim—with all the talk of disarranging clothes—we do not claim that he consummated his purpose. We claim that he attempted to accomplish a purpose, to fulfill a desire, and that his attempt resulted in the death of this girl."

This time there were no predictions of guilt or acquittal, no assurances that the good citizens of San Francisco would make the correct decision—or any decision. After one ten-to-two deadlock one way and another ten-to-two deadlock the other way, no one could be confident of either outcome or any outcome from another group of twelve.

Forty-four hours. That's approximately how long each of the first two juries was out, and neither reached a consensus. The third jury left the courtroom at 5:10 on Wednesday, April 12. They selected Edward Brown as foreman and reached their verdict by acclamation. At 5:15 came a rap from inside the jury-room door. To the astonishment of all in the courtroom, the jury had reached a decision.† Spectators who had left for a break rushed back in, refilling the seats and standing where they could. Judge Louderback warned everyone against any vocal expression of sentiment.

Acquittal.

---

* Actually, she turned seventeen that year.

† The difference between the length of the jury's deliberation and the length of time the jury was out of the box caused news reports to estimate the minutes needed to reach a verdict from less than one to as many as six.

Arbuckle let out a giant sigh. His wife sobbed quietly. After the judge gaveled the case finished and retired to his chambers, spectators erupted in a cheer. People stood on their chairs and on the railing to better see Arbuckle as he rushed to the jury box. He shook hands with the jurors, who crowded around him, patting his back, affirming their belief in his innocence, some dabbing away tears. Then Arbuckle, his attorneys, and the jurors fought through the grasping, congratulating crowd and made their way into the jury room. There a statement was read for the benefit of the press and, as camera flashes exploded, signed by each of the twelve jurors and two alternates. It read:

> Acquittal is not enough for Roscoe Arbuckle. We feel that a great injustice has been done him. We feel also that it was only our plain duty to give him this exoneration, under the evidence, for there was not the slightest proof adduced to connect him in any way with the commission of this crime. He was manly throughout the case, and told a straightforward story on the witness stand, which we all believed. The happening at the hotel was an unfortunate affair for which Arbuckle, so the evidence shows, was in no way responsible. We wish him success, and hope that the American people will take the judgement of fourteen men and women who have sat listening for thirty-one days to the evidence,* that Roscoe Arbuckle is entirely innocent and free from all blame.

Acquittal merely means the state did not prove Arbuckle guilty beyond a reasonable doubt. The unusual posttrial statement went much further in declaring Arbuckle "entirely innocent and free from all blame" and asking the American people to believe it. The jury did not have time to draft such a document during their few minutes in the jury room, nor, presumably, would they have had any inclination then to care so deeply about the beliefs of their fellow Americans. It was written before

---

* Including voir dire, the trial lasted thirty-one calender days, but there were only eighteen days of testimony.

the verdict, likely by Arbuckle's lawyers at the behest of Arbuckle and/or the movie producers whose bottom lines were dependent on resuscitating his image and career. It was, however, referred to only as the jury's statement, so not even Edward Heinrich could trace a fingerprint to its origin.

Brady later issued his own statement: "I am an American citizen, and I take off my hat to the verdict of an American jury. The District Attorney's office has done what it deemed to be its duty in this case, nothing more nor less. And I intend always to do my duty as I see it."*

If Brady's comments were intended for the voting public, Arbuckle's were tailored foremost toward moviegoers, for their verdict awaited him next. His statement declared:

> This is the most solemn moment of my life. My innocence of the hideous charges preferred against me has been proven by a jury of the best men and women of San Francisco—fourteen in all—rendering a verdict immediately after the trial. For this vindication I am truly grateful to God and my fellow men and women. My life has been devoted to the production of clean pictures for the happiness of children. I shall try to enlarge my field of usefulness so that my art shall have a wider service. It is the duty of all men to use the lessons that have been given them by experience and misfortune for the benefit of all—to make themselves more useful to humanity. This I shall do. I can only repay the trust, confidence and loyalty bestowed upon me during my trouble by millions of men and women throughout the world by rendering service in justification of their faith.

He also spoke to the press about his weight gain during the trials and his future in movies: "I am going to take a good rest and get rid of some of this surplus flesh. I must get back into physical shape before I even

* Matthew Brady never ran for higher office as many expected. He remained San Francisco DA until defeated in 1943 by future California governor Pat Brown.

think of pictures. Then I will be able to go on with my work, if the public wants me. If the public doesn't want me, I'll take my medicine. But, after the quick vindication I received I am sure the American people will be fair and just. I believe I am due for a comeback."

The night of the verdict, Paramount's Jesse Lasky said, "Our contract with Arbuckle expired at the time of his trouble. Whether or not this contract will be renewed will depend on the public. The public makes or breaks all stars. If the public receives favorably the Arbuckle pictures which we have on hand, one of which will be released at once, then we will be ready to consider the matter of a future contract."

Arbuckle did not escape all legal consequences. He pleaded guilty to a federal charge of unlawful possession of alcohol and was fined the maximum: $500. That amount would have been of no consequence to him eight months earlier, but the trial expenses (attorney fees, private investigation fees, hotel bills, travel bills . . .) coupled with his loss of income had devastated his finances. It was reported that his defense at the three trials cost more than $110,000 *not including attorney fees*. The inclusion of the substantial latter category may have ballooned his bill to over $750,000. Dream team, indeed.

Arbuckle, who returned to his Los Angeles mansion on April 15, refused an opportunity to speak to paying spectators on theater stages, saying, "I do not wish to capitalize on my good fortune so soon after achieving it. . . . I will return to my profession when I consider it proper to do so."

Crazy to Marry and *Gasoline Gus* began playing again in Los Angeles, and to strong business. Both had barely been released the previous August. *Skirt Shy* and *Freight Prepaid* had never been seen by American audiences, and Paramount was raring to get them on-screen. But the public began weighing in even before Fatty's image reached their local theaters. In the days immediately following Arbuckle's acquittal, a battle ensued between censors and their foes, between those who believed Arbuckle innocent and those who remained certain of his guilt—if not of manslaughter then of the sort of licentiousness that callously fostered a woman's death.

On the evening of April 18, six days after Arbuckle's acquittal, all Paramount movies featuring Roscoe Arbuckle were effectively banned from American theaters. It was the first proclamation by the new president of a new organization. So began the reign of the "czar of the movies," Will H. Hays.

{18}

HAYS

HAYS TO PUT FATTY THROUGH FOURTH TRIAL

—*LOS ANGELES EVENING HERALD*, APRIL 19, 1922, FRONT PAGE

For almost as long as there have been movies, there have been movie censors. In 1896 one of the first publicly screened films, Edison's forty-seven-second *The Kiss* (spoiler alert: a man and woman kiss) sparked editorial writers' demands for police department suppression, surely boosting its popularity. Investigations into the purportedly negative social influence of nickelodeons on the working class commenced in 1906, and some of the same forces that were aligning to pass Prohibition—fundamentalist morality, Progressive reform, rank nativism—conspired to regulate motion pictures. In their condemnations, temperance crusaders highlighted the intoxicating and addictive properties of movies.

In November 1907 the Chicago City Council passed the nation's first motion picture censorship law, prohibiting "immoral or obscene" movies and requiring the city's police department to issue a permit for every film shown. The law was enforced soon thereafter when two ordinary westerns were banned because the portrayal of bandits was said to promote crime. Other municipalities, including San Francisco and Los Angeles, followed Chicago's lead and drafted censorship committees, and between 1911 and 1916, state boards were established in Pennsylvania, Ohio, Kansas, and Maryland.*

After New York City closed all nickelodeons for two days in December 1908 and then barred children under sixteen from movie theaters unless accompanied by an adult, exhibitors countered by enlisting "surrogate" parents to escort kids inside and then by forming the National Board of Censorship of Motion Pictures to ferret out inappropriate movies before they were banned. The unfortunate name was changed to the National Board of Review of Motion Pictures in 1915, and by then the organization had spread to over 250 local groups throughout the country. They reviewed virtually every film America produced, classifying them "passed," "passed with changes as specified," or "condemned." Via the NBRMP's ratings, the movie industry hoped to avoid censors, but nonpassing grades flagged films for censors and forced producers to cut the objectionable material.

D. W. Griffith's 1915 blockbuster *The Birth of a Nation* was frequently banned. The NAACP challenged its screenings because of its depiction of African Americans, and it was outlawed by some communities for fear it would spark race riots. When the producers contested its Ohio banning, the case raced to the United States Supreme Court, which issued a unanimous decision comparing movies to "the theater, circus, and all other shows and spectacles." Films were "a business pure and simple, originated and conducted for profit" and thus not shielded from censorship by the First Amendment.†

This decision had its most profound effect on ambitious rookie filmmaker Robert Goldstein, who made *The Spirit of '76*, a Revolutionary War epic. It premiered shortly after America entered World War I and

* As an example of how draconian censorship rules could be, in Pennsylvania it was forbidden for a movie to portray "expectant maternity," i.e., a pregnant woman or, presumably, someone knitting baby clothes.

† This ruling would stand for thirty-seven years, until May 1952, when in what is known as "the *Miracle* decision" after the movie in question, the Supreme Court established that motion pictures are protected by the First Amendment.

was confiscated by the Chicago censorship board for potentially creating hostility toward Great Britain, then America's ally. Goldstein trimmed offending scenes, but after reinstating them for a Los Angeles run, he was tried and convicted under the Espionage Act. He served three years of a ten-year sentence before his time was commuted by President Woodrow Wilson. Ironically, his plight resulted from making a patriotic film about the American Revolution.

In 1916 the studios formed the National Association of the Motion Picture Industry, which lobbied for Constitutional and legal protections for movies. In March 1921 it issued "Thirteen Points" that the industry promised to avoid, including "suggestive bedroom and bathroom scenes" and scenes "that tend to weaken the authority of the law." NAMPI's efforts at averting film censorship were mostly unsuccessful. Meanwhile, the theater owners' NBRMP lost influence as critics accused it of whitewashing objectionable content.

After a torrent of news coverage and a protracted but ultimately failed effort by the movie industry to prevent it, on May 14, 1921, a fifth state established a censorship board—the most populous one, New York. Governor Nathan Miller said he signed the bill because "it was the only way to remedy what everyone conceded had grown to be a very great evil." Legislatures in other states introduced similar measures.

The fervor against unregulated motion pictures had been building—and then it exploded. In the days after Roscoe Arbuckle's arrest on September 10, *all* his films were pulled from *every* theater nationwide. As the parent of the sometimes rebellious film industry, Los Angeles' instinct was to protect its child, though, occasionally, when movies brought shame, it felt impelled to instill punishment. Numerous censorship ordinances were passed in Los Angeles but wielded lightly. On September 14, 1921, the city council held a "public welfare" meeting to discuss ratcheting up the regulation of films. In a discussion that grew contentious, Protestant ministers spoke in favor of censorship, and—four and a half months before his murder—the president of the Motion Picture Directors Association, William Desmond Taylor, testified for the status quo: "I have listened with amazement to the charges of these ministers that we are debauching the morals of the youth of this city. I know that the great majority of directors are building plays that are clean. . . . We have pledged ourselves not to put anything into pictures that will hurt the morals of any youth."

Afterward, Taylor issued a one-thousand-word, widely distributed statement entitled "The Nonsense of Censorship," which began:

> Censorship of motion pictures is a menace to the very principles of the Constitution of these United States of America. How strong a grasp it has obtained over the constitutional rights of America may be seen in the fact that nearly one-third of the total population of this country may now see only such motion pictures as some commission has decided they may see.

Fought at city council meetings and on editorial pages, the battle progressed in fits and starts for over a month before Los Angeles' latest censorship attempt was defeated on October 21. Numerous states also repudiated motion picture censoring measures in 1921, including California, Illinois, and Connecticut.

From the movie industry's perspective, however, the problem was larger than the prospect that a council that might ban a single title from its community or demand a scene be excised. It was the overall effect on ticket sales caused by focusing on the alleged evils of motion pictures. That's why the studios' greatest concern after September 10, 1921, was not censors; it was the perception—fueled by preachers, pundits, and politicians—that the industry was *uncensored*, that it followed no rules but merely the pursuit of wealth and pleasure, that it failed to heed the constraints of common decency. With the relentless press coverage in the weeks following Arbuckle's arrest, the opinion grew that Hollywood was the nexus of Jazz Age immorality and was capable, via both its easily transmitted products and the status of its worshipped stars, of infecting this virus throughout America. The studios had to act swiftly and decisively to show they shared the public's concern.

William Harrison Hays was born on November 5, 1879, in the farming town of Sullivan in southwestern Indiana. His father was a lawyer, a Republican, and a Presbyterian elder, and the junior Hays followed the same path, joining Dad's law firm after college, representing railroads, coal companies, and other corporations. A skilled orator with a passion for politics, he rose through the party ranks to become Indiana's Republican chairman, even as he continued to live in Sullivan with his wife and—a new addition in 1915—their son.

With elephantine ears, teeth like mixed nuts, and a nose that resembled the beak on a fruit-eating bird, Hays had—to put it kindly—a memorable face, one that would later bring much joy to editorial cartoonists. He was short and exceedingly thin, and thus whereas Arbuckle claimed to be too fat for soldiering in World War I, Hays was reportedly too frail. By then he was chairman of the Republican National Committee, a position to which the Progressive wing of the GOP elevated him in February 1918. In an era in which candidates were handpicked in smoky backrooms, party chairman was seen as a short step to a Senate seat or a governor's mansion. Hays coveted the latter as he slept in train cars and hotel rooms, traversing the country, working to elect Republicans.

He was expert at building alliances, but even if he had been lousy he would have been a success, for he had the great fortune to be Republican national chairman in 1918, when his party regained the Senate and House from the Democrats thanks to an unpopular war, and during a Depression in 1920, when his candidate, Warren G. Harding, triumphed in a landslide. Subsequently, Hays accepted the cabinet position of postmaster general in Harding's administration. From the days of America's first postmaster general, Benjamin Franklin, until the postal service was reformed in 1970, it was a powerful political job. In addition to overseeing mail delivery, the postmaster wielded much of his party's patronage, appointing supporters to postal service management positions. Though Hays moved to Washington, DC, his wife, who suffered from "lifelong frailty," and son stayed in Sullivan.

After eight years of a Democratic administration, Republican Hays came to his job with a number of postal service reforms. In a luncheon speech to the American Newspaper Publishers Association, he proclaimed, "First, it is no part of the primary business of the Post Office Department to act as a censor of the press. This should not and will not be." One month later, he granted second-class mail status to a socialist magazine, stating that Wilson's administration had relegated it to a more expensive status as a form of censorship. It was the first of several radical publications to which he bestowed mail status previously denied.

Hays was perceived as a political mastermind—an organizer, dealmaker, and publicist par excellence. He had built connections in small towns and large cities nationwide, the same communities that were now launching film censorship boards. Possible federal film censorship also loomed, and Hays was the premier power broker in the Republican Party, which now controlled Congress and the White House. He was a teetotaler and a Presbyterian elder from rural Indiana with long Dutch Irish roots into America's heartland. His background contrasted with the major film studio heads, all of whom were Jewish and most of whom were immigrants—facts not lost on Hollywood's critics, many of whom espoused anti-Semitism and nativism. And so when the movie industry was struck by a catastrophe after Labor Day 1921, it turned to Will H. Hays.

A letter was drafted to enlist Hays to the cause of minimizing the catastrophe's repercussions. It was signed by a dozen studio executives, including Adolph Zukor and Jesse Lasky, and hand-delivered to him on December 8. When word leaked, he denied accepting the offer for another month, until January 14, 1922, just before testimony began in the second Arbuckle trial. The announcement was front-page news, christening Hays "the Judge Landis of movies," in reference to the first commissioner of major league baseball, appointed in November 1920 to resuscitate the national pastime's image after 1919's Black Sox scandal.

But why would a forty-two-year-old longtime political operative with his own aspirations for higher office give up a plum cabinet position after one year to embroil himself in censorship fights, the Arbuckle trials, and an industry reeling from tales of drug-fueled orgies? The answer had six digits: $100,000—the annual salary, not including other financial incentives. His postmaster general salary was $12,000. The president made $75,000.

Hays stayed on as postmaster general until March 4. By the time he assumed his position as head of the new Motion Picture Producers and Distributors of America (which replaced the old NAMPI) in uptown Manhattan, there had been a second film scandal, the murder of William Desmond Taylor. After devoting a month to studying the movie industry, Hays outlined how he hoped to modernize it and polish its tarnished image. "As to censorship I think that will be the least of our troubles," he said. "We hope that our pictures will eliminate all causes for censorship. . . . The matter of censorship will take care of itself when our objects as to the pictures are accomplished." Let the self-censorship begin.

In the midst of the third Arbuckle trial, District Attorney Matthew Brady spoke about the reforms Hays needed to impart: "The public is tired of seeing some morally rotten but highly paid actor or actress glorified and held up as an idol. The public is tired of having sex flung in their faces. People who live decent lives, the mothers and fathers with families that they are trying to raise to be upright and decent, are tired of seeing film after film picturing infidelity and red love. They are tired of seeing the other man as a permanent fixture in the home—according to the movies. They are giving the producers their chance to reform from within. If they don't, public opinion won't do any reforming at all. It will simply annihilate the motion picture industry altogether, just as it did the saloon."

In April the Christian group Lord's Day Alliance won headlines throughout the country for publicly calling for Will Hays to "use your authority to intervene and prevent the outrage to the moral sensibilities of the citizens of this country threatened in the proposal to again exhibit any Arbuckle films."

For thirty-three years it was assumed that Hays alone decided to ban Roscoe Arbuckle from the movies on April 18—a week after Arbuckle's acquittal and a month into Hays's new job. But the year after Hays's 1954 death, his memoirs were published. Only three of the book's six hundred tedious pages mention Arbuckle, whom Hays never met, but they lay the blame for Arbuckle's banishment elsewhere. It was Joseph Schenck and Adolph Zukor, Hays claimed, who came to him after the third trial and asked him to ban their employee from their employment. He said Zukor insisted upon it, even though Paramount had two unreleased Arbuckle movies* and two that had barely been released. Hays wrote:

> With hundreds of thousands of dollars tied up in completed but unreleased films, Zukor decided to make a sacrifice rather than bring further discredit on the industry or give the slightest added impetus to public outrage. So far as he was concerned, the outrage was very real. Arbuckle had let him down—he had let the whole industry down no less than his fans—and Zukor was prepared to take the loss.

That's the best possible spin. Over the course of three trials, Paramount had likely come to terms with writing off any further North American box office grosses from Arbuckle's movies. Then came the protests, scathing editorials, and censorship calls when they rereleased *Gasoline Gus* and *Crazy to Marry* after the acquittal. During the trials, Arbuckle was rarely associated with Paramount. Now, with his movies returning to theaters, he was a Paramount star again. Zukor did the

* *Skirt Shy* and *Freight Prepaid* were never released in America, though both played in Europe in 1922. Renamed *Leap Year*, the movie formerly known as *Skirt Shy* premiered overseas during the third Arbuckle trial.

math and deduced that Paramount had more to lose in the long term by continuing its association with Arbuckle, whom much of the country disdained, than it had to gain in the short term from those who cheered or forgave him. The studio wanted a clean slate.

Hays claimed he asked Zukor to issue the statement on Arbuckle's banishment, but Zukor replied, "No, Will, let the Association give it out. That will show that the Association means business." Hays said of this gesture: "Even that early in the game Adolph Zukor had passed the stage in which profit was the primary concern of his activity. If any man had the 'alma matter' spirit for the industry which had made him, and which he had largely made, that man was he." Hays was ever expert at spinning. Profit was surely Zukor's primary concern. He was blacklisting Arbuckle from Hollywood, but rather than face any public backlash, he secretly passed that chore on to Hays, who dutifully obliged, exercising the authority so recently bestowed on him—in part, by Zukor. For the Paramount president, it was a win-win: sever ties with Arbuckle and let Hays absorb any blame. As a bonus, Hays could have the credit too, giving the appearance that the new MPPDA was rushing out of the gate to clean up Hollywood.

With the Arbuckle ban in place, Hays went about combating governmental censorship. After a May 11, 1922, Senate Judiciary Committee hearing, a proposed investigation of the movie industry fizzled. The Virginia legislature instituted a film censorship board in 1922, but Hays (and a $300,000 war chest) instituted a full-force public relations campaign against a Massachusetts referendum to censor motion pictures there. In November 1922 citizens of the Bay State voted the proposal down three to one—the only substantial popular vote on film censorship in America's history. No other state ever again instituted movie censorship, nor, despite numerous attempts, did the US Congress.

Hays utilized his political skills to form the MPPDA's Committee on Public Relations, which gave organizations a forum to voice complaints to the studios. He also instituted 1924's "the Formula," a strategy for his office to use in reviewing synopses of every movie in preproduction. Keeping with its mysterious title, the Formula was vague, until a list of eleven "Don'ts" (nudity, profanity, miscegenation, etc.) and twenty-five "Be Carefuls" (international relations, brutality, treason, etc.) was adopted in 1927. The Hays Office, as the MPPDA came to be known, claimed to reject 125 proposed movies over the six years of the Formula, but submission was voluntary, any summation could easily avoid highlighting a Don't or Be Careful, and a rejected synopsis could become a movie without consequence.

Hays regularly made newspaper headlines for everything from establishing a movie copyright bureau to unionizing film production labor to leasing the highest apartment in New York City. More than anyone else, Will H. Hays became the face of the motion picture industry, characterized as the "czar of the movies." His homely mug graced the September 13, 1926, issue of *Time* magazine (with the subtitle "Polychromatic Pollyanna"), making him one of only three people principally associated with Hollywood to receive that honor in the silent era.* Reporters never tired of presenting, if not mocking, him as a paragon of virtue, but he grew entangled in financial matters emanating from the Teapot Dome scandal—a bribery case involving President Harding's secretary of the interior. And, in the greatest contrast to his public image, Hays lived apart from his family for over a decade until divorcing his wife in 1929 and winning custody of their son—and this while Be Careful number twenty-one was "the institution of marriage" and divorce was a cinematic taboo. He remarried in 1930.

By 1930 silent films had given way to the talkies, the spoken dialogue of which greatly increased the odds of objectionable content. Momentum for federal film censorship swelled, and Hays faced renewed criticism from religious organizations. Meanwhile, civil libertarians sought ways to repeal censorship laws. Add to this the financial instability of the industry, teetering from the Great Depression and proposed antitrust legislation. All of this explains why Hays was receptive to the Motion

* The other two were Charlie Chaplin (July 6, 1925) and Adolph Zukor (January 14, 1929).

Picture Production Code. The Code was outlined by Martin Quigley, the moralistic publisher of the *Motion Picture Herald*, Hollywood's leading trade journal, and written by the aptly named Catholic theologian Daniel A. Lord. It had three general principles:

1. No picture shall be produced which will lower the moral standards of those who see it. Hence the sympathy of the audience shall never be thrown to the side of crime, wrong-doing, evil, or sin.
2. Correct standards of life, subject only to the requirements of drama and entertainment, shall be presented.
3. Law, natural or human, shall not be ridiculed, nor shall sympathy be created for its violation.

This was vague enough to dance about artfully, but the devil was in the details. The twenty-one "Particular Applications" spelled out numerous topics to avoid: everything from the obvious (sex) to the criminal (illegal drug traffic) to the profane (ridicule of religion) to the peculiar (dancing costumes). A film could feature a transgression if "compensating moral values" were introduced. For example, a plot could follow a murderer as long as he was appropriately punished.

The MPPDA adopted the Code on March 31, 1930. Both scripts and finished films were to be submitted to the Hays Office for approval. However, like previous attempts at self-censorship, this one lacked enforcement. Gangsters, monsters, and risqué humor ruled in what many now regard as a high point in movie history: pre-Code Hollywood—meaning pre–enforcement of the Code. It lasted until June 22, 1934. Then, under pressure from religious groups, the MPPDA formed the Production Code Administration. Any MPPDA member that released a movie without the PCA's seal of approval received a $25,000 fine, and no member-controlled theater could show an unapproved film. The jig was up for all those cinematic rogues. The Production Code would dictate Hollywood content for the next thirty-four years. Its authority was weakened throughout the 1960s, but it was not abandoned until November 1, 1968, when a ratings system was instituted in its place.

Hays stepped down as MPPDA president in 1945, functioned for five more years as a consultant, and retired to a life of luxury in New York City. Though he had rarely returned to Sullivan, Indiana, it was there that he died on March 7, 1954, at age seventy-four. Before and after his death, he was pilloried as the great censor of the movies. There is no doubt that the Production Code he instituted altered the history of motion pictures. It forced actors to speak via innuendos, and it frightened producers away from even broaching certain topics. Thus it was a form of censorship, but it was probably necessary to combat a more overt form. Government censors continued to function, but rarely did they even contemplate a film given the PCA's seal. The Code went too far and lasted too long, but, contrary to popular belief, this was not a result of Hays's personal morality. Will Hays's overriding motive was to protect the business of making motion pictures. And this motive had its most profound effect on one Roscoe Arbuckle.

{19}

EXILE: 1922–25

The world broke in two in 1922 or thereabouts . . .

—Willa Cather, *Not Under Forty*

Roscoe Arbuckle was devastated. His greatest hope over the preceding seven months was that once he was cleared of charges in Virginia Rappe's death he could resume his film acting career. Durfee later wrote of this period:

> Suddenly we all realized the change in Roscoe, not that it was unusual nor not to be expected. . . . Did you ever see a person whose eyes were smiling thru sorrow and tears, well that was Roscoe's condition. He who always had real mirth in his eyes, he was excessively nervous, which of course had never been a condition with him—or at least if he felt that way he had never showed it. He would sit endless hours silently patting our old darling dog Luke—and often I would hear him say: "Well, boy, do you know the future[?] I am sure I don't."

He was deeply in debt. He had deeded his West Adams mansion to Joseph Schenck as security to pay for the trials, so he and Durfee were tenants when they returned to live there. He sold his $34,000 Pierce-Arrow and other luxury cars (the Cadillac went to Buster Keaton). And still he owed his trial attorneys at least $100,000 and perhaps much more. He needed Hollywood's paydays just to get out of debt, so his unexpected banishment by Will Hays left him reeling. Five days later, on April 23, 1922, Arbuckle issued this response:

> The question of the release of my pictures is entirely within the jurisdiction of the Famous Players-Lasky Corporation, owners of these pictures, who are undoubtedly working in harmony with Mr. Will Hays. I shall do everything possible to cooperate with the leaders of the industry. In the meantime, I shall prove to the world by my conduct that I am entitled to an opportunity to earn my living in the only profession I am equipped to follow, and shall patiently and hopefully await the final opinion of the American public, in whose sense of fair play I have never lost confidence.

The most vocal segment of the American public in the wake of the Hays announcement was not interested in "fair play" toward Arbuckle—the living, breathing symbol of Hollywood licentiousness. Soon after his statement, the California Congress of Women and Parents voted in support of banning his films, and the San Francisco Federation of Women's Clubs passed a similar resolution.

In the wake of the Arbuckle trials, the public became increasingly interested in the private lives of Hollywood celebrities, and movie star coverage grew more intrusive. Gossip columns, filled with even the most pedestrian trivia, occupied a full page of many local newspapers.* In addition to savoring tales of glamour and just-like-us banalities, readers were curious about the private foibles of actors—the whisperings about what went on at parties and in bedrooms.

* Pedestrian trivia example: Doris Deane, a minor actress who would play a major role in Arbuckle's life, was featured in a March 1922 item for rescuing her mother's orange trees from "Jack Frost" by lighting dozens of smudge pots.

A book published in May 1922 entitled *The Sins of Hollywood: An Expose of Movie Vice* was authored by "a Hollywood Newspaper Man," who was revealed, by a counterattacking movie industry, to be Ed Roberts, a former editor at *Photoplay*. *The Sins of Hollywood* was ruled "too scurrilous" to be sent through the mail, which only aided its legend. Proving you can judge a book by its cover, this one is adorned with an illustration of a Hollywood starlet, a movie camera, and Satan. Inside, actors and actresses are bestowed barely disguised pseudonyms, though their phony names often are accompanied by actual photographs, just so there's no confusion.

Rudolph Valentino is "Adolpho," alleged to be a former gigolo. Mabel Normand is "Molly" and Mack Sennett is "Jack," and one chapter relates how their relationship reached its violent end with help from Mae Busch (merely called Mae). (Normand's drug use is also alluded to in the chapter "Dope!") And then there is "Rostrand," a certain movie star recently tried three times for manslaughter, who is featured in the must-read chapter "Making Sodom Look Sick." In his introduction, Roberts explained why he collected the book's "true stories":

> To the boys and girls of the land these mock heroes and heroines have been pictured and painted, for box office purposes, as the living symbols of all the virtues. An avalanche of propaganda by screen and press has imbued them with every ennobling trait. Privately they have lived, and are still living, lives of wild debauchery. . . . Unfaithful and cruelly indifferent to the worship of the youth of the land, they have led or are leading such lives as may, any day, precipitate yet another nation-wide scandal and again shatter the ideals, the dreams, the castles, the faith of our boys and girls.

And so to protect the ideals, dreams, castles, and faith of children, Roberts sought to make certain Rostrand was never again seen as the symbol of any virtue by recounting this tale of dogs gone wild:

> Rostrand, a famous comedian, decided to stage another of his unusual affairs. He rented ten rooms on the top floor of a large

> exclusive hotel and only guests who had the proper invitations were admitted. After all of the guests—male and female—were seated, a female dog was led out into the middle of the largest room. Then a male dog was brought in. A dignified man in clerical garb stepped forward and with all due solemnity performed a marriage ceremony for the dogs. It was a decided hit. The guests laughed and applauded heartily and the comedian was called a genius. Which fact pleased him immensely. But the "best" was yet to come. The dogs were unleashed. There before the assembled and unblushing young girls and their male escorts was enacted an unspeakable scene. Even truth cannot justify the publication of such details.

In newspapers, there had been previous mentions of a dog wedding at Arbuckle's house, but the preceding "unspeakable scene" seems to have been, at the least, a public consummation of canine nuptials. It furthered the image of Arbuckle living a life free of any moral restraints—precisely the sort of "mock hero" to keep off movie screens, separate from impressionable youth.

> Fatty Arbuckle says he is broke, that it took all his fortune to see him through the three trials. Perhaps he may be forced to go to work for a while.
>
> —An unsigned editorial comment in a small-town Washington newspaper, June 23, 1922

Roscoe Arbuckle declined offers to appear on vaudeville stages and instead tried to return to films. He wrote a short comedy script, "The Vision," for Buster Keaton and sold it to Joseph Schenck; Arbuckle was also set to direct. The movie was never made. When *Photoplay* editor James Quirk wrote him a letter of encouragement, Arbuckle wrote back, again stating his case but also strategizing: "You can be of real service to me by writing Mr. Hays, asking him to lift [the] ban and telling him that my innocence of the charges placed against me in San Francisco justifies your request." Not just Quirk but also representatives of the country's theater owners lobbied Hays for Arbuckle's reinstatement. Meanwhile, some felt Hays had not done enough. Senator Henry Lee Myers denounced Arbuckle on the floor of the US Senate in an argument for film censorship, stating, "At Hollywood, California, is a colony of these people, where debauchery, riotous living, drunkenness, ribaldry, dissipation, free love, seem to be conspicuous."

In June Minta Durfee left that colony and journeyed to New York City to live with her sister. Arbuckle denied that his wife had deserted him and claimed she would return when he could support himself again. He lived in the West Adams mansion with Lou Anger and Anger's wife, who were now renting it from Schenck.* He spent too much time at home, feeling sorry for himself. Al St. John later remembered his uncle sitting alone for hours in a car in the garage of the house he no longer owned, shifting gears but never moving. At Keaton's insistence, Arbuckle sometimes visited Comique and assisted his friend on his latest comedy short. But there were too many hours in a day to fill. The man who in September had sworn off booze forever was drinking again. (By this point, raucous hotel parties were known as "Arbuckle parties" and orange blossoms were called "Arbuckle cocktails.")

Arbuckle remained generous with money even when he owed more than he had. Besides Keaton, his closest friend was the suave matinee idol and notorious womanizer Lew Cody, who recalled, "Once when we were both pretty broke, I had a chance to go to New York to work. I managed to borrow enough to buy a ticket. Just before the train pulled out, Roscoe came aboard and after he'd said goodbye he handed me an envelope. 'Don't open this until after the train starts,' he said. 'It's just a letter telling you what a lousy actor I think you are.' When I opened the envelope, two $1000 bills dropped out. He'd borrowed the money here, there, and everywhere. That's the kind of a pal Fatty was."

He also found the money for a trout-fishing vacation in Vancouver, British Columbia, and in August, he sailed from San Francisco for the Ori-

---

* The house is today a Catholic rectory.

ent he had visited ten years before. Among those accompanying him was his attorney, Milton Cohen. "I need a rest and intend to take it easy and, at the same time, see some other parts of the world," he told reporters in San Francisco before departing. "I'll come back to the United States in due time and then will be my opportunity to decide what I'm going to do. It's entirely up to the people—the people who see the movies and who used to be—and I think, again will be—my friends, whether I return to the screen or not. Maybe I'll get back to making comedies, but I don't know. San Francisco doesn't make me feel very funny and I can't say right now."

He planned to visit the Middle East and Europe, but after slipping down steps and cutting a finger on the initial sea voyage, he made it no further than Japan. An infection set in, requiring surgery in Tokyo and generating a flurry of front-page stories.* Though he was greeted warmly in Japan, the injury had soured his mood, so he halted the trip and journeyed back across the Pacific. He said his time in the Orient had convinced him California was a good place to live.

> "Fatty" Arbuckle was a movie "goat." While he escaped conviction in court he was crucified by public sentiment which demanded that somebody be made to pay for the loose lives of too many of the movie stars. It was just Arbuckle's misfortune that the choice fell upon him. It might have been anyone of a number of others no better than he. A little more than usual vulgarity and an accident directed selection of Arbuckle. So he is paying for all.
>
> —From an editorial in a small-town Wisconsin newspaper, November 22, 1922

A malaise had clouded Hollywood during Arbuckle's trials and the investigation into William Taylor's murder, and it was felt most acutely at Para-

* It was later reported that his index and middle fingers on his right hand were permanently paralyzed. This was untrue.

mount, where Arbuckle had been the top actor and Taylor one of the top directors. Then came a third blow. After Arbuckle's arrest, Wallace Reid stepped in as the studio's biggest star. His six-foot-one, athletic physique and dashing good looks had elevated him to leading roles. While in Oregon in 1919, starring in a film, Reid was injured, and Jesse Lasky sent a company doctor north. The movie star was soon addicted to morphine.

Strung out, he worked at a breakneck pace, headlining in physically demanding roles for Paramount, seven each year in the first three years of the 1920s. Alcohol was another addiction. Sometimes the crew had to literally prop him up to capture shots, and his habits were well known in Hollywood and to those who got their hands on *The Sins of Hollywood*, in which "handsome Walter" is sort of patient zero in the "Dope!" chapter, supposedly hooking many of his fellow actors on cocaine and opium at his "dope parties."

On September 19, 1922, Reid's wife admitted him to a Hollywood sanitarium for treatment. And nine days before Christmas, Hollywood's worst-kept secret broke on front pages. WALLACE REID CRITICALLY ILL, "DOPE" BLAMED, screamed the *Chicago Tribune*. In Los Angeles to meet with studio executives, Will Hays visited Reid on December 19 in a padded room in the sanitarium. Hays said the cinematic heartthrob, then weighing a decimated 130 pounds, was recovering, but Reid would die a month later, on January 18, 1923.

The morning after visiting Reid, before he boarded a train with his wife and son heading to Sullivan, Indiana, for Christmas, Hays issued a statement on another matter.

As surprising as it was for Hays to bar Arbuckle from movie screens, it was more shocking when he reinstated him eight months later. On December 20, 1922, Arbuckle received what the press called an early Christmas present when Hays dropped a grenade disguised as a statement:

> Every man in the right way and at the proper time is entitled to his chance to make good. It is apparent that Roscoe Arbuckle's conduct

> since his trouble merits that chance. So far as I am concerned, there will be no suggestion now that he should not have his opportunity to go to work in his profession. In our effort to develop a complete co-operation and confidence within the industry, I hope we can start this New Year with no yesterdays. "Live and let live" is not enough; we will try to live and help live.

The grenade would go off shortly thereafter.

In his memoirs, Hays claimed he reinstated Arbuckle only after long deliberation:

> It was not my wish that he again become a movie actor, as many at the time professed to believe, nor was I exuding sentimentality for a comedian whom I had never met. I merely refused to stand in the man's way of earning a living in the only business he knew. . . . It did seem to me that if work could be found for the man as a comedy director, perhaps, or as a technician, it was not my job to bar him from such a chance. In a spirit of American fair play, and I hope of Christian charity, I proposed that he be given a chance.

In fact, the April 18 banishment had been vague, merely stating that at Hays's request Paramount had "cancelled all showings and all bookings of the Arbuckle films." That said, with Paramount shelving two unreleased Fatty features, the implication was clear: don't work with Arbuckle. The December 20 "pre-Christmas pardon" was clearer: Arbuckle's films are again welcome on-screen, and producers are free to employ him.

Hays had received pressure to make this reversal from theater owners eager to screen Fatty films; from studios other than Paramount, worried about the precedent of the MPPDA hampering profits; from editorialists; and from letter-writing members of the public. Still, there was no major groundswell of public support. Perhaps Hays had simply heard from enough sympathetic industry people while in Los Angeles. With the trials long over and Arbuckle's association with Paramount a faded memory, Zukor and company had gotten what they wanted from the banishment and likely had no concerns about their previous comedy superstar beginning an association with a new studio.

Hays later professed, "It seemed a relatively commonplace decision to me, and I anticipated no such excitement as ensued. . . . But for the next three months it became a *cause célèbre* . . . as newspaper editorials and civic leagues presented me with every public building in the country, brick by brick."

Those bricks, and lots of them, would start to bombard Hays before December 20 was done, but first there was euphoria. Arbuckle rushed into Schenck's office at 10 AM, seeking confirmation of what he had heard from reporters and so excited that he was, the *Los Angeles Times* reported, shaking and "stammering so badly that he had difficulty in making himself understood." What he'd heard was true. A brief formal statement from Arbuckle was drafted and handed out to the press: "Mr. Hays has made his decision. It is my intention in every way to live up to what Mr. Hays expects of me." A perfectly bland pronouncement, stripped of any sense of triumph, from a man who was then experiencing the heights of exuberance.

"I cannot say just now how soon we can get a picture for him or what kind of pictures he will make," Schenck said. "Stories do not come out of thin air, and we must have something suitable to him, something in his character. I have received many telegrams today from all parts of the country congratulating me and Arbuckle. People have been saying nice things over the phone. I believe the American public is just, and that it has come to realize that Arbuckle should be back on the screen."

Around the time Schenck said that, the Los Angeles Federation of Women's Clubs held an emergency meeting and passed a motion calling for Arbuckle to never again appear on-screen. The Illinois Motion Picture Association promptly announced that Fatty movies would not play in any of its theaters. His cinematic image wasn't welcome in Michigan's theaters either. Or in Boston or Indianapolis. And on and on. In many cases, municipalities merely reasserted bans that had been in place since shortly after his arrest. Protesting telegrams deluged Hays—from religious groups, women's groups, teachers' groups.

Two days after their hasty statement, Illinois theater owners reversed it, deciding to let Arbuckle's films screen—if the public wanted to see them. The same "let the people decide" edict was enacted in New York and California. The Motion Picture Directors Association, which under the late William Taylor had been ardently anticensorship, held a lengthy emergency meeting and, after a contentious debate, passed a controversial resolution that did not mention Arbuckle but stated "that under no circumstance should any person or persons who by their actions have proven a menace to the well-being of our industry be tolerated or excused." Responding to pressure from women's clubs, the mayor of Los Angeles vowed to keep Arbuckle off his city's screens. He telegraphed his protest to Hays, as did many other politicians. On December 23 Hays responded with telegrams of his own, claiming he was not reinstating Arbuckle but would not stand in the way of him making a living. The equivocation pleased no one.

Arbuckle released a statement that appeared in newspapers on Christmas morning. "All I ask is the rights of an American citizen—American fair play," it began, before rehashing his acquittal and then arguing that those "who are unjustly, untruthfully, maliciously and venomously attacking me are refusing to abide by the established law of the land" as well as "a higher law." In regards to the latter, the previously irreligious Arbuckle (or whoever wrote his statement) had much to say, quoting scripture and accusing his ministerial critics of ignoring the spirit of the Bible. He asked what his opponents would have thought of Jesus forgiving the penitent thief: "Would not some of these persons have denounced Christ and stoned him for what he said?" Arbuckle asked if Christianity was about charity or "a thing of only teeth and claws." In conclusion: "The sentiment of every church on Christmas Day will be 'Peace on Earth and good will to all mankind.' What will be the attitude the day after Christmas to me?"

The day after the day after Christmas, the San Francisco Federation of Women's Clubs met to urge Hays's banishment of Arbuckle in order to make an example "of those who brazenly violate the moral code of a Christian nation."

Theatrical producer Arthur Hammerstein offered Paramount $1 million for the two never-released feature films as well as the barely released *Gasoline Gus*. When that was refused, he offered to exhibit the features for only 10 percent of their profits, so confident was he that they would be successful. Referencing a screening of an Arbuckle movie in New York City two days earlier, Hammerstein said, "The crowd was so anxious to see him that they nearly broke down the doors. Whenever people are told they ought not to see a certain thing that's the very thing they are most eager to see." Paramount did not budge.

Over the final days of 1922, Arbuckle journeyed to San Francisco. There his former defense attorney Gavin McNab and financiers organized a company with $100,000 of funding to produce Fatty movies in Los Angeles. Subsequently, Arbuckle wrote the script for a two-reel comedy, *Handy Andy*.

The debate raged into the new year. Hays selected the members of an advisory group of religious and civic leaders, but he disagreed with their resolution urging him to advise producers against releasing any Fatty movies. After a long conference with the committee, Hays issued his "final statement," saying that he was leaving it up to the public, Arbuckle's employers, and Arbuckle himself, and that in doing so he was removing himself as judge.

Perhaps it would have been different had Arbuckle never been banned. Perhaps he could have weathered the initial outrage regarding his return to movies, and the protesters would have grown quieter over time and silenced with the popularity of new Fatty features. Instead, he had escaped punishment from the courts only to receive it from the movie industry, and by reversing its sentence eight months later it appeared as if that industry suddenly condoned his booze-fueled "orgy." The two decisions together could seem like a whitewash: let Arbuckle have some time off to jaunt about the world and then let him return to cinematic stardom like nothing had happened.

If it had been about just one man, even one as famous as Roscoe "Fatty" Arbuckle, his presumptive return never would have created the momentous firestorm it did. This was about much more. It was America's first great battle in a culture war. Society was changing fast—too fast for many—and Hollywood, with its drugs, its sexual libertinism, its flaunting of Prohibition, its disrespect for authority, and its moral relativism, was at the forefront of this change. Or so the editorialists said, over and over again—and with renewed vigor once Wallace Reid's drug addiction became common knowledge. Motion pictures themselves were a new and powerful force, having soared to prominence within the previous decade, and people were still coming to terms with a technology that permitted Fatty to ogle a young woman on thousands of screens. The outrage was great that a man who now represented the worst of Hollywood immorality could be welcomed back onto those screens.

Arbuckle's heights of euphoria on December 20 were supplanted by depths of despair the following weeks when he realized his hopes of returning to the life he knew before had been dashed. An article in January portrayed Arbuckle as depressed. He had gone from the stately West Adams mansion, his home during the height of his fame and fortune, to "a little obscure cabin in Hollywood" where he lived with Luke the loyal dog. "I just want to work and to make people laugh—and to eat," he said. The day that article ran, January 10, was the day he began acting in *Handy Andy*. It was never released and likely never finished.

Arbuckle would retreat behind the camera. On January 31 came the announcement that he had signed to direct five shorts for Reel Comedies, Joseph Schenck's new company, incorporated the day prior. Among those backing the venture were Lou Anger, Buster Keaton, and, again, Gavin McNab. The movies would be distributed by Educational Pictures, a small company previously known for instructional films. Arbuckle said that directing was "a chance to make good in the right way"—and that he was done with acting. A reporter who talked with the ostracized actor several times during this period remembered, "He was very bitter over what he believed was injustice, which financially and professionally ruined him. I had never seen a more hopeless man."

Arbuckle did appear in a film in 1923—and for Paramount. James Cruze, director of five of his Paramount features, made *Hollywood*, a comedy feature about the struggles to find movie industry success. It was loaded with cameos by celebrities, including Charlie Chaplin, Douglas Fairbanks, and Mary Pickford. But one uncredited bit part stole the show. When the hapless heroine joins a casting cattle call, an unrevealed overweight man steps aside to give the nervous wannabe his place. After she strikes out, the man steps up to the casting director's window for his turn, only to have the window slammed in his face. He stares at CLOSED on the window before the camera reveals his identity: Roscoe Arbuckle. "It was a superbly forcible touch, inserted in the picture without comment," a reviewer opined. "Whether one feels sympathy or contempt for Arbuckle, one cannot deny that this was a vitally dramatic moment in *Hollywood*." The movie played with no notable protests. Instead, Arbuckle's appearance was applauded at screenings, including in San Francisco, two years after Labor Day.

Ultimately, Arbuckle was not credited for his work directing, writing, and producing shorts for Reel Comedies, as publicizing his involvement would provide little upside and raise the potential for protests. His unacknowledged efforts began in February 1923 with *Easter Bonnets*, which allowed him to finally cast the now-twenty-three-year-old actress Doris Deane, whom he had met and courted on the steamship *Harvard* the day after Labor Day 1921. The next five shorts starred Edwin "Poodles" Hanneford, a circus clown noted for his horse-riding tricks. The work occupied Arbuckle's time and provided a creative outlet, but it brought little of the joy he had experienced as a movie star.

He still desired the spotlight, and he needed the large paychecks that came with it to pay down his debts. In May he signed on for a four-week stint at Chicago's upscale Marigold Gardens cabaret club, telling corny jokes punctuated with singing and dancing. When Arbuckle the vaudevillian first acted in the then-debased medium of motion pictures in 1909, it was the equivalent of slumming. Now he had traveled full circle: he was a former movie star from glamorous Hollywood returning to the decaying world of vaudeville. The money was good—a guaranteed $2,500 per week and more if the gate was strong—but all but

$500 of that went straight to the IRS, to which he owed $30,000 in back taxes.

The first time the crowd of two thousand at Marigold Gardens saw Arbuckle at the debut performance on June 4, he was in a movie on a screen running toward the camera, growing ever larger, and then the real man burst through the paper screen in three dimensions. The resulting ovation lasted fifteen minutes. "This is the first smile I've had in a long, long time," he told the audience. The show's producer remembered opening night: "A little girl strolled over to present him with a rose. The comedian went down on his knees and with tears streaming down his face he kissed the child in gratitude. The entire audience, including myself, was in tears." That producer admitted he had friends planted about the auditorium on opening night to foster applause in case the crowd was cold; the ringers were not needed.

The show was popular, but the attempt to transfer some of Fatty's slapstick antics to the stage was not deemed an artistic success. "The people have been very kind," Arbuckle said. "They have come out to see me and they have been extremely generous in their applause. In return I have done my best to amuse them in a poor act." The poor act included him in a ballerina dress and the return of Keystone's custard pies. Failing to shy away from misogynistic humor, he sang, "Our women are lean and fat, and some are darn good-looking. But the only use we have for them is when they do our cooking."

He took the act east to a boardwalk cabaret in Atlantic City, where he pulled in $6,000 weekly. Minta Durfee was set to perform at a competing club, billing herself as "Mrs. Fatty Arbuckle." This angered the owner of the club hiring Mr., and he tried to forbid Mr. from seeing Mrs. When the club owner requested that Arbuckle sue his wife for using his full name, Arbuckle told the press, "She stood by me in my time of trouble. Sue her? I'll be at the train [when she arrives] with a bouquet of roses." He was.

The couple had remained close friends, but there was no chance of them resuscitating their marriage. On November 2, 1923, Durfee filed for divorce in Providence, Rhode Island. The state was then the Reno of the East, noted for its relatively easy divorces—but not easy enough for Durfee. Her preliminary divorce was rescinded when she failed to prove she had lived in Rhode Island for four years.

In a letter from Arbuckle to Durfee dated November 18, 1923, it's clear he was regularly sending her money as contractually obligated by their separation agreement. The tone is affectionate toward his divorcing wife and her family, and he reveals a bluer strain of humor than his films could capture, closing with "Well kid don't get discouraged, keep a stiff upper lip, that's the only thing of mine that is stiff, I think somebody put salt peter in my coffee. Kisses and flowers, will write soon. Dingle-tit Roscoe." Earlier in the letter, he explained why he had "been busier than a dog with turpentine in his ass": "I have been thrown in at the last minute to direct Buster's next picture and I have been very busy trying to get the story ready."

> Fatty Arbuckle is now a Buster Keaton director under the name Will B. Good, so maybe he will.
>
> —*Herald-Star* (Steubenville, Ohio), January 17, 1924

Released in April 1924, *Sherlock Jr.* was Buster Keaton's third feature film,* the first on which he alone was credited as director, and today it is regarded as one of the masterpieces of silent cinema. In this surreal comedy, Keaton plays a movie projectionist who dreams that he climbs into a projected movie and enters its storyline. The action and stunts are breakneck; the effects are astonishing. And the original codirector was Keaton's close friend and mentor, Roscoe Arbuckle. In his autobiography, Keaton wrote:

> We were about to start *Sherlock Jr.* in 1924 when I decided that I must do something for my pal, Roscoe. . . . Roscoe was down in the

* It is arguably not feature length. Keaton recut it after poor previews, shrinking it to forty-five minutes.

> dumps and broke. . . . I suggested to Lou Anger that we give Roscoe a job directing *Sherlock Jr.* Lou said it could be arranged, but that we better get him to use some other name. I suggested "Will B. Good," but this was considered too facetious, so we changed it to "Will B. Goodrich."* The experiment was a failure. Roscoe was irritable, impatient, and snapped at everyone in the company. He had my leading lady, Kathryn McGuire, in tears dozens of times a day. One day, after Roscoe went home, the gang of us sat around trying to figure out what to do next. It was obvious that we couldn't make the picture with a man directing whose self-confidence was gone, whose nerves were all shot.

In one of the two scenes Arbuckle likely directed with McGuire, she is abducted by her butler and taken to a shack where the implication is the butler is about to rape her. Helming this scene may have been particularly stressful for Arbuckle, as he would have perceived that everyone was focused on him. He lasted no more than three weeks codirecting *Sherlock Jr.* before his best friend fired him. "He hadn't recovered from those trials, of being accused of murder and nearly convicted," Keaton said. "It just changed his disposition. In other words, it made a nervous wreck out of him."

Arbuckle wrote and directed four comedy shorts in 1924. All starred Al St. John, who was credited as writer and director in his uncle's place. All also featured Arbuckle's new (and long-delayed) love interest, Doris Deane. She was thirteen years his junior, born Doris Dibble in Wisconsin in 1900. Deane was the only child of peripatetic parents: in 1910

* William Goodrich was the given name of Arbuckle's father, so it is likely this was Arbuckle's first choice for a nom de plume and the Will B. Good pun followed. In the November 18, 1923 letter to Durfee, Arbuckle wrote: "I am taking my father's name to direct by and from now on to the screen I will be known as William Goodrich. Ain't that the cat's nuts. Sounds like a tire." However, the Will B. Good pseudonym was told to the press, who reported it in January 1924.

the family was renting a house in Iowa, where her father worked in a saloon, but by her high school years they lived in Butte, Montana, then a copper-mining boomtown. Subsequently, they relocated to Southern California.

There, under her new name, nineteen-year-old Deane nabbed her first film role. She was a tall and thin brunette with dimples and an easy smile. She dreamed of movie stardom. Things were looking up when she met Arbuckle on the *Harvard* in 1921. One week prior, her second film, Universal's *The Shark Master*, was released, and she had a major part. But only two additional roles followed before Arbuckle began casting her in comedy shorts in 1923.

She was best known for a flurry of publicity in December 1922 because of her rumored engagement to Jack Dempsey, then the world's heavyweight boxing champion. Chummy photos of the pair appeared on sports pages. The rumor was neither confirmed nor denied, but she would marry another heavyweight.

"Weeks ago I saw Fatty alone in a boat fishing off Catalina shore. Before that several times I had encountered him on solitary walks in the Hollywood Hills." So wrote a journalist in the summer of 1924. "He was getting a grip on himself. By such lonely vigils he achieved readjustment to begin once more where he started years since." Bolstered by his young love interest, steady work, and improving financial strength, Arbuckle's mood lifted. When he wasn't walking in the hills, he again drove a luxury automobile, as he owned a $9,000 McFarlan Knickerbocker Cabriolet, fire-engine red with FATTY license plates.*

In June 1924 thirty-seven-year-old Roscoe Arbuckle returned to Alexander Pantages's vaudeville troupe, which he had first traveled with

* The still-stunning car is displayed today in the Nethercutt Museum in Sylmar, California.

as a teen twenty years prior.* Now he would perform a comic monologue as the lineup's star attraction. At his first show, at the Pantages Theatre in San Francisco, he was greeted by an eleven-minute ovation. Even Matthew Brady backed off, saying the three trials were "the only way an accused man could be cleared of a horrible charge" and "I would rather build up than tear down and help than hurt, and Arbuckle has been condemned and hurt enough."

"San Francisco's reception of me is, I think, just evidence of the American fair play spirit that never dies—given time," Arbuckle said. "I've had my dose of foul play. Now it's fair play." When asked if his films would now be released, he answered, "I hope not. They would be old stuff now. . . . I want to make new comedies. Better pictures. I'm more serious now than I was in the old days." He exercised daily, and he claimed to have lost twenty pounds in the previous three weeks, all in an effort to get in shape for his "reappearance on the screen."

In Utah, he didn't avoid the topic on everyone's mind, joking, "No, I don't belong to either the Republicans or Democrats; no more parties for me." He said he hoped to return to movie stardom "just as soon as I recover from the Hays fever."

It wasn't all joviality and applause. In some communities, censors fought to keep him off stages just as they had screens. In Kansas City, Missouri, as a resolution was being read before the city council to bar him from local theaters, the subject of the ban appeared and asked to speak. Permission granted. He asked the council for a "chance to live a clean, decent life and pay my debts" and concluded with, "I come to you as Mary Magdalene—asking forgiveness." After the council peppered him with questions, the resolution was defeated ten to five. When

* In a parallel to Arbuckle's life, in 1929 Alexander Pantages would be accused of raping a seventeen-year-old aspiring actress. He claimed it was a setup but was convicted and sentenced to fifty years imprisonment. On appeal, the conviction was overturned. Pantages was financially devastated by court costs and the Depression before his death in 1936.

his appearances in Quincy, Illinois, were protested by a local minister, he asked to testify from that minister's pulpit about his own turn to Christianity since the famous party. Permission denied.* The Quincy shows drew large crowds.

In Cleveland, he headlined a bill filled out by a local singing/dancing/comedy duo that included a twenty-one-year-old British immigrant named Lester Hope. Arbuckle was impressed enough by the youngsters' blackface act to recommend them to a vaudeville producer. Lester later changed his name to Bob and became one of the most famous entertainers who ever lived.

On his way to shows in Louisville, Kentucky, the train that carried Arbuckle stopped in Logansport, Indiana, long enough for him to talk with an enterprising local reporter and to receive three telegrams (all collect, two from Durfee) from a messenger boy who called him "Mr. Fatty." He bummed a cigarette and a light from the reporter, but he had difficulty finding a single among his roll of hundreds when he paid the messenger. He said he envied the creative freedom of Charlie Chaplin, who could dote on his very occasional projects at United Artists, and he stated he would be returning to Los Angeles to act in a movie (untrue) and that he had sworn off booze (untrue) and women (untrue).

This had become his practiced storyline over the previous two and a half years, for to him his return was all about his reform. If people believed he was a changed man, why couldn't they accept him again as a comedic film character? A telegram to a Toledo theater showed Arbuckle's strategy at work:

---

* The minister asked for "written evidence of Christian life and fruitage during the three years that have elapsed since your tragic ordeal." Arbuckle responded: "I did not know it was customary to get a written receipt from God when you decided to follow Him. Furthermore, I am not asking you for salvation. I have already received that. However, if you must have a written recommendation, get in touch with Rev. Brougher of Los Angeles. I have taken God into my heart, but did not know that it was necessary to advertise it, but since I have decided to go straight with God I have learned to turn the other cheek. God bless you." The evidence of Arbuckle's supposed turn to a Christian lifestyle is limited to his embracing it during censorship battles, for then he did find it necessary to advertise.

> Appeal to you as one of several in motion picture industry to help me place before followers of motion picture screen my request for permission to return to pictures. May I ask privilege of use of your stage for a few minutes daily for one week to talk personally to motion picture fans and if possible obtain consensus of opinion regarding my return to my life work, motion pictures.

The theater responded in the affirmative. "I don't claim to be an angel," Arbuckle told the appreciative audience three days later, just before reading them the third trial jury's statement regarding his innocence. "I was a young fellow whose head had been turned around by success. I had plenty of money and there were plenty of fair weather friends to 'yes' me. I simply was led into bad company—and for that I already have paid dearly."

This spin was different from his strategy during the trials. Under oath, he had claimed to be an "angel," assisting an ill Rappe. Now he said that he'd been ushered down the wrong path, seemingly blaming his connection to the tragedy on his playboy lifestyle. As to him being a "young fellow" in September 1921, he was thirty-four.

Durfee once stated that early in her marriage her husband did not share her love of books, but in a letter to her dated September 13, 1924, he mused on literary matters. He panned Émile Zola's *L'assommoir* ("Of all the morbid, filthy, dirty smelly books I ever read, it is the worst") and claimed he was going to buy Edward Gibbon's gargantuan *The History of the Decline and Fall of the Roman Empire* when he returned to Los Angeles, joking, "I would certainly delight to read about something that fell harder than I did."

Arbuckle's tour through the Pacific Northwest was a bust. By a unanimous vote, the Portland, Oregon, city council banned him. When the censorship board forbade him from stages in Tacoma, Washington, he and the theater sought a court injunction. Injunction denied. Appealed to the federal court. Injunction denied. He returned to Los Angeles and performed at the Pantages Theatre there.

On September 4, 1924, Arbuckle wrote Durfee. Referring to her by his term of endearment "Mint," he said he "received contract okay" and went on to discuss a crucial component of it: how he intended to send a check to her each week. This appears to have been a new financial arrangement. They agreed that he would pay her 15 percent of his earnings for the first year and 20 percent thereafter, and "not less than $200 per week" until she remarried or until death terminated the contract. (Their 1919 separation agreement had paid her $500 weekly, but he had a lucrative movie deal then.) He mentioned that she would be sailing on the ocean liner *Majestic* and said, "I envy you that trip"—which he was financing. That November, Durfee was in Paris, where she would find it easier to end her marriage. She had, at Arbuckle's behest, traveled thirty-six hundred miles to file for divorce from her husband of sixteen years.

On December 5 came the announcement that Arbuckle would marry Doris Deane. Alluding to the death of Virginia Rappe, one acerbic headline read, DORIS IS DARING. The wedding was originally set for February, and a March ceremony was scrapped hours before it was to go off because the divorce could not be formalized. Finally, on May 16, 1925, Roscoe Arbuckle and Doris Deane married at her mother's home. Buster Keaton was the best man, and Keaton's wife, Natalie Talmadge, was the maid of honor. Joseph Schenck (who by now was chairman of United Artists) and Lou Anger were among the thirty-five guests.* Hundreds attended the reception at Keaton and Talmadge's new Beverly Hills home. Subsequently, the newlyweds moved into a nearby house they rented from Schenck, but not before they went on a honeymoon at a location reportedly "hidden away in the country."

---

* By this point, Anger had nothing to do with managing Arbuckle's career and had formed his own production company. After Schenck became president of United Artists in 1927, he hired Anger. In 1933 Schenck helped found 20th Century Pictures, which merged with ailing Fox two years later. Schenck went on to become chairman and then head of production at 20th Century-Fox, and Anger worked in management at the studio.

Shortly before the wedding ceremony, one of the guests, producer Roland West, gave Arbuckle a most unique present: a contract worth $100,000 to direct ten two-reel comedies. The press made much of the gesture, but it was essentially a continuation of his current occupation, directing low-budget shorts in an age of features. He had already made thirteen for Reel Comedies, the last seven starring Al St. John, including *The Iron Mule*, a spoof of John Ford's railroad epic *The Iron Horse*. His name appeared on none of them.* The new comedies starred either Johnny Arthur or Lupino Lane, former vaudevillians destined for busy but undistinguished celluloid careers. Despite the initial publicity for the contract, when the shorts were released, "William Goodrich" was credited, not Arbuckle.

It is unknown why Arbuckle chose his father's first and middle names to direct under. It may have been a tribute—a means of forgiving the man who had died a half-decade prior and had been mostly absent or abusive when Roscoe was young. But it could have been a slander—a way of tying his dad to forgettable flicks, even if only Arbuckle and his family knew. Perhaps it was just a convenient moniker that had no greater meaning. Regardless, "William Goodrich" was destined to become a very prolific director. It was as though Arbuckle had returned to his unglamorous, anonymous movie work of 1909, doing chores for paychecks. As Charlie Chaplin and Buster Keaton won great acclaim for creating innovative features, Arbuckle saw little benefit to having his name attached to shorts starring second-string talent.

However, a first-stringer made a cameo. For *The Iron Mule*, Buster Keaton let Arbuckle use the exact replica of a pioneering steam engine built for Keaton's feature *Our Hospitality*, and Keaton also appeared in the short as an Indian, uncredited and virtually unrecognizable. The roles were reversed a few months later when Arbuckle appeared in drag in Keaton's 1925 feature *Go West*. As Keaton's character tries to control a cattle stampede through Los Angeles, Arbuckle plays a frightened

* The first six were uncredited, the next four were credited to Al St. John, and the final three were credited to Grover Jones, a prolific screenwriter.

mother in a department store; the rotund actress Babe London is his daughter. Neither role was credited, and it was easy for audiences to miss Fatty in drag. But the cameo was more than just another practical joke for Arbuckle and Keaton. London remembered, "It was their way of thumbing their noses at the people who had decreed that Roscoe could not appear on the screen."

Keaton wasn't the only industry friend who stuck by Arbuckle. The Masquers, an all-male social club of mostly actors, was born in May 1925 as sort of a West Coast version of the Friars Club. Arbuckle was made an official member on October 7 of that year. Other early members included Keaton, Joseph Schenck, Tom Mix, and Lionel Barrymore.* It was a little over four years since the Los Angeles Athletic Club voted Arbuckle out, so being voted by his peers into another exclusive club—while still blacklisted as an actor by Hollywood—was a satisfying triumph.

But he soon found out how little some things had changed. On October 16 the Masquers were set to give a comedy revue at Hollywood High School, but after receiving protests, the school demanded Arbuckle be dropped from the cast. The Masquers stood by their newest member, canceled the high school show, and instead rented the Philharmonic Auditorium, where the revue played to a packed house full of movie professionals. Arbuckle's appearance in the first skit elicited a long ovation, and when it faded and some hisses were heard, the ovation began again.

In December 1925 Hollywood heavyweights Cecil B. DeMille, Charlie Chaplin, and every studio head were among the six hundred who gathered for a banquet in honor of Sid Grauman. Maybe, as he sat at a table with wife Doris Deane and his friends, Roscoe Arbuckle was remembering those teenage days long ago when he worked for the Graumans: singing illustrated songs on a vaudeville bill at the Unique in San Jose and then soloing at the Portola Café in San Francisco, back when

* Among the many legends who later joined: Frank Sinatra, Henry Fonda, Humphrey Bogart, Sir Laurence Olivier, and Johnny Carson.

the Hotel St. Francis was going up, back when he could walk the streets and no one recognized him, and strangers neither loved nor loathed him.

Writer Rupert Hughes, the master of ceremonies, introduced some of the notables at the banquet. When he came to Arbuckle, he asked him to stand. "Here is the sad spectacle of a man being punished by so-called democracy!" Hughes shouted. Arbuckle's head bowed. "A man who was acquitted of a trumped-up charge by three American juries! But our militant *good people* arose to crucify, to persecute an innocent man! They dragged him down from the topmost pinnacle of being the clean and funny comedian that he was and made of him the world's most tragic figure!" The applause thundered. It was much louder for Roscoe Arbuckle than anyone else. Hollywood showered with love the man blacklisted by Hollywood.

{20}

ENDURANCE: 1926–32

> Have you ever realized that actors are mere public toys, playthings for the people to handle and grow tired of, toys that amuse for a time, toys that lure with the brightness of their paint, to be patronized just so long as the paint is new and bright and attractive, dropped and forgotten when it is worn off and the toy is broken and old? Dead, never to be resurrected; discarded and thrown aside for a toy more amply shaded with varnish and crimson, forgotten for a new face, a newer, larger smile, a greater capacity for tears.
>
> —MOVIE STAR JOHN BUNNY, ONE MONTH BEFORE HIS DEATH IN 1915

We can never know how frequently or how fully Roscoe Arbuckle was capable of forgetting the event that, above all others, came to define his life. But there were many good times. A front-page article in February 1926 entitled "'Fatty' Arbuckle Does Comeback!" portrayed a happily married man, making $2,000 weekly as a director, living in a "palatial home in Beverly Hills, with two servants to make his life easy for him." An accompanying photograph captured him and wife Doris Deane and their St. Bernard (Luke had recently died). The article noted that he had paid off $50,000 of $182,000 in debts and planned to have the remainder erased in three years. "With my wife and my new work I have found happiness," he said.

In March, he, Buster Keaton, and their wives drove to Yosemite National Park in Arbuckle's new convertible Lincoln Phaeton and, perhaps with movie stars' sense of entitlement, disregarded orders not to use an automobile entrance still under construction. In retaliation, the road was blocked, preventing their exit from the park. So with movie stars' money, they hired a train to ship themselves and the Phaeton out. It seemed like a plot from one of their Comique shorts—the merry pranksters one-upping the humorless officials. Front-page headline: MOVIE STARS ESCAPE FROM PARK PRISON.

Other times it was Lew Cody who accompanied Arbuckle on his adventures—especially the sort that involved alcohol. At 3 AM on September 17, 1926, Cody married Mabel Normand, supposedly on a drunken dare.*

Arbuckle's first attempt at directing a feature, *Sherlock Jr.*, had failed. His second opportunity came in 1926, courtesy of an unlikely source: newspaper tycoon William Randolph Hearst, who had sold many editions five years prior with screaming FATTY headlines. Though he never divorced the wife he married in 1903, Hearst lived openly with his mistress, actress Marion Davies, thirty-four years his junior. Through his own Cosmopolitan Productions, he cast Davies as the star of comedies and costume dramas, churning through a pool of directors in the process. Working as "William Goodrich," Arbuckle was merely another.

A romantic comedy based on a musical play, *The Red Mill* was shot in California but set in rural Holland. From the beginning, the tyrannical Hearst was anxious about getting his desired results from Arbuckle, so he assigned MGM director King Vidor to oversee the production. Actress Colleen Moore remembered, "The intrigues on the set of *The Red Mill* would have made a good thriller. Everyone was aware that they were being watched. Arbuckle watched Marion, Vidor watched Arbuckle, and

* By then Normand's health was in decline and her career was nearly over (she acted in her final two comedy shorts in 1927). She died of tuberculosis in 1930 at thirty-seven.

Mr. Hearst watched all three of them. Roscoe had a nice way of making everyone on the set feel relaxed. He was very workmanlike and had no problems communicating what he wanted his cast to do."

Released by MGM, *The Red Mill* was a box office flop, leading Hearst to again hire a new director for Davies's next vanity project. Nevertheless, the visually rich film may have encouraged Arbuckle's old home of Paramount to give him another shot, for they hired him to helm *Special Delivery*, a comedy feature starring theater legend Eddie Cantor, whose vocal talents were lost in silent cinema. Mailman Cantor is pitted against a suave con man (then-little-known William Powell) for the affections of a young woman. Another down-on-his-luck comedy legend, Larry Semon, was Arbuckle's assistant director.* The final chase is especially well-staged, both funny and exciting, proving "William Goodrich's" directing acumen. *Special Delivery*'s advertising sometimes touted the former star behind the name: "Directed by Roscoe 'Fatty' Arbuckle, alias William Goodrich."

Unfortunately, the public was no more interested in a mailman comedy starring a silenced singer than they were a Dutch comedy starring William Hearst's girlfriend. Arbuckle never again worked for Paramount.

From a January 4, 1927 gossip column item regarding a film industry dinner dance:

> In the gathering sitting obscurely and dancing only occasionally was Fatty Arbuckle who is rounding out what is left of his career as a director under the name Will B. Good.† There is a noticeable hurt, stricken look in his eyes. He is a cloistered clown paying scandal's terrible price. He probably does not need my pity but I pitied him just the same.

---

* To fend off creditors after making the financially disastrous *The Wizard of Oz* (1925), Semon mirrored Arbuckle, directing two-reel comedies for Educational and returning to vaudeville. He died in 1928 at age thirty-nine.

† He never actually used this pseudonym.

Arbuckle returned to front pages on March 15, 1927, when he reportedly signed a deal worth $2.5 million over five years to direct and perform in feature films financed by Abe Carlos, formerly with Fox.* At last, six years after his arrest, Arbuckle would again star on the big screen. Doris Deane was to act opposite her husband in the films, and the first production was to begin in Germany on October 1.

In the meantime, Arbuckle set out on what was billed as his final vaudeville tour, a farewell to the stage before going back in front of the camera. A Los Angeles review noted the large ovations for him before and after his set but wished that his act of "quips and wisecracks" had focused less on his "various misfortunes" and "hard luck."

After the spring tour, Arbuckle starred in a Broadway revival of the farce *Baby Mine*. Humphrey Bogart had a supporting role. Arbuckle's opening-night ovations were rousing, but he appeared awkward. "Mr. Arbuckle is not much of an actor," noted one review. It didn't aid the play when between acts, its star broke character to speak to the audience about his troubled attempts to return to cinema and his impending comeback. *Baby Mine* closed after only twelve performances. One more "misfortune."

There were others. When he made an appearance on a New York vaudeville stage, the National Educational Association protested. A lien was placed against him for failure to pay all of his 1926 taxes. Alerted by the tax figures, Minta Durfee sued him for $25,000, later settling for $16,500.† Arbuckle offered no public comment regarding the suit or the settlement. By now the reported October start date of his new film had come and gone.

Arbuckle's theatrical appearances continued into 1928, in what was still being advertised as "his last vaudeville tour prior to re-entering the

* The deal reportedly had a $5,000-per-week salary; the other half of the estimated payday would come from Arbuckle's share of profits.

† Durfee claimed she was getting the minimum $200 weekly payments from Arbuckle but not 20 percent of his earnings as agreed.

movies." Delegations of ministers in Clarksburg, West Virginia, protested Arbuckle's appearance at a theater there. He was banned from stages in Minneapolis because he "might corrupt public morals." And a performance in Waterloo, Iowa, was canceled after protests. The career-resuscitating, financially lucrative movie deal never materialized.

These negatives tended to drown out the positives, such as a Kansas City, Missouri, theater showing a Keystone Fatty comedy in April 1928 in "defiance of the Hays organization." The movie morality czar was now so tarnished by the Teapot Dome scandal that Senator James A. Reed quipped in a presidential campaign speech, "I have never paraded as a reformer, but I propose that the motion picture industry remove Will Hays and put back Fatty Arbuckle." The crowd roared in agreement.

A French crowd had a different reaction. Arbuckle traveled first to Cherbourg and then to Paris to perform his comedy at the prestigious Empire music hall. "Some of my old films have been shown abroad successfully and on my trip here some years ago I met with every courtesy," he said in an article entitled "'Fatty' Arbuckle Goes to Paris to Regain Esteem." This time the crowd was so hostile toward his act that a riot call was made to the police and the stage manager turned off the lights for eight minutes "hoping the audience would cool off." News of the disastrous "riot" spread throughout America.

His love life fared no better. In May 1928 Arbuckle—who had spent the previous twelve months in hotels and on trains and steamships—returned to Los Angeles and moved into the Hollywood Hotel, where Virginia Rappe, Buster Keaton, and many other cinematic hopefuls had lived. After three years of marriage, he and Deane had separated. "We haven't got along happily for some time, and if I've got to be lonesome I might as well be lonesome here," the forty-one-year-old said of the popular hotel.

When Deane filed for divorce in August 1928, she set off an explosive charge: the couple had attended a party in April 1926 at the home of a "prominent resident" of Hollywood where, she claimed, Arbuckle became "terribly intoxicated" and forcibly attempted to get physical with a female guest. Allegedly, the screaming woman was rescued by

Deane and others. The accusation was never brought to court, and other than a smattering of headlines such as 'NOTHER WILD PARTY FOR FATTY ARBUCKLE, the press showed scant interest. Made public more than two years after the alleged event, the unsubstantiated charge was likely an attempt by Deane to paint her husband in the worst possible light. She sought $750 monthly in alimony and also claimed her husband had been "vicious, cruel, morose and nagging." The divorce was delayed; the marriage continued, unhappily.

Viola Dana remembered Arbuckle as occasionally verbally abusive to Deane (as he sometimes was to Keaton and Alice Lake as well): "You know, Roscoe was an easy man to like, *if you let him be in charge*. After that third trial, he believed everyone was going to let bygones be bygones. But that isn't the way things work in the movie industry, even if you're *liked*. He took all of his frustrations, personal and professional, out on poor Doris until she couldn't take it anymore."

Maybe it was a way to start the party again, a way for a middle-aged has-been to return to those glorious days before Prohibition when nights were filled with dancing and drinking, eating and laughing in Vernon and Venice and Hollywood. The world then had been a blur of practical jokes and pretty starlets, boxing matches and poker games, steaks, clams, and—always—drinking. There were famous friends, whole packs of them, but none more famous than him. Everyone knew him. Everyone wanted to be his pal. Going back seems the sort of thing he would dream up in the lobby of the Hollywood Hotel. The acting, the money, the prestige—the best part of it all then was those nights when, as Buster Keaton said, "the world was ours."

And so Roscoe Arbuckle bought his own nightclub. Ironically, initial reports claimed he was launching a nationwide chain of coffee shops. It must have been the name: Roscoe Arbuckle's Plantation Cafe. Launched under different ownership in the summer of 1922, the Plantation Cafe, with its row of eight Corinthian columns and its regal white facade, resembled a Southern mansion, as did buildings at MGM and Culver

Studios, both just up the street. The club was located in Culver City, an incorporated municipality virtually surrounded by Los Angeles but with little enthusiasm for Prohibition.

Culver City's main thoroughfare, Washington Boulevard, was crowded with a long string of nightclubs with flashing signs—Ford's Castle, Kit Kat Club, Doo Doo Inn, Lyon's Den, Monkey Farm. Thousands flocked to this strip nightly for the live jazz from future legends like Lawrence Brown and Lionel Hampton, but also for the dancing, gambling, prostitution, and booze. Much of the alcohol was brewed up in the backyards of nearby houses, further aiding the local economy. The hottest joint on Washington was Sebastian's Cotton Club (where Louis Armstrong would headline in 1930–31), but the Plantation Cafe also developed a reputation as an upscale destination, because of its quality jazz bands and comedy revues and the actors who were frequent masters of ceremony. Since Culver City did not completely condone violations of the Volstead Act, raids were a regular feature at the Plantation. Arrests were made, bottles destroyed, fines paid, only to have the nightclub open again—and be raided again. DRY STORM RAGES OVER PLANTATION, read a typical *Los Angeles Times* headline from January 1926.

By the time Arbuckle and his fellow investors purchased the Plantation Cafe in July 1928, the club's aura had faded. Arbuckle set out to change that. On opening night, August 2, the colonial foyer was stuffed with floral tributes, including a giant likeness of Arbuckle from Mabel Normand, and celebrities dined on the ten-dollar-a-plate dinner (about $130 in today's dollars). After more typical cabaret acts, Arbuckle, Buster Keaton, Al St. John, Tom Mix, and vaudeville comedian Jack Pearl performed slapstick antics, including custard pie tossing. A report said, "Every screen star of note now in Hollywood was present with ears pinned back and hair well larded. And if their hosannas is [*sic*] a criterion, the future of Arbuckle as a restaurateur is assured."

The newly revived club was a hit from the start, selling out nightly to "a strange crowd of big-time movie stars, would-be stars and tourists." "I guess I'll go back to the stage," Arbuckle said soon after the opening. "But for now I'll do my entertaining here." Jazz greats played the Plantation, but Fatty was the biggest attraction in his own club. He also inspired its new theme: fat farmers. The waiters, hat check girls, and parking attendants were all corpulent, and befitting plantation workers and reminiscent of Arbuckle's country bumpkin character, they wore bib overalls.

The month after Roscoe Arbuckle's Plantation Cafe opened, England's Prince George, a notorious playboy, was in Los Angeles and partying with an actress, first at the estate of Hollywood power couple Douglas Fairbanks and Mary Pickford and then at Gloria Swanson's house. Sometime in the early morning hours, everyone journeyed to the Plantation and persuaded Arbuckle to keep it open. The shindig there ended at 5 AM but continued back at Swanson's. This was the lifestyle Arbuckle wanted to preserve: to be a member of royalty, Hollywood or otherwise, in a party that seemed like it would never end. It was the lifestyle he had publicly sworn off six years prior when what he desired most was a return to movie stardom, but now that his return had been denied, he embraced it more openly than before.

Two days before Christmas 1928, the Plantation was raided, and ten men, not including Arbuckle, were arrested for Prohibition violations. In January 1929 the club was cited after neighbors complained about its sleep-preventing sounds, but Arbuckle ignored the quieting order until the Culver City mayor visited and threatened to close the club. Alcohol busts and code violations were one thing, but in May 1929 a riot broke out at the Plantation, and when police tried to disperse it the brawlers turned on the men in blue—but without the pulled punches of a Keystone comedy. A policeman was critically injured.

This was the sort of publicity that repelled customers. Then came the stock market crash of October 1929 and the subsequent Depression. Arbuckle sold his share in 1930, and shortly thereafter the Plantation Cafe closed for good.

After his two features fizzled, Arbuckle's directing career had stalled, and he spent the next three years working on vaudeville stages and greeting guests at his Plantation. Meanwhile, without him, the motion picture industry was finding its voice.

For the three decades that movie actors were rendered mute, their silence was a peculiarity that everyone—performers, filmmakers, viewers—had adopted as the new normal. It was both limiting and, in the way someone who loses one sense appreciates more her other senses, liberating. Some complexities of storytelling and characterization were lost, but silent cinema in the 1920s developed an exuberant expressiveness to compensate. Writing in *Photoplay* in 1921, editor in chief James Quirk rhapsodized:

> In [motion pictures'] silence it more nearly approximates nature than any arts save painting and sculpture. The greatest processes of the universe are those of silence. All growth is silent. The deepest love is most eloquent in that transcendent silence of the communion of souls. . . . The talking picture will be made practical, but it will never supercede the motion picture without sound. It will lack the subtlety and suggestion of vision—that vision which, deprived of voice to ears of flesh, intones undisturbed the symphonies of the soul.

From nearly the beginning, inventors had attempted to make motion pictures talk. In 1895, two years after unveiling his viewing-box Kinetoscope, Thomas Edison introduced the Kinetophone, which added sound via a phonograph player (which Edison had invented in 1877). Viewers listened to music and effects via earphones as they peered into the cabinet, observing moving pictures unsynchronized to the audio—the nineteenth-century equivalent of using an iPad with earbuds to experience *Avatar*. Only forty-five such machines were sold, and film projection soon rendered even audio-equipped viewing boxes obsolete.

Many inventors attempted to synchronize projected films with phonograph records. Competing systems had names like the Chronophone, the Synchroscope, and, nearly a century before the word took on another meaning, the Cameraphone. Edison kept to his original name, relaunching a Kinetophone in 1913 that utilized a complex pulley system pairing a cylindrical phonograph player and a film projector to marry image and sound. Ads claimed it "startles the civilized world and revolutionizes the picture business," but synchronization was spotty and sound amplification was lousy. It flopped.

Meanwhile, others were blazing a different path. In 1901 German physics professor Ernst Ruhmer wrote an article for *Scientific American* about his new Photographophone, which played back sounds recorded as waves on film strips. The volume of those sounds could be manipulated via increasing or decreasing the amount of light used during playback. Ruhmer had created the first optical tape recorder and player, but it was former Edison employee Eugene Lauste who made the greatest advances in the recording, projection, and amplification of sound and picture on strips of film. He (and two others) secured the patent for his system in 1907, and he shot America's first true sound movie in 1911. Lauste worked to improve the technology, but World War I and a lack of financing stifled his dreams of commercialization.

In 1919 Lee de Forest patented an improved method for recording sound and moving images simultaneously on film. His De Forest Phonofilm Corporation commercially screened eighteen short sound movies (mostly of vaudeville acts) on April 13, 1923, in New York City. The "talking picture" industry was born. The major studios yawned. In 1924 a small animation company began using de Forest's process for singalong cartoons, but after business arrangements with two fellow inventors crumbled, Phonofilm declared bankruptcy. Those fellow inventors, Freeman Owens and Theodore Case, sold their sound patents to Fox Film Corporation, and Fox, in turn, released *Sunrise* on October 23, 1927, with the first feature-length sound-on-film soundtrack. Still, those sounds were only music and effects; dialogue was subtitled.

In the same way some still swear by vinyl recordings in the digital age, Edison's concept of marrying a phonograph record with a motion picture persisted even as men on both sides of the Atlantic innovated and improved sound-on-film techniques. D. W. Griffith employed the disc technology for singing and effects in his 1921 feature *Dream Street*, which bombed. Struggling Warner Bros. utilized the Bell Telephone Company's sound-on-disc process, which Warners dubbed Vitaphone. The initial result was *Don Juan*, released on August 6, 1926; the otherwise silent feature boasted a synchronized soundtrack of music and effects. *Don Juan*'s screenings were preceded by Vitaphone shorts, including one with a man hyping the sound process. That man was Will Hays.

Sound-on-disc motion pictures were cheaper to make than sound-on-film productions and had superior audio fidelity, but their synchronization was a continuous challenge, as was the distribution of the necessary discs, which wore out quickly and were prone to skipping and breaking. Therefore, a coalition of studios—not including Warners and Fox—agreed on a standard sound-on-film technology in early 1927.

But it was Warners' second sound-on-disc feature that launched the "talking pictures" phenomenon. *The Jazz Singer*, starring singer Al Jolson, was released on October 6, 1927. Though most of the audio was a score recorded separately and most of the "talking" was singing, Jolson's songs and some dialogue were recorded live on the set—a first in a feature film. It was a huge success.

Still, the studios in the sound-on-film coalition were hesitant to produce their own talkies. With the addition of audio, motion pictures became a new medium, with new challenges and expenses. Dialogue became a screenwriter's paramount concern instead of an intertitle afterthought. Delivering those words became the crucial function of actors—many of whom, by the late 1920s, had never before spoken a line heard by an audience. Directors and cameramen were bound to the constrictions of recording via microphones and a bulkier camera (padded to muffle its hum from the mic). Studios needed to invest in audio equipment and personnel. Theaters needed to purchase and install sound systems. Fending off the inevitable, there was a brilliant burst of creativity in the silent movies of 1927 and 1928; many films were filled with lyrical cinematography and nearly devoid of intertitles. They were the final poems of a dying language.

Warner Bros. continued to release sound-on-disc movies,* including the first "all-talking" feature, *The Lights of New York*, on July 28, 1928. It was another blockbuster. "Talking pictures" were all the rage. The other studios were no longer hesitant. Even James Quirk, seven years after glo-

* The last holdout, Warners would switch to sound-on-film technology in early 1930.

rifying silence, was resigned to sound: "It's up to us to sit tight, cross our fingers, and let the scientists tinker," he wrote in October 1928.

By the end of February 1929, all of the major studios had released at least one sound feature, and the final entirely silent feature by a major studio came out that August. Mute movies did not survive to greet the new and troubled decade. The art form and industry of D. W. Griffith and Mack Sennett, of Buster Keaton and Mabel Normand, and of Roscoe "Fatty" Arbuckle was extinct. Cinema had a new language.

Arbuckle must have thought the movies had left him behind for good. But in November 1929 came the announcement that the great silent film actor would star in a talkie feature directed by the ever-loyal James Cruze, who had helmed Arbuckle's final four features before Labor Day 1921 and sneaked him into 1923's *Hollywood.* Cruze had launched his own production company. "Now Hollywood wonders—and expects soon to learn—whether the passing of years has softened these opinions," one article mused about the women's clubs' condemnations of Arbuckle. But Hollywood did not soon learn, for the Cruze-directed feature was never produced.

Instead, Arbuckle returned to the industry he loved by writing uncredited gags for comedy sound shorts produced by RKO. Later that year, "William Goodrich" was directing comedy shorts starring Lloyd Hamilton and other lesser lights. Over the next two years, "Goodrich" directed (and frequently wrote) twenty-seven talkies for Educational, and during his downtime he made five more for RKO. It was a Keystone pace of approximately one new movie every three weeks. In two of the RKO shorts, Arbuckle took aim at the incident that led to his banishment: *That's My Line* and *Beach Pajamas* both feature a scheming female trapping an innocent traveling salesman in a compromising position.

Another Hollywood outcast, actress Louise Brooks,* starred in the ninth of the twenty-seven films, 1931's *Windy Riley Goes to Hollywood.*

* Brooks was a star in comedies at Paramount and a flapper icon, but in 1928 the twenty-two-year-old snubbed the studio and went to Europe, where she starred in the sexually charged classic *Pandora's Box* (1929).

She later recalled, "[Arbuckle] made no attempt to direct this picture. He sat in his chair like a man dead. He had been very nice and sweetly dead ever since the scandal that ruined his career. But it was such an amazing thing for me to come to make this broken down picture, and to find my director was the great Roscoe Arbuckle. Oh, I thought he was magnificent in films."

Windy Riley Goes to Hollywood was one of seven of Arbuckle's new shorts with *Hollywood* in the title, which typically focused on a starlet breaking into the film business.* They allowed Arbuckle to poke fun at the studios that prevented him from appearing on-screen. *Windy Riley* is awful, and it immediately followed another actress-breaking-into-Hollywood short, so it's easy to believe Brooks's contention that Arbuckle mostly collected a paycheck.

However, if you watch *Bridge Wives*, made a year later and starring Al St. John as the neglected husband of a woman addicted to the national craze of bridge, you see Arbuckle utilizing sound creatively (via a radio that can neither be turned off nor destroyed), dishing up original camera moves (St. John seemingly kicks the camera's focus onto his wife), and expertly capturing St. John's mania. Perhaps the clever script and the fact that it starred his nephew invigorated the director. *Bridge Wives* transcended its minuscule budget, and in pacing and originality it has aged well—in marked contrast to many early sound films.

It leaves us to wonder what its director could have accomplished with more money, more time, and longer stories. He directed his final movie, *Niagara Falls*, in the summer of 1932. It was the 129th film Roscoe Arbuckle or "William Goodrich" was known to have helmed.

Some of Arbuckle's later films lampooned the foibles of married life, a topic he likely had a bleak view of after two failed marriages. In September 1929 Doris Deane filed a second divorce complaint, this time

* At least two of these featured a teenage Betty Grable (using the pseudonym Frances Dean), who became a major movie star in the 1940s.

making no mention of another wild party but instead claiming desertion and cruelty: "He left me and went to a Hollywood hotel. I called him and asked him to come back, but he wouldn't. He said he was through." The marriage, though, was not officially through for another thirteen months. Around the time of the divorce, Arbuckle met his next wife. Like his first two, she was a young actress.

Born in 1905, Addie Dukes spent her early childhood in Kentucky before relocating to Chicago with her family. There the teenage Dukes won singing competitions. In 1922, the week after she turned seventeen, she married a musician. A daughter, Marilyn, was born. The couple separated, and in 1925, Addie McPhail moved with her family to Los Angeles, where she swiftly landed her first film role. She was a slim brunette with a striking jawline and, like Deane, a dimpled smile. She signed with a low-budget company and was featured prominently in two series of comedy shorts and played smaller roles in features.* "I was a stranger in Hollywood, so it was only my appearance that opened doors, although they never opened very wide," she remembered. McPhail worked steadily, but the glamorous life eluded her. In the 1930 census, she was living in a Hollywood apartment with her father and her daughter.

Roscoe Arbuckle claimed he fell in love with Addie McPhail, eighteen years his junior, after seeing her in 1930 in two features. He cast her in Educational shorts. "I had feelings for Roscoe," McPhail recalled, but "we worked together for several months at the studio before we even had lunch together." By the time of that lunch, Arbuckle's future wife, McPhail, had acted in a movie with his ex-wife, Deane, that he wrote and directed. Little is known of this lost comedy short beyond its fitting title: *Marriage Rows*. As it was Deane's first film in six years and the last of her career, in retrospect it looks like a farewell present from Arbuckle to his ex.† Arbuckle cast McPhail in more films, including the aforementioned *Beach Pajamas*.

---

* Among the features was 1931's *Girls Demand Excitement*, the second film starring John Wayne.

† In March 1932 Deane married a banker; they divorced two years later. She died in Hollywood in 1974.

As their romance blossomed, Arbuckle and McPhail dined at the Brown Derby and danced at the Ambassador Hotel and the rooftop garden of the Roosevelt Hotel. He turned forty-four in 1931, and most of the "beautiful people" at the Hollywood hot spots—the new stars of the talkies—were, like McPhail, young enough to be his children, but Arbuckle still lived the high life. He still spent generously on food and drinks for himself and his friends—and any faux friends who might glom on to him. He still went out clubbing. (He was then living in an apartment a block from the heart of the Sunset Strip in what is today West Hollywood but was then unincorporated. Immune from Los Angeles police raids, the Strip was a playground of Prohibition-era nightclubs.) He still had to have a flashy luxury automobile. (In June 1929, he listed his monthly income at $500. If true, he spent his annual gross and then some on a new Lincoln town car, which cost $6,105.57.) He still enjoyed his extended adolescence. (A dubious item in a syndicated column in December 1931 featured a drawing of a nervous Arbuckle carrying a giant rolled rug and read: "'Fatty' Arbuckle, on a wager, stole the lobby rug of a Los Angeles hotel! He was aided by two accomplices who staged a fake murder in an adjoining room to draw attention of employees and guests of the hotel.") And McPhail, for whom acting meant a modest income, was thrust into a world of Hollywood gossip columns, the VIP areas of exclusive clubs, and black-tie gatherings.

The biggest of those gatherings was held on November 7, 1931, when a who's who of film notables congregated at the Biltmore Hotel ballroom for the opening event of the movie industry's social season, Great Depression be damned. Dinner was served at 10 PM, and dancing ended sometime around dawn. A highlight "was the dancing of the serpentine by all the guests, during which Roscoe (Fatty) Arbuckle became the drummer in the orchestra in an impromptu display of jazz-band talent."

As for the exclusive clubs, none was more exclusive than the Embassy Club, an opulent two-story space in Hollywood with a glass-enclosed rooftop lounge. The three hundred members included Charlie Chaplin, Sid Grauman, Gloria Swanson, and Roscoe Arbuckle, and only members and their guests could enter. The Embassy was the place for celebrities—especially fading silent stars—to eat, drink, and dance. On September 19, 1931, Arbuckle was there with a screenwriter and two unidentified women, one of whom was likely McPhail. After leaving at 2 AM, a policeman prevented Arbuckle from driving because he thought he was intoxicated. Arbuckle smashed a bottle of alcohol that had been in his car, saying, "There goes the evidence."* At the police station, he and the screenwriter passed sobriety tests, and Arbuckle insisted the officer take the same test. He did and passed. In court, Arbuckle paid a twenty-five-dollar fine for breaking the bottle. Ten years prior, his name was splashed across front pages for a very different arrest. Now, when many had forgotten him, he made a dubious comeback: FATTY ARBUCKLE JOKES ABOUT MORNING ARREST was on the front page of the *Los Angeles Times*.

Before then, in August 1931, it was announced that Arbuckle and McPhail would marry—though she was not yet divorced. Some of the coverage led with the actress's engagement and made no mention of her fiancé's career—as if the reporter was unaware. For others, time had only coarsened their memories. An editorial in an Iowa newspaper opined, "There ought to be a law prohibiting the marriage of such types of men as Fatty Arbuckle. He has forfeited the right to the esteem of all right-thinking people."

In the March 1931 *Photoplay*, an article about Arbuckle appeared under the title "Just Let Me Work." It summarized his struggle against censorship and his attempts to clear his name and reclaim his place in front of the cameras. "For years, his name and the news of the fight were good copy," the article mused. "But then, inevitably, came the indifference that is worse, in 'Fatty's' profession, than the most rabid condemnation. 'Fatty' was left to be forgotten." The article concluded with Arbuckle making another argument for his return:

* He later claimed to have no knowledge of where the bottle came from, saying, "I thought someone was playing a practical joke on me and, when the officer addressed me, I threw it out merely as a precaution."

> All I want is to be allowed to work in my field. It isn't for money. I'm not broke. . . . My conscience is clear, my heart is clean. I refuse to worry. I feel that I have atoned for everything. You know, people can be wrong. I don't say I'm *all* right. I don't believe the other side is *all* right. And anyway, so much worse has happened in history to people vastly more important than I am that my little worries don't matter, in comparison. So why should I kick? People have the right to their opinions. The people who oppose me have the right to theirs. I have the right to mine—which is that I've suffered enough, and been humiliated enough. I want to go back to the screen. I think I can entertain and gladden the people that see me. All I want is that. If I do get back, it will be grand. If I don't—well, okay.

Two months later, *Motion Picture Classic* published "Isn't Fatty Arbuckle Punished Enough?" which explained that one recent plan for Arbuckle's return had been deterred by the protestations of women's clubs. Still, the article tried to rally readers: "Statisticians have figured out a life sentence in prison is commuted on an average of ten years. Isn't a decade a long sentence for any man to serve? Hasn't Fatty suffered enough? Is he to be forever denied a chance to stage a comeback?"

Meanwhile, *Photoplay*'s James Quirk went on a radio program and asked listeners to weigh in on Arbuckle's possible return. Over three thousand letters poured in to the magazine, overwhelmingly in the affirmative. Among the letter writers was Matthew Brady, who averred, "Arbuckle should be allowed to make his own living in his own way." A third fan magazine, *Motion Picture*, chimed in with two articles: "Doesn't Fatty Arbuckle Deserve a Break?" and "The Fans Want Fatty Arbuckle Back on the Screen."

The subject of these articles had had his hopes dashed too often. In June 1931 he said, in an obvious play for sympathy, "I have no desire to return as an actor. In the dark hours of my life it was a consolation to know that I had given happiness to millions of people. There doesn't seem to be much chance of happiness for me. No man can live and be happy without work, and all I want to do is to be permitted to use whatever talents and training I have in the writing and direction of pictures under my own name."

Arbuckle continued to make stage appearances, embarking on a vaudeville tour of eastern Canada with fiancée McPhail as his female lead. "Roscoe was warmly received, even in Montreal and Quebec, and met with only a little opposition," she remembered. In early May 1932, he was booked for six weeks in and around New York City. Broadway's Palace Theatre featured a sign above the marquee with two outsized names: QUEENIE SMITH and ROSCOE ARBUCKLE.* Below were six additional names, including Milton Berle. Arbuckle was also part of a vaudeville benefit show at the Metropolitan Opera, where Berle, who often performed in drag, was "master or mistress of ceremonies."

As their vaudeville tour hopscotched Eastern cities, McPhail's divorce finally went through. After difficulties in two other states, she and Arbuckle married in Erie, Pennsylvania, on June 21—at 2:30 AM, after rousing the court reporter and justice of the peace out of their beds.

A month later, when the couple was back in New York City and performing in a Brooklyn vaudeville house, Arbuckle learned from his agent, Joe Rivkin, that Warner Bros. wanted him to star in a sound short. Filming was to take place at the Vitaphone studio in Brooklyn. "Roscoe felt like he had been given his life back," McPhail remembered. "It was the call he had been waiting eleven years for."

He signed the contract in New York City on July 27. A photo of that moment, with his new bride and a studio executive watching, was titled "Star Emerging from Eclipse." An Associated Press story effused, "Frankly gambling on Fatty's chances for success, the producers decided to risk just one picture. If the Arbuckle box office power of the past is apparent, Fatty will be on a high road to the most spectacular 'comeback' in film history."

* The rare absence of "Fatty" surely pleased Arbuckle. Queenie Smith was a Broadway actress.

"It's kind of like home to me, you know—pictures," Arbuckle told a reporter, and he explained that comedy styles were constantly changing. "You gotta adapt," he said, but then added, reflexively, "But I can promise they'll be good, clean, wholesome pictures. Broad comedy, with something for the children." Yes, clean and wholesome for the children, since the event that drove him from screens nearly eleven years prior was never far from his thoughts. It was never far from most anyone's thoughts when they thought of him.

"They got all the money I had. I ended up a quarter of a million dollars in debt. I've paid it back in vaudeville. Did they cram it down my throat? Hun . . . plenty." *They* was everyone who made him out to be a monster: the prosecutors, the press, the protestors, the censors. Then, as if to answer the question before it was asked, the question that was always there, almost never asked but forever lurking, Roscoe "Fatty" Arbuckle said, "I never did anything. I've got a clear conscience and a clean heart."

{21}

LEGENDS

> "I suppose history never lies, does it?" said Mr. Dick, with a gleam of hope.
>
> "Oh dear, no, sir!" I replied, most decisively. I was ingenious and young, and I thought so.
>
> —Charles Dickens, *David Copperfield*

For decades, the narrative of the events of Labor Day 1921 and their aftermath did not change but merely faded, shrinking to the size of unfortunate but enduring epitaphs: "ruined by wild party," "tried for rape death of actress," "scandal-plagued," "thrown out of Hollywood." Proving some would never forget, in 1948, twenty-six years after Arbuckle's acquittal, the Women's Club of Hopkinsville, Kentucky, "passed a strong resolution expressing their opposition to the showing of any Fatty Arbuckle films."

Arbuckle's greatest defender at that time was celebrity journalist Adela Rogers St. Johns. In 1950 she penned a remembrance entitled, tellingly, "The Arbuckle Tragedy" for the *American Weekly*, a magazine widely circulated as a newspaper supplement, and she quoted her own male housekeeper, who said he cleaned for Rappe until the day the naked actress ran outside shouting for help and lying that the housekeeper had attacked her. "The neighbors said whenever she got a few drinks in her she did that," according to the unnamed housekeeper, and unnamed neighbors supposedly confirmed this. Rogers also framed the legal proceedings as a slam dunk for Arbuckle by not mentioning the first two trials but quoting the innocence statement of "the jury which acquitted him in less than a minute."

In 1957 movie power broker Donald Crisp claimed Arbuckle was framed: "He was no more guilty of killing that girl than the man in the moon. He wasn't even in San Francisco. Her dead body was discovered at three in the afternoon. He didn't get to San Francisco until eight that evening." If nothing else, Crisp proved how effortlessly the case could be rewritten.

As favorably as St. Johns and Crisp slanted his "tragedy," they ignored Arbuckle's artistry. With each passing year, knowledge of his comic expertise faded, as did the status of silent cinema. In a 1949 public opinion poll on the top fifteen funniest comedians of all time, Charlie Chaplin was the only silent star to make the list, and only at fifteenth, though Arbuckle did receive some votes.* That same year, in an extensive cover story in *Life* magazine titled "Comedy's Greatest Era," respected critic James Agee championed silent-era slapstick. One sentence of the sixteen-page article was dedicated to Arbuckle, mentioning his talents without noting his travails. Then, in separate, lengthy tributes, "the four most eminent masters" were christened: Charlie Chaplin, Buster Keaton, Harold Lloyd, and Harry Langdon.† The history was being written without Roscoe Arbuckle.

There were exceptions. "They get American movies here," wrote Bob Hope from Moscow in a newspaper column in 1957. "But they're a little late. Several people asked me if Fatty Arbuckle is up for an academy award this year." It was the rare reference to Arbuckle that made no mention of his scandal; Hope never forgot his early debt to the ostracized star. Arbuckle

* So did Buster Keaton and Harold Lloyd. Bob Hope won the poll by a wide margin.

† Langdon was another Mack Sennett protégé (post-Keystone), and he rose to prominence starring in comedy features in the mid-1920s. His star has since faded as well, leaving only Chaplin, Keaton, and Lloyd in the silent comedy pantheon. But if the triumvirate was ever a quaternity, Arbuckle had to be the fourth. It's also debatable whether Lloyd's contributions to silent comedy were greater than Arbuckle's, despite the latter's pantomime career ending in 1921.

was also one of the original 1,558 people chosen by the motion picture selection committee for the Hollywood Walk of Fame. These initial sidewalk stars were laid in 1960 and 1961 without ceremonies, and Arbuckle's honor sparked no protest.* Likewise, Fatty footage was included in the 1960 feature documentary on silent slapstick *When Comedy Was King* and its 1961 sequel *Days of Thrills and Laughter*. His scenes in both are a celebration of his artistry, void of any mention of controversy.

It was forty-one years after his arrest before the first (ridiculous) book-length attempt at retelling the story of Arbuckle's case was published. (By contrast, within two years after the conclusion of another "trial of the century," the market was glutted with more than forty books on the O. J. Simpson case.) The absence of Arbuckle books was in marked contrast to the abundance of book announcements from his ex-wives. The first, from Doris Deane, came in 1935: a biography and possible movie. Neither materialized. Four years later came the news that Minta Durfee had written a play about her former husband: "The Clown Speaks." In 1951 she said she was penning a book of the same name. By 1955 the title had changed to "My Clown Cried." By 1971 a news item would state that the book was finished and "Bob Hope is said to be interested in buying the movie rights." No such book was ever published.†

In 1960 a lengthy United Syndicate article focused on the trials. Its greatest impression is summarized in this sentence: "Then, in 1921, Funny Fatty became involved in a sordid sex affair and all the people who loved him suddenly and mercilessly decided to hate him." Just how sordid that alleged "sex affair" was rumored to have been remained a whispered secret for decades after its occurrence, not even published in "underground" exposés like *The Sins of Hollywood*. By the early 1960s, however, these rumors had begun to find a new life in print.

---

* In contrast, Charlie Chaplin was rejected because of his leftist politics. Arbuckle's inclusion and Chaplin's exclusion prompted "one Hollywood observer" to quip, "It is apparently all right to rape and murder, but it's not all right to be a pinko." Chaplin got his star in 1972.

† Sections of Durfee's unpublished book manuscripts reside in the Margaret Herrick Library of the Academy of Motion Picture Arts and Sciences. They are the source for many of Durfee's recollections quoted in this book.

In 1952 Robert Harrison launched *Confidential* magazine. Its slogan was "Tells the Facts and Names the Names," though facts and names were typically attached to caustic innuendo. Mostly by emphasizing celebrity sexuality, *Confidential*'s circulation soon soared to over three and a half million, and its huge success spawned more than a dozen imitators, their garish colors and SHOCKING headlines screaming for attention. Facing a phalanx of libel suits, the magazine was effectively tamed by the studios in 1958, and Harrison sold it. As his scandal had retreated into history, Arbuckle was never featured in *Confidential*, but later coverage of the case owes much to this free-speech pioneer. For better and worst, *Confidential* blazed a trail so that future publishers could explore Hollywood sex scandals—including Roscoe Arbuckle's.

"HERE IS THE SHOCKING, SOMETIMES SORDID, AND ALWAYS FASCINATING STORY OF ONE OF THE MOST FAMOUS CRIMINAL TRIALS OF ALL TIME—THE FATTY ARBUCKLE CASE." So screams, with caps locked, *The Fatty Arbuckle Case* just inside a cover complete with a giant, frowning Arbuckle head blocking out the disrobed parts of a brunette beauty lounging beside a bottle of liquor. Surely one of the most famous criminal cases of all time deserved better than this 1962 paperback penned by pulp fictionist Leo Guild, whom in 2007, on the tenth anniversary of his death, a newspaper dubbed "the Worst Pulp Novelist Ever." Guild was once a columnist for the *Hollywood Reporter*, and over a lengthy career he churned out all manner of dreck, including gambling guides (he called himself "the Wizard of Odds"), horror (*The Werewolf vs. Vampire Woman*), humor (*Bachelor's Joke Book*), and several blaxploitation/sexploitation tomes with titles like *Street of Ho's*, *Black Bait*, and *The Girl Who Loved Black: White Girls Who Love Black Pimps*. Guild also fashioned himself a celebrity biographer, penning lazy books about such legends as Josephine Baker, Darryl Zanuck, and Liberace.*

* *The Loves of Liberace* (1956) was an attempt to paint the flamboyant pianist as the ultimate ladies' man. How straight was Liberace? Guild wrote, "Liberace is the perfect specimen of a well-groomed gentleman, he doesn't chew tobacco or drive a truck; but he is as hairy as Rosselini, and who has ever questioned his masculinity? He can move a piano by himself, he chops wood for exercise; and he has always, since he was a very small child, liked to be clean."

In *The Fatty Arbuckle Case*, Guild wrote, "These are the rumors, the facts and the theories, sifted and arranged in what seems to this author the most reasonable and probable re-creation of that fateful day." In his version, Arbuckle and Maude Delmont conspired in Los Angeles to get Virginia Rappe to a party in San Francisco so Arbuckle could have sex with her. The party livened up when Delmont stripped to only her panties for the amusement of all and compared her bare breasts with those of an unnamed and equally topless showgirl. Soon thereafter, Rappe, who called Arbuckle "despicable," went willingly with him into 1219. With regard to what followed, the Wizard of Odds hedged his bet. The most "sane explanation," he reported, is that Arbuckle and Rappe had intercourse and "by force or roughness, Virginia's bladder was broken." But he also wrote, "One rumor was that the drunken Arbuckle had ravaged her with a coke bottle. Another said he used a jagged stick of ice."

Here, then, forty-one years after Arbuckle's arrest, is the now-legendary supposition: he ruptured Rappe's bladder while raping her with a bottle.* The broader rumor was that Arbuckle was unable to achieve an erection and thus substituted another item for his phallus, most often identified as a Coca-Cola bottle. Never mind that there was no evidence of this, and never mind that one could not puncture a bladder thusly without doing grave injury to the upper vaginal wall. Indeed, there was no evidence of any vaginal contact by Arbuckle, and no such contact was ever alleged in court (other than his application of ice). Rappe was clothed while he was alone with her in 1219. But four decades later, a persistent myth took root and grew.

And it wasn't merely relegated to pulp paperbacks. The following year, Charles Beaumont (best known for penning scripts for *The Twilight Zone*) revisited the case in a book of nostalgic essays, and though he made it clear he felt Arbuckle got a raw deal, he dished the dirt in a parenthetical aside: "(Three versions of the incident were in office and alley circulation: Arbuckle had raped the girl, killing her with thrusts of his

* A less explicit intimation of this rumor had been published when Arbuckle was still alive. According to a 1931 *Time* article, "Because many suspicious persons thought he might have caused the death of Cinemactress Rappe by attacking her, perhaps with a beer bottle, no cinema producers dared antagonize their audiences by hiring Funnyman Arbuckle."

presumably enormous penis;* he had used a coca cola bottle or a dildo; he had impaled her on a broom handle. Most people devotedly believed all three stories.)"

The bottle rumor began its journey from whispers to legend even earlier than 1962. Leo Guild seems to have expanded on a version of the story contained in another lurid volume, which he probably consulted in its original, French-language edition when he wrote *The Fatty Arbuckle Case*. Its subsequent English translation would have the greatest impact on the public's perception of the events in room 1219.

> If a book such as this can be said to have charm, I think it lies in the fact that here is a book without one single redeeming merit.
>
> —From the *New York Times* review of *Hollywood Babylon*

Born Kenneth Anglemyer in 1927 and raised in Los Angeles, Kenneth Anger made his first experimental short films when a child and his homoerotic *Fireworks* at age twenty. His avant-garde movies, which often explored occultism and/or sexuality, generated both praise and protest and made Anger a minor celebrity in the cinematic underground—but supplied scant income. He had been living in Paris since 1950 when he collected stories of movie industry depravity, and, influenced by *Confidential* and the blunt writing style of occultist Aleister Crowley, he penned a photo-laden book of scandals, *Hollywood Babylone*, published in French in 1959. An item in American newspapers in 1961 read, "Vacationers returning from Europe are smuggling in a book called *Hollywood Babylone*, written entirely in French but apparently well worth translating."

American Marvin Miller specialized in publishing quick knockoffs of successful sex-themed European books, and he encouraged Anger to translate *Hollywood Babylone* into English. The filmmaker translated

* This version of the story had an equally unsubstantiated contrapositive. For example, the 1989 book *Movieland* presumed, "And when Fatty died it was discovered that his sexual parts had never matured: he had the genitals of a child."

two-thirds, but Miller rendered the other third in a more vulgar style and added stories. *Hollywood Babylon* came out in 1964, and despite being sold in a plain brown wrapper like the pornography of the era, it made the shelves of mainstream American bookstores and appeared in newspaper ads. Estimates are that this "bootleg version" sold as many as two million copies, but none of the profits were returned to its author. Miller also turned the book into a 1972 sexploitation "documentary" with cheap recreations of tawdry scenes, including the 1921 Labor Day party.

Anger sued Miller, demanding over $500,000 in royalties and damages, and eventually won a small settlement, but he never collected from the elusive publisher. Made aware of the enduring interest in his poisonous tome, Anger Americanized and updated the text. Rereleased in 1975, *Hollywood Babylon* was again a success, and Anger took "the Hollywood Babylon Show" on the road, reading theatrically from the text and screening appropriately inappropriate silent film clips.

Stuffed with photos, some of shockingly gory crime scenes, *Hollywood Babylon* stands as a 305-page compendium of all the ways fame can defeat you: drug addiction, murder, sexual dysfunction, public humiliations, depression, suicide. As such, it has memorialized long-gone stars—but only via innuendo, rumors, or lies. F. W. Murnau is remembered not as a great, poetic director but for dying in a car crash while allegedly performing fellatio on his fourteen-year-old valet as the boy drove. Clara Bow is commemorated not as a leading actress of the late 1920s or the quintessential flapper but as a nymphomaniac who had group sex with the USC football team (including John Wayne).* Likewise, generations know nothing of Roscoe Arbuckle's comedic artistry, but they were certain he had once killed an actress by raping her with a bottle—a legend promulgated foremost by *Hollywood Babylon*.

The book's very title harks back to the Arbuckle case, and its third chapter, "Fat Man Out," is devoted to that subject. From its first line about Mack Sennett discovering "plumber's helper" Arbuckle "when

---

* This story was debunked in the 1980s via interviews with the football players.

he came to unclog the comedy producer's drain," the chapter is littered with falsehoods. Arbuckle supposedly stripped with the prostitutes in "Mishawn [*sic*] Manor," and Rappe worked in minor roles at Keystone, where she "did her fair share of sleeping around and gave half the company crabs. This epidemic so shocked Sennett that he closed down his studio and had it fumigated."

Anger tells a lively if false version of the Labor Day party. Maude Delmont (who is misidentified with a photo of Minta Durfee) is Arbuckle's "friend" whom, as in Leo Guild's account, he enlists to bring Rappe to San Francisco. Of what occurred in 1219 Anger offers no opinion but instead promulgates the rumors (italics and ellipses are his):

> As headlines screamed, the rumors flew of a *hideously unnatural rape:* Arbuckle, enraged at his drunken impotence, had ravaged Virginia with a Coca-Cola bottle, *or* a champagne bottle, then had repeated the act with a jagged piece of ice . . . *or*, wasn't it common knowledge that Arbuckle was *exceptionally well endowed?* . . . *or*, was it just a question of 266-pounds-too-much of Fatty flattening Virginia in a *flying leap?*

It's clear which rumor Anger prefers when, in reference to Arbuckle's acquittal, he highlights "the lack of specific evidence (such as a bloody bottle)," as if a bottle theory had been examined in court. And at the chapter's end, he presents the 1931 incident outside the Embassy Club when Arbuckle destroyed evidence of illegal drinking, and asks, "Was he thinking of another bottle that went sailing out the 12th floor window of the Hotel St. Francis on Labor Day 1921?"

The myth of "Fatty's bottle party" spread like a contagious disease. For a visceral image of said myth, 1971's self-published *Fatty* by Gerald Fine set the standard with a scene wherein a drunk and still drinking Maude Delmont privately tells Matthew Brady and Nat Schmulowitz about entering 1219 just after Arbuckle was alone there with Rappe: "She was all beat up and bruised . . . lyin' on th' floor between the two beds. There was a coke bottle on the floor. Fatty had shoved it up her cunt, the son of a bitch. . . . She said that when she wouldn't give in that he used the coke bottle to force her open. Then she said when he took the bottle out, he mounted her." (Brady dismisses Delmont's drunken account because "she had been bought or had some powerful hatred for Fatty.") The book—labeled a "novel," presumably for scenes like the preceding—is mostly sympathetic to Arbuckle.

An unsympathetic view can by found in the 1974 memoir of silent-era screenwriter Anita Loos, *Kiss Hollywood Goodbye*. She declared that Arbuckle caused Rappe's death "when she was trying to fight off his unorthodox lovemaking." A 1994 *Newsweek* article, tied to O. J. Simpson's arrest for double murder, concocted facts and cruel Arbuckle quotes to paint the silent star guilty, and it ran with another of Anger's rumors: "Arbuckle had told others that he had jabbed a large, jagged piece of ice into [Rappe's] vagina. Three days later she died from a ruptured bladder, having been literally raped to death." And a 1998 article in London's the *Independent* entitled "When Apes Put Men to Shame" chose the third and final rumor: "Hollywood has always had its share of call-girl scandals. In 1921, the American actor Fatty Arbuckle was charged with crushing to death a starlet during an orgy in San Francisco."

One of the most perniciously false descriptions of the alleged assault was in a 1993 edition of the scholarly *Journal of Popular Culture* and penned by pioneering TV host Steve Allen:*

> The popular comedian Fatty Arbuckle, in the 1920s, never worked again in the motion picture business after his arrest in conjunction with an incident in which a prostitute died, apparently because Arbuckle, in a sexual context, had inserted in the poor woman's body a Coca-Cola bottle, which broke and cut her internally, after which she bled to death. If such a thing were to happen today, I would not be surprised if Arbuckle ended up doing a TV commercial for Pepsi.

---

* Allen should have been better informed about his fellow comedian, for he wrote the songs for the 1985 Los Angeles musical *Fatty*, which took a sympathetic view of its namesake.

As the preceding references to "call-girl scandals" and a "prostitute" demonstrate, Virginia Rappe's reputation has also been assaulted by history. Adela Rogers St. Johns doubled down on her previous vitriol. In her 1978 book *Love, Laughter and Tears*, she placed all the blame on the victim: "During this vacation an extra girl named Virginia Rappe got some alcohol in her system, stripped off her clothes and plunged Fatty and Hollywood into our first major scandal."

Minta Durfee was the other chief Rappe antagonist. Of her unpublished book, the *Los Angeles Times* said after her death, "Her manuscript was too circumspect to interest publishers."* Nevertheless, her circumspect remembrances interested other writers, and by readily granting interviews, she contributed to their books. Durfee—who never remarried and appeared as an extra or bit player in over two dozen movies and TV shows from the mid-1930s to the early 1970s—had the advantage of longevity, living by modest means in Los Angeles until her death in 1975 at age eighty-five. She even chatted on TV's *The Merv Griffin Show* in 1970 (advertised as "widow of film star Roscoe 'Fatty' Arbuckle"). In a 1964 interview, she said Rappe "was suffering from several diseases," one of which resulted in Sennett fumigating Keystone. This quote appears in Kevin Brownlow's monumental history of silent film *The Parade's Gone By*, published in 1968.

Durfee's interviews were the greatest influence on Fine's *Fatty* as well as on Stuart Oderman's 1994 biography *Roscoe "Fatty" Arbuckle*. In the latter, she's quoted as saying, "Virginia Rappe was one of those poor young girls who came to Hollywood looking for a career and who wound up being *used* more in the dressing room or in some executive's office than in front of the camera. At Sennett's, she spread syphilis all over the studio, and Mr. Sennett had to have the place fumigated!" Note how Durfee in this 1969 interview upped the ante of Kenneth Anger's

* She is very circumspect in regards to the Arbuckle case and its participants, but her manuscript pages and interviews proved much more verifiably reliable in regards to her ex-husband's biography, and they helped fill in many details of his early life and their marriage.

anecdote, turning crabs into syphilis, as if a venereal disease could be eliminated by an insect exterminator. There is no evidence that Rappe ever suffered from either crabs or a venereal disease. Also, Rappe never worked at Keystone. Facts be damned.

In a 1973 interview, Durfee said, "Mr. Sennett had to close the studio down for several days while he had everything repainted and fumigated" because Rappe had "spread syphilis all over the studio." So painters, too, were enlisted in the health crusade. The interview, published as a chapter in 1975's *You Must Remember This,* is laced with falsehoods, such as "Our lawyers proved with medical records that Virginia died of cystitis, an inflammation of the bladder. She had such a severe case that she had to use a catheter to eliminate. Her sphincter muscle wouldn't work." It's likely Durfee didn't know the lies from the truth by this point, so long had she been confusing the two to paint Arbuckle in the best light and all who opposed him in the worst.

In the same published interview, she picked off her former husband's perceived accusers one by one, and her spurious attacks jaundiced much of the case's history until now. . . .

On Maude Delmont: She "had seventy-two affidavits out against her for being a professional correspondent, a woman that's found in bed with a husband when a photographer bursts into the room and takes a picture. That was when they had these setup divorces and the only grounds for divorce was adultery. Maude Delmont had gone to the well too often, she'd made it into a racket, and so the cops were down on her. When the cops found out Maude Delmont had been at the party at the Hotel St. Francis, she must have made a deal with the district attorney. They'd forget about the seventy-two affidavits if she'd frame Roscoe."

Truth: There were many rumors about Delmont, some stemming from her alleged relationship with Earl Lynn, but there is not one known affidavit as described.

On the Women's Vigilant Committee: "Roscoe was in handcuffs when he was taken from his cell and walked through a hallway to the courtroom for that [first] hearing. There were people milling around who'd seen this man on the screen. They knew him and started to applaud.

But there was one woman in the crowd, the head of a vigilante women's group with thousands of members, who had a lot of her followers with her. As soon as she saw Roscoe, she said, 'Women, do your duty.' And they all spat at Roscoe. His face and clothes were covered with spit."

Truth: The press would have made much of this event had it occurred.

On William Randolph Hearst: He was "that dreadful, dreadful old man" who attacked Arbuckle relentlessly in his newspapers to extract revenge against Hollywood for not making his mistress Marion Davies a star.

Truth: Between 1918 and 1929, Davies starred in twenty-nine films, financed by Hearst and released by Hollywood studios, so the publisher had no reason for a vendetta against Hollywood in 1921. Also, Durfee failed to mention that Arbuckle directed one of those twenty-nine films for that "dreadful, dreadful" man.

On Will H. Hays: "This awful Will Hays, who was the censor in our business, instead of standing up like a man and declaring Roscoe absolutely guiltless, was absolutely ruthless. . . . I've never seen a man in all my lifetime that looked more like a rat dressed up in men's clothing than Will Hays."

Truth: As previously discussed, Hays banished but then reinstated Arbuckle. He did look like a rat.

But back to Virginia Rappe. In most accounts of the case, she is diminished to a bit part, as if it was not her tragedy. She's a showgirl, an extra, a slut if not a whore. A 1994 Associated Press story on the case was typically jaundiced: Arbuckle hired the "notorious" Maude Delmont "to supply party girls," one of whom was Rappe, who had been fired by Sennett "after she allegedly infected several actors with a venereal disease. An alcoholic, she drifted in the Hollywood lowlife."

In 1976, at last, came the first book-length biography of Arbuckle and the first extensively researched (though unsourced) portrait of the trials, David Yallop's *The Day the Laughter Stopped: The True Story of Fatty Arbuckle*. Once again, we're treated to the tale of Rappe's venereal disease causing the fumigation of Keystone. Yallop also has Dr. Melville Rumwell concluding that Rappe had gonorrhea—though Rumwell never stated this at any of the three trials, nor did any other doctor who examined her before or after her death. Likewise, the following game-changer was never mentioned by the medical experts, witnesses, or attorneys of the time: Rappe hit Arbuckle up for "a great deal of money" at the Labor Day party because (Yallop's italics) "*She was pregnant, and she was sick. She needed money to have an abortion, and she wanted to have the abortion as soon as possible.*" Explaining away the lack of physical evidence, Yallop conveniently suggests Rumwell performed an illegal autopsy to cover up an illegal abortion he'd performed on the dying Rappe. Yallop pegs the bladder tear on either a spontaneous rupture or a catheter used to treat a prior medical condition. (There was no evidence to suggest that a catheter caused the tear.) He also pins an unspecified scheme to blackmail Arbuckle on Delmont and suggests that Rappe may have initially been involved, seeking money for her abortion.

The next book on the subject, 1991's *Frame-Up!: The Untold Story of Roscoe "Fatty" Arbuckle* by Andy Edmonds, collapses under its own conspiracy theory (it too lacks source notes). Again, Durfee is listed as a principal source,* and again we get her portrait of Rappe—the ultimate version: "I couldn't stand that girl. She was sweet enough, naive. But had no morals whatsoever. She'd sleep with any man who asked her. In fact, Mack Sennett had to shut the studio down twice because of her . . . because she was spreading lice and some sort of venereal disease. She was a sad case."

Then Edmonds tops Yallop. Rappe, who had had "at least five abortions by the time she was sixteen" and a baby at seventeen (placed in a foster home), wasn't just in San Francisco for her latest "hatchet job" abortion—though the procedure, performed by Rumwell before the party, "account[ed] for the tenderness of her abdomen." In room 1220 Rappe supposedly tickled Arbuckle, who then reflexively kneed her in the abdomen. Pained, she ran into 1219; her bladder was ruptured. Arbuckle later found her in the bathroom, as he explained. As farfetched

* Curiously, Edmonds claims to have been introduced to Durfee by someone the author met in 1976, but Durfee died in September 1975. This may be a mere mistake, one of numerous dates, names, and events that are botched.

as Edmonds's version of the party is, it's not as bizarre as the author's contention that Adolph Zukor designed a frame-up and Fred Fishback pulled it off, bringing together "a nightgown salesman [Ira Fortlouis], an actress who was known to strip [Rappe], and a woman who would take compromising pictures and say anything in court for the right price [Delmont]." Zukor supposedly wanted to obtain compromising photos of Arbuckle to use against him in contract negotiations. The plan failed—or worked too well—when the actress who was known to strip died. Edmonds's outrageous theory seems devised to justify the book's exclamatory title.

There has never been a movie version of Roscoe Arbuckle's story, on the big or small screen, despite interest dating back to the 1930s.* Durfee first optioned the film rights to her version in 1957, and that same year a TV network was planning a musical about Arbuckle. Then and for a decade afterward, Jackie Gleason was the first choice for the role. The lead in a proposed big-screen biopic might have gone to John Belushi, who was eyeing the part before his 1982 death. Likewise, John Candy was studying for the role in 1993; he died in 1994. And in the sort of coincidence that seems a curse, Chris Farley met with playwright/screenwriter David Mamet in January 1997 to plan an Arbuckle biography in which he would star; Farley died that December. The closest thing to a Fatty movie was 1975's *The Wild Party*, a Merchant Ivory production starring James Coco as "Jolly Grimm," an aging silent star who stages an orgy in the late 1920s and ends up killing his mistress (Raquel Welch) and her actor boyfriend. The movie might have done much to confuse the facts of 1921's real "wild party" had it not been such a box office dud.

* There have, however, been several stage adaptations of Arbuckle's life and/or the trials, including the 1982 London play *Fatty*; 1990's *Arbuckle* and *The Death of a Clown*, both staged in San Francisco; 1998's Chicago "multi-media treatment" *Fatty*; and at least seven different plays staged in Los Angeles. (In 1966 came a flurry of stories about a Broadway musical named *Fatty* starring the previously mentioned junior Jackie Coogan in the eponymous role. Coogan, then famous as Uncle Fester on TV's *The Addams Family*, gained weight and rehearsals began that fall, but *Fatty* never played.)

In the 1990s the Arbuckle case did make it to television in other forms: on the syndicated series *Hollywood Babylon*, based officially but loosely on Anger's book; on an episode of *E! Mysteries and Scandals*; and on A&E's *Biography*, which served up a spoiler in the episode's title: "Fatty Arbuckle: Betrayed by Hollywood." In the 2000s it was the focus of two novels: Ace Atkins's *Devil's Garden*, which follows the trials as observed by private detective Dashiell Hammett, and Jerry Stahl's fictional Arbuckle autobiography *I, Fatty*, which greatly exaggerated Fatty's drug addiction.

Still, most Americans who recognize the name Fatty Arbuckle know it only as the punch line to a dirty joke, even if they're foggy about the setup.* They heard he raped someone with a bottle, but they're unsure of who he was or why he mattered. *The Simpsons* captured this with a wink when Krusty the Clown asks, "What has Fatty Arbuckle done that I haven't done?"

Almost always, the press provides only one answer. In the December 31, 1999, issue of *Time*, Arbuckle was included in the "People of the Century," but only as one of four "lethal cocktails" of "crime and fame" in a section called "Murder, Inc." Its mangled single-sentence remembrance: "In 1921, the comic was charged with, but never convicted of, the rape and murder of a starlet he met at an orgy." Eight years later, Arbuckle's "scandal" was featured in a *Time* special issue on the "Crimes of the Century." The paragraph summation implied that he was charged with puncturing the bladder of "a naive young actress" during "forced sex (with a beer bottle!)." It also said that he died "after falling into alcoholism and lurid obscurity." If it's possible to be both lurid and obscure, that has only befallen him in the years after his death.

Cinematic stardom offers the ability to stay forever young, captured in moving images and viewed by generations long after perishing. Ros-

* Things are different in England for those who remember a restaurant chain called Fatty Arbuckles American Diner (sans apostrophe). They likely associate Fatty Arbuckle with "very generous portions of quality American style food." Fatty Arbuckles launched in 1983 and grew to more than forty franchises in the 1990s. The eponymous actor/director peered into a movie camera on its signs. The name was later shortened, and only one Arbuckles remains open today.

coe Arbuckle achieved such immortality, but it has been far exceeded by a different sort. Always, it seems, when there's a celebrity scandal of sex or violence, he returns, if only briefly, to the news. And not only then. He garners mentions when there are censorship battles and obscenity questions, when there is a sensational trial or the tragic death of an actress or a Hollywood celebrity arrest. A severely abbreviated list of the events his name has been associated with includes the 1943 paternity suit against Charlie Chaplin, the 1947 Black Dahlia murder, the TV quiz show scandal of the 1950s, the 1962 suicide of Marilyn Monroe, the 1969 Manson Family murder of Sharon Tate, the 1988 videotaped sexcapades of Rob Lowe, the arrests of Pee-wee Herman and Hugh Grant for lewd contact, O. J. Simpson's arrest for double murder, the Clinton impeachment, Michael Jackson's molestation trial, and Janet Jackson's wardrobe malfunction.

The names of even silent film superstars like Mabel Normand and Buster Keaton are largely unknown today, for they have little reason to appear in the press and their movies are watched mostly by a loyal but small cadre of silent film aficionados. In contrast, the name Roscoe Arbuckle—or, much more likely, Fatty Arbuckle—reappears when there is a scandal or controversy as big as an impeachment or as small as a nipple slip. He is forever the life of the party, forever a defendant, forever a villain or a victim or both, forever remembered—when he is remembered—for his tremendous and devastating fall from grace.

{22}

LABOR DAY REVISITED

> Oh, that day! One kept waiting—as if a morning would arrive from before that day to take them away all along a different track. One kept waiting for that shattering day to unhappen, so that the real—the intended—future, the one that had been implied by the past, could unfold. Hour after hour, month after month, waiting for that day to not have happened. But it had happened. And now it was always going to have happened.
>
> —Deborah Eisenberg, "Twilight of the Superheroes"

Before

This is what occurred on September 5, 1921, in room 1220 prior to whatever happened when Virginia Rappe and Roscoe Arbuckle were alone together in room 1219. The state and the defense reached a consensus regarding most of these events, though they differed on one significant element.

Consensus

Rappe had been at the party in room 1220 for three hours, drinking orange blossoms, conversing, and dancing, when shortly before 3 PM she tried to enter the bathroom of room 1221 (Lowell Sherman's room), but

Maude Delmont was in there with Sherman. Rappe then passed through 1220 and into 1219 (the room shared by Arbuckle and Fred Fishback). There was no indication that Rappe appeared ill or distressed at the party before entering 1219.

State

The prosecution claimed that Arbuckle watched Rappe enter 1219 and followed her.

Defense

The defense claimed Arbuckle was unaware that Rappe entered 1219 and that he only entered 1219 and locked its door to 1220 in order to change out of his pajamas and into a suit before taking Mae Taube for their scheduled car ride.

Analysis

To get from 1221 to 1219 Rappe crossed through 1220—a room then occupied by Alice Blake, Zey Prevost, and Arbuckle. It seems unlikely Arbuckle would have missed Rappe walking from one door to the other. That said, Rappe may not have gone directly from door to door, Arbuckle may have been distracted by the other two women, or he may have been facing one of the room's two outer walls, both of which featured a window.*

During

There are two conflicting versions of what occurred in 1219 to cause Rappe's injury. Here we examine both accounts as presented in the closing arguments of the third and final trial, in which each side had the benefit of the pretrial hearings, the previous two trials, and the third trial's testimony to help them formulate their strongest cases.

* He had previously joked about jumping out one of those windows.

State's Account

"The defendant followed Virginia Rappe into room 1219, and he closed and locked the door. There was no one else in the room. Miss Rappe did not get an opportunity to go to the bathroom. Evidently, he said something or touched her in some way. . . . Miss Rappe would be standing near the bathroom; the defendant would be between Miss Rappe and the door leading into room 1220. So Miss Rappe, to avoid whatever the defendant said he was going to do, or had attempted to do, at that time, ran to the door leading into the hall. . . . He followed her to the door, he pulled her away from the door, he threw her upon the [double] bed. . . . At that precise moment when the defendant forced her toward the bed Virginia Rappe was in the most perfect condition to have her bladder ruptured if any force was applied to her. All that was necessary was a distended bladder."

The state agreed with the defense that Rappe had a distended bladder at this point, but whether the distension was caused by her cystitis (a condition that had been confirmed during the first trial by the court-appointed panel of doctors), her ingestion of orange juice and gin (both of which are more diuretic than water), or any other catalyst was immaterial to them, because it didn't explain how that distended bladder ruptured. They claimed that cystitis had nothing to do with the rupture (this may or may not have been true) and that spontaneous bladder ruptures are very rare (true). Thus, some external force caused her bladder to rupture.

"The defendant then threw his weight upon her, her bladder ruptured, and she passed into a state of shock. . . . So Miss Rappe lost consciousness, and of course the defendant knew that she had lost consciousness, and he attempted to revive her. He used the ice, and he succeeded in reviving her. And when he had revived her, and when the bed was wet, then and not until then did he open the door into room 1220."

Because the state did not contend that Arbuckle's attempt at sexual assault proceeded beyond throwing her to the bed and throwing himself upon her, there was no physical evidence of those actions beyond rumpled sheets.

Defense Challenge

The defense challenged the state's account in three principal ways:

Hairs

Hairs thought to match Rappe's were found by the state's forensics expert Edward Heinrich between the two beds and in the bathroom. The defense contended that this validated their story and invalidated the state's.

Analysis: Because the state argued that Rappe was moved from one bed to the other and later moved into the bathroom, the hairs support both conflicting suppositions of what occurred in 1219. Forget the hairs.

Fingerprints

The defense vigorously challenged the state's claim that two handprints on 1219's hallway door demonstrated that Arbuckle placed his hand over Rappe's to prevent her escape.

Analysis: The handprints were much debated and were largely responsibile for one of the jurors holding out for a guilty verdit in the first trial. However, modern forensic experts consulted for this book determined that the state's logic behind the dual prints would not hold up in a criminal court today, because such fingerprints cannot even be dated, let alone timed to the same moment, to prove that one hand was pressing the other. Forget the fingerprints.

Timeline

The defense made much of the timeline, claiming there was insufficient time—approximately ten minutes—for everything to have occurred as the state said.

Analysis: It could have taken only a few minutes for Arbuckle's assault and revival of Rappe as the state alleged—surely no more time than it would have taken Arbuckle to do all he claimed to have done in 1219. Forget the timeline.

Defense's Account

The primary way the defense countered the state's story was via a very different tale—told (in the first and third trials) by the only surviving person who knew for certain what occurred. "When I walked into

1219," Arbuckle explained, "I closed and locked the door, and I went straight to the bathroom and found Miss Rappe on the floor in front of the toilet, holding her stomach and moving around on the floor. She had been vomiting." The defense postulated two ways Rappe's bladder could have ruptured: spontaneous and via some external force.

Spontaneous

After suggesting that her bladder had been weakened by many years of cystitis and overextended by hours of drinking without urinating and that her abs were "exceedingly well-developed" due to physical training, the defense proposed, "Now, a violent contraction of the abdominal muscles produced by an act of vomiting, the medical experts advise you, might cause a rupture of an overextended bladder. And if Miss Rappe's bladder was ruptured while in an act of vomiting, would the rupture be the result of any act of the defendant in this case?"

Analysis: Instances of spontaneous bladder ruptures are rare, though most are preceded by alcohol consumption, which both fills the bladder and, by dulling nerve impulses, reduces the feeling that one needs to empty it. A chronic case of cystitis could also have weakened her bladder walls, making her more susceptible to such a rupture. Still, the odds were greatly against a spontaneous rupture, and it would most probably have required atypical stress. Vomiting would qualify as such stress. But Rappe's vomiting—such an important component of the defense's story—was witnessed only by Arbuckle. No physical evidence was found. No other witness noted any indication of it. Rappe, by accounts, never told other witnesses she was or had been nauseous. Arbuckle claimed he gave her two glasses of water soon after she vomited, and that water did not come back up and out.

Spontaneous bladder rupture remains a possible explanation, but a very unlikely one.

Some External Force Not Witnessed

The defense conjectured that Rappe could have struck the side of the door upon entering the bathroom, or she could have fallen and hit her abdomen on the side of the bathtub or toilet seat. Or the rupture may have occurred after Arbuckle initially tried to assist her.

"Mr. Arbuckle assisted Miss Rappe from the [bathroom] floor and placed her upon the toilet seat. Later he gave her some water. She expressed a desire to leave the bathroom and lie down for a moment. Mr. Arbuckle assisted her into room 1219, set her upon the smaller of the two beds, lifting her feet up, and she reclined upon the bed. At that moment Mr. Arbuckle left the room and went into the bathroom. He came out into room 1219 within a few moments, and he failed to find Miss Rappe upon the smaller of the two beds; he found her upon the floor.

"True, we do not know exactly how she got on the floor, but it is not unreasonable to suppose that, suffering from a spasm of the bladder while lying on the bed, writhing in pain, she fell off the bed onto the floor." (Bladder spasms are a complication of cystitis, and those sharp, intense pains could have caused Rappe to fall.) The defense then conjectured, quoting doctors, that Rappe could have fallen on her abdomen or "upon other parts of her body," and either way it "might produce sufficient force to rupture an overextended bladder."

Analysis: Striking her abdomen against the side of the bathroom door with sufficient force seems wholly unlikely—unless she was stumbling drunk, and the testimony stated otherwise. Falling in the bathroom and striking her abdomen on the bathtub or toilet seat is less dubious but still improbable. It would have been difficult to fall in such a way that her abdomen got the worst of it. In addition, there were no bruises or marks on her midsection as from striking a hard surface, and perhaps most tellingly, Arbuckle never claimed she mentioned such a fall. His testimony at the first trial regarding the time they were both in the bathroom emphasized her nausea, though he did say that she was "holding her stomach" and that after he assisted her, she was "gasping and had a hard time getting her breath." He implied she was in greater pain in the bedroom later: "I found Miss Rappe between the two beds rolling about on the floor and holding her stomach and crying and moaning."*

---

* In contrast, when "Roscoe Arbuckle Tells His Own Story" was published a month later, Rappe's apparent pain when she was in the bathroom and when she was between the beds were described in the same terms, making it seem more likely she was injured in the bathroom.

As for a fall to the floor of 1219 causing the rupture, this too is doubtful. It would have been difficult for her to belly flop off the bed and to the floor approximately two feet down. A fall "upon other parts of her body" could have possibly caused an abdominal constriction that ruptured the bladder, but this removes us from blunt trauma and returns us to the statistical oddity of a spontaneous rupture.

State Challenge

The state challenged the defense's account primarily by questioning Arbuckle's immediate actions in assisting Rappe and his comments and lack of comments about those actions soon thereafter and then days later.

Immediate Actions

The state asked why Arbuckle, upon finding Rappe ill in the bathroom, did not immediately seek assistance.

Analysis: Arbuckle said he thought Rappe was merely nauseous from alcohol consumption, so his actions, as he described them, seem appropriate.

Actions Soon Thereafter

The state further questioned why Arbuckle never told anyone at the party nor the hotel's assistant manager, Harry Boyle, nor the first doctor summoned, Dr. Olav Kaarboe, that he had found Rappe in the bathroom nauseous, that he had helped her to a bed, and that she had likely fallen from that bed. That first day, he told no one anything about what occurred in 1219. "Is that human nature? Is that the way an innocent man would act?" the state asked.

Analysis: It does seem suspicious—*if Arbuckle thought Rappe was seriously injured.* By his account, he did not. Neither did anyone else at the party, nor Dr. Kaarboe, who attended to her that evening. All assumed that she had had too much to drink and she would sleep it off. Given that, it would not be especially notable that Rappe had vomited and probably fallen, and it would have been ungentlemanly at the time to mention it.

Actions Days Later

The state made much of the fact that Arbuckle did not recount his story of assisting a nauseous Rappe until on the witness stand at the first trial—that he had avoided telling the story to the press, the police, and the district attorney, as well as at a coroner's inquest, a grand jury, and a preliminary hearing. "Is that the way a man who had nothing to fear would act?" the state asked. The state postulated that Arbuckle's team only formulated their story after first hearing the state's witnesses, devising the tale to both complement and counter those witnesses' accounts.

Further, the state pointed out that Arbuckle did in fact speak on the evening of September 9 soon after learning of Rappe's death, and he gave a story very different from the one he later told under oath. Over the telephone, he told a *San Francisco Chronicle* reporter "there were no closed or locked doors [to 1219]," and "Virginia Rappe threw her fit in the presence of everyone, and that it was after she had thrown her fit she was taken into the other room and disrobed." That corresponds to what he told the *Los Angeles Times* that same evening, and it was his story for the next approximately twenty-four hours. Before he came to San Francisco, he gave a telephone statement to the San Francisco police: "We sat around and had some drinks and pretty soon Miss Rappe became hysterical and complained she could not breathe and began to tear her clothes off. . . . At no time was I alone with Miss Rappe. There were half a dozen people in the room all the time." This also matches the statement he released to the press upon arriving in San Francisco on the evening of September 10.

Analysis: Arbuckle's delay in telling his second version of events may have been a strategy to concoct an appropriate tale for the criminal trial, but he may also have wanted to tell the authorities and preliminary juries about his assisting an ill Rappe but been cautioned not to by his counsel, since it was a tale fraught with more land mines than his original never-alone-with-her deflection. Either way, he was exercising his right to remain silent, as instructed by his first defense attorney, Frank Dominguez, and his silence should not weigh on opinions of his truthfulness.

It's much more significant that his second version of events (the only one told under oath) does not resemble his first and that the first version is patently false. These are major strikes against Arbuckle's credibility. The initial lies of September 9 and 10 may have simply been the quickest way he could think of to hopefully dodge bad publicity, and thus they do not necessarily negate his later, more complicated, and much different version of events. Still, since he was lying from the start, it leads one to wonder when, if ever, he was telling the truth.

After, Part 1

Accounts of what occurred after Arbuckle opened the locked door to 1219 begin with a key disagreement.

State

Delmont, Prevost, and Blake stated that Arbuckle only opened the door after Delmont kicked it repeatedly.

Defense

Arbuckle insisted he opened the door without provocation in order to find Delmont, who was not located right away.

Analysis

As Delmont never testified in the criminal trials and many questions were raised about Prevost and Blake's multiple statements, it is difficult to determine the truth. Certainly, Arbuckle had a greater motivation to lie than Prevost or Blake. However, he and Rappe had been behind a locked door a relatively short period of time (despite Delmont first claiming an "hour," as if to motivate her actions), and no cries or other noises were heard from Rappe to provoke Delmont's alleged door-kicking. Still, Delmont may have been influenced by her own drunkenness (she admitted to drinking "eight or ten" whiskeys), and she may have lost track of time while in 1221's bathroom with Sherman. The kicking story is likely more truthful, but it remains in doubt.

After, Part 2

Next, Delmont, Prevost, and Blake entered 1219 to find Rappe on the double bed in great pain and barely conscious. The events that immediately followed are only partly agreed upon.

Consensus

The women moved Rappe from the double bed to the single bed because the double bed was wet, and when Rappe began tearing at her clothes, they helped her remove them. Arbuckle reentered the room, followed by Fred Fishback, who had just returned to the hotel. Arbuckle helped Rappe remove her arm from a sleeve of her dress because she was tearing at it. He left the room again.

With assistance from Prevost and Delmont, Fishback carried the naked Rappe into the bathroom for a cold bath, meant to comfort her pains. Afterward, he carried Rappe back to the single bed. (In some versions, he holds her upside down by her feet.) What occurred next is disputed.

State

When Arbuckle reentered 1219, the moaning Rappe supposedly said, "He hurt me," to which Arbuckle said, "Aw, shut up. I'll throw her out the window if she doesn't stop yelling." When ice was used by Delmont to comfort the naked Rappe, Arbuckle inserted an ice cube into Rappe's vagina, saying, "That will make her come to."

Defense

When Arbuckle reentered 1219, Delmont was rubbing the naked Rappe with ice. There was a piece of ice on or near Rappe's vagina. He picked it up and asked, "What's this doing here?" "Leave it here. I know how to take care of Virginia," Delmont answered. He put it back and started to cover Miss Rappe with a sheet. Delmont told him to leave, and Arbuckle told her, "Shut up, or I'll throw you out the window." Then he left.

Analysis

Here we have two of the most notorious features of the case, the ice incident and the "Throw her out the window" comment. Neither version reflects particularly well on Arbuckle, but as witnesses attesting to the state's version included Al Semnacher, who heard Arbuckle commenting about the ice in a crude manner the next day, it seems most likely the state's version is truer. Whether Arbuckle placed the ice in, on, or near Rappe's vagina remains in doubt, but the defense tacitly accepted that their client initiated the "icing" in the first trial as they dismissed it as a "collateral incident." In addition, such an act fit with Arbuckle's sense of humor, which could be much coarser than what viewers saw in his movies.

It is true that a wanton disrespect for Rappe's body could be consistent with a sexual predator. However, if he had injured Rappe while initiating a sexual assault, it seems unlikely he would soon thereafter have demonstrated to witnesses such disrespect for her body. Ultimately, it was indeed a collateral incident, indicating something about Arbuckle's character but nothing about his guilt or innocence. Similarly, the "Throw her out the window" comment could highlight a disregard for the pained Rappe, but it might also be the sort of crass comment—whether directed at Rappe or Delmont—a man concealing his guilt would not make.

After, Part 3

The two sides largely agreed on what transpired after the "icing."

Consensus

Arbuckle and Delmont put a bathrobe on Rappe. Mae Taube had arrived. She called the front desk, and assistant manager Harry Boyle came up to the suite. From Boyle, Arbuckle secured another room, 1227, just down the hall, and he carried Rappe most of the way there before handing her to Boyle, who carried her the remainder of the way to 1227's bed. Boyle called the hotel doctor, Dr. Kaarboe, who attended to Rappe in 1227 and diagnosed that she had drunk too much alcohol and merely needed to sleep it off.

Down the hall in 1220, the party continued. There Boyle told Arbuckle the doctor had seen Rappe and concluded nothing was wrong. Boyle left. Arbuckle took Taube for the long-promised ride in his Pierce-Arrow. Others came to the party. Delmont and the hotel detective finished off the gin and orange juice. Arbuckle returned to the party and that evening went out for dinner and dancing. He didn't check on Rappe or inquire about her. The next he heard of her, four days later, she was dead.

Analysis

The state portrayed Arbuckle's partying while Rappe lay dying as criminal callousness, but if he assumed, as an innocent man would and as he had been told, that Rappe was sleeping off her alcohol, his actions were not inappropriate. A guilty man might be more concerned about Rappe's health and what she might be saying to others about what occurred in 1219, but by outward appearances she slipped from Arbuckle's mind.*

Conclusion

Ultimately, the state's version of events seems more likely than the defense's, and yet it fails to hold up on the crucial question of Arbuckle's criminality. What is most curious is that Rappe lived for four days after Labor Day, and yet she never implicated Arbuckle in the sort of assault the state alleged. She never said she tried to escape out 1219's other door, where the handprints were supposedly so damning. She was never heard to scream or shout for help while in there either. Even Virginia

* Arbuckle made this point in his initial statement to the *Los Angeles Times* the day Rappe died: "To show how serious we thought it was, I and the other men danced in the hotel that night."

Breig, the Wakefield secretary, who only came forward at the third trial, did not claim to have heard Rappe say in the hours before her death that Arbuckle acted without consent. "Arbuckle took me by the arm and threw me on the bed and put his weight on me, and after that I do not know what happened," Rappe allegedly told Breig. Was it an act of violence or an act of mutual passion? Maid Josephine Keza claimed to overhear a female in 1219 saying "No, no, oh my God" and a man telling her to "shut up." But even if true, this did not necessarily indicate a crime. The judge at the preliminary hearing suggested these words might instead indicate the shifting boundaries of passion.

Over the two days that Rappe lay in a bed in room 1227, she was treated by three nurses: Jean Jameson, Vera Cumberland, and Martha Hamilton. Here we have witnesses, sober professionals, with whom Rappe, after sustaining her injury, may have been inclined to talk candidly. They had no known biases toward either the state or the defense. Hamilton testified to hearing nothing specific about the cause of the injury. Jameson and Cumberland testified at the coroner's inquest, there providing the most reliable accounts of Virginia Rappe's "testimony." (As their accounts differed from both the state's and the defense's contentions about what occurred in 1219, neither side called them to testify at the three criminal trials. Furthermore, their coroner's inquest testimony was never highlighted in the press.)

According to Jameson, "Miss Rappe told me that relations with her sweetheart were responsible for the ailment from which she had been suffering. She was very anxious that the party and what had occurred there be kept from Henry Lehrman, who she said was her sweetheart. As she expressed it, he would throw her down if he found out. She said she had been suffering for six weeks from internal trouble. She frequently asked me, 'What could have broken inside of me?' She asked me several times to determine if she had been assaulted. She said she was unconscious."

Said Cumberland, "The patient admitted to me that her relations with Arbuckle in the room had not been proper. She did not say whether her actions had been voluntary or involuntary. She said that she had been living with Henry Lehrman for some time and that several months ago she and Lehrman had had a quarrel and that he had gone to New York. She was very anxious that what happened be kept from him."

It is unclear what Rappe could have meant in Jameson's account when she brought up "relations with her sweetheart." But she likely thought her pain was emanating from her vagina, and thus she may have believed it was caused by previous sexual relations with Lehrman, or she may have wanted the nurse to think that. The "internal trouble" was likely her cystitis. Cumberland's account is more telling, as Rappe admitted she and Arbuckle had improper relations, likely meaning kissing and caressing. The fact that she did not say such relations were involuntary means they were more likely consensual. Interestingly, both accounts emphasize her being "very anxious" about keeping her behavior at the party from the volatile Lehrman.

This is likely what occurred between Roscoe Arbuckle and Virginia Rappe on Labor Day of 1921. They had been seated together and talking in room 1220, he in his pajamas and purple robe, she in her jade skirt and blouse. They were flirting. When she couldn't get into the bathroom in 1221, he watched her enter 1219, the bedroom he shared with Fishback. He followed her in there and locked the door. She had not yet entered 1219's bathroom, or she had just entered and she exited when Arbuckle made his presence known. They began to kiss. They may have pressed against the hallway door, leaving handprints there. Passions inflamed. Kissing, embracing, he guided her to the double bed and shoved her onto it, and he fell on top of her. Then, when his weight came down on her abdomen—or soon thereafter when, in the throes of passion, he elbowed or kneed her in the abdomen—her distended bladder ruptured.

And she blacked out. Her loss of consciousness, mentioned in one way or another by virtually everyone who spoke to her subsequently, may seem an unlikely and convenient coincidence, but as the state correctly pointed out, loss of consciousness immediately after the rupture of a distended bladder is a common occurrence, because of the resulting drop in blood pressure.

Arbuckle used water (frozen or not) in an attempt to revive her. She came to, groggy and pained. And, whether or not it was being kicked, he opened the locked door. Having blacked out moments after her bladder ruptured, Rappe was uncertain what had happened to her. She would naturally question whether something had been done to her while she was unconscious to cause her subsequent pains. "*She asked me several times to determine if she had been assaulted.*" Further, the actions she could remember were ones she did not want to be known beyond the nurses in whom she confided. She especially did not want them known by Lehrman. "*The patient admitted to me that her relations with Arbuckle in the room had not been proper.*"

After Rappe's death when the press and police were enquiring, Arbuckle feared that the truth was a slippery slope. Would they believe that his interaction with Rappe was consensual? What would the moviegoing public think of this still-married man engaging in boozy foreplay with a starlet in a hotel room? He must have even wondered how she could have been terminally injured and why she had blacked out. There had to be some other explanation. And so he first lied that he had never been alone with her. Later, when it fit the testimony of the state's witnesses, there came another explanation, a more elaborate lie—the story of Arbuckle aiding the nauseous Rappe.

The preceding scenario would not fit the definition of involuntary manslaughter—homicide committed without malice but in the perpetration of an unlawful act. That was the charge ultimately leveled against Arbuckle when the murder charge didn't stand. The unlawful act in the state's allegation was a sexual assault that was halted by Rappe's injury and resulting loss of consciousness, but the state produced no evidence, not the bruises nor the handprints nor the ruptured bladder, directly tying Arbuckle to such an assault. Other witness accounts of what Rappe allegedly said, such as "He hurt me," did not preclude that their interaction was consensual.

That's not to say he was entirely blameless. He was guilty of perjury for his concocted Good Samaritan story. He may have been worthy of some condemnation for his alcohol-fueled (Prohibition-era) pajama party with showgirls, and he certainly was for the ice incident if, as seems most likely, he made inappropriate contact as a joke. Indeed, he may have been guilty of all the state charged. Or something less. The interactions of Arbuckle and Rappe may have been consensual until the final moments, and then signals may have been misinterpreted or disregarded. The "assault" may have started and ended with a fall on a bed.

In any case, based on what the prosecution knew and did not know, Roscoe Arbuckle should never have been tried for manslaughter and certainly never branded a murderer and a rapist. Further, he should never have been painted as a monster by the press and blacklisted by the film industry.

There were but two people in that room, and neither of them knew that one of them had suffered a bladder tear until after she was dead. We can never know for certain what happened behind the locked door of 1219 on Labor Day of 1921, other than the fact that one person endured an injury there that resulted four days later in the loss of her life and eventually led to the destruction of her reputation. The other person suffered horribly for that death, perhaps justly, perhaps even escaping true justice, but most likely unjustly. Most likely, in the scope of society's condemnation, it is one of the greatest injustices to a career and a reputation ever perpetrated.

{23}

DENOUEMENT: 1932–33

ARBUCKLE FILM BRINGS ARREST
The board of motion-picture censors of Portland [Oregon] today ordered the arrest of Andrew Saso, manager of a theater, on the ground that he had shown a motion-picture featuring Roscoe (Fatty) Arbuckle. Films featuring Arbuckle have been barred by city ordinance since October 15, 1924.

—*Los Angeles Times*, December 14, 1932, front page

Arbuckle had enjoyed an accomplished and lengthy career onstage, first singing and later telling jokes. His rich voice would have been ideal for radio, if anyone had dared to give him such a chance, but most of his American fans never heard him utter a word before his initial sound film was released in November 1932. *Hey, Pop!* was his first starring movie role in over eleven years. Warner Bros. had been especially careful, returning him to his customary on-screen getup (oversized pants, undersized bowler) and frequent secondary costume (a dress) and a slapstick plot and gags reminiscent of his two-reelers from the 1910s. The only addition was dialogue, which Arbuckle handled admirably.

Shorts like *Hey, Pop!* ran before feature attractions and typically weren't advertised on marquees or in newspapers. Thus, Arbuckle's comeback film created little controversy, garnering some positive reviews but mostly screening unnoticed. There was by now a new generation of movie stars and movie fans. The transition from silence to sound had marked a gaping demarcation, marginalizing silent comedians and their sight gags.*

Arbuckle made three comedy shorts for Warner Bros. in the final five months of 1932, each shot in less than a week at Brooklyn's Vitaphone studio (the old Vitagraph studio where teenage Mabel Normand acted). The second of these, *Buzzin' Around*, featured Al St. John and a swarm of animated bees.† It was the final of sixty-three films known to include the uncle and nephew. The third short, *How've You Bean?*, paired Arbuckle with the smaller, blank-eyed Fritz Hubert to form a new comedy duo, with the latter serving mostly as straight man to the former's shenanigans. (Destined for a brief career, twenty-four-year-old Hubert had only just debuted with a small role in *Hey, Pop!*) The pair mishandle Mexican jumping beans; as with the bees in *Buzzin' Around*, the beans are animated to good effect. This heralded a change, because with the rise of Mickey Mouse, short comedy was increasingly an animated medium. And slapstick, which had gone from vaudeville to silent films to sound films during Arbuckle's lifetime, was finding a new and lasting home in cartoons.

A New York gossip column item in October 1932 read, "Quite the most man-about-town-ish man-about-town at the moment is Fatty Arbuckle who, liberated from an old stigma, seems to be having the time of his life. He appears in all the night spots, invariably accompanied by his attractive wife." The party continued for Arbuckle, who had first been a regular at Manhattan nightclubs with Keaton fifteen years prior. But, now-middle-aged, he had shed the all-male entourage to spend time with his new wife. He and McPhail danced at such legendary joints as the Cotton Club, the Onyx Club, and Roseland Ballroom.

---

* With sound, Buster Keaton also returned to low-budget comedy shorts, starring in twenty-six between 1934 and 1941. He later resuscitated his career better than any other silent star, scoring roles in feature films, plays, and television programs until his death in 1966 at age seventy.

† St. John also had a prolific sound career, including more than eighty supporting roles in westerns as the bearded, comical "Fuzzy." He died in 1963 at sixty-nine. Over a forty-year career, Al St. John acted in over 340 films.

A suite at Manhattan's elegant Park Central Hotel was the home for Arbuckle, McPhail, McPhail's then-eight-year-old daughter, Marilyn, and their African American maid. Arbuckle never had a child of his own, but he loved playing with kids, and kids quickly warmed to him. For the first time since he lived with Durfee's family in the early 1910s, there was a child in his home. He doted on Marilyn.

In early 1933 the family of three returned to Los Angeles on a vacation. Afterward, when they boarded a train and headed east again, it was the last time Arbuckle, who called himself a "100% Californian," saw the Golden State. During Mardi Gras week in March 1933, he played a weeklong vaudeville engagement to packed houses in New Orleans, assisted by McPhail. Also that month, a newspaper item read, "Roscoe Arbuckle has given up dieting. He says he's not going to starve himself to death just for the sake of living a few years longer."

In April he was back at the Vitaphone studio, starring in the comedy short *Close Relations*, which featured Shemp Howard of Three Stooges fame. Then he was again paired with Fritz Hubert in *Tomalio* and *In the Dough*. Arbuckle had no love interest in his six comeback movies, thus avoiding any association with the scandal of 1921. Instead, *In the Dough*, his final film, recalls more innocent times. Its relentless pie fight is reminiscent of Arbuckle's Keystone days, when every scene was a potential custard eruption and Fatty's fame was climbing weekly. Production began on June 22 and wrapped on the afternoon of June 28.

On the evening of June 28, Arbuckle and McPhail belatedly celebrated their one-year wedding anniversary at Billy La Hiff's Tavern, a popular hangout for Broadway and film notables in midtown Manhattan. Alcohol was served at La Hiff's with a wink at Prohibition, which was by that summer evening crawling feebly toward its official demise on December 5. Arbuckle and McPhail ate and drank. She played backgammon. He talked with friends, including former world boxing champ Johnny Dundee. Arbuckle had tickets to the world heavyweight championship fight the following evening at the Madison Square Garden Bowl, a seventy-two-thousand-seat outdoor arena in Queens. Arbuckle and his agent, Joe Rivkin, discussed his Midwest vaudeville tour scheduled to begin in four days and the fact that Warner Bros. was exercising its option to produce eight additional sound Fatty shorts. A feature film was a possibility. It's appropriate that the final full day in the life of Roscoe Arbuckle was spent acting in a film and then out on the town, eating, drinking, and socializing with friends—for those were the things that made him happiest.

"I've made my comeback," Arbuckle said. "There are lots of stars not doing as well as I am right now."

Arbuckle and his wife had planned to go to a nightclub, but he was more tired than usual. It was the rare time he turned down an opportunity to keep the party going. At around 11:30 PM, he and McPhail took a cab the seven blocks to their home at the Park Central Hotel. He was in bed by 12:30 on the morning of June 29, 1933. Between then and 2:15, Roscoe Arbuckle died peacefully of a heart attack at age forty-six.

Dressed in a gray suit, white shirt, and a dark bow tie, Arbuckle's body was laid in a gray casket in the ornate Gold Room of Frank E. Campbell's Funeral Church on Broadway on Manhattan's Upper West Side. As many as a thousand mourners and curious onlookers paid their final respects to him on June 29 and 30.

Campbell's had then (and maintains now) a reputation for discreetly and securely handling the mortuary needs of the rich and famous.* Funeral services were conducted by officers of an Elks Lodge (Arbuckle was an Elk) at 1:00 PM on Saturday, July 1, at the Funeral Church. Three hundred people attended. Honorary pallbearers included Billy La Hiff, Joe Rivkin, Ray McCarey (the director of Arbuckle's final three movies), and comic actor Bert Lahr (later the Cowardly Lion in *The Wizard of Oz*). Because only two days elapsed between his death and his funeral, Arbuckle's famous friends in California didn't have time to traverse the country via train. Buster Keaton, Charlie Chaplin, and Joe Schenck were among those who sent flowers.

---

* Campbell's secured this reputation when it handled the services of Rudolph Valentino in 1926.

"We think of his love of children and how he brought a surcease of sorrow to those in pain," the Elks elder said in the eulogy. "There is nothing in the world like laughter, and so we may say that he made the world laugh. And now that the end has come we know he will be judged by the good he has done." After the service, a crying McPhail, wearing all white, followed the flower-topped casket outside to the hearse while police held back the rubbernecking crowd of five hundred. Then, by car, she followed the hearse to Fresh Pond Crematory in Queens. Soon thereafter, McPhail, her daughter, and her maid returned to Los Angeles.

Within weeks of his death, his older brother Harry and younger half-brother Clyde contested Roscoe Arbuckle's will, claiming they had a right to over $100,000 in stocks and bonds. In July 1934 a New York court ruled that the estate's assets totaled $2,000. Minus debts, $396 was awarded to Addie McPhail.*

On September 6, 1934, Arbuckle's ashes were shipped to McPhail in Los Angeles, and shortly thereafter she alone committed them to the Pacific Ocean off Santa Monica—the waters in which Roscoe Arbuckle had swum on those blissful days two decades earlier when his fame and fortune had only just begun to grow, when he could never have imagined the highs and lows his life would reach.

His obituaries mostly focused on the lows. In the briefest of hatchet jobs, *Time* told readers as much about Will Hays's career as Arbuckle's: "Died. Roscoe Conkling ("Fatty") Arbuckle, 46, globular oldtime cinemactor; of a heart attack; in Manhattan. Although acquitted of manslaughter after the death of one Virginia Rappe eleven years ago, the malodorous evidence brought out at the trial dropped him to obscurity; resulted in the appointment of President Harding's Postmaster General Will H. Hays as public apologist for Hollywood."

Some obituary writers painted a cautionary tale: "Instead of being the innocent and jovial blunderer he so amusingly depicted, Arbuckle

* McPhail acted only a few more times in bit parts. She remarried and lived in Los Angeles until her death at ninety-seven in 2003.

was disclosed as a weakling who couldn't stand prosperity and who, under the influence of intoxicants, became a coarse vulgarian. But now there can only be a feeling of pity for 'Fatty' Arbuckle—a man who muffed a wonderful opportunity in life. Young people should be able to learn something from a study of his life—it is as important to know the road to avoid as the road to take."

Others told a tragic story: "Arbuckle got a rough deal in life. He was yanked from the heights and shot to the depths so that I sometimes wondered how he managed to survive the ordeal. And for what? For doing something that happens in every city, in every state, in every hotel on every day of the year. For staging a drunken party. But Arbuckle got the rap that most party-goers are fortunate enough to miss. In his case a sick girl died. And the holier-than-thous swooped down upon the man with such vengeance that they deprived him of a livelihood for many years."

Will Rogers echoed this sentiment more poetically: "Those who demanded their pound of flesh, finally received their satisfaction. 'Fatty' Arbuckle accommodated 'em by dying, and from a broken heart."

His heart literally broke, but Arbuckle was as happy when he died as he had been in twelve years. He was married again, happily, and a first-time stepfather. He was working onstage and acting in movies. He was no longer burdened by great debts. He was optimistic about his future, but June 29, 1933, may have been as good as it would get. His cinematic comeback would have continued, but judging by the careers of most silent stars, it likely would have expired within a few years, and it almost certainly never would have approached the heights of his previous peak. In that regard, his may well have been the right time to exit life's stage.

Arbuckle's final movies continued to play after he was gone. He continued to fall and chase and hurl pies, and audiences continued to laugh at him, forgetting for a while the tragedy and trials, and forgetting, like always, the reality outside the dark theater. They laughed with an old friend like old times, after he was gone.

ACKNOWLEDGMENTS

Numerous people and institutions assisted in the research of this book. I would especially like to thank the staffs of the Margaret Herrick Library of the Academy of Motion Picture Arts and Sciences, the Louis B. Mayer Library of the American Film Institute, the Library of Congress, the Los Angeles Public Library and the County of Los Angeles Public Library, the San Francisco Public Library, the Harry Ransom Center of the University of Texas at Austin, the San Francisco County Clerk's Office, the San Francisco District Attorney's Office, the County of San Francisco Criminal Court, the California Department of Public Health, the National Archives and Records Administration, the San Francisco Museum and Historical Society, the Orange County Archives, the Bisbee Mining & Historical Museum, the West Adams Heritage Association, the Culver City Historical Society, the Blackhawk Museum, the Nethercutt Museum, the International Buster Keaton Society, the Interstitial Cystitis Network, and the Westin St. Francis hotel—the enduring home of room 1219.

The following online databases proved especially useful: Ancestry.com, Chronicling America (the Library of Congress newspaper archive, at http://chroniclingamerica.loc.gov), the Google News archives, the Internet Archive (www.archive.org), NewspaperArchive.com, ProQuest.com, and *Taylorology* (www.taylorology.com). Some Arbuckle movies and video documentary material were viewed via the Internet Archive and YouTube.

The many individuals who assisted with research include Bruce Long (the force responsible for *Taylorology*), Dean Budnick (author of a doctoral thesis on the Arbuckle case, "Directed Verdict"), Howard Mutz (official historian of the Westin St. Francis), Don Wilson (Route 101 historian), Marilyn Slater (Mabel Normand scholar), Thomas Reeder (Henry Lehrman scholar), Henry E. Scott (author of *Shocking True Story*), Marion Gregston of the Montecito Association History Committee (for busting the myth that the Montecito Inn was owned by Arbuckle and Chaplin), and Kenneth Moses and Larry Stewart (fingerprint experts). A special thanks to Robert Young Jr., Don Schneider, and Stuart Oderman, all of whom interviewed Minta Durfee, and to Paul E. Gierucki for his work restoring Arbuckle's films.

Thanks also to Yuval Taylor, Devon Freeny, Mary Kravenas, and everyone else at Chicago Review Press, Eric Myers of the Spieler Agency, Rose Bubert, Joe Weider, Roger Ebert, Charles Mitchell, Arnold Lipkind, James Hosney, Peter McGough, Shawn Perine, Kevin Horton, and the clerk at Book Alley (Pasadena) who remembered she filed *Anger: The Unauthorized Biography of Kenneth Anger* in the "Psychology" section.

NOTES

1. Labor Day

a custom-built right-hand-drive Pierce-Arrow . . . "Conspicuous Consumption: Fatty Arbuckle's Fabulous Pierce-Arrow," *Special Interest Auto*, February 1990, 44–46.

"To attempt to describe in cold, unfeeling print . . ." Variety, August 5, 1921.

"Paramount Week" . . . Advertisement, *Literary Digest*, September 3, 1921, 8.

They invited Arbuckle . . . Eleanor Keaton and Jeffrey Vance, *Buster Keaton Remembered* (New York: Harry N. Abrams, 2001), 84.

"'most polished villain'" . . . From the Studio Lot, *Oakland Tribune*, September 5, 1921.

an article attributed to Roscoe "Fatty" Arbuckle . . . Roscoe Arbuckle, "Love Confessions of a Fat Man," *Photoplay*, September 1921, 22–23.

twenty bottles were along for the ride . . . "Probers Identify Men Who Carried Arbuckle's Booze," *Oakland Tribune*, September 17, 1921.

The St. Francis . . . History and details via David Siefkin, *Meet Me at the St. Francis: The First Seventy-Five Years of a Great San Francisco Hotel* (San Francisco: St. Francis Hotel Corp., 1979), 10–11, 38.

His menu was noted . . . Linda Civitello, *Cuisine and Culture: A History of Food and People* (Hoboken, NJ: Wiley, 2011), 287.

Breakfast options . . . Siefkin, *Meet Me at the St. Francis*, 39.

The hotel's brochure in the early 1920s . . . Ibid., 46.

a deliveryman carried four bottles . . . "Liquor Source Found," *St. Joseph News-Press*, October 5, 1921.

a fully stocked speakeasy in the basement . . . Charles Fracchia, "San Francisco During Prohibition," forum with Michael Krasney, KQED radio broadcast, December 5, 2008.

she made the news for her elopement . . . "Young Romance Is Short-Lived," *Oakland Tribune*, December 7, 1912.

he had filed for divorce . . . "Semnacher, Who Attended Party, Seeking Divorce," *Oakland Tribune*, September 14, 1921.
"Virginia Rappe, the movie actress" . . . "Put Miss Rappe in Tub, Fishbach [*sic*] Testifies," *New York Times*, November 24, 1921.
"I'll go up there . . ." "Dead Girl's Accusation Is Repeated," *Oakland Tribune*, September 13, 1921.
she wore the same self-made clothes . . . "Fate Sealed by Dress She Made," *Los Angeles Times*, September 15, 1921.
At the time of the 1920 census . . . US Census Bureau, *Fourteenth Census of the United States, 1920*, population of San Francisco, CA, precinct 38, dist. 33, sup. dist. 4, enum. dist. 264, January 7 & 8, 1920 (Washington, DC: Government Printing Office, 1921).
"Let's have some music . . ." "Arbuckle on Grill Tells of S.F. Party," *Oakland Tribune*, November 28, 1921.
Arbuckle later described her as "peeved" . . . "Virginia Rappe Film May Be Offered as Evidence in Trial," *Pittsburgh Press*, November 29, 1921.
"Who are all these people?" . . . Ibid.
The deliveryman from Gobey's Grill . . . "Liquor Source Found."
"Roscoe liked nothing better . . ." Buster Keaton with Charles Samuels, *My Wonderful World of Slapstick* (Garden City, NY: Doubleday, 1960), 158.
"If I would jump out of the twelfth-story window . . ." "Comedian Ready to End Life, Party Guest Says," *Oakland Tribune*, September 14, 1921.

2. Journeys: 1887–1908

Roscoe Arbuckle purportedly weighed sixteen pounds . . . "Nobody Loves a Fat Man?," *Movie Pictorial*, June 13, 1914, 20.
This much is true . . . Parents' and siblings' ages estimated based on their ages on June 22, 1880, via US Census Bureau, *Tenth Census of the United States, 1880*, population of Pawnee Township, Smith County, KS, sup. dist. 3, enum. dist. 302, June 22, 1880 (Washington, DC: Government Printing Office, 1881).
The town in 1883 . . . William G. Cutler, *History of the State of Kansas* (Chicago: A. T. Andreas, 1883), www.kancoll.org/books/cutler/.
"a sod house of the most primitive kind" . . . Nevada Daily Mail, September 12, 1921.
Its population had blossomed . . . "General Population by City: Orange County, 1860–1900," OC Almanac, www.ocalmanac.com/Population/po25.htm.
Roscoe later said he never felt loved . . . Minta Durfee, unpublished manuscript, 13, Minta Durfee Arbuckle Collection, Margaret Herrick Library, Academy of Motion Pictures Arts and Sciences, Beverly Hills, CA.
Schoolmates would remember him . . . "Nicknamed 'Fatty' When Six Years Old," *Oakland Tribune*, September 13, 1921.
Still, others would recall . . . "Grave of Arbuckle's Mother Is Neglected," *Los Angeles Times*, September 13, 1921.
Teasing children bestowed on him . . . "Nicknamed 'Fatty' When Six Years Old."
"My stage career was thrust upon me . . ." "The Solemn Mr. Arbuckle," *New York Tribune*, May 6, 1917.

Bacon had been a sheepherder . . . "Frank Bacon, Actor, Tired Out, Is Dead," *New York Times*, November 20, 1922.
"For years and years he barnstormed . . ." "Frank Bacon, the Creator of 'Lightnin',' Dies," *New York Herald*, November 20, 1922.
So greasepaint was used to blacken . . . Roscoe Arbuckle, interview by Ray Frohman, *Los Angeles Herald*, October 28, 1919.
Hours later, a railroad worker . . . Durfee, unpublished manuscript, 15–16.
Entering an amateur contest at the local theater . . . Ibid., 19–22.
the 1900 census listed . . . US Census Bureau, *Twelfth Census of the United States, 1900*, population of Santa Clara, CA, sup. dist. 2, enum. dist. 77, June 9, 1900 (Washington, DC: Government Printing Office, 1904).
"Whenever a baseball went over the fence . . ." "Former 'Kid Pals' of Arbuckle Tell of Early Scrapes," *Evening Independent* (Massillon, OH), September 13, 1921.
dancing jigs or belly-flopping . . . "Story of a Farm Boy's Rise to Film Star," *New York American*, September 13, 1921.
"He was aggravatingly lazy . . ." "Here's Interesting 'Cut-Back' on Life of 'Fatty' Arbuckle," *Evening Independent* (Massillon, OH), September 20, 1921.
"His father used to beat him . . ." "Film Comedian Forgets His Two Blind Sisters," *Oakland Tribune*, September 12, 1921.
In San Francisco two years later . . . Susan Saperstein, "Grauman's Theaters," *Guidelines: Newsletter for San Francisco City Guides and Sponsors*, www.sfcityguides.org/public_guidelines.html?article=200&submitted=TRUE.
In February 1903 . . . Clyde Arbuckle, *Clyde Arbuckle's History of San Jose* (San Jose, CA: Smith & McKay, 1985), 454.
Between their first public projections . . . David Robinson, *From Peep Show to Palace: The Birth of American Film* (New York: Columbia University Press, 1996), 61.
The Unique has a unique history . . . Saperstein, "Grauman's Theaters."
the Hotel St. Francis opened its doors . . . David Siefkin, *Meet Me at the St. Francis: The First Seventy-Five Years of a Great San Francisco Hotel* (San Francisco: St. Francis Hotel Corp., 1979), 11, 18–21.
Alexander Pantages . . . Daniel Statt, "Pantages, Alexander," HistoryLink.org, www.historylink.org/index.cfm?DisplayPage=output.cfm&File_Id=2999.
"who persuaded me that I had a voice . . ." Wil Rex, "Behind the Scenes with Fatty and Mabel," *Picture-Play*, April 1916, 50.
"taught me several valuable things . . ." "Turning Pounds into Laughs Not Arbuckle's Ideal," *Sun*, June 17, 1917.
a new woman appeared onstage . . . Durfee, unpublished manuscript, 23.
Arbuckle turned again to Alexander Pantages . . . Ibid., 24.
His rotation of characters . . . Eric L. Flom, *Silent Film Stars on the Stages of Seattle: A History of Performances by Hollywood Notables* (Jefferson, NC: McFarland, 2009), 119–123.
One day, while returning to Long Beach . . . Minta Durfee, interview by Don Schneider, July 21, 1974, excerpted at Mabel Normand Home Page, www.mn-hp.com/minta1.html; further details from other Durfee interviews.
"I don't know what got into me" . . . Minta Durfee, interview by Walter Wagner, July 4, 1973, in *You Must Remember This* (New York: Putnam, 1975), 31.
"His ability to do everything . . ." Durfee, unpublished manuscript, 34.

"Will you marry me?" . . . Ibid., 8.
the couple married in the Byde-A-Wyle . . . "Stage Wedding Draws Crowds," *Los Angeles Times*, August 6, 1908.
Durfee was bedridden . . . Durfee, unpublished manuscript, 13.

3. Virginia

Virginia never knew her father . . . "Origin of Miss Rappe," *Los Angeles Times*, September 20, 1921.
"a pretty girl of nineteen" . . . "Locked in the Veterans' Building," *Chicago Tribune*, December 23, 1892.
"the most dangerous gang of forgers . . ." "Forger Pullman Boys' Friend," *New York Times*, December 31, 1898.
her "grandmother," Caroline Rapp . . . Nat Schmulowitz, closing statement of third Arbuckle trial, in *Classics of the Bar: Stories of the World's Great Legal Trials and a Compilation of Forensic Masterpieces*, vol. 8, ed. Alvin V. Sellers (Washington, DC: Washington Law Book, 1942), 38.
Rappe's "adopted aunt" . . . Ibid.
Mabel Rapp's deathbed wish . . . "Adopted Aunt of Actress Denies Operation Rumor," *Oakland Tribune*, September 12, 1921.
a "rollicking schoolgirl . . ." "Friends Defend Miss Rappe," *New York Tribune*, November 7, 1921.
A 1908 article in the Chicago Tribune . . . "Are the Artists' Models of Chicago More Beautiful Than the Famous Models of Paris?," *Chicago Tribune*, November 22, 1908.
she entered into a pact . . . "Mrs. Arthur Greiner to Re-wed Husband," *Cedar Rapids Daily Republican*, October 25, 1912.
"attracting considerable attention . . ." Ibid.
"Miss Rappe spends most of her time . . ." Editorial, *Omaha Exclesior*, September 20, 1913.
Rappe's advice to young women . . . "New Jobs Await Working Women," *Los Angeles Times*, January 3, 1913.
when only 18 percent of American women . . . US Census Bureau, *Thirteenth Census of the United States, 1910* (Washington, DC: Government Printing Office, 1912–14).
the average annual salary for employed men and women . . . Ibid.
A front-page news story early in 1914 . . . "Girls in Pink Bloomers Mystify Ship's Passengers," *Fort Wayne News*, January 13, 1914.
"the spider-web hat . . ." "'Won't You Come into My Parlor?' Says Spider to Butterflies of Fashion," *Reno Evening Gazette*, May 18, 1915.
"monoplane hat" . . . "Trim Little Craft Is the Monoplane, Is Now Soaring 'Cross the Fashion Skies," *Reno Evening Gazette*, May 22, 1915.
"summer muff" . . . "With Muffs In Summer Girls Remain Cool," *Reno Evening Gazette*, May 29, 1915.

"Equal clothes rights with men! . . ." "Here's the Tuxedo Girl, How Do You Like Her?," *Reno Evening Gazette*, May 10, 1915.
"'The women of America want world peace' . . ." "Peace Hat! And It's Crownless Too!," *Reno Evening Gazette*, June 19, 1915.
"a man's diamond ring . . ." "Operated on Rappe Girl, Says Doctor," *Bakersfield Californian*, March 10, 1922.
"member of an old aristocratic family . . ." "Fashion Model to Wed," *Daily-News Record*, July 31, 1915.
"nice but old enough to be my grandfather" . . . "'Cold and Unresponsive' Is Men's Description of Miss Rappe," *Evening Record*, September 21, 1921.
She struck poses in an Atlanta department store . . . "Pretty Victim in Arbuckle Gin-Frolic Remembered as Model in Atlanta Store," *Atlanta Constitution*, September 13, 1921.
"'Paradise Garden,' a seven-part Metro . . ." Review of *Paradise Garden*, *Variety*, October 12, 1917.
"tears her dress in the rear . . ." Ibid.
director Henry Lehrman . . . Biographical details via Thomas Reeder, "And He That Strives to Touch the Stars: Henry Lehrman and the Fledgling Film Industry," *Galitzianer*, November 2009, 16–24.
she was listed as "boarder" . . . US Census Bureau, *Fourteenth Census of the United States, 1920*, population of Los Angeles, CA, precinct 394, January 10, 1920 (Washington, DC: Government Printing Office, 1921).
"one of the wealthiest and most beautiful . . ." "Wealthy Young Woman to Be Screen Actress," *Fort Wayne Journal-Gazette*, September 21, 1919.
Lehrman released a terse statement . . . Anthony Balducci, *Lloyd Hamilton: Poor Boy Comedian of Silent Cinema* (Jefferson, NC: McFarland, 2009), 77.
Arbuckle said his renting . . . "Film Actor on Stand," *Los Angeles Times*, November 29, 1921.
This lengthy headline and subhead . . . "Back to Quakerland!," *New Castle News*, March 4, 1920.
she won prizes for such . . . "Miss Rappe Winning Fame as Screen Star," *Oakland Tribune*, September 11, 1921.
He signed on to direct four films . . . Reeder, "And He That Strives," 21.
she paid Kate Hardebeck . . . "Deny Miss Rappe Ill," *Los Angeles Times*, April 8, 1922.
"Her chief delight . . ." "Lauds Character of Miss Rappe," *Evening Public Ledger* (Philadelphia, PA), September 13, 1921.
his death certificate lists . . . California State Board of Health, standard certificate of death for William Monroe Ritchie, July 8, 1921, state index number 13748.
Semnacher would later claim . . . "Blackmail Charged," *Los Angeles Times*, September 27, 1921.
sandwiches and coffee in vacuum bottles . . . "Lauds Character of Miss Rappe."
Delmont later claimed she brought a pint of whiskey . . . "Dead Girl's Accusation Is Repeated," *Oakland Tribune*, September 13, 1921.
a "very pleasant time" . . . "Adopted Aunt of Actress Denies Operation Rumor."

4. Sanitarium

the hotel's house physician, Dr. Arthur Beardslee . . . Beardslee's actions via "Arbuckle's Aim Short," *Los Angeles Times*, November 20, 1921.

Rappe said she did not recollect anything . . . "Dying Statement of Movie Actress Read by Doctor," *Atlanta Constitution*, November 26, 1921.

Arbuckle spoke with Al Semnacher . . . "Arbuckle Defense Opens; State Rests," *New York Times*, November 23, 1921.

Arbuckle picked up the $611.13 tab . . . "Arbuckle's Three Day Party Cost Actor $611.13," *Sacramento Bee*, September 23, 1921.

the steamship Harvard . . . Gordon Ghareeb and Martin Cox, *Hollywood to Honolulu: The Story of the Los Angeles Steamship Company* (Palo Alto, CA: Glencannon, 2009), 13–20.

he met on the Paramount lot . . . Minta Durfee, unpublished manuscript, unnumbered pages, Minta Durfee Arbuckle Collection, Margaret Herrick Library, Academy of Motion Pictures Arts and Sciences, Beverly Hills, CA.

Spreckels came to Rappe's side . . . "Mrs. Spreckels, Jr., Friend of Dead Girl Pays Tribute," *Oakland Tribune*, September 12, 1921.

"Oh, to think I led . . ." "Party Guests Give Evidence Before Coroner," *Indianapolis Star*, September 13, 1921.

prayed for the comatose woman's recovery . . . "Pastor Wants Facts on Arbuckle Party," *Oakland Tribune*, September 19, 1921.

5. Hollywood: 1909–12

Key works consulted for early motion picture history: David Robinson, *From Peep Show to Palace: The Birth of American Film* (New York: Columbia University Press, 1996); Robert Sklar, *Movie-Made America: A Cultural History of American Movies* (New York: Vintage, 1975); Gordon Hendricks, "The History of the Kinetoscope," in *The American Film Industry*, ed. Tino Balio (Madison: University of Wisconsin Press, 1976).

The actual first . . . William M. Drew, "The Prehistory of Hollywood," Early Hollywood Films and Movie Stars, 2009, http://william-m-drew.webs.com/prehistoryofhollywood.htm.

Ben's Kid, a western . . . Andrew A. Erish, *Col. William N. Selig, the Man Who Invented Hollywood* (Austin: University of Texas Press, 2012), 83.

Arbuckle's second film, Mrs. Jones' Birthday . . . Ibid.

"The Jones of the picture is a fat fellow . . ." Review of *Mrs. Jones' Birthday*, *New York Dramatic Mirror*, September 11, 1909.

"My God! . . ." Minta Durfee, unpublished manuscript, 81, Minta Durfee Arbuckle Collection, Margaret Herrick Library, Academy of Motion Pictures Arts and Sciences, Beverly Hills, CA.

"Then, there was nobody breaking in . . ." "'Fatty' Arbuckle Went into the Movies, He Confesses, Because He Likes to Eat," *Baltimore American*, February 13, 1921.

at Los Angeles' Auditorium Theater . . . Arbuckle's roles via theater review, *Los Angeles Herald*, January 19, 1909; ibid., February 3, 1909; ibid., March 16, 1909.

"[He] sings much better than he acts" . . . The Drama, *Los Angeles Times*, March 2, 1909.
"You wanted him, you married him . . ." Durfee, unpublished manuscript, 13.
staging such plays as . . . Theater listings, *Bisbee Daily Review*, June 17, 1909; ibid., September 5, 1909; ibid., December 7, 1909; ibid., December 14, 1909.
Elks Club funeral . . . "Elks Honor Dead's Memory," *Bisbee Daily Review*, December 5, 1909.
Eagles Club affair . . . "Eagles Do Selves Proud with Smoker," *Bisbee Daily Review*, October 20, 1909.
country club "dinner and smoker" . . . "Country Club Has Big Time at Feast," *Bisbee Daily Review*, December 11, 1909.
Orpheum wrestling match . . . "Stone Proves Too Fast for Indian," *Bisbee Daily Review*, November 30, 1909.
Arbuckle guest umpired one game . . . "C.Q. Ball Teams Will Battle Today," *Bisbee Daily Review*, October 3, 1909.
"Roscoe Arbuckle and the rest of the Orpheum bunch . . ." "Muckers Defeated by the Demons," *Bisbee Daily Review*, September 9, 1909.
The other entertainment . . . "Country Club Has Big Time at Feast."
"At the close of the performance . . ." "Man from Boston Scores Big Hit in Two Performances," *Bisbee Daily Review*, December 28, 1909.
cranking out three shows daily . . . Theater advertisement, *Los Angeles Herald*, April 26, 1910.
"I remember [Arbuckle] when he was . . ." Harry Carr, Grouchy Remarks, *Los Angeles Times*, December 9, 1921.
"It may have been slammed together . . ." Review of *The Sanitarium*, *Variety*, October 15, 1910.
At home, Arbuckle and his wife were sharing . . . US Census Bureau, *Thirteenth Census of the United States, 1910*, population of Los Angeles, CA, sup. dist. 7, enum. dist. 11, April 29, 1910 (Washington, DC: Government Printing Office, 1912–14).
"Roscoe's swinging off the street car . . ." Durfee, unpublished manuscript, 48.
the second film company . . . "David Horsley: How the First Independent Started," *Moving Picture World*, March 10, 1917, 1518–19.
its first major tragedy . . . "Maddened Japanese Slays," *Oakland Tribune*, October 27, 1911.
"Special Appearance . . ." Advertisement, *Evening News* (San Jose), August 18, 1911.
She soon discovered she was pregnant . . . Durfee, unpublished manuscript, 50, 58.
a critically and commercially successful run . . . Positive reviews from four Chicago newspapers are excerpted in "How Chicago Received 'The Campus,'" *The Shield* 28, no. 1 (February 10, 1912): 48–49.
"a nice little chap . . ." Theater review, *Oakland Tribune*, June 29, 1912.
"Roscoe and I made it a habit . . ." Durfee, unpublished manuscript, 65.
"serenaded by bands and royally entertained" . . . "Ferris Hartman Company Made the Orientals Laugh," *Oakland Tribune*, March 16, 1913, 23.
"a quaint old negro servant" . . . Review of *The Mikado*, *North-China Herald*, October 19, 1912.
"barked at a dog who barked at me" . . . "Roscoe Arbuckle, Mountain of Flesh, Achieves Fame," *Morning Oregonian*, April 4, 1920.

6. Postmortem

Document notes are from California State Board of Health, standard certificate of death for Virginia Rappe, September 15, 1921, local registered number 5182. Typical autopsy procedures are from various sources.

He noted two bruises . . . "Testify to Bruises on Virginia Rappe," *New York Times*, September 23, 1921.

Blood had congested . . . "Describe Injuries of Film Actress," *Evening Public Ledger* (Philadelphia, PA), September 23, 1921.

The lower lobes of one . . . "Arbuckle Hit Hard," *Los Angeles Times*, September 23, 1921.

The peritoneum was inflamed . . . Coroner's inquest testimony, in K. Sellers Kennard, MD, "Rupture of the Female Urinary Bladder," *Medico-Legal Journal*, May/June 1923, 74.

It was unusually small . . . "Film Actor Is Nervous," *Los Angeles Times*, November 19, 1921.

Dr. Ophüls made an incision . . . Kennard, "Rupture of the Female Urinary Bladder," 74.

a small clot of blood . . . Ibid., 73.

described by Ophüls as "a clean break" . . . Ibid.

He noted eleven bruises . . . "Testify to Bruises on Virginia Rappe."

Viewing through a microscope . . . Kennard, "Rupture of the Female Urinary Bladder," 74.

He sent the stomach . . . "Arbuckle Held Without Bail as Murderer," *Chicago Tribune*, September 12, 1921.

caused by "some external force" . . . "Testify to Bruises on Virginia Rappe."

7. Rise: 1913–14

"But let's be practical . . ." Mack Sennett with Cameron Shipp, *King of Comedy* (Garden City, NY: Doubleday, 1954), 26.

"The round, fat girls . . ." Ibid., 28–29.

"He was my day school . . ." Ibid., 51.

Baumann and Kessel supplied $2,500 . . . Doings at Los Angeles, *Motion Picture World*, September 14, 1912.

"Overnight our place . . ." Sennett, *King of Comedy*, 88.

Keystone's dubious press releases . . . "Chaos at Keystone," *Motion Picture World*, November 30, 1912; Doings at Los Angeles, *Motion Picture World*, October 26, 1912; ibid., September 7, 1912; ibid., July 26, 1913.

one true eccentric . . . Adela Rogers St. Johns, *Love, Laughter and Tears: My Hollywood Story* (Garden City, NY: Doubleday, 1978), 30.

"a university of nonsense . . ." Sennett, *King of Comedy*, 140.

"Woman is rarely ridiculed . . ." "It Is to Laugh," *Moving Picture World*, December 21, 1912. 1166.

the readers of Photoplay would vote her . . . "Victory on the Last Lap," *Photoplay*, June 1914.

a notice in August 1914 . . . *Motion Picture News*, August 15, 1914.

"Big Otto" . . . Minta Durfee, interview by Don Schneider, July 21, 1974, excerpted at Mabel Normand Home Page, www.mn-hp.com/minta1.html.

"All my mechanical knowledge . . ." Roscoe Arbuckle, interview by Ray Frohman, *Los Angeles Herald*, October 28, 1919.

an upbringing worthy of the adjective "Dickensian" . . . Details of the early life of Charlie Chaplin and the lives of his parents via Stephen Weissman, *Chaplin: A Life* (New York: Arcade, 2008), 9–97.

named something like "Chapman" . . . Sennett, *King of Comedy*, 151.

"I was not terribly enthusiastic . . ." Charlie Chaplin, *My Autobiography* (New York: Simon & Schuster, 1964), 138.

"I'm too shy, and I feel uncomfortable . . ." Minta Durfee, interview by Walter Wagner, July 4, 1973, in *You Must Remember This* (New York: Putnam, 1975), 33.

The Essanay Film Manufacturing Company was a minor studio . . . Ted Okuda and David Maska, *Charlie Chaplin at Keystone and Essanay: Dawn of the Tramp* (Lincoln, NE: iUniverse, 2005), 108.

"Mr. Sennett asked Roscoe . . ." Durfee, interview by Schneider.

"But outside of falling . . ." "Nobody Loves a Fat Man?," *Movie Pictorial*, June 13, 1914, 20.

their pit bull, Luke . . . Raymond Lee, *Not So Dumb: The Life and Times of the Animal Actors* (South Brunswick, NJ: Barnes, 1970), 52–54.

His love of cars bound him . . . William F. Nolan, *Barney Oldfield: The Life and Times of America's Legendary Speed King* (New York: Putnam, 1961), 115–16.

"Mabel and I were engaged . . ." Sennett, *King of Comedy*, 103.

"So one Sunday morning . . ." Durfee, interview by Schneider.

"If either of us . . ." Minta Durfee, "The True Story About My Husband," *Movie Weekly*, December 24, 1921.

8. The Next Weekend

The giant DETAIN ARBUCKLE banner . . . Evening News quotes, Blake's affidavit, and Arbuckle's statement via "Detain Arbuckle," *Evening News* (San Jose), September 10, 1921.

the Daily News had over a hundred thousand readers . . . John D. Stevens, *Sensationalism and the New York Press* (New York: Columbia University Press, 1991), 125.

To meet the growing demand . . . Michael Simon Bessie, *Jazz Journalism: The Story of the Tabloid Newspapers* (New York: Dutton, 1938), 99.

"In making 'arrests,' the reporters . . ." A. J. Liebling, "The Case of the Scattered Dutchman," *New Yorker*, September 24, 1955.

"Hollywood dope ring" . . . Los Angeles Record, September 16, 1921, quoted in Rob Leicester Wagner, *Red Ink, White Lies: The Rise and Fall of Los Angeles Newspapers 1920–1962* (Upland, CA: Dragonflyer Press, 2000), 30.

"After Miss Rappe . . ." "Mystery Death Takes Actress," *Los Angeles Times*, September 10, 1921.

"This is assuming serious proportions" . . . Leo Friedman, closing statement of third Arbuckle trial, in *Classics of the Bar: Stories of the World's Great Legal Trials and a Compilation of Forensic Masterpieces*, vol. 8, ed. Alvin V. Sellers (Washington, DC: Washington Law Book, 1942), 124.

"there were no closed or locked doors" . . . "Girl Dead After Wild Party in Hotel," *San Francisco Chronicle*, September 10, 1921.

"His face was grave . . ." "Lauds Character of Miss Rappe," *Evening Public Ledger* (Philadelphia, PA), September 13, 1921.

"We all thought it was very unfortunate . . ." "More Guests of Arbuckle Will Testify," *Oakland Tribune*, September 25, 1921.

"ill feelings" toward him . . . "Detain Arbuckle."

"For God's sake . . ." Viola Dana, interview in "Single Beds and Double Standards," episode 3 of *Hollywood*, BBC documentary miniseries, 1980.

"She had a few drinks . . ." "Fatty Arbuckle to Be Arrested in Girl's Death," *Palm Beach Post*, September 11, 1921.

"I am coming here . . ." "'Fatty' Arbuckle in Wild Dash to Explain Death of Movie Girl," *Sunday Morning Star*, September 11, 1921.

"They're saying some rotten things . . ." "'Fatty Arbuckle Charged with Actress' Murder," *Oakland Tribune*, September 11, 1921.

"I don't know why . . ." Ibid.

Arbuckle released a statement . . . "Roscoe Arbuckle Faces an Inquiry on Woman's Death," *New York Times*, September 11, 1921.

"Roscoe Arbuckle will not even admit . . ." "Arbuckle Being Held in a Six-Foot Cell," *Salt Lake Tribune*, September 12, 1921.

"Not on an occasion of this sort" . . . "Arbuckle Shows Signs of Worry," *Spokesman-Review* (Spokane, WA), September 12, 1921.

His weight was 266 pounds . . . "Arbuckle Dragged Rappe Girl to Room, Woman Testifies," *New York Times*, September 13, 1921.

"This woman without a doubt . . ." "Arbuckle Is Jailed on Murder Charge in Woman's Death," *New York Times*, September 12, 1921.

It was six by six . . . "Formal Murder Charge Is Filed Against Film Comedian," *Berkeley Daily Gazette*, September 12, 1921.

"Are you going to give me a partner in here?" . . . "Arbuckle Held Without Bail as Murderer," *Chicago Tribune*, September 12, 1921.

"The shame of it all" . . . "Clean-Up of Film Industry Needed, Say Clergymen," *Oakland Tribune*, September 12, 1921.

The first cancellation . . . "Arbuckle Silent When Questioned by Police," *Oakland Tribune*, September 11, 1921.

"There's nothing like that . . ." "Not Like Fatty, Says Charlie," *Milwaukee Journal*, September 12, 1921.

"I'm through with booze . . ." "Arbuckle Being Held in a Six-Foot Cell."

"He's a regular guy" . . . Ibid.

Semnacher said he found them . . . "Movie Society in Los Angeles Split by Arbuckle Case," *Pittsburgh Press*, September 12, 1921.

Rappe's outer garments . . . "Arbuckle Is Jailed on Murder Charge in Woman's Death."

"It's too lonesome alone" . . . "Formal Murder Charge Is Filed Against Film Comedian."

"I've heard often of . . ." "Falstaff of Movies Engages Big Array of Legal Talent," *Pittsburgh Press*, September 12, 1921.

9. Muddle: 1915–16

Frequently banned and legally challenged . . . Edward de Grazia and Roger K. Newman, *Banned Films: Movies, Censors and the First Amendment* (New York: R.R. Bowker, 1982), 5–6.

unprecedented box office gross . . . $18 million figure via Russell Merritt, "Dixon, Griffith, and the Southern Legend," *Cinema Journal* 12, no. 1 (Autumn 1972), 27; $60 million figure via Richard Schickel, *D. W. Griffith: An American Life* (New York: Simon & Schuster, 1984), 281.

At its peak in 1920, colorization . . . Richard Koszarski, *An Evening's Entertainment: The Age of the Silent Feature Picture, 1915–1928* (Berkeley: University of California Press, 1990), 127.

thirteen additional magazines . . . Steven Lomazow, "Movie Magazine Bibliography," *Magazine History: A Collector's Blog*, November 2, 2008, http://magazinehistory.blogspot.com/2008/11/movie-magazine-bibliography.html.

An article in the August 1915 edition . . . "Heavyweight Athletics," *Photoplay*, August 1915, 35–38.

sat in the St. Francis lobby for an interview . . . Kitty Kelly, "Keystone Stars Chat with Kitty," Flickerings from Film Land, *Chicago Tribune*, April 9, 1915.

Roscoe bought me a Rolls Royce . . . Minta Durfee, interview by Walter Wagner, July 4, 1973, in *You Must Remember This* (New York: Putnam, 1975), 35.

Valentine's Day ball . . . "Photoplayer's [*sic*] Club Ball," *Motography*, March 6, 1915, 350.

"We were both busy . . ." Minta Durfee, "The True Story About My Husband," *Movie Weekly*, December 24, 1921.

"He wasn't a man who could say . . ." Durfee, interview by Wagner, 42–43.

"While medical science waged . . ." "Mabel Normand Fighting Death," *Los Angeles Herald*, September 20, 1915.

they finally, but privately, became engaged . . . Mack Sennett with Cameron Shipp, *King of Comedy* (Garden City, NY: Doubleday, 1954), 191.

According to Minta Durfee's account . . . Minta Durfee, interview by Stuart Oderman, July 1969, in *Roscoe "Fatty" Arbuckle: A Biography of the Silent Film Comedian, 1887–1933* (Jefferson, NC: McFarland, 1994), 75.

"It was learned yesterday . . ." Santa Monica Outlook, September 21, 1915.

killed a rattlesnake, stopped a studio burglar . . . Keystone Studio News, *Photoplayers' Weekly*, July 29, 1915, 12.

a five-mile ocean swim race . . . Variety, September 10, 1915.

fended off an octopus . . . "Octopus Seizes Mabel Normand," *Photoplayers' Weekly*, September 4, 1915, 12.

"Roscoe sat on my head . . ." Randolph Bartlett, "Why Aren't We Killed?," *Photoplay*, April 1916, 83.

Hartman subsequently directed . . . "Spotlight Dims on Oakland Idol of Comedy," *Oakland Tribune*, August 23, 1931.

they attended the Broadway musical . . . "Fatty and Mabel's New Year," *Moving Picture World*, January 18, 1916, 251.

"Then I'll find a hotel . . ." Minta Durfee, interview by Stuart Oderman, July 1969, in *Roscoe "Fatty" Arbuckle: A Biography*, 81.

"Roscoe knew he was good for publicity . . ." Ibid.

"The studio was bristling with activity . . ." Wil Rex, "Behind the Scenes with Fatty and Mabel," *Picture-Play*, April 1916, 46–53.

a "burial party" aboard her yacht . . . Motion Picture Magazine, October 1916.

"What's the worst thing . . ." "Fatty Off Guard," *Film Fun*, March 1916, 15.

"The world has Chaplinitis . . ." "Chaplinitis," *Motion Picture Magazine*, July 1915, 121.

they wouldn't take hold in the film industry . . . Tom Kemper, *Hidden Talent: The Emergence of Hollywood Agents* (Berkeley: University of California Press, 2010), 5.

the leading vaudeville talent rep . . . "Max Hart, 76, Dies," *New York Times*, May 24, 1950.

a contract with Metro Pictures . . . An unpublished 1958–59 manuscript by Minta Durfee, cited in Robert Young Jr., *Roscoe "Fatty" Arbuckle: A Bio-Bibliography* (Westport, CT: Greenwood, 1994), 52.

As late as February 1916 . . . "The First Night Calendar," *New York Times*, February 20, 1916.

Born in Russia in 1878 . . . Joseph Schenck bio via Alan Hynd, "The Rise and Fall of Joseph Schenck," pts. 1–3, *Liberty*, June 28, 1941, July 5, 1941, and July 12, 1941.

the "notorious" Arbuckle's arrival . . . Sennett, *King of Comedy*, 195.

"It is hard to believe . . ." Ibid., 215.

"To this day, I guess . . ." Roscoe Arbuckle, interview by Ray Frohman, *Los Angeles Herald*, October 28, 1919.

Schenck paid Hart . . . "Arbuckle's Film Value," *Oakland Tribune*, April 2, 1922.

"I was greatly upset . . ." Durfee, interview by Oderman, July 1969, in *Roscoe "Fatty" Arbuckle: A Biography*, 90.

News of Arbuckle's leaving . . . "Roscoe Arbuckle to Quit Keystone," *Chicago Tribune*, September 27, 1916.

the name of his production company . . . "Arbuckle to Leave Keystone," *Motography*, October 7, 1916, 832.

Arbuckle pronounced it "Cumeeky" . . . Rudi Blesh, *Keaton* (New York: MacMillan, 1966), 87.

Arbuckle's "moving picture concern" . . . "May Build Movie Comedy Concern," *Los Angeles Times*, December 13, 1916.

a skin infection near Arbuckle's left knee . . . Minta Durfee, unpublished manuscript, 103, Minta Durfee Arbuckle Collection, Margaret Herrick Library, Academy of Motion Pictures Arts and Sciences, Beverly Hills, CA.

The intern injected Arbuckle with morphine . . . Ibid.

"*In the last decades of the nineteenth century . . .*" Details of morphine's history and effects via David T. Courtwright, *Dark Paradise: A History of Opiate Addiction in America* (Cambridge, MA: Harvard University Press, 2001); C. B. Pearson, M.D, "What Should Be the Attitude of the Medical Profession and of Society Towards the Morphine Addict?," *Medical Review of Reviews*, July 1918, 406–13.

one in every four hundred Americans . . . "Uncle Sam Is the Worst Drug Fiend in the World," *New York Times Magazine*, March 12, 1911.

When the intern determined that amputation . . . Durfee, unpublished manuscript, 104.

If he was to kick his jones for opiates . . . Ibid., unnumbered; details of the effects of morphine addiction treatment via William L. White, *Slaying the Dragon:*

The History of Addiction Treatment and Recovery in America (Bloomington, IL: Chestnut Health Systems, 1998).

Fatty lost over eighty pounds . . . Durfee, unpublished manuscript, unnumbered.

10. Indictment

"rough clothes . . ." "Formal Murder Charge Is Filed Against Film Comedian," *Berkeley Daily Gazette*, September 12, 1921.

"Nothing I could say now . . ." "Sensations Develop in Comedian's Case," *Evening News* (San Jose), September 12, 1921.

"Roscoe Arbuckle, murder" . . . Ibid.

Delmont alleged that Arbuckle had lured . . . "Says 'Fatty' Used Stardom as Lure," *Evening Public Ledger* (Philadelphia, PA), September 14, 1921.

her less incendiary affidavit . . . "'Fatty's' Fatal Folly," *NZ Truth* (New Zealand), October 22, 1921.

"Oh, please don't make me . . ." "Arbuckle Dragged Rappe Girl to Room, Woman Testifies," *New York Times*, September 13, 1921.

hands clasped, face twitching . . . "Formal Murder Charge Is Filed Against Film Comedian."

"I desire to state . . ." "Throng Crowds Court to Hear Prisoner Plead," *San Francisco Call and Post*, September 12, 1921.

"From information I received . . ." "Miss Rappe's Fiancé Threatens Vengeance," *New York Times*, September 13, 1921.

"I know of no legal method . . ." "700 New York Theaters Bar Arbuckle Films," *New York Tribune*, September 14, 1921.

a demand grew for films . . . "Films Featuring Miss Rappe Shown," *Los Angeles Times*, September 14, 1921.

"We want the full facts . . ." "Court Holds Arbuckle as Girl's Slayer," *New York Tribune*, September 13, 1921.

Rumwell claimed he called the coroner's office . . . "Arbuckle Dragged Rappe Girl to Room, Woman Testifies."

"an almost unnoticed figure . . ." "Jury Adjourns Without Indicting Film Comedian," *Los Angeles Times*, September 13, 1921.

Those at Paramount said nothing . . . "Employers Silent on Death Case," *Los Angeles Times*, September 13, 1921.

Alice Lake emphasized . . . "Film People Tell Views," *Los Angeles Times*, September 13, 1921.

Buster Keaton was unequivocal . . . Ibid.

"Arbuckle is a great big, good-natured, lovable sort of chap . . ." "Officials Seeking Notoriety Try to Hang Arbuckle, Says Schenck" *Los Angeles Times*, September 12, 1921.

"I have little to say . . ." "Athletic Club Ousts Arbuckle," *Los Angeles Times*, September 13, 1921.

"due to the shock . . ." "Five Witnesses Heard," *Quebec Telegraph*, September 13, 1921.

"He looked nervous . . ." "Famous Comedian Silent on Wild Party and Violent Death of Virginia Rappe," *Pittsburgh Press*, September 13, 1921.

"My attorneys have advised me . . ." Ibid.
"District Attorney Brady more time . . ." "Five Witnesses Heard."
"We have sent Miss Zey Prevon . . ." "Witnesses Are Disappearing in Arbuckle Case, Charge," *Pittsburgh Press*, September 13, 1921.
Arbuckle's housekeeper . . . "'Just a Big Boy,' Housekeeper Says," *Oakland Tribune*, September 13, 1921.
the inmate in the cell next to his . . . "Arbuckle Will Lose Neighbor in Jail," *Los Angeles Times*, September 13, 1921.
Another headline stated . . . "Grave of Arbuckle's Mother Is Neglected," *Los Angeles Times*, September 13, 1921.
Arbuckle's sister Nora . . . "Sister Talks for Arbuckle," *Miami News*, September 13, 1921.
his brother Harry's "no comment" . . . "Brother Is Neutral," *Los Angeles Times*, September 14, 1921.
"Fatty Arbuckle has one sincere mourner . . ." "Bulldog Mourns for Arbuckle," *Los Angeles Times*, September 14, 1921.
A headline promised . . . "Other Illegal Acts Charged to Film Star," *San Francisco Chronicle*, September 13, 1921.
Another header asserted . . . "Second Girl Escapes Fate of Miss Rappe," *Los Angeles Examiner*, September 13, 1921.
An article in a Flagstaff newspaper . . . "Fatty Arbuckle Treats Wife Rough in Arizona," *Coconino Sun*, September 16, 1921.
first appeared in bold print . . . "Dying Girl Laid Blame on Comedian," *Los Angeles Examiner*, September 11, 1921.
A headline in Tuesday's Baltimore Sun . . . "Arbuckle Affair No Surprise After Orgies of Film Colony," *Baltimore Sun*, September 13, 1921.
Tales of his sickening orgies . . . "Old Rules for Girls Supplanted by New Now," *San Francisco Examiner*, September 14, 1921.
Positioned on the page . . . "Hollywood Orgies Exposed by Police," *Evening Public Ledger* (Philadelphia, PA), September 16, 1921.
in the Denver Post that Thursday . . . "Narcotics Needles Turned Tame Party at Hollywood into Astounding Success," *Denver Post* September 15, 1921.
A short United Press story . . . "Miss Rappe's Death Brings Movie World Scandals to Climax," *Pittsburgh Press*, September 12, 1921.
"For three or four years . . ." "The Arbuckle Incident," *Los Angeles Times*, September 13, 1921.
The next day, the same paper . . . "Arbuckle's Fat Is to Blame for His Trouble, Declares Famous Psycho-analyst," *Denver Post*, September 14, 1921.
"Arbuckle is a gross, common, bestial, drunken individual . . ." Editorial, *Dayton Daily News*, reprinted in *Herald of Gospel Liberty*, October 6, 1921.
An editorial in the Atlanta Constitution . . . "Ruined by Wealth," *Atlanta Constitution*, September 13, 1921.
Photo montages . . . "Once in Happy Repose," *New York American*, September 15, 1921; "Beautiful, Laughing Virginia Rappe in Film Scenes," *Chicago Herald and Examiner*, September 13, 1921.
This striking image . . . "They Walked into His Parlor," *San Francisco Examiner*, September 15, 1921.

Open up the New York American . . . "Hope for Fame Lured Actress to Her Death," *New York American*, September 14, 1921.

"But in his innermost soul . . ." "Yesterday's Jester a Fallen Idol; Phantom Bacchus Leaves His Halo; Apathy Settles on Actor's Face," *San Francisco Examiner*, September 14, 1921.

"Roscoe Arbuckle is just a great big . . ." "Wife to Help Arbuckle," *New York Times*, September 13, 1921.

"I am going to him . . ." "Arbuckle Innocent, Declares His Wife," *New York Times*, September 14, 1921.

the coroner's inquest . . . Details of the September 13 coroner's inquest via "Fatty Arbuckle Indicted," *Chicago Tribune*, September 14, 1921; "Arbuckle Is Indicted for Girl's Death," *New York Tribune*, September 13, 1921; "Arbuckle Indicted for Manslaughter in Actress Death," *New York Times*, September 14, 1921; "Grand Jury Called, Refuses to Indict Arbuckle on Charge," *Eugene Register-Guard*, September 13, 1921.

"beauty specialist" . . . "'Avenger' Denied Cash for Bills, Swings on Man," *Oakland Tribune*, September 14, 1921.

reporters captured the confrontation . . . Ibid.

Semnacher claimed . . . "Denies Woman 'Smashed' Him," *Los Angeles Times*, September 15, 1921.

Henry Lehrman wired Delmont . . . "Lehrman Sends $150 to Help Mrs. Delmont," *New York Times*, September 15, 1921.

"Never had any" . . . "Arbuckle Denies Having Liquor," *Sacramento Bee*, September 14, 1921.

claimed she had gone into hiding . . . "Manslaughter Indictment Placed Against Arbuckle," *Evening Public Ledger* (Philadelphia, PA), September 14, 1921.

Prevost's new recollection . . . "Show Girl Tells Intimate Details of Arbuckle Party," *Bakersfield Californian*, September 16, 1921.

The chorus girls backed up . . . "Proceedings of the Day," *Los Angeles Times*, September 14, 1921.

He made no remark . . . "Fate Sealed by Dress She Made," *Los Angeles Times*, September 15, 1921.

"I protest in the name . . ." "Clash Marks Inquest on Girl's Death," *Oakland Tribune*, September 14, 1921.

Arbuckle tried to light a cigarette . . . "Arbuckle Spirit Shows Sign of Slump," *Oakland Tribune*, September 15, 1921.

"Said rupture was caused . . ." "Arbuckle Accused of Manslaughter by Coroner's Jury," *New York Times*, September 15, 1921.

a gang of at least eight young men . . . "All Assailants of Girls Known, Police Declare," *Oakland Tribune*, November 27, 1920.

"I, the undersigned juror . . ." "One Juror Files Dissenting Verdict," *Oakland Tribune*, September 15, 1921.

Understandably, headlines like . . . "Girl, 20, Sobs Recital of Attack by 19," *San Francisco Examiner*, December 11, 1920.

more than seventy-five San Francisco women's clubs . . . Louis S. Lyons and Josephine Wilson, eds., *Who's Who Among the Women of California* (San Francisco: Security, 1922), 197.

"no better than the Howard Street gangsters . . ." "'Like Howard Street Gang Case,' Says Leader," *San Francisco Examiner*, September 14, 1921.
Another WVC member said . . . "Vigilant Women Condemn Wild Orgy of Arbuckle," *San Francisco Examiner*, September 15, 1921.
"Women After Arbuckle" . . . "Star to Be Vigorously Prosecuted," *Los Angeles Times*, September 16, 1921.
Pierce-Arrow was parked . . . "Probers Identify Men Who Carried Arbuckle's Booze," *Oakland Tribune*, September 17, 1921.
Arbuckle's net worth . . . "$5000 per Week Is Arbuckle's Salary; Is Great 'Spender,'" *Evening News* (San Jose), September 12, 1921.
a furniture company had filed a lien . . . "Arbuckle Property Attached," *Schenectady Gazette*, September 15, 1921.
an interior decorator filed an attachment . . . Ibid.
"For the sake of God and justice to men . . ." "Bail To-day for Arbuckle Is Forecast," *New York Tribune*, September 16, 1921.
"army of special police" . . . "Arbuckle to Go on Trial for Murder," *New York Tribune*, September 17, 1921.
Joyce "Dollie" Clark . . . "Arbuckle Guest Put on Probation," *Los Angeles Times*, September 17, 1921.
"The next case is number five . . ." "Arbuckle Will Be Tried for Murder," *San Francisco Examiner*, September 17, 1921.
"The people are ready to proceed . . ." Ibid.
"We want to be courteous . . ." Ibid.
"The District Attorney's office . . ." "Arbuckle to Be Tried on Murder Charge," *Los Angeles Times*, September 17, 1921.
"On the beautiful face . . ." "Golden Gate City Showers Virginia Rappe with Flowers," *Detroit Free Press*, September 16, 1921.
Per Lehrman's wired instructions . . . "Body to Be Shipped To-day," *New York Tribune*, September 16, 1921.

11. Glory: 1917–18

he loped about with a cane . . . Minta Durfee, unpublished manuscript, 102, Minta Durfee Arbuckle Collection, Margaret Herrick Library, Academy of Motion Pictures Arts and Sciences, Beverly Hills, CA.
The sendoff party . . . "Banquet for Arbuckle," *Los Angeles Times*, February 11, 1917.
An ad in a Salt Lake City newspaper . . . Scrapbook pages, undated, Minta Durfee Arbuckle Collection.
"At night, there was always a banquet . . ." Minta Durfee, interview by Stuart Oderman, July 1969, in *Roscoe "Fatty" Arbuckle: A Biography of the Silent Film Comedian, 1887–1933* (Jefferson, NC: McFarland, 1994), 102.
Arbuckle told an incredulous Chicago reporter . . . "Minus Pies and Torn Pants," *Chicago Tribune*, February 28, 1917.
"Arbuckle had a carbuncle . . ." "Elgin Car Carries Fatty Arbuckle When He Visits Chicago," *Deseret Evening News* (Salt Lake City, UT), March 10, 1917.

he placed a wreath on the Liberty Bell . . . "City Opens Its Arms for 'Fatty' Arbuckle," *Evening Public Ledger* (Philadelphia, PA), March 3, 1917.
dinner was served at . . . "Fatty Arbuckle Greeted," *Boston Globe*, March 7, 1917.
What Fatty ate . . . "City Opens Its Arms for 'Fatty' Arbuckle."
She recounted one rampage . . . Tape-recorded 1958–59 memoirs of Minta Durfee, cited in Robert Young Jr., *Roscoe "Fatty" Arbuckle: A Bio-Bibliography* (Westport, CT: Greenwood, 1994), 55.
"Well, if he can be stubborn . . ." Minta Durfee, "The True Story About My Husband," *Movie Weekly*, December 24, 1921.
paid her $500 weekly . . . "Wife of Film Star who Starts Across Country to Aid Him," *Bakersfield Californian*, September 14, 1921.
A cyclone blew away the town . . . Buster Keaton with Charles Samuels, *My Wonderful World of Slapstick* (Garden City, NY: Doubleday, 1960), 20.
"a pretty strenuous day" . . . Keaton, *My Wonderful World of Slapstick*, 21.
given to him by Harry Houdini . . . Buster Keaton, interview by Herbert Feinstein, October 6, 1960, in *Buster Keaton: Interviews*, ed. Kevin W. Sweeney (Jackson, MS: University Press of Mississippi, 2007), 128.
the original version of the story . . . Marion Meade, *Buster Keaton: Cut to the Chase* (New York: HarperCollins, 1995), 18.
"The tiny comedian is perfectly at ease . . ." Theater review, *New York Clipper*, July 20, 1901.
On October 4, 1909, an ad . . . Advertisement, *Variety*, October 4, 1909.
He signed with Max Hart . . . Meade, *Buster Keaton*, 57.
he ran into Lou Anger . . . Ibid., 60.
watching Tillie's Punctured Romance . . . "Anything Can Happen—and Usually Did," *Image*, December 1974, 24.
"Between one thing and another" . . . Keaton, *My Wonderful World of Slapstick*, 92–93.
"Roscoe—none of us who knew him . . ." Ibid., 93.
"You're late" . . . Rudi Blesh, *Keaton* (New York: MacMillan, 1966), 89.
his "gross contour" and "supremely terrible face" . . . "Fatty Sheds Tear over Shakespeare," *Los Angeles Times*, August 31, 1919.
Keaton claimed he had never . . . Keaton, *My Wonderful World of Slapstick*, 94.
Reisenweber's . . . "J. Reisenweber Dies of Stroke," *Standard Union*, August 10, 1931; William Grimes, *Appetite City: A Culinary History of New York* (New York: North Point, 2009), 179.
the Motion Picture Charity Ball . . . "Big Film Ball," *Motography*, May 5, 1917, 936.
opening night of a minor league baseball game . . . "Portland Club to Whoop Things Up," *Day* (New London, CT), May 9, 1917.
"in doubt as to his practical usefulness . . ." "No Slackers with 'Fatty' Arbuckle," *Delmarva Star* (Wilmington, DE), July 1, 1917.
he and Keaton registered for the draft . . . Roscoe C. Arbuckle, World War I registration card, FHL roll number 1530898, draft board 17; Joseph F. Keaton, World War I registration card, FHL roll number 1766041, draft board 116; both at National Archives and Records Administration, Washington, DC.

Arbuckle sold his Rolls-Royce . . . "Fatty's Profit," *Variety*, August 31, 1917.
"Roscoe was a poor boy . . ." Minta Durfee, interview by Walter Wagner, July 4, 1973, in *You Must Remember This* (New York: Putnam, 1975), 35.
"Roscoe loves company" . . . Louella Parsons, In and Out of Focus, *New York Morning Telegraph*, March 3, 1919.
"He likes nothing better . . ." Durfee, "The True Story About My Husband."
"There's nothing in the world . . ." "'Fatty' Arbuckle off the Screen," *Literary Digest*, July 14, 1917, 41.
the average annual household income . . . Michael L. Dolfman and Denis M. McSweeney, *100 Years of U.S. Consumer Spending: Date for the Nation, New York City, and Boston*, US Bureau of Labor Statistics Report 991, 9.
"Mr. Arbuckle has probably the most complete . . ." New York Sun, July 29, 1917.
Improvisation . . . "'Fatty' Arbuckle off the Screen," 41.
Acting . . . "The Solemn Mr. Arbuckle," *New York Tribune*, May 6, 1917.
Production . . . "'Fatty' Arbuckle off the Screen," 42.
Editing . . . Ibid.
Comedy . . . First two paragraphs in "The Solemn Mr. Arbuckle"; third paragraph in "'Fatty' Arbuckle off the Screen," 42.
Balboa Studio . . . History via Jean-Jacques Jura and Rodney Norman Barden II, *Balboa Films: A History and Filmography of the Silent Film Studio* (Jefferson, NC: McFarland, 1999).
an exact reproduction . . . "Visiting Roscoe Arbuckle in Village of Jazzville," *Los Angeles Times*, November 25, 1917.
A typical Tuesday night . . . Louella Parsons, In and Out of Focus, *New York Morning Telegraph*, March 3, 1919; "Tea Parties at Vernon," *Los Angeles Times*, September 21, 1919.
"Some men might resent . . ." Parsons, In and Out of Focus, March 3, 1919.
"It borders over much . . ." Review of *Good Night Nurse*, *Motion Picture Magazine*, August 1918.
"The longer I worked with Roscoe . . ." Keaton, *My Wonderful World of Slapstick*, 95.
gratis vaudeville shows . . . The Vaudeville Show, *Los Angeles Times*, December 23, 1917.
Arbuckle was one of five . . . "Kings of Movies Raise $787,000 for Loan Bonds," *New York Tribune*, April 18, 1918.
Long Beach war bond parade . . . "Arbuckle Falls into Liberty Parade," *Los Angeles Times*, May 5, 1918.
"to gather in smokes for the boys . . ." "Fatty Receives Poem from 'Over There,'" *Bridgeport Telegram*, June 22, 1918.
article that focused on the latter practice . . . "Patriotic Arbuckle," *Los Angeles Times*, December 2, 1917.
Comique threw him a farewell dinner . . . New York Telegraph, August 11, 1918.
Keaton was visited by Natalie Talmadge . . . Keaton, *My Wonderful World of Slapstick*, 98–99.
He was transferred to a town near Bourdeaux . . . Meade, *Buster Keaton*, 81.
"Roscoe Arbuckle shares comedy honors . . ." "An Analytical Review of the Year's Acting," *Photoplay*, November 1918, 106.

Arbuckle spent two weeks . . . Shadow on the Screen, *New York Tribune*, December 29, 1918.
the Arbuckle/Lake relationship . . . Viola Dana, interview by Stuart Oderman, July 1974, in *Roscoe "Fatty" Arbuckle: A Biography*, 131.
"The people adored 'Fatty' . . ." "An Analytical Review," 106.

12. Preliminaries

An angry mob of 150 . . . "Wyoming Mob Shoots Up Fatty," *Wyoming State Tribune*, September 17, 1921.
"Will do best I can" . . . William Randolph Hearst, telegram to Adolph Zukor, September 22, 1921, Adolph Zukor Collection, Margaret Herrick Library, Academy of Motion Pictures Arts and Sciences, Beverly Hills, CA.
He was visited by his brothers . . . "Brothers Visit Arbuckle," *Los Angeles Times*, September 19, 1921.
"Some of the mail . . ." Minta Durfee, interview by Walter Wagner, July 4, 1973, in *You Must Remember This* (New York: Putnam, 1975), 40.
"to get the lay of the land" . . . "State Re-enacts Fatal Party in Arbuckle Suite," *New York Tribune*, September 19, 1921.
a sermon delivered that same Sunday . . . "Fatty Stands Before Nation with Leering Grin While His Hands Drip Blood—Straton," *Denver Post*, September 19, 1921.
"He has assaulted public decency . . ." "Pastors Show Peril of Arbuckle Party," *Los Angeles Examiner*, September 19, 1921.
"I feel sorry for 'Fatty' Arbuckle . . ." "Billy Sunday Lays Blame on Actress, Thinks Charge Against 'Fatty' Unfounded," *Detroit Free Press*, September 19, 1921.
Virginia Rappe appeared angelic . . . Visitation details via "Thousands See Body of Dead Girl," *Los Angeles Times*, September 19, 1921; "8000 See Rappe Girl's Body," *New York Times*, September 19, 1921.
On Monday morning . . . Details of Rappe's burial via "Virginia Rappe in Final Rest," *Los Angeles Times*, September 20, 1921.
The count varies . . . "Thousands See Body of Dead Girl"; "8000 See Rappe Girl's Body."
"I'm ready for the defense . . ." "Wife Pleads for Arbuckle," *Reading Eagle*, September 19, 1921.
she had admitted her testimony at the coroner's inquest . . . *Los Angeles Evening Herald*, September 16, 1921, quoted in Rob Leicester Wagner, *Red Ink, White Lies: The Rise and Fall of Los Angeles Newspapers 1920–1962* (Upland, CA: Dragonflyer Press, 2000), 38.
Arbuckle embraced his wife . . . "'Hello Roscoe, Honey Dear!': Wife's Greeting, Strong Mutual Respect Revealed at Reunion," *San Francisco Examiner*, September 20, 1921.
"Ada Gillifillian . . ." "Cash Plot Charge in Arbuckle Case," *Evening Public Ledger* (Philadelphia, PA), September 20, 1921.
"There is money in this Arbuckle case . . ." "Police Here Asked to Watch Witness in Arbuckle Case," *New York Tribune*, September 21, 1921.

"Tell the truth" . . . Ibid.

"forcibly applied a piece of ice . . ." "'Confession' in Arbuckle Death Case Questioned," *Los Angeles Times*, September 22, 1921.

On the hysterical end . . . "Declares Arbuckle Told of Using Foreign Substance in Attack on Miss Rappe," *Lewistown Daily*, September 22, 1921.

in an automobile driven by a red-headed woman . . . "Sleuths Waiting for Sherman Get Only Merry Laugh," *New York Tribune*, September 22, 1921.

a deposition swearing that Arbuckle was never alone . . . "Sherman Aids Arbuckle," *New York Times*, November 2, 1921.

Universal became the first studio to institute a morality clause . . . "Morality Clause for Films," *New York Times*, September 22, 1921.

"The drunken orgy at the St. Francis . . ." "Crime That of a Fiend," *Ellensburg Daily Record*, September 22, 1921.

"Women began showing up at the Hall of Justice . . ." "Women Throng First Hearing of Arbuckle Case," *New York Tribune*, September 23, 1921.

"Men are being excluded everywhere . . ." "Arbuckle Hit Hard," *Los Angeles Times*, September 23, 1921.

"some force from outside" . . . "With Puzzled Air, Arbuckle Hears Evidence," *San Francisco Chronicle*, September 23, 1921.

Al Semnacher was the only witness . . . Semnacher's testimony via People v. Arbuckle, Superior Court of California, County of San Francisco, preliminary hearing transcript, 165–68.

Red-faced Arbuckle . . . "Testimony Is Vulgar," *Los Angeles Times*, September 25, 1921.

fussing with a long stream . . . Ibid.

The United Press correspondent described . . . "Witness Testifies Arbuckle Confessed He Tortured Actress," *Sunday Morning Star*, September 25, 1921.

Dominguez got Semnacher to admit . . . "Testimony Is Vulgar."

"under the influence of alcohol or morphine" . . . "Blackmail Charged," *Los Angeles Times*, September 27, 1921.

Semnacher was not Rappe's manager . . . Ibid.

"on" Rappe's "snatch" . . . People v. Arbuckle, preliminary hearing transcript, 264.

Dominguez explained the relevance . . . "'Blackmail' to Be Arbuckle's Defense Plea," *New York Tribune*, September 27, 1921.

Judge Lazarus declared . . . "Blackmail Charged."

his original intent was "joshing" Rappe . . . People v. Arbuckle, preliminary hearing transcript, 128.

by the time of the 1910 census . . . US Census Bureau, *Thirteenth Census of the United States, 1910*, population of New York City, NY, sup. dist. 1, enum. dist. 1301, April 27, 1910 (Washington, DC: Government Printing Office, 1912–14).

The groom was John C. Hopper . . . "Mrs. Bambina Delmont Former Wife of Canadian Farmer and Ex-Soldier," *Oakland Tribune*, September 14, 1921.

she lived for a time in Wichita, Kansas . . . "Mrs. Delmont Known in Kansas," *Los Angeles Times*, September 18, 1921.

authorities asked her to leave Catalina . . . "Begin Inquiry Here on Life of Mrs. Delmont," *Los Angeles Times*, September 18, 1921.

The 1920 census had found her . . . US Census Bureau, *Fourteenth Census of the United States, 1920,* population of Los Angeles, CA, precinct 40, sup. dist. 8, enum. dist. 262, January 3, 1920 (Washington, DC: Government Printing Office, 1921).

wedding Cassius Clay Woods . . . "New Arbuckle Charge Looms," *Los Angeles Times,* October 1, 1921.

both recalling, with minor variations . . . "Use of Ice Mentioned," *New York Tribune,* September 28, 1921.

"That'll bring you to" . . . People v. Arbuckle, preliminary hearing transcript, 336.

"No, no, oh my God!" . . . Ibid., 341–42.

"Do you mean to say . . ." Ibid., 346–48.

"You are traveling very close . . ." Ibid., 350.

the judge was ready to deliver his decision . . . "Arbuckle Out on Bail; Held for Manslaughter," *Los Angeles Times,* September 29, 1921.

The courtroom of mostly female observers . . . Courtroom reaction via "Arbuckle Out on Bail; Held for Manslaughter"; "Arbuckle Freed on Bail; Murder Charge Dropped," *New York Tribune,* September 29, 1921.

"Roll a cigarette . . ." "Arbuckle Freed on Bail; Murder Charge Dropped."

if Arbuckle "were unknown . . ." "Brady Attacks Decision," *New York Times,* September 29, 1921.

he was stopped by women well-wishers . . . "Arbuckle Due in City Today," *Los Angeles Times,* September 30, 1921.

the conductor, porters, and many passengers . . . Ibid.

a large crowd of friends and curious spectators . . . "1500 at Train Station as Comedian Arrives; Kissed by Women," *Los Angeles Herald,* September 30, 1921.

an editorial questioning it . . . "Some Problems for the Psychologists," *New York Times,* October 1, 1921.

"I've only seen him . . ." "Blackmail Plot Against Arbuckle Charged at Trial," *Atlanta Constitution,* September 27, 1921.

her "tense trip to Los Angeles . . ." Minta Durfee, unpublished manuscript, 52, Minta Durfee Arbuckle Collection, Margaret Herrick Library, Academy of Motion Pictures Arts and Sciences, Beverly Hills, CA.

There was a mild backlash . . . "Feasting and Vigilance," *Los Angeles Times,* September 27, 1921.

the guest of honor at a homecoming party . . . "Arbuckle Celebrates in Los Angeles Home," *New York Times,* October 1, 1921.

"He has seen fair-weather friends . . ." Minta Durfee, "The True Story About My Husband," *Movie Weekly,* December 24, 1921.

"Half the people there . . ." Rudi Blesh, *Keaton* (New York: MacMillan, 1966), 80.

13. Bliss: 1919–20

"Dear Mr. Arbuckle . . ." "Roscoe Arbuckle Visits Prison Birds," *Detroit Free Press,* June 15, 1919.

"a certain little girl . . ." Louella Parsons, In and Out of Focus, *New York Morning Telegraph,* March 3, 1919.

"Anyhow, you can see . . ." "Fatty Arbuckle to Get Three Million," *Los Angeles Times*, February 23, 1919.

screamed one front page . . . "$1,000,000 a Year for Movie 'Fatty,'" *Washington Times*, February 23, 1919.

"I have watched Doc . . ." Parsons, In and Out of Focus, March 3, 1919.

"[A fat man] is regarded . . ." "On the Advantages of Embonpoint," *Photo-Play Journal*, February 1919, 52.

A tongue-in-cheek article in the Los Angeles Times . . . "Is Fate Stacking Up the Refinement on 'Fatty'?," *Los Angeles Times*, June 16, 1919.

the PCL's Vernon Tigers . . . Team history via Dennis Purdy, *Kiss 'Em Goodbye: An ESPN Treasury of Failed, Forgotten, and Departed Teams* (New York: ESPN, 2010), 338–39; "Roscoe 'Fatty' Arbuckle's Vernon Tigers," Sports Hollywood, www.sportshollywood.com/vernontigers.html.

"the longest bar in the world" . . . Kiss 'Em Goodbye, 336.

"I'm just going into it for the sport . . ." "Arbuckle Is Now Magnate," *Los Angeles Times*, May 6, 1919.

"just bought them to please Anger" . . . Roscoe Arbuckle, interview by Ray Frohman, *Los Angeles Herald*, October 28, 1919.

"San Francisco won a ball game . . ." "Pitchers Are Very Scarce," *Los Angeles Times*, May 16, 1919.

The actors performed baseball sketches . . . "Fatty Makes 'Em Like Defeat," *Los Angeles Times*, August 11, 1919.

He estimated ahead of time . . . "Arbuckle Party Off for North," *Los Angeles Times*, August 8, 1919.

Arbuckle and Keaton reveled in practical jokes . . . Buster Keaton with Charles Samuels, *My Wonderful World of Slapstick* (Garden City, NY: Doubleday, 1960), 113–22.

"Few of us in that whole Hollywood gang . . ." Ibid., 155–56.

Arbuckle interacted with Virginia Rappe . . . "Film Actor on Stand," *Los Angeles Times*, November 29, 1921.

"I mean to have some real drama . . ." "The Sad Tale of Arbuckle," *Los Angeles Times*, November 16, 1919.

the Directors Ball . . . West Coast News, *New York Telegraph*, December 7, 1919.

performing on a New York stage . . . Theater and Arts, *New York Times*, December 21, 1919.

"Instead of passing from us . . ." "John Barleycorn Died Peacefully at the Toll of 12," *New York Times*, January 17, 1920.

"The reign of tears is over . . ." Daniel Okrent, *Last Call: The Rise and Fall of Prohibition* (New York: Scribner, 2011), 2.

"Had to do it to save my cellar!" . . . "Buys Home to Save Cellar," *Los Angeles Times*, January 12, 1920.

According to the census . . . US Census Bureau, *Fourteenth Census of the United States, 1920*, population of Los Angeles, CA, precinct 188, sup. dist. 8, enum. dist. 443, January 2, 1920 (Washington, DC: Government Printing Office, 1921).

"He and the big St. Bernard . . ." Minta Durfee, "The True Story About My Husband," *Movie Weekly*, December 24, 1921.

He continued decorating the house . . . West Adams house details via Minta Durfee, unpublished manuscript, 53, Minta Durfee Arbuckle Collection, Margaret Herrick Library, Academy of Motion Pictures Arts and Sciences, Beverly Hills, CA.

the mammoth skeleton and innards of a Pierce-Arrow . . . "Conspicuous Consumption: Fatty Arbuckle's Fabulous Pierce-Arrow," *Special Interest Auto*, February 1990, 44–46.

"a special squad of police" . . . "Arbuckle's Car Is a Genuine Knockout," *Los Angeles Times*, May 2, 1920.

a dog wedding . . . "Arbuckle Held Without Bail as Murderer," *Chicago Tribune*, September 12, 1921.

"a 'spirited' program . . ." "Mexican Halloween," *Los Angeles Times*, October 30, 1920.

"It is evident that Fatty Arbuckle . . ." Review of *The Round Up*, *Variety*, October 10, 1920.

Passport application of Roscoe Arbuckle . . . Via National Archives and Records Administration, Washington, DC.

His bitter stepmother claimed . . . "Film Comedian Forgets His Two Blind Sisters," *Oakland Tribune*, September 12, 1921.

marrying a former Ziegfeld Follies showgirl . . . "Arbuckle Marrying?," *Variety*, November 19, 1920.

he literally missed the boat . . . *Variety*, November 26, 1920.

Arbuckle joked that he might . . . Ibid.

"Paris went wild . . ." Plays and Players, *Photoplay*, March 1921, 89.

Four thousand Parisians crowded . . . "Arbuckle Besieged," *New York Times*, December 1, 1920.

he laid a bouquet on the spot . . . "French Receive 'Fatty' Warmly," *New York Herald*, Paris ed., December 1, 1920.

a dinner attended by 150 British notables . . . *New York Herald*, Paris ed., December 6, 1920.

14. First Trial

"Now that the wave of insanity . . ." "Plot Is Thinning," *Los Angeles Times*, October 3, 1921.

"Enclosed in the following space . . ." "The Arbuckle Case," *Moving Picture World*, October 1, 1921, 513.

a screening in Sing Sing prison . . . "Sing Sing Bars Arbuckle Film," *New York Tribune*, October 7, 1921.

"I want you to have explicit faith . . ." Roscoe Arbuckle, letter to Joseph Schenck, October 1, 1921, Adolph Zukor Collection, Margaret Herrick Library, Academy of Motion Pictures Arts and Sciences, Beverly Hills, CA.

San Francisco detectives tailed Arbuckle . . . "Brady Sleuths Dog Arbuckle," *Los Angeles Times*, November 10, 1921.

"A palatial residence was to be our home . . ." Minta Durfee, unpublished manuscript, 52, Minta Durfee Arbuckle Collection, Margaret Herrick Library, Academy of Motion Pictures Arts and Sciences, Beverly Hills, CA.

"We slept in separate bedrooms . . ." Minta Durfee, interview by Stuart Oderman, September 1969, in *Roscoe "Fatty" Arbuckle: A Biography of the Silent Film Comedian, 1887–1933* (Jefferson, NC: McFarland, 1994), 174.

the official story was that he had quit . . . "Chief Counsel Quits Case and Lauds Arbuckle," *San Francisco Chronicle*, October 6, 1921.

"a million-dollar array of counsel" . . . "No Verdict Returned," *Los Angeles Times*, December 3, 1921.

Rappe had left a daughter . . . "Daughter Is Left by Virginia Rappe," *Los Angeles Times*, October 16, 1921.

"If [Rappe's] estate is of any value . . ." "Virginia Rappe Had a Daughter," *Spokesman-Review* (Spokane, WA), October 23, 1921.

others in Chicago had more sensational tales . . . "'Fatty' to Get Depositions of 3 Chicago Witnesses," *Chicago Tribune*, October 27, 1921.

lambasted the San Francisco prosecutor . . . "Ho, Hum, 'Wild Parties' Tame," *Los Angeles Times*, October 21, 1921.

Al Stein, an assistant director to Fred Fishback . . . "Dead Movie Man in Arbuckle Case," *Evening Public Ledger* (Philadelphia, PA), October 11, 1921.

Her estate consisted of . . . "Virginia Rappe Had a Daughter."

Gobey's Grill . . . "Case Up Today," *Los Angeles Times*, October 5, 1921.

Jack Lawrence, the deliveryman . . . "Man Under Arrest Admits Vending Arbuckle Liquor," *Chicago Tribune*, October 18, 1921.

What the microscope reveals . . . "Microscope's Evidence May Determine Arbuckle's Fate," *Evening Independent* (Massillon, OH), October 31, 1921.

"a drugstore is a veritable laboratory . . ." Eugene B. Block, *The Wizard of Berkeley* (New York: Coward-McCann, 1958), 32.

After obtaining a chemistry degree . . . Heinrich background and details of kidnapping case via Katherine Ramsland, "He Made Mute Evidence Speak: Edward O. Heinrich," *Forensic Examiner*, fall 2007, 62–64.

Visiting the room on three occasions . . . "Microscope's Evidence."

"I'm certainly glad my trial . . ." "Arbuckle Ready for Trial," *New York Times*, November 13, 1921.

headlines appeared such as . . . "Women May Try Arbuckle," *Toledo News-Bee*, November 16, 1921.

"When the jury finally is completed . . ." "Brady Bans Matron from Actor's Panel," *San Francisco Examiner*, November 17, 1921.

While the male occupations varied . . . "11 Jurors to Try 'Fatty' Passed by Attorneys," *Chicago Tribune*, November 16, 1921.

McNab asked Dr. Arthur Beardslee . . . "Arbuckle's Aim Short," *Los Angeles Times*, November 20, 1921.

"I do not know what she was doing . . ." People v. Arbuckle, Superior Court of California, County of San Francisco, first trial transcript, 962.

Prevost recounted how . . . Ibid., 882–84.

"a big roll of money . . ." "Zey Prevost, Alice Blake in Witness Chair," *San Francisco Examiner*, November 22, 1921.

When Blake returned to the stand . . . Ibid.

Al Semnacher told of seeing Rappe . . . People v. Arbuckle, first trial transcript, 1043–45.

"No, no, oh my God!" . . . "Arbuckle's Side Opens," *Los Angeles Times*, November 23, 1921.

Edward O. Heinrich's presentation . . . People v. Arbuckle, first trial transcript, 1106–23.

a front-page headline would scream . . . "'Avenger' May Testify Against Arbuckle," *Pittsburgh Post-Gazette*, November 30, 1921.

Delmont would be arrested . . . "Mrs. Delmont Held in Bigamy Charge," *Pittsburgh Press*, December 3, 1921.

the defendant's nervous tics . . . "Film Actor Is Nervous," *Los Angeles Times*, November 19, 1921.

purposefully distracting himself . . . "Girls Help Arbuckle," *Los Angeles Times*, November 22, 1921.

"There was but one feature . . ." "Name of Mrs. Delmont Out of Star's Case," *San Francisco Examiner*, November 20, 1921.

"Society women continue to make up . . ." "Arbuckle Likely to Go on Stand in Own Defense," *Atlanta Constitution*, November 25, 1921.

an article sympathetic to Arbuckle . . . Anthony Slide, *Inside the Hollywood Fan Magazine: A History of Star Makers, Fabricators, and Gossip Mongers* (Jackson, MS: University Press of Mississippi, 2010), 157.

Screenland asked on its cover . . . "Is Virginia Rappe Still Alive?," *Screenland*, December 1921, 20–21.

"The state has miserably failed . . ." "Arbuckle's Side Opens."

Is it not an insult . . . "Arbuckle's Battle On," *Los Angeles Times*, December 2, 1921.

Arbuckle offered "girlie" . . . People v. Arbuckle, first trial transcript, 1163.

was said to appear "thoughtful" . . . "Arbuckle, with Jury, Visits Scene of Orgy," *New York Tribune*, November 24, 1921.

feasted on turkey stuffed with oysters . . . "Arbuckle Last Witness," *Los Angeles Times*, November 25, 1921.

in the cold rain to a restaurant . . . "Film Folk Summoned," *Los Angeles Times*, November 28, 1921.

Rumwell had been arrested . . . "Physician Is Held in Arbuckle Case," *Los Angeles Times*, November 2, 1921.

In the latter group were . . . "Angelenos on Stand," *Los Angeles Times*, November 26, 1921.

referring to himself as "Sherlock Holmes" . . . "Film Actor to Testify," *Los Angeles Times*, November 27, 1921.

The defense had one final witness . . . Arbuckle testimony and courtroom behavior via People v. Arbuckle, first trial transcript, 1659–89; "Film Actor on Stand," *Los Angeles Times*, November 29, 1921; "Big Crowd Storms Hall of Justice to Hear Arbuckle," *San Francisco Chronicle*, November 29, 1921; "Arbuckle on Stand, Denies Harming Rappe Girl, Says He Aided Her," *San Francisco Chronicle*, November 29, 1921.

the deposition of Dr. Maurice Rosenberg . . . "Film Actor on Stand."

the state began calling rebuttal witnesses . . . "Witness Is Arrested," *Los Angeles Times,* November 30, 1921.
The final witnesses in the trial . . . "Jurors Get Case Soon," *Los Angeles Times,* December 1, 1921.
the one centered on Irene Morgan . . . "Arbuckle's Battle On"; "Nurse, Witness for Arbuckle, Found Poisoned," *New York Tribune,* December 2, 1921.
the state's closing argument . . . People v. Arbuckle, first trial transcript, 2127–80; "Arbuckle's Battle On."
"She alternated their journeys . . ." "Arbuckle's Battle On."
McNab began the defense's closing . . . People v. Arbuckle, first trial transcript, 2188–268; "No Verdict Returned."
It returned to the state . . . People v. Arbuckle, first trial transcript, 2271–93.
"It is considered a forgone conclusion . . ." "Death Threat Made Against Big Comedian," *Warsaw Daily Times,* December 2, 1921.
headlines like the San Francisco Examiner's . . . "Woman Votes Actor Guilty Says Report," *San Francisco Examiner,* December 3, 1921.
saw Arbuckle joking with reporters . . . "Arbuckle's Jury Hung," *Los Angeles Times,* December 4, 1921.
Arbuckle played hide-and-seek . . . "Jury Fails to Agree," *Los Angeles Times,* December 5, 1921.
"We had some wild times . . ." "Jury 10 to 2 for Acquittal of Movie Star," *San Francisco Chronicle,* December 5, 1921.
"We felt the case . . ." Ibid.
"The ten members of the jury . . ." "Foreman of Jury Makes Statement," *San Francisco Examiner,* December 4, 1921.
It was reported that he voted . . . "Woman Juror Balks Verdict for Arbuckle," *New York Tribune,* December 5, 1921.
"It was the matter of fingerprints . . ." "Mrs. Hubbard Declares She Did Her Duty," *San Francisco Chronicle,* December 5, 1921.
"The jury was subjected . . ." "Anent Mixed Juries," *San Francisco Chronicle,* December 7, 1921.
"It is a fair presumption . . ." "Possibly Old Fashioned But—," *Chicago Tribune,* December 5, 1921.
"Regardless of the guilt or innocence . . ." "Juror Praised, Arbuckle Scored by Vigilants," *San Francisco Call and Post,* December 7, 1921.
"I just want to congratulate . . ." "Woman Juror Balks Verdict."
"The poor boy" . . . Ibid.
"While this is not a legal acquittal . . ." "Arbuckle Says Juror's Stand Real Acquittal," *San Francisco Chronicle,* December 5, 1921.

15. Overture: 1921

Eight hundred fifty-four feature films . . . "The Dream Merchants: 1920–1928," episode 3 of *Moguls and Movie Stars: A History of Hollywood,* TCM documentary miniseries, November 15, 2010.
nearly 40 percent of Americans . . . Ibid.
"Last March I traveled on the same train . . ." O. O. McIntyre, New York Day by Day, *Pittsburgh Press,* September 28, 1921.

"Under the prismatic spell . . ." O. O. McIntyre, New York Day by Day, *Reading Eagle*, March 2, 1934.

"While most of us are struggling . . ." Notice for *Brewster's Millions*, *Logansport Pharos-Tribune*, May 28, 1921.

"For His Uncle Samuel . . ." Advertisement for *The Dollar-A-Year-Man*, *Milwaukee Sentinel*, April 24, 1921.

"Did you ever hear of slapstick drama?. . ." Review of *The Traveling Salesman*, The Shadow Stage, *Photoplay*, July 1921, 68.

"I can't sleep nights . . ." Delight Evans, West Is East, *Photoplay*, June 1920, 44.

"It would be hard to imagine . . ." Jesse L. Lasky with Don Weldon, *I Blow My Own Horn* (Garden City, NY Doubleday, 1957), 153.

Arbuckle's recurrent speeding stops . . . "Fatty's History Is Spectacular," *Los Angeles Examiner*, September 11, 1921.

On April 15 Daniels arrived . . . "Out of the Past: Film Star Nabbed in Orange County," *Orange Coast Magazine*, April 1985, 170–71; "Jail Term for Bebe Daniels," *Los Angeles Times*, March 29, 1921; "Bebe Daniels Has Busy Day," *Los Angeles Times*, April 18, 1921.

Arbuckle appeared in the movie-themed comic . . . Strips reprinted in *Fatty Arbuckle and His Funny Friends* (Fantagraphics Books, December 2004).

a now-famous Ralph Barton caricature . . . "When the Five O'Clock Whistle Blows in Hollywood," *Vanity Fair*, September, 1921, 50.

"Since he had made his fortune" . . . "'Fatty' Arbuckle Good to Family, Says Sister," *New York Tribune*, September 14, 1921.

"I know of many cases . . ." Minta Durfee, "The True Story About My Husband," *Movie Weekly*, December 24, 1921.

"Roscoe Arbuckle helped lead . . ." Plays and Players, *Photoplay*, May 1921, 80.

"Roscoe Arbuckle—not being much of a horseman . . ." Plays and Players, *Photoplay*, October 1921, 112.

"road-" standing in for "whore-" . . . "'Fatty' Not at Party in Roadhouse," *Los Angeles Times*, July 13, 1921.

Mishawum Manor "chicken and champagne orgy" . . . Details of the event via "Tufts Gives Facts of Movie Dinner," *New York Times*, July 28, 1921.

"The orgy was described as . . ." "Can't Find Providence Man Whose Name Was Used to Obtain Big Hush Money in the Tufts Scandal," *Providence News*, July 12, 1921.

Kingston was tried and convicted . . . "Attorney General v. Tufts," *Northeastern Reporter* 132 (August 30–December 27, 1921): 331–34.

Paramount hush money . . . "Coakley Tells How He Spent Movie Men's $100,000 Hush Fund," *Evening Tribune* (Providence, RI), July 14, 1921.

Coakley admitted . . . Ibid.

removed Tufts from office . . . "Supreme Court Removes Tufts," *Boston Globe*, October 2, 1921.

frequently described as a party in his honor . . . "District Attorney Pelletier and Three Boston Lawyers Are Before Court on Charges," *Providence News*, September 30, 1921.

"Though the first reel was a riot . . ." "'Fatty' Arbuckle $50 Out After Having Real Fight," *Baltimore Sun*, July 21, 1921.

a very different version of the Congress Hotel story . . . "Fatty's History Is Spectacular."
"the row [Arbuckle] had . . ." Louella Parsons, In and Out of Focus, *New York Morning Telegraph*, August 7, 1921.
"This is an actual photograph . . ." Advertisement for Omar cigarettes, *Milwaukee Sentinel*, August 3, 1921.
premiere of The Three Musketeers . . . "3 Musketeers Showing," *Los Angeles Express*, September 1, 1921.
announced the local premiere of another film . . . "Gasoline Gus Arbuckle Show at Grauman's," *Los Angeles Times*, September 4, 1921.

16. Second Trial

"This case has put . . ." "Arbuckle Home; Hits at Brady," *Los Angeles Times*, December 7, 1921.
brooch and a $1,000 jeweled purse . . . "Fatty Arbuckle in Court Again," *Norwalk Hour*, January 11, 1922.
"My wife has proven . . ." "Arbuckle Broke, Plans to Return to the Movies Feb. 1," *Evening Independent* (Massillon, OH), January 6, 1922.
the first trial cost . . . Ibid.
For its last two issues . . . Minta Durfee, "The True Story About My Husband," *Movie Weekly*, December 24, 1921; Roscoe Arbuckle, "Roscoe Arbuckle Tells His Own Story," *Movie Weekly*, December 31, 1921.
speaking with reporters in a corridor . . . "Arbuckle Fears to Lose Public Liking," *Evening News* (San Jose), January 17, 1922.
"It was the day before . . ." Dashiell Hammett, "Seven Pages," 1926 manuscript, Harry Ransom Center, University of Texas at Austin.
"The whole thing . . ." Ibid.
Voir dire proved more difficult . . . "Woman, 11 Men in New Rappe Trial," *San Francisco Examiner*, January 12, 1922.
The very definition of a reluctant witness . . . Blake testimony via "Miss Rappe's Friend Is a Poor Witness," *San Francisco Chronicle*, January 19, 1922.
A photo of her appeared . . . "Her Memory Gone," photo, *Providence News*, January 26, 1922.
On cross-examination, McNab focused . . . "Attorneys for Film Star Confuse State's Witnesses," *Pittsburgh Press*, January 19, 1922.
Prevost was even less of an asset . . . Prevost testimony via "Arbuckle Girl 'Hostile Witness,'" *San Francisco Call and Post*, January 19, 1922.
"The case against Roscoe . . ." "Arbuckle Witness Fails Prosecutor," *New York Times*, January 20, 1922.
Rumors that Brady would drop the case . . . "Lack of Memory Is Owned by Witness," *Evening Herald*, January 20, 1922.
"The Roscoe Arbuckle manslaughter trial . . ." "Second Arbuckle Show Falls Flat; Not So with Actor," *Milwaukee Journal*, January 22, 1922.
When Heinrich returned . . . "Identifies Fingerprints as Made by Arbuckle and Girl," *Bakersfield Californian*, January 23, 1922.

Warden Woolard, the Los Angeles Times reporter . . . "New Arbuckle Testimony," *Los Angeles Times*, January 24, 1922.
the defense brought forth two experts . . . "Finger Prints Were 'Faked' Says Expert," *San Francisco Examiner*, January 26, 1922.
she grew embroiled in a new legal subplot . . . "Refuses to Bar Story of Woman," *Bakersfield Californian*, January 26, 1922.
New witnesses spoke of Rappe's . . . "Arbuckle Case Defense May Close Today," *San Francisco Chronicle*, January 27, 1922.
"That Roscoe (Fatty) Arbuckle will be acquitted . . ." "Arbuckle's Acquittal Is Freely Predicted," *Pittsburgh Press*, January 27, 1922.
"excellence of health" . . . "Rappe Girl's Health Stirs Controversy," *San Francisco Examiner*, January 29, 1922.
a large story appeared . . . "Nero's Orgies Rivaled on Coast Folk," *Border Cities Star* (Windsor, Ontario), January 28, 1922.
U'Ren began the state's closing argument . . . "Arbuckle Case to Jury Late Today," *Bakersfield Californian*, February 1, 1922.
"Whatever you do is all right" . . . "Jury Quits for Night, 11 to 1 for Arbuckle," *Chicago Tribune*, February 2, 1922.
"If the court please . . ." Ibid.
"This is the end . . ." Ibid.
William Desmond Taylor lay on his back . . . Body discovery and aftermath via Ed. C. King, "I Know Who Killed Desmond Taylor," *True Detective Mysteries*, October and November 1930; Rick Geary, *Famous Players: The Mysterious Death of William Desmond Taylor* (New York: ComicsLit, 2009).
"nervous breakdown" . . . "Mabel Normand Better," *Variety*, November 11, 1920.
running the banner headline . . . "Women Feature Film Murder," *San Francisco Chronicle*, February 3, 1922; "Arbuckle Jury Still Out, 10 for Aquittal," *San Francisco Chronicle*, February 3, 1922.
"Taylor was the best fellow . . ." "Taylor Best Man on Lot, Says Arbuckle," *San Francisco Bulletin*, February 2, 1922.
a statement attributed to Arbuckle . . . "Fatty Philosophizes on Taylor Case," *Los Angeles Record*, February 15, 1922.
In its front-page story . . . "Arbuckle Abandons Hope," *Los Angeles Times*, February 3, 1922.
Deliberation was cut short . . . "Arbuckle Jury Still Debates," *St. Petersburg Times*, February 3, 1922.
engaged to marry a vaudeville actor . . . "Arbuckle Witness Will Wed Thespian," *Telegraph-Herald* (Dubuque, IA), February 3, 1922.
A buzz of shocked mutterings . . . "Comedian Will Be Tried Again, Brady Asserts," *San Francisco Chronicle*, February 4, 1922.
"The jurors believed that the defense's failure . . ." "Arbuckle's Story Not Believed: Jurors Tell Why They Decided," *San Francisco Examiner*, February 4, 1922.
"The defense presented a very weak case . . ." Ibid.
"From the reading of Arbuckle's testimony . . ." Ibid.
some creative accounting . . . "Comedian Will Be Tried Again."
"Had the majority of the jury . . ." Ibid.

"In this life you've got to take a punch . . ." "Will Retry Arbuckle," *Los Angeles Times*, February 4, 1922.

17. Third Trial

a deposition from a "surprise witness" . . . "Arbuckle to Los Angeles," *Aurora Daily Star*, February 8, 1922.

"A young woman thought by police . . ." "Waited for Zeh Prevost," *New York Times*, February 14, 1922.

after the questioning of fifty-one citizens . . . "12 in Jury Box for Retrial of Arbuckle," *San Francisco Examiner*, March 16, 1922.

juror Edward Brown . . . "Juror Sworn to Try Fatty Under Fire," *San Francisco Examiner*, March 21, 1922.

they delved into the health . . . Nat Schmulowitz, closing statement of third Arbuckle trial, in *Classics of the Bar: Stories of the World's Great Legal Trials and a Compilation of Forensic Masterpieces*, vol. 8, ed. Alvin V. Sellers (Washington, DC: Washington Law Book, 1942), 56–58.

Blake couldn't recall seeing . . . "Breaks Down on Stand," *Los Angeles Times*, March 23, 1922.

Her telegram to Brady . . . San Francisco court records, People v. Arbuckle, quoted in Eric Dean Budnick, "Directed Verdict: The Roscoe 'Fatty' Arbuckle Trial Discourse" (PhD dissertation, Harvard University, 2000), 58.

Arbuckle hung his head . . . "Miss Rappe's Death Fills Trial Record," *San Francisco Examiner*, March 23, 1922.

"I don't think I'll answer . . ." "Actor's Trial Continues," *Los Angeles Times*, March 25, 1922.

"I don't see why . . ." "Arbuckle Broke Now, He Declares," *Boston Daily Globe*, March 26, 1922.

applying the word "shyster" . . . "Arbuckle Judge Roused," *Los Angeles Times*, March 27, 1922.

Brady had a surprise final witness . . . Breig's testimony via "Surprise Witness Heard," *Los Angeles Times*, March 28, 1922.

It came to thirty-four dollars . . . Leo Friedman, closing statement of third Arbuckle trial, in *Classics of the Bar*, 119.

"trying to blacken . . ." "Declares Past of Arbuckle Demands Probe," *Vancouver Sun*, March 27, 1922.

Chicago nurse Virginia Warren . . . "Past of Rappe Girl Bared by Chicago Nurse," *San Francisco Chronicle*, March 31, 1922.

"I first saw Virginia Rappe . . ." "Arbuckle Defense Built in Chicago," *Milwaukee Sentinel*, November 1, 1921.

Friedman treated her very name . . . Friedman, closing statement, 131.

"according to her own testimony . . ." Ibid., 109–10, 131.

he could speak to Norgaard's morals . . . "Fresh Problem in Fatty Case," *Los Angeles Times*, March 31, 1922.

a woman named Helen Whitehurst testified . . . "Virginia Rappe Tore Clothing Say Witnesses," *San Francisco Chronicle*, April 1, 1922.

Fred Fishback could no longer recall . . . "Fishbach [*sic*] Loses Memory on Stand," *Telegraph-Herald* (Dubuque, IA), April 2, 1922.
described as "less enthusiastic" . . . "Arbuckle Takes Stand," *Los Angeles Times*, April 6, 1922.
Arbuckle retold the tale . . . Ibid; "Arbuckle on Stand, Fights Wordy Battle," *San Francisco Chronicle*, April 6, 1922.
In its rebuttal, the state . . . "Deny Miss Rappe Ill," *Los Angeles Times*, April 8, 1922.
In surrebuttal, the defense . . . "Fatty's Case Near End," *Los Angeles Times*, April 11, 1922.
"And that night Belshazzar . . ." Milton U'Ren, closing statement of third Arbuckle trial, in *Classics of the Bar*, 13–33.
First, Nat Schmulowitz reiterated . . . Nat Schmulowitz, closing statement of third Arbuckle trial, in *Classics of the Bar*, 33–62.
the emotional speech . . . Gavin McNab, closing statement of third Arbuckle trial, in *Classics of the Bar*, 62–98.
Countering for the state. . . Leo Friedman, closing statement of third Arbuckle trial, in *Classics of the Bar*, 98–135.
The third jury left the courtroom . . . Details of Arbuckle's acquittal via "Jury Sets Film Artist Free in 2 1/2 Minutes," *San Francisco Chronicle*, April 13, 1922.
"Acquittal is not enough for Roscoe Arbuckle . . ." "Jurors Write Exoneration," *San Francisco Examiner*, April 13, 1922.
"I am an American citizen . . ." "Jury Sets Film Artist Free."
"This is the most solemn moment . . ." Ibid.
"I am going to take a good rest . . ." "Remaining Arbuckle Charge Dismissed as Star Acquitted of Manslaughter by Jurors," *Bakersfield Californian*, April 13, 1922.
"Our contract with Arbuckle . . ." "To Release Fatty Film," *Los Angeles Times*, April 13, 1922.
He pleaded guilty . . . "Drops Second Charge Against Arbuckle," *New York Times*, April 13, 1922.
It was reported that his defense . . . "Arbuckle Expense Costly," *New York Times*, April 15, 1922.
"I do not wish to capitalize . . ." Ibid.
effectively banned from American theaters . . . "Ban Put on Arbuckle," *Los Angeles Times*, April 19, 1922.

18. Hays

there have been movie censors . . . Information on local and state censorship boards via Lee Grieveson, *Policing Cinema: Movies and Censorship in Early-Twentieth-Century America* (Berkeley: University of California Press, 2004), 23.
National Board of Censorship of Motion Pictures . . . Edward de Grazia and Roger K. Newman, *Banned Films: Movies, Censors and the First Amendment* (New York: R.R. Bowker, 1982), 10–11.
issued a unanimous decision . . . Mutual Film Corporation v. Industrial Commission of Ohio, 236 US 230 (February 23, 1915).

filmmaker Robert Goldstein . . . "The Unluckiest Man in Movie History," *Slate*, June 13, 2000, www.slate.com/articles/news_and_politics/chatterbox/2000/06/the_unluckiest_man_in_movie_history.html.

an example of how draconian . . . "Humanizing the Movies," *New York Times*, January 18, 1922.

National Association of the Motion Picture Industry . . . De Grazia and Newman, *Banned Films*, 21–23.

"it was the only way to remedy . . ." "Movie Censor Law Signed by Miller," *New York Times*, May 15, 1921.

"I have listened with amazement . . ." "'Fatty' Made Issue in Censorship Row," *Los Angeles Examiner*, September 15, 1921.

"Censorship of motion pictures is a menace . . ." William Taylor, "The Nonsense of Censorship," September 14, 1921, reprinted in *Taylorology* 88 (April 2000): www.public.asu.edu/~bruce/Taylor88.txt.

William Harrison Hays was born . . . Details of Hays's early life via Thomas J. Wolfe, ed., *A History of Sullivan County, Indiana* (New York: Lewis, 1909), 1–3.

reportedly too frail . . . "Will Hays: The Moses Who Hopes to Lead the G.O.P. Out of the Woods," *Current Opinion*, September 1919, 156–57.

who suffered from "lifelong frailty" . . . Will Hays Jr., *Come Home with Me Now: The Untold Story of Movie Czar Will Hays by His Son* (Indianapolis: Guild Press of Indiana, 1993), 3.

First, it is no part of the primary business . . . "Executive Changes Outlined by Hays," *New York Times*, April 29, 1921.

second-class mail status to a socialist magazine . . . "Hays Removes Ban on the Liberator," *New York Times*, May 26, 1921.

"the Judge Landis of movies" . . . "Will Hays to Quit Cabinet for Films; Harding Consents," *New York Times*, January 15, 1922.

"As to censorship . . ." "No Politics," *American Cinematographer*, April 1, 1922, 14.

"The public is tired of seeing . . ." "Pungent Hint from Experience," *Continent*, March 30, 1922, 382.

"use your authority to intervene . . ." "Alliance Asks Hays to Stop Arbuckle Films," *Milwaukee Sentinel*, April 16, 1922.

"With hundreds of thousands . . ." Will H. Hays, *The Memoirs of Will H. Hays* (Garden City, NY: Doubleday, 1955), 360–61.

"No, Will, let the Association . . ." Ibid., 361.

"Even that early in the game . . ." Ibid.

against a Massachusetts referendum . . . Gregory D. Black, *Hollywood Censored: Morality Codes, Catholics, and the Movies* (New York: Cambridge University Press, 1996) 32–33.

claimed to reject 125 proposed movies . . . Ibid., 33.

until divorcing his wife in 1929 . . . "Movie Czar Granted Divorce," *Chicago Tribune*, June 22, 1929.

the Motion Picture Production Code . . . Information on the formation of the Code and its principles via de Grazia and Newman, *Banned Films*, 32–34.

19. Exile: 1922–25

"Suddenly we all realized . . ." Minta Durfee, unpublished manuscript, 81, Minta Durfee Arbuckle Collection, Margaret Herrick Library, Academy of Motion Pictures Arts and Sciences, Beverly Hills, CA.

He was deeply in debt . . . Inside Stuff on Pictures, *Variety*, May 28, 1922.

he owed his trial attorneys . . . "Fatty Arbuckle Broke, Is Report," *Star Journal* (Sandusky, OH), June 12, 1922.

"The question of the release . . ." "Arbuckle Bows to Ruling of Film Dictator," *Los Angeles Times*, April 23, 1922.

California Congress of Women and Parents . . . "Mother Clubs After Fight Vote Down Films," *San Francisco Call and Post*, April 26, 1922.

San Francisco Federation of Women's Clubs . . . "Arbuckle Film Condemned as Women End Meet," *San Francisco Call and Post*, April 29, 1922.

Doris Deane, a minor actress . . . Picture Personalities, *Oakland Tribune*, March 5, 1922.

Ed Roberts, a former editor . . . Introduction, *Taylorology* 30 (June 1995): www.public.asu.edu/~ialong/Taylor30.txt.

ruled "too scurrilous" . . . "Bars 'Sins of Hollywood,'" *New York Times*, May 24, 1922.

"To the boys and girls . . ." Ed Roberts ("A Hollywood Newspaper Man"), *The Sins of Hollywood: An Expose of Movie Vice* (Los Angeles: Hollywood Publishing, 1922), reprinted in *Taylorology* 30 (June 1995): www.public.asu.edu/~ialong/Taylor30.txt.

"Rostrand, a famous comedian . . ." Ibid.

"Fatty Arbuckle says he is broke . . ." Editorial, *Chehalis Bee-Nugget*, June 23, 1922.

He wrote a short comedy script . . . "Arbuckle Writes Comedy for Buster," *Los Angeles Times*, May 19, 1922.

Arbuckle was also set to direct . . . "Fatty Arbuckle Becomes Motion Picture Director," *Wichita Daily Times*, June 3, 1922.

"You can be of real service . . ." "The Six 'Fatty' Arbuckle Vitaphones," *Griffithiana: Journal of Film History*, October 1993, 55.

Senator Henry Lee Myers . . . *Congressional Record* 62, pt. 9 (June 14–29, 1922): 9657.

Minta Durfee left that colony . . . "Mrs. Arbuckle Leaves Again," *Los Angeles Times*, July 1, 1922.

Al St. John later remembered . . . "Another Big 'Speak' Opens," *Youngstown Vindicator*, December 15, 1932.

known as "Arbuckle parties" . . . Jefferson Williamson, *The American Hotel: An Anecdotal History* (New York: Knopf, 1930), 143.

"Once when we were both . . ." Screen Life in Hollywood, *Sandusky Register*, July 2, 1933.

"I need a rest . . ." "Arbuckle Sets Sail From S.F. on World Tour," *Oakland Tribune*, August 16, 1922.

after slipping down steps and cutting . . . "'Fatty' Arbuckle Has Infected Finger," *Oakland Tribune*, September 2, 1922.

He said his time in the Orient . . . "'Fatty' Back from Trip to Orient," *Oakland Tribune*, September 27, 1922.
"'Fatty' Arbuckle was a movie 'goat' . . ." Editorial, *Stevens Point Daily Journal*, November 22, 1922.
reported that his index and middle fingers . . . "'Fatty Loses Use of Finger After Injuries," *Oakland Tribune*, October 31, 1922.
"handsome Walter" . . . Roberts, *The Sins of Hollywood*.
Hollywood's worst-kept secret broke . . . "Wallace Reid Critically Ill, 'Dope' Blamed," *Chicago Tribune*, December 16, 1922.
Will Hays visited Reid . . . "Hays Visits Sick Actor," *Los Angeles Times*, December 20, 1922.
"Every man in the right way . . ." "Storm Breaks on Arbuckle," *Los Angeles Times*, December 21, 1922.
"It was not my wish . . ." Will H. Hays, *The Memoirs of Will H. Hays* (Garden City, NY: Doubleday, 1955), 360–61.
"cancelled all showings . . ." "Ban Put on Arbuckle," *Los Angeles Times*, April 19, 1922.
Hays later professed . . . Hays, *Memoirs*, 361.
"stammering so badly . . ." "Storm Breaks on Arbuckle."
"Mr. Hays has made his decision . . ." Ibid.
"I cannot say . . ." Ibid.
Around the time Schenck said that . . . Initial reactions to Arbuckle's reinstatement via ibid; "Storm of Protest at Hays Restoring Arbuckle to Films," *New York Times*, December 22, 1922.
Illinois theater owners reversed it . . . "Arbuckle Will Get His Chance," *Los Angeles Times*, December 22, 1922.
"that under no circumstance . . ." "Directors Not for Arbuckle," *Los Angeles Times*, December 23, 1922.
Hays responded with telegrams . . . "Hays Insists Stand Right," *Los Angeles Times*, December 24, 1922.
"All I ask is the rights . . ." "Appeal Made by Arbuckle," *Los Angeles Times*, December 25, 1922.
"of those who brazenly violate . . ." "Club Women of S.F. Area Plead Ban on Arbuckle," *Oakland Tribune*, December 28, 1922.
Arthur Hammerstein offered Paramount . . . Arthur Hammerstein, letter to Adolph Zukor, December 16, 1922, Adolph Zukor Collection, Margaret Herrick Library, Academy of Motion Pictures Arts and Sciences, Beverly Hills, CA.
"The crowd was so anxious . . ." "Million Bid for Arbuckle Films," *Los Angeles Times*, December 27, 1922.
McNab and financiers organized a company . . . "M'Nab Backing Arbuckle Film," *Los Angeles Times*, December 30, 1922.
he disagreed with their resolution . . . "Hays's Committee Opposes Release of Arbuckle Films," *Hartford Courant*, January 5, 1923.
his "final statement" . . . "Hays Gives Final Word on Fatty," *Los Angeles Times*, January 6, 1923.
"a little obscure cabin in Hollywood" . . . "Fatty Starts Upon $750,000 Comeback Film," *Ogden Standard-Examiner*, January 10, 1923.
"I just want to work . . ." Ibid.

acting in Handy Andy . . . "No Pies in Arbuckle's Comeback," *Eau Claire Leader*, January 23, 1923.

"a chance to make good . . ." "'Fatty' Arbuckle to 'Come Back'; New Role," *Joplin News Herald*, January 31, 1923.

"He was very bitter . . ." "Fatty Arbuckle Is Starting Over," *Appleton Post-Crescent*, July 5, 1924.

"It was a superbly forcible touch . . ." Robert E. Sherwood, *The Best Moving Pictures of 1922–23* (Boston: Small, Maynard, 1923), 78–85.

Arbuckle's appearance was applauded . . . "Fatty Arbuckle Quietly Enters Filmland Again," *Sioux City Journal*, September 23, 1923.

a guaranteed $2,500 per week . . . "Fatty Arbuckle to Dance in Cabaret for $2500 Per Week," *Telegraph-Herald* (Dubuque, IA), May 13, 1923.

"This is the first smile . . ." "Fatty Arbuckle Stages Comeback in Chicago Cafe," *Traverse City Record-Eagle*, June 6, 1923.

The show's producer remembered . . . "Pioneer Fair Revue Producer Was 50% of What Today Is MCA," *Billboard*, February 28, 1948, 91.

"The people have been very kind" . . . "Arbuckle Fails in Cabaret Act but Keeps Hope," *Syracuse Herald*, June 17, 1923.

"Our women are lean and fat . . ." "Fatty Arbuckle in Revue House of David Burlesque," *Chillicothe Constitution*, June 6, 1923.

he pulled in $6,000 weekly . . . "About Roscoe Arbuckle," *Oakland Tribune*, July 29, 1923.

"She stood by me . . ." "'Fatty' Arbuckle Smashes Up Cabaret, Socks Manager, to Meet His Wife at Train," *Evening Independent* (Massillon, OH), July 19, 1923.

"Well kid don't get discouraged . . ." Roscoe Arbuckle, letter to Minta Durfee, November 18, 1923, manuscript from the estate of Charles Williamson and Tucker Fleming, auctioned April 20, 2011.

"We were about to start . . ." Buster Keaton with Charles Samuels, *My Wonderful World of Slapstick* (Garden City, NY: Doubleday, 1960), 194.

In one of the two scenes . . . David B. Pearson, "Playing Detective: Possible Solutions to the Production Mysteries of *Sherlock Jr.*," in *Buster Keaton's Sherlock Jr.*, ed. Andrew Horton. (Cambridge: Cambridge University Press, 1997), 146.

"He hadn't recovered from those trials . . ." Kevin Brownlow, *The Parade's Gone By . . .* (Berkeley: University of California Press, 1968), 486.

"I am taking my father's name . . ." Arbuckle to Durfee, November 18, 1923.

in 1910 the family . . . US Census Bureau, *Thirteenth Census of the United States, 1910*, population of Dubuque City, IA, sup. dist. 3, enum. dist. 126, April 18, 1910 (Washington, DC: Government Printing Office, 1912–14).

they lived in Butte, Montana . . . "Arbuckle Again Sued by Former Butte Student," *Montana Standard*, September 18, 1929.

her rumored engagement to Jack Dempsey . . . "Jack Dempsey Reported Engaged," *Appleton Post-Crescent*, December 16, 1922.

"Weeks ago I saw Fatty . . ." "Fatty Arbuckle Is Starting Over."

he was greeted by an eleven-minute ovation . . . "Arbuckle Opens at Pantages," *Los Angeles Times*, June 15, 1924.

"the only way an accused man . . ." Ibid.

"I would rather build up . . ." "'Fatty' Arbuckle," *Ogden Standard-Examiner*, July 15, 1924.

"San Francisco's reception of me . . ." "Arbuckle Draws Capacity Crowds," *Ogden Standard-Examiner*, July 17, 1924.

"I hope not . . ." Ibid.

get in shape for his "reappearance . . ." Patrolling the Sport Highway, *Ogden Standard-Examiner*, July 18, 1924.

"No, I don't belong to either . . ." "'Fatty' Arbuckle Wants Comeback," *Ogden Standard-Examiner*, July 18, 1924.

"chance to live a clean . . ." "Arbuckle Plea Defeats Ban in Kansas City," *Oakland Tribune*, July 29, 1924.

British immigrant named Lester Hope . . . Bob Hope and Pete Martin, *Have Tux, Will Travel: Bob Hope's Own Story* (New York: Simon & Schuster, 1954), 40.

He said he envied the creative freedom . . . "'Fatty' Arbuckle Soon to Return to Movie Game, He Tells the Morning Press," *Logansport Morning Press*, August 29, 1924.

"I did not know . . ." "'Fatty' Arbuckle Would Preach Sermon but Minister Objects," *Pittsburgh Post-Gazette*, August 13, 1924.

"Appeal to you as one of several . . ." Untitled clipping, *Toledo Blade*, September 6, 1924, in scrapbook pages, Minta Durfee Arbuckle Collection, Margaret Herrick Library, Academy of Motion Pictures Arts and Sciences, Beverly Hills, CA.

"I don't claim to be . . ." Untitled clipping, *Toledo Blade*, September 10, 1924, scrapbook pages, Minta Durfee Arbuckle Collection.

he mused on literary matters . . . Roscoe Arbuckle, letter to Minta Durfee, September 13, 1924, auctioned at Bonhams, December 14, 2011, www.bonhams.com/auctions/19431/lot/4001/.

the Portland, Oregon, city council banned him . . . "Fatty Arbuckle's Films Opposed by City of Portland," *Eugene Guard*, October 16, 1924.

forbade him from stages in Tacoma . . . "'Fatty' Arbuckle Kept From Giving Tacoma Monologue," *Twin Falls Daily News*, October 21, 1924.

Arbuckle wrote Durfee . . . Roscoe Arbuckle, letter to Minta Durfee, September 4, 1924, document for sale on eBay, accessed May 15, 2011.

They agreed that he would pay . . . "Amount of Arbuckle's Wealth Brought Up; to Pay Ex-Wife $200 Week," *Joplin Globe*, March 28, 1924.

the announcement that Arbuckle would marry . . . "Doris Deane to Wed Arbuckle," *Oakland Tribune*, December 5, 1924.

one acerbic headline . . . "Doris Is Daring," *Linton Daily Citizen*, January 31, 1925.

a March ceremony was scrapped . . . "Arbuckle Wedding, Slated for Tonight, Halted Month by Law," *Oakland Tribune*, March 24, 1925.

married at her mother's home . . . "Roscoe Arbuckle and Doris Deane Married," *Albuquerque Morning Journal*, May 17, 1925.

"hidden away in the country" . . . "'Fatty' Arbuckle and Doris Deane Are Wed," *Titusville Herald*, May 18, 1925.

a contract worth $100,000 . . . "Fatty Arbuckle Weds Doris Deane at Pasadena," *Cook County Herald* (Arlington Heights, IL), May 22, 1925.

"It was their way of thumbing . . ." David Yallop, *The Day the Laughter Stopped: The True Story of Fatty Arbuckle* (New York: St. Martin's, 1976), 283.

the school demanded Arbuckle be dropped . . . "Film Actors to Stand Back of Roscoe Arbuckle," *Sioux City Journal*, October 16, 1925.

elicited a long ovation . . . "Fatty Given Ovation at Masquers," *Los Angeles Times*, October 23, 1925.

"Here is the sad spectacle . . ." Russell J. Birdwell, Hollywood!, *Ogden Standard-Examiner*, December 13, 1925.

20. Endurance: 1926–32

A front-page article in February 1926 . . . "'Fatty' Arbuckle Does Comeback!," *Olean Evening Times*, February 3, 1926.

In March, he, Buster Keaton, and their wives . . . "Movie Stars Escape from Prison," *Nevada State Journal*, March 25, 1926.

"The intrigues on the set . . ." Colleen Moore, interview by Stuart Oderman, August 1967, in *Roscoe "Fatty" Arbuckle: A Biography of the Silent Film Comedian, 1887–1933* (Jefferson, NC: McFarland, 1994), 206.

advertising sometimes touted . . . Advertisement for *Special Delivery*, *Syracuse Herald*, June 25, 1927.

"In the gathering sitting obscurely . . ." O. O. McIntyre, New York Day by Day, *Record Argus* (Greenville, PA), January 4, 1927.

a deal worth $2.5 million . . . "'Outlaw' of Film Signs Deal for $2,500,000," *San Francisco Chronicle*, March 15, 1927.

A Los Angeles review noted . . . "Pantages Sets High Standard," *Los Angeles Times*, April 19, 1927.

Arbuckle's opening night ovations . . . "Baby Mine Revived After 17 Years," *New York Times*, June 10, 1927.

"Mr. Arbuckle is not much of an actor" . . . Features of New York Stage, *Salt Lake Tribune*, June 19, 1927.

National Educational Association . . . "Protest Appearance of Fatty Arbuckle," *Free Press* (Carbondale, IL), August 19, 1927.

A lien was placed against him . . . "Tax Liens Filed Against Carey and Arbuckle," *Los Angeles Times*, December 1, 1927.

Minta Durfee sued him . . . "Arbuckle Pay to Be Attached," *Los Angeles Times*, December 28, 1927.

"his last vaudeville tour prior to re-entering . . ." Advertisement for vaudeville performance, *Altoona Mirror*, February 25, 1928.

ministers in Clarksburg, West Virginia . . . "Ministers Protest Arbuckle Visit," *New Castle News*, January 26, 1928.

"might corrupt public morals" . . . "Minneapolis Bans Fatty Arbuckle," *Decatur Daily Review*, April 28, 1928.

a performance in Waterloo, Iowa . . . "Protests Cancel Fatty Arbuckle's Appearance Here," *Waterloo Evening Courier*, May 10, 1928.

"defiance of the Hays organization" . . . "Fatty Arbuckle Plans Comeback While Political Scandals Have Darkened the Fame of Will Hays," *Vidette Messenger* (Valparaiso, IN), April 20, 1928.

"I have never paraded as a reformer . . ." "Senator Reed Flays Graft in Politics," *Tipton Daily Tribune*, April 12, 1928.
"Some of my old films . . ." "'Fatty' Arbuckle Goes to Paris to Regain Esteem," *Sioux City Journal*, March 19, 1928.
"hoping the audience would cool off" . . . "Arbuckle a Riot in Paris; but O, the Kind of Riot!," *Manitowoc Herald News*, March 26, 1928.
"We haven't got along happily . . ." "'Fatty' Arbuckle and Wife Are Separated," *Warsaw Union*, May 28, 1928.
at the home of a "prominent resident" . . . "Doris Dean [*sic*] Would Divorce Fatty," *Helena Daily Independent*, August 7, 1928.
a smattering of headlines such as . . . "'Nother Wild Party for Fatty Arbuckle," *Lubbock Morning Avalanche*, August 7, 1928.
"vicious, cruel, morose and nagging" . . . "Doris Dean Would Divorce Fatty."
"You know, Roscoe was an easy man . . ." Viola Dana, interview by Stuart Oderman, July 1974, in *Roscoe "Fatty" Arbuckle: A Biography*, 208.
initial reports claimed he was launching . . . "Arbuckle Plans Coffee Inn Chain," *Ogden Standard-Examiner*, August 2, 1928.
a long string of nightclubs . . . Culver City clubs' history via "Colorful Nightlife Thrived in Westside," *Los Angeles Times*, May 7, 1981.
a typical Los Angeles Times headline . . . "Dry Storm Rages over Plantation," *Los Angeles Times*, January 26, 1926.
"Every screen star of note . . ." On the Pacific Coast, *Miami News*, September 6, 1928.
"a strange crowd of big-time movie stars . . ." "Arbuckle's Cafe Employs Only Persons of Large Proportions," *Sheboygan Press*, July 30, 1928.
"I guess I'll go back to the stage" . . . Ibid.
England's Prince George . . . "Prince's Brother Danced with One Girl All Night Long," *Lowell Sun*, September 29, 1928.
the Plantation was raided . . . "Roscoe Arbuckle's Night Club Raided," *San Antonio Express*, December 24, 1928.
the Culver City mayor visited . . . "Cafes Put on Probation," *Los Angeles Times*, January 24, 1929.
a riot broke out at the Plantation . . . "More Participants in Arbuckle Care Brawl Are Sought," *Record-Chronicle* (Denton, TX), May 21, 1929.
the motion picture industry was finding its voice . . . Information on the transition from silent films to sound primarily via Donald Crafton, *The Talkies: American Cinema's Transition to Sound, 1926–1931* (Berkeley: University of California Press, 1999); William K. Everson, *American Silent Film* (New York: Oxford University Press, 1978), 334–47; Scott Eyman, *The Speed of Sound: Hollywood and the Talkie Revolution, 1926–1930* (Baltimore: Johns Hopkins University Press, 1999).
"In [motion pictures'] silence it more nearly . . ." James Quirk, editorial, *Photoplay*, May 1921, 19.
"startles the civilized world . . ." Advertisement for Kinetophone, *Motion Picture World*, January 25, 1913.
"It's up to us to sit tight . . ." James Quirk, editorial, *Photoplay*, October 1928, 28.

"Now Hollywood wonders . . ." "Plan to Make Talkies of Crime Confessions," *Capital Times* (Madison, WI), November 22, 1929.
"[Arbuckle] made no attempt to direct . . ." Kevin Brownlow, *The Parade's Gone By . . .* (Berkeley: University of California Press, 1968), 363.
"He left me and went to a Hollywood hotel . . ." "'Fatty' Should Wed Pugilist, Says Wife," *Ogden Standard-Examiner*, October 5, 1929.
Born in 1905, Addie Dukes . . . Obituary for Addie McPhail, *Independent* (London), May 1, 2003.
"I was a stranger in Hollywood . . ." "Addie McPhail, 97; Actress, Last Wife of 'Fatty' Arbuckle," *Los Angeles Times*, May 5, 2003.
"I had feelings for Roscoe" . . . Ibid.
he listed his monthly income at $500 . . . Conditional Contract of Sale, June 12, 1929, Mack Sennett Collection, Margaret Herrick Library, Academy of Motion Pictures Arts and Sciences, Beverly Hills, CA.
a new Lincoln town car, which cost . . . Ibid.
A dubious item . . . Captain Roscoe Fawcett, Screen Oddities, *Logansport Pharos-Tribune*, December 16, 1931.
A highlight "was the dancing of the serpentine . . ." "Film Folk Frolic at Gay Party," *Los Angeles Times*, November 9, 1931.
The three hundred members included . . . Gregory Paul Williams, *The Story of Hollywood: An Illustrated History* (Los Angeles: BL Press, 2006), 180.
"There goes the evidence" . . . "Fatty Arbuckle Jokes About Morning Arrest," *Los Angeles Times*, September 21, 1931.
"There ought to be a law . . ." Editorial, *Pella Chronicle*, August 6, 1931.
an article about Arbuckle appeared . . . "Just Let Me Work," *Photoplay*, March 1931, 65, 127–28.
"I thought someone was playing . . ." "Fatty Arbuckle Pays Fine for Precaution," *Los Angeles Times*, September 22, 1931.
Two months later, Motion Picture Classic published . . . "Isn't Fatty Punished Enough?," *Motion Picture Classic*, May 1931.
"Arbuckle should be allowed . . ." "Again Arbuckle?," *Time*, July 29, 1931.
A third fan magazine . . . "Doesn't Fatty Arbuckle Deserve a Break?," *Motion Picture*, September 1931, 40–41; "The Fans Want Fatty Arbuckle Back on the Screen," *Motion Picture*, November 1931, 16.
"I have no desire to return . . ." "Return of Arbuckle to Screen Voiced Pro, Con," *Circleville Herald*, June 22, 1931.
"Roscoe was warmly received . . ." Obituary for McPhail, *Independent*.
"master or mistress of ceremonies" . . . News and Comment of Stage and Screen, *Fitchburg Sentinel*, May 7, 1932.
after rousing the court reporter . . . "'Fatty' Finally Married," *Rochester Evening Journal*, June 21, 1932.
"Roscoe felt like he had been given . . ." Obituary for McPhail, *Independent*.
A photo of that moment . . . "Star Emerging from Eclipse," *Mansfield News*, August 8, 1932.
"Frankly gambling on Fatty's chances . . ." "'Fatty' Arbuckle to Attempt Comeback," *Salt Lake Tribune*, July 28, 1932.

"It's kind of like home to me . . ." "Fatty Arbuckle Is Coming Back," *Joplin Globe*, July 29, 1932.

21. Legends

"passed a strong resolution . . ." Looking Backward, *Kentucky New Era* (Hokinsville, KY), January 13, 1948.

she penned a remembrance . . . Adela Rogers St. Johns, "The Arbuckle Tragedy," *American Weekly*, October 22, 1950.

"He was no more guilty . . ." "Donald Crisp Fine Figure After Making 400 Movies," *Calgary Herald*, April 3, 1958.

a 1949 public opinion poll . . . "Adults Rate Hope Funniest Comedian," *Los Angeles Times*, September 19, 1949.

an extensive cover story . . . James Agee, "Comedy's Greatest Era," *Life*, September 5, 1949, 70–88.

"They get American movies here" . . . Bob Hope, "A Bodyguard? Ridiculous! No One's Seen My Films," *Deseret News* (Salt Lake City, UT), March 21, 1958.

The first, from Doris Deane . . . Behind the Scenes in Hollywood, *Steubenville Herald Star*, July 1, 1935.

Minta Durfee had written a play . . . May Mann, Going Hollywood, *Ogden Standard-Examiner*, August 24, 1939.

penning a book of the same name . . . "Sennett Alumni Recall Kops and Pies in Eyes," *Los Angeles Times*, July 30, 1951.

the title had changed to . . . Hollywood, *Kingsport Times*, April 22, 1955.

"Bob Hope is said to be interested . . ." Jackie the Author, *Post-Standard* (Syracuse, NY), August 14, 1971.

"Then, in 1921, Funny Fatty . . ." "Scandal and the Stars: Fatty Arbuckle," *Daily Reporter* (Dover, OH), September 27, 1960.

"one Hollywood observer" . . . Ezra Goodman, *The Fifty-Year Decline and Fall of Hollywood* (New York: MacFadden, 1961), 337.

Confidential magazine . . . Henry E. Scott, *Shocking True Story: The Rise and Fall of Confidential, "America's Most Scandalous Scandal Magazine"* (New York: Pantheon, 2010).

Arbuckle was never featured in Confidential . . . E-mail exchange between author and Henry E. Scott, June 11, 2011.

"Here Is the Shocking . . ." Leo Guild, *The Fatty Arbuckle Case* (New York: Paperback Library, 1962).

pulp fictionist Leo Guild . . . Paul Collins, "The Worst Pulp Novelist Ever: Remembering Leo Guild," *Stranger*, March 14, 2007.

"Liberace is the perfect specimen . . ." Leo Guild, *The Loves of Liberace* (Avon, 1956), quoted in *Odd Books* blog, September 26, 2010, http://oddbooks.co.uk/oddbooks/loves-liberace.

"These are the rumors . . ." Guild, *Fatty Arbuckle Case*, 27.

who called Arbuckle "despicable" . . . Ibid., 35.

The most "sane explanation". . . Ibid., 40.

"One rumor was . . ." Ibid., 41.

"Three versions of the incident . . ." Charles Beaumont, *Remember? Remember?: A Nostalgic Backward Glance at Some of Yesteryear's Most Beloved Features of Our National Profile* (New York: Macmillan, 1963), 208.
A less explicit intimation . . . "Again Arbuckle?," *Time*, July 29, 1931.
"If a book such as this . . ." "Hollywood Babylon," *New York Times*, August 31, 1975.
"Vacationers returning from Europe . . ." Voice of Broadway, *News Tribune* (Fort Pierce, FL), September 19, 1961.
"And when Fatty died . . ." Jerome Charyn, *Movieland: Hollywood and the Great American Dream Culture* (New York: New York University Press, 1989), 65.
Miller rendered the other third . . . Bill Landis, *Anger: The Unauthorized Biography of Kenneth Anger* (New York: HarperCollins, 1995), 122.
as many as two million copies . . . Ibid., 123.
"plumber's helper" Arbuckle . . . Kenneth Anger, *Hollywood Babylon* (New York: Dell, 1975), 27.
This story was debunked . . . David Stenn, *Clara Bow: Runnin' Wild* (New York: Cooper Square, 1988), 107–15.
"Mishawn [sic] Manor" . . . Anger, *Hollywood Babylon*, 27.
"did her fair share of sleeping around . . ." Ibid., 29.
misidentified with a photo of Minta Durfee . . . Ibid., 38.
Arbuckle's "friend" . . . Ibid., 30.
"As headlines screamed . . ." Ibid., 39.
"the lack of specific evidence . . ." Ibid., 42.
"Was he thinking of another bottle . . ." Ibid., 45.
"She was all beat up . . ." Gerald Fine, *Fatty* (self-published, 1971), 94.
"she had been bought . . ." Ibid., 95.
"when she was trying to fight off . . ." Anita Loos, *Kiss Hollywood Goodbye* (New York: Viking, 1974), 107.
"Arbuckle had told others . . ." "Tales of Celebrity Babylon," *Newsweek*, June 27, 1994, 26.
"Hollywood has always had its share . . ." "When Apes Put Men to Shame," *Independent* (London), February 27, 1998.
"The popular comedian Fatty Arbuckle . . ." Steve Allen, "Madonna," *Journal of Popular Culture* 27 (Summer 1993): 1.
"During this vacation . . ." Adela Rogers St. Johns, *Love, Laughter and Tears: My Hollywood Story* (Garden City, NY: Doubleday, 1978), 62–63.
"Her manuscript was too circumspect . . ." "Minta Durfee—Always in Arbuckle's Corner," *Los Angeles Times*, September 21, 1975.
"widow of film star . . ." TV listings, *Tucson Daily Citizen*, October 28, 1970.
"suffering from several diseases" . . . Kevin Brownlow, *The Parade's Gone By . . .* (Berkeley: University of California Press, 1968), 39.
"Virginia Rappe was one of those poor . . ." Minta Durfee, interview by Stuart Oderman, September 1969, in *Roscoe "Fatty" Arbuckle: A Biography of the Silent Film Comedian, 1887–1933* (Jefferson, NC: McFarland, 1994), 152.
"Mr. Sennett had to close the studio . . ." Minta Durfee, interview by Walter Wagner, July 4, 1973, in *You Must Remember This* (New York: Putnam, 1975), 36.

She "had seventy-two affidavits . . ." Ibid., 38–39.
"Roscoe was in handcuffs . . ." Ibid., 39.
"that dreadful, dreadful old man" . . . Ibid., 38.
"This awful Will Hays . . ." Ibid., 41.
the "notorious" Maude Delmont . . . "Two Hollywood Cases Bear Likeness to Simpson's," *Daily Courier* (Yavapai County, AZ), July 3, 1994.
Once again, we're treated . . . David Yallop, *The Day the Laughter Stopped: The True Story of Fatty Arbuckle* (New York: St. Martin's, 1976), 110.
"a great deal of money" . . . Ibid., 112.
"She was pregnant . . ." Ibid.
an illegal autopsy to cover up an illegal abortion . . . Ibid., 128.
an unspecified scheme to blackmail Arbuckle . . . Ibid., 125.
"I couldn't stand that girl . . ." Andy Edmonds, *Frame-Up!: The Untold Story of Roscoe "Fatty" Arbuckle* (New York: William Morrow, 1991), 156.
"at least five abortions . . ." Ibid., 155
"hatchet job" abortion . . . Ibid., 252.
Curiously, Edmonds claims . . . Ibid., 7–8.
Zukor designed a frame-up . . . Ibid., 253.
Durfee first optioned the film rights . . . "TV's Gleason Sought to Portray Arbuckle," *Los Angeles Times*, February 18, 1957.
a TV network was planning a musical . . . Broadway, *Reading Eagle*, April 23, 1957.
for a decade afterward, Jackie Gleason . . . "TV's Gleason Sought."
John Belushi, who was eyeing the part . . . "The Lost Roles of John Belushi," *Splitsider*, March 3, 2011, www.splitsider.com/2011/03/the-lost-roles-of-john-belushi/.
John Candy was studying for the role . . . Martin Knelman, *Laughing on the Outside: The Life of John Candy* (New York: Thomas Dunne, 1996), 199.
Chris Farley met with playwright/screenwriter David Mamet . . . Tom Farley and Tanner Colby, *The Chris Farley Show: A Biography in Three Acts* (New York: Viking, 2008), 267–68.
Chicago "multi-media treatment" . . . "Chicago Fatty Follows 1920s Arbuckle Scandal, Mar. 3" *Playbill*, March 2, 1998.
a Broadway musical named Fatty . . . "Coogan Lands Broadway Role," *Daily Review* (Hayward, CA), May 10, 1966.
In 1921, the comic was charged . . . "Murder, Inc.," *Time*, December 31, 1999.
"a naive young actress" . . . "The Fatty Arbuckle Scandal, 1920," *Time*, March 1, 2007.
Fatty Arbuckles American Diner . . . "Fatty Arbuckles," Franchise Business, www.franchisebusiness.co.uk/fatty-arbuckles.

22. Labor Day Revisited

"The defendant followed Virginia Rappe . . ." Leo Friedman, closing statement of third Arbuckle trial, in *Classics of the Bar: Stories of the World's Great Legal Trials and a Compilation of Forensic Masterpieces*, vol. 8, ed. Alvin V. Sellers (Washington, DC: Washington Law Book, 1942), 121–22.
modern forensic experts consulted for this book . . . Author's interviews with Kenneth Moses on July 18, 2011, and Larry Stewart on July 18–19, 2011.

"When I walked into 1219 . . ." People v. Arbuckle, first trial transcript, 1668–69.
her abs were "exceedingly well-developed" . . . Nat Schmulowitz, closing statement of third Arbuckle trial, in *Classics of the Bar*, 49.
"Now, a violent contraction . . ." Ibid.
"Mr. Arbuckle assisted . . ." Ibid., 49–50.
she was "holding her stomach" . . . People v. Arbuckle, Superior Court of California, County of San Francisco, first trial transcript, 1669–76.
described in the same terms . . . Roscoe Arbuckle, "Roscoe Arbuckle Tells His Own Story," *Movie Weekly*, December 31, 1921.
"Is that human nature? . . ." Milton U'Ren, closing statement of third Arbuckle trial, in *Classics of the Bar*, 24.
"Is that the way a man who had nothing to fear . . ." Ibid., 24.
"there were no closed or locked doors . . ." "Girl Dead After Wild Party in Hotel," *San Francisco Chronicle*, September 10, 1921.
"We sat around and had some drinks . . ." "Detain Arbuckle," *Evening News* (San Jose), September 10, 1921.
"To show how serious we thought . . ." "Mystery Death Takes Actress," *Los Angeles Times*, September 10, 1921.
"Arbuckle took me by the arm . . ." "Surprise Witness Heard," *Los Angeles Times*, March 28, 1922.
"Miss Rappe told me . . ." "Fatty Arbuckle Indicted," *Chicago Tribune*, September 14, 1921.
"The patient admitted to me . . ." Ibid.

23. Denouement: 1932–33

"Quite the most man-about-town-ish . . ." New York Letter, *Brownsville Herald*, October 14, 1932.
"100% Californian" . . . Roscoe Arbuckle, letter to Mrs. Lee, dated December 1, 1932, document for sale on eBay, accessed August 16, 2011.
"Roscoe Arbuckle has given up dieting . . ." Medbury Witticisms, *Herald-Star* (Stubenville, OH), March 9, 1933.
Arbuckle and McPhail belatedly celebrated . . . Details of Arbuckle's final night at La Hiff's via "1000 Pay Tribute at Arbuckle Bier," *New York Times*, July 1, 1933; "Throngs Pass Arbuckle Bier," *Los Angeles Times*, June 30, 1933.
"I've made my comeback" . . . "1000 Pay Tribute at Arbuckle Bier."
"We think of his love of children . . ." "Stage Folk Mourn at Arbuckle Bier," *New York Times*, July 2, 1933.
claiming they had a right . . . "Arbuckle Will Contest Planned by Brothers," *Los Angeles Times*, July 19, 1933.
a New York court ruled . . . "Roscoe Arbuckle Once Paid $1000 Daily, Leaves $400," *Syracuse Herald*, July 27, 1934.
she alone committed them to the Pacific Ocean . . . Robert Young Jr., "Where Fatty Arbuckle Is and Isn't Buried," Arbucklemania, www.silent-movies.com/Arbucklemania/Burial.html.
Time told readers as much . . . Milestones, *Time*, July 10, 1933.
"Instead of being the innocent . . ." "Consider 'Fatty' Arbuckle," *Mansfield News-Journal*, July 1, 1933.

"Arbuckle got a rough deal . . ." Mark Hellinger, All in a Day, *Lowell Sun*, July 5, 1933.

"Those who demanded their pound of flesh . . ." Will Rogers, Will Rogers Says, *Traverse City Record-Eagle*, June 30, 1933.

SELECT BIBLIOGRAPHY

Adams, Charles F. *Murder by the Bay: Historical Homicide in and About the City of San Francisco*. Sanger, CA: Word Dancer, 2005.

Allen, Frederick Lewis. *Only Yesterday: An Informal History of the 1920's*. New York: Harper & Row, 1931.

Allen, Robert C. *Vaudeville and Film 1895–1915: A Study in Media Interaction*. New York: Arno, 1980.

Anger, Kenneth. *Hollywood Babylon*. New York: Dell, 1975.

Arbuckle, Roscoe. "Love Confessions of a Fat Man." *Photoplay*, September 1921, 22–23.

———. "Roscoe Arbuckle Tells His Own Story." *Movie Weekly*, December 31, 1921.

Bartlett, Randolph. "Why Aren't We Killed?" *Photoplay*, April 1916, 80–84.

Black, Gregory D. *Hollywood Censored: Morality Codes, Catholics, and the Movies*. New York: Cambridge University Press, 1996.

Blesh, Rudi. *Keaton*. New York: MacMillan, 1966.

Block, Eugene B. *The Wizard of Berkeley*. New York: Coward-McCann, 1958.

Bowser, Eileen. *The Transformation of Cinema, 1907–1915*. New York: Scribner, 1990.

Brownlow, Kevin. *The Parade's Gone By* . . . Berkeley: University of California Press, 1968.

Budnick, Dean Eric. "Directed Verdict: The Roscoe 'Fatty' Arbuckle Trial Discourse." PhD dissertation, Harvard University, 2000.

Chaplin, Charlie. *My Autobiography*. New York: Simon & Schuster, 1964.

Collins, Paul. "The Worst Pulp Novelist Ever: Remembering Leo Guild." *Stranger*, March 14, 2007.

Crafton, Donald. *The Talkies: American Cinema's Transition to Sound, 1926–1931*. Berkeley: University of California Press, 1999.

de Grazia, Edward, and Roger K. Newman. *Banned Films: Movies, Censors and the First Amendment*. New York: R.R. Bowker, 1982.

Durfee, Minta. Interview by Don Schneider, July 21, 1974. Excerpted at Mabel Normand Home Page, www.mn-hp.com/minta1.html.

———. "The True Story About My Husband." *Movie Weekly*, December 24, 1921.

———. Unpublished manuscript. Minta Durfee Arbuckle Collection, Margaret Herrick Library, Academy of Motion Pictures Arts and Sciences, Beverly Hills, CA.

Edmonds, Andy. *Frame-Up!: The Untold Story of Roscoe "Fatty" Arbuckle*. New York: William Morrow, 1991.

Ellis, Tom. "Just Let Me Work." *Photoplay*, March 1931, 65, 127–28.

Erish, Andrew A. *Col. William N. Selig, the Man Who Invented Hollywood*. Austin: University of Texas Press, 2012.

Everson, William K. *American Silent Film*. New York: Oxford University Press, 1978.

Eyman, Scott. *The Speed of Sound: Hollywood and the Talkie Revolution, 1926–1930*. Baltimore: Johns Hopkins University Press, 1999.

Fine, Gary Alan. *Difficult Reputations: Collective Memories of the Evil, Inept, and Controversial*. Chicago: University of Chicago Press, 2001.

———. "Scandal, Social Conditions, and the Creation of Public Attention: Fatty Arbuckle and the 'Problem of Hollywood,'" *Social Problems*, August 1997, 297–321.

Fleming, E. J. *Wallace Reid: The Life and Death of a Hollywood Idol*. Jefferson, NC: McFarland, 2007.

Geary, Rick. *Famous Players: The Mysterious Death of William Desmond Taylor*. New York: ComicsLit, 2009.

Grant, Robert, and Joseph Katz. *The Great Trials of the Twenties: The Watershed Decade in America's Courtrooms*. Cambridge, MA: Da Capo, 1998.

Grieveson, Lee. *Policing Cinema: Movies and Censorship in Early-Twentieth-Century America*. Berkeley: University of California Press, 2004.

Guild, Leo. *The Fatty Arbuckle Case*. New York: Paperback Library, 1962.

Hays, Will H. *The Memoirs of Will H. Hays*. Garden City, NY: Doubleday, 1955.

Hynd, Alan. "The Rise and Fall of Joseph Schenck." Pts. 1–3. *Liberty*, June 28, 1941, July 5, 1941, and July 12, 1941.

Jura, Jean-Jacques, and Rodney Norman Barden II. *Balboa Films: A History and Filmography of the Silent Film Studio*. Jefferson, NC: McFarland, 1999.

Keaton, Buster, with Charles Samuels. *My Wonderful World of Slapstick*. Garden City, NY: Doubleday, 1960.

Keaton, Eleanor, and Jeffrey Vance. *Buster Keaton Remembered*. New York: Harry N. Abrams, 2001.

Kennard, K. Sellers, MD. "The Rupture of the Female Urinary Bladder." *Medico-Legal Journal*, May/June 1923, 71–77.

King, Rob. *The Fun Factory: The Keystone Film Company and the Emergence of Mass Culture*. Berkeley: University of California Press, 2009.

Kramer, Peter. "'Clean, Dependable Slapstick': Comedy Violence and the Emergence of Classical Hollywood Cinema." In *Violence and American Cinema*, edited by David J. Slocum. New York: Routledge, 2001.

Lahue, Kalton C., and Terry Brewer. *Kops and Custards: The Legend of Keystone Films*. Norman: University of Oklahoma Press, 1968.

Landis, Bill. *Anger: The Unauthorized Biography of Kenneth Anger*. New York: HarperCollins, 1995.

Lasky, Jesse L., with Don Weldon. *I Blow My Own Horn*. Garden City, NY: Doubleday, 1957.

Leff, Leonard J., and Jerold L. Simmons. *The Dame in the Kimono: Hollywood, Censorship, and the Production Code*. 2nd ed. Lexington: University Press of Kentucky, 2001.

Leicester, Rob. *Red Ink, White Lies: The Rise and Fall of Los Angeles Newspapers 1920–1962*. Upland, CA: Dragonflyer Press, 2000.

Lewis, Philip C. *Trouping: How the Show Came to Town*. New York: Harper & Row, 1973.

Literary Digest. "'Fatty' Arbuckle off the Screen." July 14, 1917, 40–42.

Louvish, Simon. *Keystone: The Life and Clowns of Mack Sennett*. New York: Faber and Faber, 2003.

Meade, Marion. *Buster Keaton: Cut to the Chase*. New York: HarperCollins, 1995.

Neibaur, James L. *Arbuckle and Keaton: Their 14 Film Collaborations*. Jefferson, NC: McFarland, 2007.

———. *Early Charlie Chaplin: The Artist as Apprentice at Keystone Studios*. Lanham, MD: Scarecrow, 2011.

Oderman, Stuart. *Roscoe "Fatty" Arbuckle: A Biography of the Silent Film Comedian, 1887–1933*. Jefferson, NC: McFarland, 1994.

Okrent, Daniel. *Last Call: The Rise and Fall of Prohibition*. New York: Scribner, 2010.

Okuda, Ted, and David Maska. *Charlie Chaplin at Keystone and Essanay: Dawn of the Tramp*. Lincoln, NE: iUniverse, 2005.

Pearson, David B. "Playing Detective: Possible Solutions to the Production Mysteries of *Sherlock Jr.*" In *Buster Keaton's Sherlock Jr.*, edited by Andrew Horton. Cambridge: Cambridge University Press, 1997.

Purdy, Dennis. *Kiss 'Em Goodbye: An ESPN Treasury of Failed, Forgotten, and Departed Teams*. New York: ESPN, 2010.

Ramsland, Katherine. "He Made Mute Evidence Speak: Edward O. Heinrich." *Forensic Examiner*, fall 2007, 62–64.

Rapf, Joanna E. "Both Sides of the Camera: Roscoe 'Fatty' Arbuckle's Evolution at Keystone." In *Slapstick Comedy*, edited by Tom Paulus and Rob King. New York: Routledge, 2010.

Reeder, Thomas. "And He That Strives to Touch the Stars: Henry Lehrman and the Fledgling Film Industry." *Galitzianer*, November 2009, 16–24.

Rex, Wil. "Behind the Scenes with Fatty and Mabel," *Picture-Play*, April 1916, 46–53.

Roberts, Ed ("A Hollywood Newspaper Man"). *The Sins of Hollywood: An Expose of Movie Vice*. Los Angeles: Hollywood Publishing, 1922. Reprinted in *Taylorology* 30 (June 1995): www.public.asu.edu/~ialong/Taylor30.txt.

Robinson, David. *From Peep Show to Palace: The Birth of American Film*. New York: Columbia University Press, 1996.

Sellers, Alvin V., ed. *Classics of the Bar: Stories of the World's Greatest Legal Trials and a Compilation of Forensic Masterpieces*. Vol. 8. Washington, DC: Washington Law Book, 1942.

Sennett, Mack, with Cameron Shipp. *King of Comedy*. Garden City, NY: Doubleday, 1954.

Sherman, William Thomas. *Mabel Normand: A Source Book to Her Life and Films*. 6th ed. Scribd.com, 2012.

Siefkin, David. *Meet Me at the St. Francis: The First Seventy-Five Years of a Great San Francisco Hotel*. San Francisco: St. Francis Hotel Corp., 1979.

Sklar, Robert. *Movie-Made America: A Cultural History of American Movies*. New York: Vintage, 1975.

Slide, Anthony. *Inside the Hollywood Fan Magazine: A History of Star Makers, Fabricators, and Gossip Mongers*. Jackson, MS: University Press of Mississippi, 2010.

St. Johns, Adela Rogers. *Love, Laughter and Tears: My Hollywood Story*. Garden City, NY: Doubleday, 1978.

Stoloff, Sam. "Fatty Arbuckle and the Black Sox: The Paranoid Style of American Popular Culture, 1919–1922." In *Headline Hollywood: A Century of Film Scandal*, edited by Adrienne L. McLean and David A. Cook. New Brunswick, NJ: Rutgers University Press, 2001.

———. "Normalizing Stars: Roscoe 'Fatty' Arbuckle and Hollywood Consolidation." In *American Silent Film: Discovering Marginalized Voices*, edited by Gregg Bachman and Thomas J. Slater. Carbondale, IL: Southern Illinois University Press, 2002.

Sweeney, Kevin W., ed. *Buster Keaton: Interviews*. Jackson, MS: University Press of Mississippi, 2007.

Ulaby, Neda. "Roscoe Arbuckle and the Scandal of Fatness." In *Bodies Out of Bounds: Fatness and Transgression*, edited by Jana Evans Braziel and Kathleen LeBesco. Berkeley: University of California Press, 2001.

Wagner, Walter. *You Must Remember This*. New York: Putnam, 1975.

Walker, Brent E. *Mack Sennett's Fun Factory*. Jefferson, NC: McFarland, 2009.

Weissman, Stephen. *Chaplin: A Life*. New York: Arcade, 2008.

White, William L. *Slaying the Dragon: The History of Addiction Treatment and Recovery in America*. Bloomington, IL: Chestnut Health Systems, 1998.

Williams, Gregory Paul. *The Story of Hollywood: An Illustrated History*. Los Angeles: BL Press, 2006.

Yallop, David. A. *The Day the Laughter Stopped: The True Story of Fatty Arbuckle*. New York: St. Martin's, 1976.

Young, Robert, Jr. *Roscoe "Fatty" Arbuckle: A Bio-Bibliography*. Westport, CT: Greenwood, 1994.

INDEX

B ARBUCKLE

Merritt, Greg, 1965-

Room 1219

SEP - 4 2013